THE
DEADLY
SISTERHOOD

THE
DEADLY
SISTERHOOD

A STORY OF WOMEN, POWER, AND INTRIGUE
IN THE ITALIAN RENAISSANCE, 1427–1527

LEONIE FRIEDA

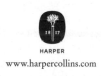

HARPER
www.harpercollins.com

HarperCollins books may be purchased for educational,
business, or sales promotional use. For information, please write:
Special Markets Department, HarperCollins Publishers,
10 East 53rd Street, New York, NY 10022.

First published in Great Britain in 2012
by Weidenfeld & Nicolson.

FIRST U.S. EDITION PUBLISHED 2013

Library of Congress Cataloging-in-Publication Data
has been applied for.

ISBN: 978-0-06-156308-9

13 14 15 16 17   OFF/RRD   10 9 8 7 6 5 4 3 2 1

To my late father, who inspired me with his passion for history;
to my mother, who inspires me with her courage;
and to my sister, Anna, who is my best friend.
To we four.

Contents

PART THREE: 1500–1527

List of Illustrations

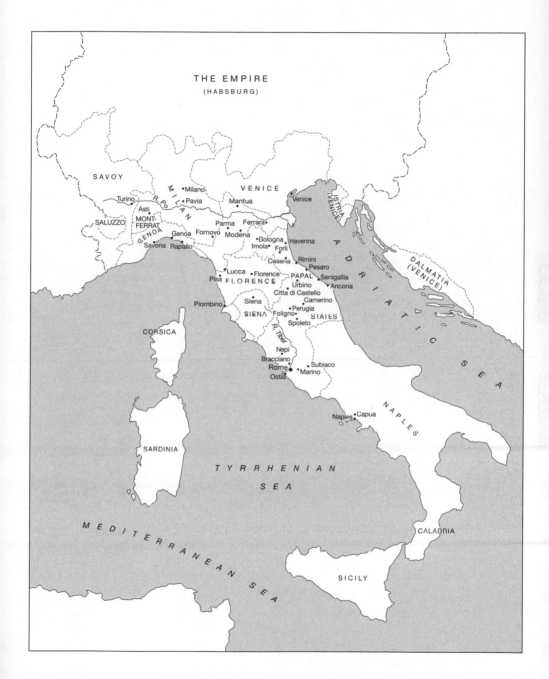

Italy in the late fifteenth century

The House of Medici

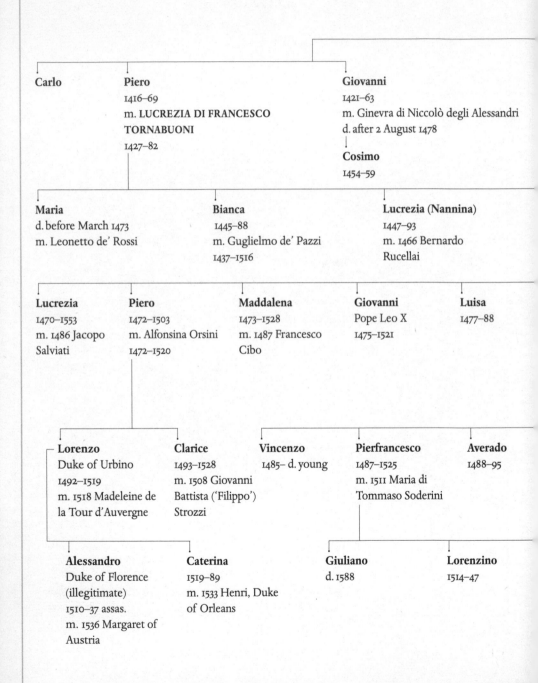

Carlo	Piero		Giovanni
	1416–69		1421–63
	m. **LUCREZIA DI FRANCESCO**		m. Ginevra di Niccolò degli Alessandri
	TORNABUONI		d. after 2 August 1478
	1427–82		
			Cosimo
			1454–59

Maria	Bianca	Lucrezia (Nannina)
d. before March 1473	1445–88	1447–93
m. Leonetto de' Rossi	m. Guglielmo de' Pazzi	m. 1466 Bernardo
	1437–1516	Rucellai

Lucrezia	Piero	Maddalena	Giovanni	Luisa
1470–1553	1472–1503	1473–1528	Pope Leo X	1477–88
m. 1486 Jacopo	m. Alfonsina Orsini	m. 1487 Francesco	1475–1521	
Salviati	1472–1520	Cibo		

Lorenzo	Clarice	Vincenzo	Pierfrancesco	Averado
Duke of Urbino	1493–1528	1485– d. young	1487–1525	1488–95
1492–1519	m. 1508 Giovanni		m. 1511 Maria di	
m. 1518 Madeleine de	Battista ('Filippo')		Tommaso Soderini	
la Tour d'Auvergne	Strozzi			

Alessandro	Caterina	Giuliano	Lorenzino
Duke of Florence	1519–89	d. 1588	1514–47
(illegitimate)	m. 1533 Henri, Duke		
1510–37 assas.	of Orleans		
m. 1536 Margaret of			
Austria			

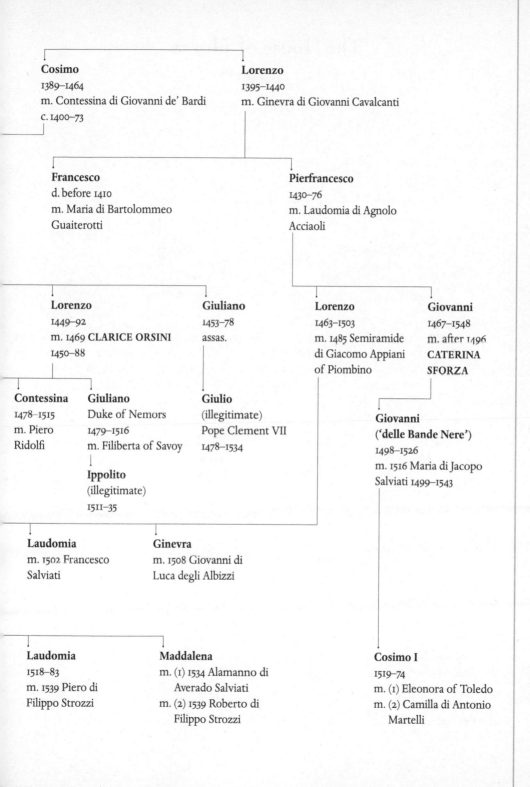

Cosimo
1389–1464
m. Contessina di Giovanni de' Bardi
c. 1400–73

Lorenzo
1395–1440
m. Ginevra di Giovanni Cavalcanti

Francesco
d. before 1410
m. Maria di Bartolommeo
Guaiterotti

Pierfrancesco
1430–76
m. Laudomia di Agnolo
Acciaioli

Lorenzo
1449–92
m. 1469 CLARICE ORSINI
1450–88

Giuliano
1453–78
assas.

Lorenzo
1463–1503
m. 1485 Semiramide
di Giacomo Appiani
of Piombino

Giovanni
1467–1548
m. after 1496
CATERINA
SFORZA

Contessina
1478–1515
m. Piero
Ridolfi

Giuliano
Duke of Nemors
1479–1516
m. Filiberta of Savoy

Giulio
(illegitimate)
Pope Clement VII
1478–1534

Giovanni
('delle Bande Nere')
1498–1526
m. 1516 Maria di Jacopo
Salviati 1499–1543

Ippolito
(illegitimate)
1511–35

Laudomia
m. 1502 Francesco
Salviati

Ginevra
m. 1508 Giovanni di
Luca degli Albizzi

Laudomia
1518–83
m. 1539 Piero di
Filippo Strozzi

Maddalena
m. (1) 1534 Alamanno di
Averado Salviati
m. (2) 1539 Roberto di
Filippo Strozzi

Cosimo I
1519–74
m. (1) Eleonora of Toledo
m. (2) Camilla di Antonio
Martelli

The House of Sforza

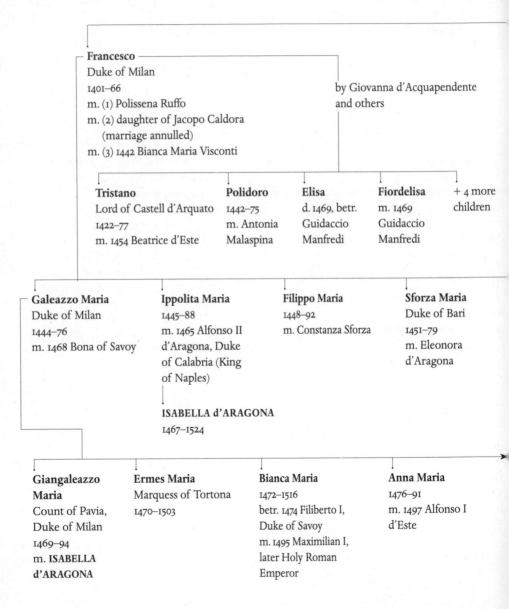

Francesco
Duke of Milan
1401–66
m. (1) Polissena Ruffo
m. (2) daughter of Jacopo Caldora
  (marriage annulled)
m. (3) 1442 Bianca Maria Visconti

by Giovanna d'Acquapendente
and others

Tristano
Lord of Castell d'Arquato
1422–77
m. 1454 Beatrice d'Este

Polidoro
1442–75
m. Antonia
Malaspina

Elisa
d. 1469, betr.
Guidaccio
Manfredi

Fiordelisa
m. 1469
Guidaccio
Manfredi

+ 4 more
children

Galeazzo Maria
Duke of Milan
1444–76
m. 1468 Bona of Savoy

Ippolita Maria
1445–88
m. 1465 Alfonso II
d'Aragona, Duke
of Calabria (King
of Naples)

ISABELLA d'ARAGONA
1467–1524

Filippo Maria
1448–92
m. Constanza Sforza

Sforza Maria
Duke of Bari
1451–79
m. Eleonora
d'Aragona

**Giangaleazzo
Maria**
Count of Pavia,
Duke of Milan
1469–94
m. **ISABELLA
d'ARAGONA**

Ermes Maria
Marquess of Tortona
1470–1503

Bianca Maria
1472–1516
betr. 1474 Filiberto I,
Duke of Savoy
m. 1495 Maximilian I,
later Holy Roman
Emperor

Anna Maria
1476–91
m. 1497 Alfonso I
d'Este

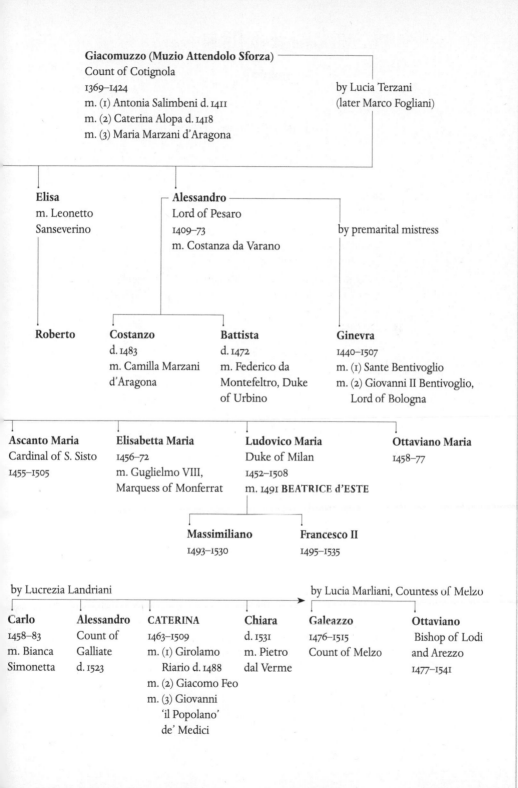

Giacomuzzo (Muzio Attendolo Sforza)
Count of Cotignola
1369–1424
m. (1) Antonia Salimbeni d. 1411
m. (2) Caterina Alopa d. 1418
m. (3) Maria Marzani d'Aragona

by Lucia Terzani
(later Marco Fogliani)

Elisa
m. Leonetto
Sanseverino

Alessandro
Lord of Pesaro
1409–73
m. Costanza da Varano

by premarital mistress

Roberto

Costanzo
d. 1483
m. Camilla Marzani
d'Aragona

Battista
d. 1472
m. Federico da
Montefeltro, Duke
of Urbino

Ginevra
1440–1507
m. (1) Sante Bentivoglio
m. (2) Giovanni II Bentivoglio,
Lord of Bologna

Ascanto Maria
Cardinal of S. Sisto
1455–1505

Elisabetta Maria
1456–72
m. Guglielmo VIII,
Marquess of Monferrat

Ludovico Maria
Duke of Milan
1452–1508
m. 1491 BEATRICE d'ESTE

Ottaviano Maria
1458–77

Massimiliano
1493–1530

Francesco II
1495–1535

by Lucrezia Landriani

by Lucia Marliani, Countess of Melzo

Carlo
1458–83
m. Bianca
Simonetta

Alessandro
Count of
Galliate
d. 1523

CATERINA
1463–1509
m. (1) Girolamo
Riario d. 1488
m. (2) Giacomo Feo
m. (3) Giovanni
'il Popolano'
de' Medici

Chiara
d. 1531
m. Pietro
dal Verme

Galeazzo
1476–1515
Count of Melzo

Ottaviano
Bishop of Lodi
and Arezzo
1477–1541

The House of della Rovere

Leonardo della Rovere
fl. 1400

Francesco
Sixtus IV
1414–84

Luchina
m. Giovanni Basso

Bianca
m. Paolo Riario

Raffaello

Count Girolamo
1438–88
m. CATERINA
SFORZA

Violante
m. Antonio
Sansoni

Pietro
Cardinal 1471

Girolamo
Cardinal
1477

Agostino
Archbishop

Maria
m. Antonio
Grosso

Raffaele
Sansoni Riario
Cardinal 1477
(held 16
archbishoprics)

Leonardo
Cardinal

Clemente
Cardinal

Giuliano
Cardinal 1471
(Pope Julius II)

Bartolomeo
Bishop of Massa
and Ferrara

Leonardo
Rome Prefect
(then Duke of
Sora)
m. Giovanna
d' Aragona

Giovanni
(succeeds Leonardo
to Rome Prefecture
and Dukedom of
Sora)
m. Giovanna da
Montefeltro

Francesco
Maria

The House of Gonzaga

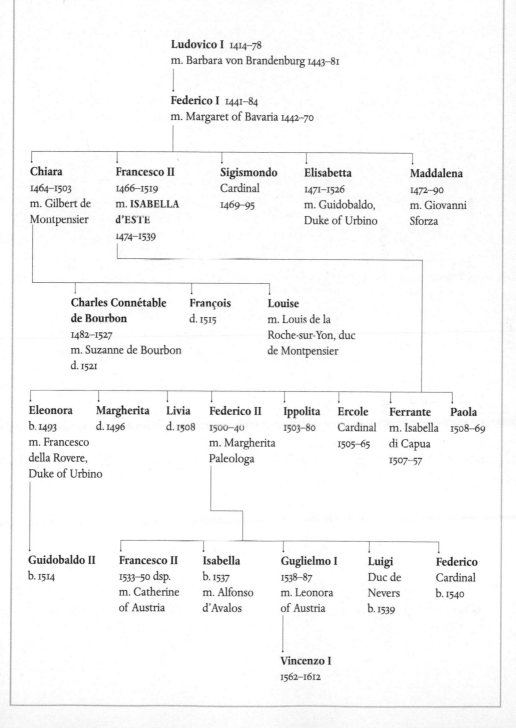

Ludovico I 1414–78
m. Barbara von Brandenburg 1443–81

Federico I 1441–84
m. Margaret of Bavaria 1442–70

Chiara	**Francesco II**	**Sigismondo**	**Elisabetta**	**Maddalena**
1464–1503	1466–1519	Cardinal	1471–1526	1472–90
m. Gilbert de	m. **ISABELLA**	1469–95	m. Guidobaldo,	m. Giovanni
Montpensier	**d'ESTE**		Duke of Urbino	Sforza
	1474–1539			

Charles Connétable	**François**	**Louise**
de Bourbon	d. 1515	m. Louis de la
1482–1527		Roche-sur-Yon, duc
m. Suzanne de Bourbon		de Montpensier
d. 1521		

Eleonora	**Margherita**	**Livia**	**Federico II**	**Ippolita**	**Ercole**	**Ferrante**	**Paola**
b. 1493	d. 1496	d. 1508	1500–40	1503–80	Cardinal	m. Isabella	1508–69
m. Francesco			m. Margherita		1505–65	di Capua	
della Rovere,			Paleologa			1507–57	
Duke of Urbino							

Guidobaldo II	**Francesco II**	**Isabella**	**Guglielmo I**	**Luigi**	**Federico**
b. 1514	1533–50 dsp.	b. 1537	1538–87	Duc de	Cardinal
	m. Catherine	m. Alfonso	m. Leonora	Nevers	b. 1540
	of Austria	d'Avalos	of Austria	b. 1539	

Vincenzo I
1562–1612

The House of Este

Leonello
(illegitimate /
legitimized)
13th Marquis
of Ferrara
1407–50
m. (1) Margherita
  Gonzaga
m. (2) Maria d'Aragona

Francesco
(illegitimate)
b. before 1430

Borso
(illegitimate)
1413–71
1st Duke of
Modena 1452
and Ferrara
1471

Niccolò
1438–76

Gurone Maria
(illegitimate)
d. 1484

Alberto
(illegitimate)
1415–1502

Lucia
1419–37

Ginevra
1419–40
m. Sigismondo
  Malatesta

Isotta
(illegitimate)
1425–56)
m. (1) Oddo Antonio da
  Montefeltro
m. (2) Stjepan III
  Frankopan Modruški,
  prince of Krk Senj
  and Modruš

Girolano
(illegitimate)

Battista
(illegitimate)

Vincenzo
(illegitimate)

Lucrezia
(illegitimate)
b. before 1473
d. 1516 or 1518
m. Annibale Bentivoglio

ISABELLA
1474–1539
m. Gian Francesco
Gonzaga

BEATRICE
1475–97
m. Ludovico
Sforza

Alfonso I
3rd Duke of Ferrara
and Modena 1476–1534
m. (1) Anna Sforza
m. (2) 1502 **LUCREZIA BORGIA**
  d. 1519

Ercole II
1508–59
m. Reneé, dau.
Louis XI

Ippolito II
1509–72, Cardinal
1539

Eleanora
1515–75

Anna
1531–1607

Alfonso II
1533–97
m. (1) Lucrezia de Medici
m. (2) Barbara von Habsburg
m. (3) Margherita Gonzaga

Lucrezia
1585–98

Eleanara
1537–81

Luigi
1538–86

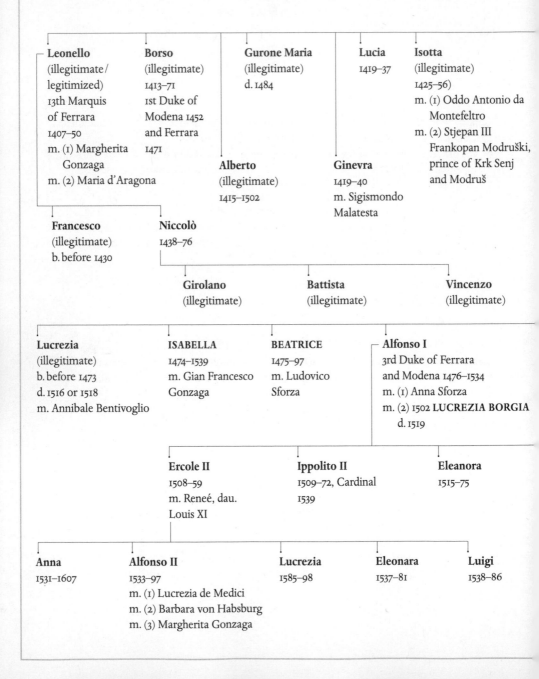

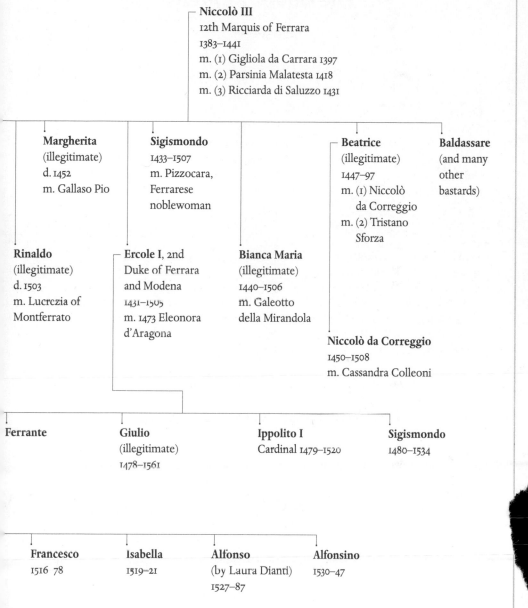

Niccolò III
12th Marquis of Ferrara
1383–1441
m. (1) Gigliola da Carrara 1397
m. (2) Parsinia Malatesta 1418
m. (3) Ricciarda di Saluzzo 1431

Margherita
(illegitimate)
d. 1452
m. Gallaso Pio

Sigismondo
1433–1507
m. Pizzocara,
Ferrarese
noblewoman

Beatrice
(illegitimate)
1447–97
m. (1) Niccolò
da Correggio
m. (2) Tristano
Sforza

Baldassare
(and many
other
bastards)

Rinaldo
(illegitimate)
d. 1503
m. Lucrezia of
Montferrato

Ercole I, 2nd
Duke of Ferrara
and Modena
1431–1505
m. 1473 Eleonora
d'Aragona

Bianca Maria
(illegitimate)
1440–1506
m. Galeotto
della Mirandola

Niccolò da Correggio
1450–1508
m. Cassandra Colleoni

Ferrante

Giulio
(illegitimate)
1478–1561

Ippolito I
Cardinal 1479–1520

Sigismondo
1480–1534

Francesco
1516–78

Isabella
1519–21

Alfonso
(by Laura Dianti)
1527–87

Alfonsino
1530–47

The House of Borgia

Cesare
(illegitimate)
1476–1509
Cardinal 1493,
Duke of Romagna
m. Charlotte d'Albret

Juan
(illegitimate)
1478–97
Duke of Gandia
m. Maria Enriquez
de Luna

LUCREZIA
(illegitimate)
1480–1519
m. (1) Giovanni Sforza
m. (2) Alfonso d'Aragona
m. (3) Alfonso d'Este

Louise
1500–53
m. (1) Louis de
la Tremouille
m. (2) Philippe
de Bourbon

Girolamo
(illegitimate)
m. (1) Isabella
Pizzabernari
m. (2) Isabella
Pio di Carpi

**Camilla
Lucrezia**
(illegitimate)
Abbess of
S. Bernardino,
Ferrara
d. 1573

Rodrigo
Duke of
Bisceglie
1499–1512

Ercole II
Duke of
Ferrara 1509–59
m. Renée of
France

Ippolito
Cardinal
1509–72

The House of Aragona (Naples)

Alfonso II
Duke of Calabria
1448–95
m. Ippolita Sforza 1446–86

Eleonora
1450–93
m. 1473 Ercole d'Este,
Duke of Ferrara

Federico IV
1452–1504
m. (1) Anne of Savoy
m. (2) Isabella del Balzo

Ferrante II (Ferrandino)
1467–96
m. Giovanna d'Aragona,
his father's half sister

ISABELLA
1470–1524
m. Giangaleazzo Sforza

Pietro
1472–91

Rodrigo Borgia
Cardinal 1456,
Pope Alexander VI 1492
mistresses include Vanozza Cattanei
and Giulia Farnese 1474–1524

Joffre
(illegitimate)
1482–1518
Prince of Squillace
m. (1) Sancia d'Aragona
m. (2) Maria Milan de Aragón
    y de Villahermosa

Giovanni
(illegitimate)
1498–1548
Infans Romanus,
Duke of Camerino

Rodrigo
(illegitimate)
1503–

Eleonora
Abbess of
Corpus Domini,
Ferrara
1515–75

Francesco
Marquis of
Massalom-
Barda
1516–78

Francesco
2nd Prince of
Squillace
m. (1) Isabella
    Piccolomini
m. (2) Isabella d´
    Aragona

Lucrezia
m. Giovanni
Battista Carafa,
Marquis of
Castelvetere

Antonia
m. Antonio
Todeschini
Piccolomini,
Marquis of
Delicete

Maria
m. Michele
Ayerba
d'Aragona,
Count of
Simari

Ferrante I
1423–94
m. (1) Isabella di Chiaromonte 1424–65
m. (2) Joan of Aragon

Giovanni
Cardinal
1456–85

Beatrice
1457–1508
m. Matthias Corvinus,
King of Hungary

Francesco
1461–86

Sancìa
(illegitimate)
1478–1504
m. Joffre Borgia

Alfonso
(illegitimate)
Duke of Bisceglie
1481–1500
m. **LUCREZIA BORGIA**
1480–1519

Rodrigo
1499–1512

'So thick was the undergrowth of alliances among the seigniorial families that to strike one branch was to break another. Like the dogs in the woods of Suicides.'

P. Partner, The Lands of St Peter (1972)

Introduction

Even after the passage of more than five hundred years, fifteenth-century Italy, that dangerous and exhilarating place, still glitters. Its power to dazzle remains undimmed. At the time, Italy provided little more than a geographical expression for the boot-shaped peninsula divided into 250 disparate and individual states, each with their own language or dialect, laws, currency, customs and idiosyncrasies. They varied greatly, not least in size. The Duchy of Milan and the Republic of Venice, both at the northern end of the peninsula, were among the largest, though, territorially, neither could rival the Kingdom of Naples, usually referred to simply as 'the Kingdom'. These lands of the Aragonese kings stretched along the entire length of the country south of Rome, down to the tip of Italy.

These large, powerful states contrasted dramatically with the smaller domains. The Duchy of Mirandola, near Modena, owned by the Pico, Lords of Concordia, comprised little more than a forti-fied town surrounded by water, and could have fitted neatly into London's Hyde Park with room to spare, especially at low tide. The people spoke Miràndla, had their own currency, the 'diemi', and venerated their own patron saint, Posidonio. Whether large or small, each dominion blazed with its own unmistakable hue. Some could be described as progressive, others as repressive, all of them as unpredictable as the frequently colourful personalities of their princely autocrats.

The rulers went by all manner of names. Great and noble families dominated, though exceptional houses such as the mercantile de' Medici had also won their place alongside the princely clans. Several feudal dynasties still prospered, whose families and fortunes had been built on their martial skills. The great tales of virtue and courage that circulated about the earliest Orsini knights or the brave warriors of the Colonna had long since passed into the folklore of Christendom. Important families with warrior-princes carried much glamour, such as the glittering d'Este of Ferrara, the royal house of Aragon, the Sforza and the Gonzaga. The ranks of leading princes swelled during the course of our story, as the names of Borgia, Farnese and della Rovere took their places among the foremost families of Italy.

The papacy had returned in 1376 after its almost seventy-year sojourn in Avignon, a period which was followed by the Western Schism and a time of internal strife, of popes and anti-popes. At one stage three men claimed the papal tiara, followed by a two-year interregnum with no pontiff at all. The confusion and chaos ended in 1417 when Odonne Colonna became Pope Martin V.

In the fourteenth century Rome had fallen into a state of decay and, unsurprisingly, lost its allure to pilgrims and prelates alike. The wide, ancient avenues stood quiet, blocked at intervals by markets and shacks. Temple pediments and fine columns lay collapsed, their once fluted elegance spread out on the ground beside the shattered carvings. Criminal gangs worked the old city, seizing anything that could be carried off, carted away and sold. They stripped the marble floors and limestone blocks, leaving the old ruins naked but for the verdant creepers. Empty alcoves seemed to gape in open-mouthed lament for the stolen busts of former emperors. Grassy meadows had sprung up as though attempting to recover some modesty for the once proud centre of the civilized world. Smallholdings dotted the land, as goats and sheep grazed contentedly, undisturbed by the bloodier battles between the Colonna and the Orsini, while the rest of the population fled, leaving the city all but deserted. It seems extraordinary today to think that the Almighty's holy and anointed chosen home for his Church had once been ready to slide into oblivion, lost for ever to vice and sin.

Gaining mastery over Rome and returning the place to order provided an immediate challenge for Martin, and for those who followed after his death in 1431. Francesco della Rovere was elected Pope Sixtus IV in 1471 and started an ambitious rebuilding and modernization programme. The feudal clans of Orsini and Colonna nursed a deep-seated hatred for each other and fought out their ancient battle for the domination of the city well into the early part of the sixteenth century. The papacy invariably depended upon one or other of the two families for support in its elections, and would use the soldiers of the chosen house as enforcers, or peacekeepers – often two entirely opposing initiatives – depending on who was pope at the time.

As Rome began to achieve some measure of order by the mid-fifteenth century, the pontiffs attempted to extend their monarchical grasp over the temporal Territories of Saint Peter with mixed results. The vast swathe of land from the Romagna in the north-east of Italy across the Apennine Mountains and south to Rome had been the scene of bitter fighting during the near-necrotic period of the papacy. Entrepreneurial local magnates and warlords seized power, and by the time the pontiff turned his attention beyond the walls of Rome the tempestuous and unruly Apennine and Romagnol dominions had fallen into independent hands. The Ferrarese region, for instance, ruled by the respected house of d'Este, could not be controlled from Rome, nor did the pope have a treasury to support a campaign of reconquest. It is this period that demonstrated how paradoxical and irreconcilable the pontiffs' dual roles as spiritual leaders of the Christian Church, and temporal monarchs of the Papal Territories, could be.

Around the Holy Father and papal monarch, other magnates carried titles of assorted rank, ranging from the King of Naples, to dukes, marquises, counts, barons, as well as assorted brigands and robber-princes, all bestriding a territory over which they claimed hegemony. Some served as genuinely enlightened rulers; others qualified as no more than psychotic tyrants. Yet, following the spirit of the age, even the cruellest prince among them had usually managed to acquire finely honed artistic sensibilities.

The seigniorial families, such as the Visconti Sforza, the d'Este and the Gonzaga, proud of their ancient heritage, held sway over their states through their long tenure and personal prestige. As their own domains enjoyed periods of domestic tranquillity, these battle-hardened rulers put their martial experience to commercial use, turning their armies into mercenary forces for hire. Italy, after all, never lacked for local wars and bloody conflagrations.

Conflict among the peninsula's princes was endemic. The arriviste petty tyrants, with their hurriedly devised escutcheons, tried hard to fit in, but feared the well-established rulers might catch an occasional unpleasant whiff of drying paint from these newly conceived heraldic adornments. Driven by a mixture of paranoia and ambition, they had yet to acquire the self-assured ways of the greatest princes of the peninsula, and, though their talents might have counted for something in the twilight world of thieves, confidence tricksters and occasional soldiers, few had acquired the aptitude, or the power, to lead a well-organized armed force. To boost their courage and swell their armies in the persistent jockeying for position among the other states, they parleyed but hardly dared bargain with the experienced soldier-princes. These parvenus became *ingénus* as the grizzled patrician *condottieri* casually asked for, and received, extortionate sums for their services. A newly minted prince would rarely argue, fearing that any negotiating might suggest a lack of means, and lead to his own death sentence.

The Renaissance was an age when display meant plenty, and abundance equalled strength; a new arrival would pay whatever he must to hire a great *condottiere* and his men. These sums earned a sizeable income for the *condottieri* states. Others, such as the Medici, the *de facto* princes of Florence, used the mercenary leaders and their armies when necessary, but their preferred alliance lay with the Sforza of Milan. However, these ever-rational Florentines disliked the irreversible justice of the death penalty. When troubled by internal problems, they abjured the sword when possible, preferring to rid themselves of their enemies by means of fiscal strangulation and the might of the accounting book.

Whatever the methods, these potentates' lives were committed to three things above all others: survival, expansion and self-glorification. The last of these, the insatiable urge for glory and immortality, partly explains the extraordinary architectural and artistic feats of the Italian Renaissance. The rediscovery of ideas and techniques lost since the disintegration of the ancient Greek and Roman civilizations led to a flood of commissions. Many of the great sculptures, churches, frescoes adorned with the faces of their patrons, and other precociously daring works of the period, remain familiar today. The popes, dukes, cardinals, bankers and soldiers applied their utmost efforts to immortalize their names through their patronage of the Humanist artists, architects, poets, and writers. Leonardo da Vinci, Luigi Pulci, Marsilio Ficino, Filippo Brunelleschi, Giovanni Boccaccio, Donato di Niccolò di Betto Bardi, known as Donatello, Michelangelo di Buonarroti and Agnolo Polizano, were but a few of their number.

The decision to design a new Medici palace in the 1440s evoked a huge amount of interest. It would not be the largest palace in the city (a deliberate decision on the part of Lorenzo the Magnificent's grandfather, Cosimo de' Medici); but Brunelleschi lost the commission when he drew the cover off his maquette to reveal a design that would translate the building into a vast and grandiose edifice thereby quickly reawakening the ticklish city's republican sensibilities. Brunelleschi added a crowning solecism by placing the main doors of the palazzo directly facing those of the church of San Lorenzo. The precise juxtaposition of church and palace doors lay in the strict preserve of bishops and kings alone. The whole concept provided the architechual antithesis of the subtle and successful Medici method that had afforded them leadership of Florence. Cosimo rebuffed the idea impatiently, at which Brunelleschi reportedly knocked his maquette to the floor, smashing it into countless pieces.

The eventual design by Michelozzo triggered the building of a number of apparently similar palazzi among the city's magnates. Yet few managed more than a pale imitation of the original. They lacked the detail and particular dimensions that cleverly made the Medici palace appear light and elegant but at the same time disguised its sturdy ground floor. The new headquarters of the ruling family became the ultimate Florentine showplace, a family home, that could quite easily house official visitors council meetings.

Even the chapel had a double purpose: after finishing his morning prayers, Cosimo could conduct his most secret business in this exquisite and sound-proof place of worship. Most importantly, in the event of political unrest the palazzo had a further and most particular strength as a fortress. Michelozzo had worked hard to make theirs a home for all seasons.

The palazzo was originally built to house the four direct descendants of Cosimo and his wife Contessina. These included their sickly heir, Piero the Gouty, and daughter-in-law, Lucrezia Tornabuoni. A long-nosed, plain-faced girl, Lucrezia seemed to have been born with an innate understanding of human power dynamics, particularly the complex rules favoured by Florentine patriarchs that forced her gender out of the lime light. The first of our 'deadly sisterhood', she would live on to rule alongside her eldest son, Lorenzo, as Queen Mother of Florence.

Lucrezia received many foreign and fellow Italian rulers, their families and ambassadors at the Medici palazzo. Without exception, the guests fell into raptures of delight when they saw the palace for the first time. They thoroughly approved of the building's mixture of innovation with important defensive qualities, its many comforts juxtaposed with treasures from Cosimo's art collection. It also served as an unofficial new centre of government. As Cosimo and his sons could only rarely make the short journey to the Palazzo Vecchio, the official seat of the Florentine government, it became common to see officials hurrying to the Medici headquarters to discuss their business and take advantage of its many places to walk and talk in privacy. In summer the cool of a double courtyards afforded respite from the blistering summer heat, the second opening upon an enchanting garden fragranced by boxed lemon trees. The graceful lines of Michelozzo's mansion also gave the family a heating system to ward off the penetrating cold of the Florentine winters, water for washing, and a rudimentary waste disposal system.

History, it seems, has a sense of humour. Despite the efforts of the rich princes, popes and bankers to immortalize their names in the works they commissioned, few among them are remembered today, yet the poly-talented artists who had accidentally created their own personal memorials, are venerated the world over. The humble words of Petrarch suggested he believed otherwise when he wrote:

> It is possible that some word of me may have come to you, though even this is doubtful, since an insignificant and obscure name will scarcely penetrate far in either time or space. If, however, you should have heard of me, you may desire to know what manner of man I was, or what was the outcome of my labours.

Of course, Petrarch's name and the splendour of the world he inhabited has penetrated far into our time. This is the famous world of the fifteenth-century Italian Renaissance. What we know far less about is the real and still hidden history of that time – one that did not feature in these great monuments, inscriptions or official accounts. The events of this secret history could as likely have taken place in a small palace chapel, crossing a Florentine piazza, in the ballrooms, bedchambers, and the whispering recesses of great palace corridors, as on the fields of battle or before stout fortress walls. It is a history driven by some of the bravest and most brilliant women of the age. This book recreates the tempestuous lives and careers of eight of them.

These consorts and ducal daughters figure less prominently in official documents, except as human postscripts affixed first to their father's name and regal declarations, then seamlessly to those of their princely husbands. Even upon the birth of a son and heir, letters of congratulations would arrive written to the ruler and father of a male child. Muted commiserations or a tactful silence often followed the delivery a baby girl, whose birth might even have been left unrecorded in the official accounts. As for the mother, if she survived, the prescribed post-partum recovery dictated that she remain in her bed for many weeks, taking broth and lying in a darkened chamber.

Yet these baby girls, whose births went largely uncelebrated, are the subject of this book. All were connected by the dense family relations and interwoven dynastic politics of fifteenth-century Italy; indeed it would have been impossible to stand apart. As one historian has noted: 'So thick was the undergrowth of alliances among the seigniorial families, that to strike one branch was to break another.'

The eight princesses of our deadly sisterhood give their own account of the hidden history of their time in their daily letters: letters crammed with family news, quotidian events and other apparent trivia. Whether they were friends or rivals, sisters or strangers married into the family, the actions and exchanges of these women tell us far more than any formal accounts.

A visit to the pawnbroker followed by the apparent profligacy of shopping for gold brocade made perfect sense in a world where outward display was central to survival. Sharing the family jewels and gold plate held no shame. The ruling house of Mantua, for instance, would gather all their golden ornaments together to be worn and displayed by the wife of the ruling marquis Isabella d'Este, who came from neighbouring Ferrara. A greedy magpie when it came to collecting for herself, she acted sensibly by borrowing the pooled family jewels for making an appearance, especially on her frequent visits to the court of Milan where her younger sister and rival, Beatrice, reigned supreme. Isabella had a well-earned reputation for making an entrance. She had learned how to stand apart, and appear cleverly modish without stooping to vulgarity. Lavish embroidery with gold and silver thread could display her academic talents at the back of her skirts. An ancient Greek wisdom would be picked out in precious pearls near the hem, only to reveal another meaning altogether when the wide and hidden pleats opened as she danced, turning and twirling. The full extent of her wit would be admired by all. Isabella managed, with thrift and ingenuity, to match or outdo her sister Beatrice with her seemingly endless round of balls, banquets, masques and other festivities that she devised and at the court of her husband's rich duchy of Milan. The gems sparkling in Isabella's hair lent much-needed lustre to her husband's military reputation. Fellow princely guests concluded that the fortune of the Marquis must be vast, for how else could he bedeck his wife in such costly splendour?

Often betrothed at birth, the sisterhood married in their early teens. Their husbands had frequently to depart, most often to fight for their states, and the number of hungry-looking bastards sloping around the court, waiting for an opportunity to remove their half-sibling or cousin from his throne, made the princely departure a riskier business than going into battle. So their young wives were often left to act as regents, usually with an elder of the court to give counsel. In some notable cases, miserable and mistreated wives did throw their lot in with plotters. Fortunately, among the sisterhood, the ruling couples' joint desire to protect their children and future inheritance prevailed.

As she waved to her departing husband, often for many months at a time, a new, probably teenage, perhaps homesick regent, had a back-breaking task ahead of her. Entertaining foreign potentates with suitable pomp and tone according to their status and the relationship with between the two states, planning and leading court festivities, and taking part in the chase, all fell into a young regent's remit. Whether parrying witticisms with foreign ambassadors or composing tributes at the death of a neighbouring potentate, she would also have to find the time to fulfil her duty as loving mother to their princely – and any illegitimate – children. As illegitimacy proved no bar to success in the Renaissance, known as the golden age of bastards, expectation fell to the wives to raise their husbands' natural children with their own.

Dutiful servants had to be found to care for occupants of the nursery, as well as appropriate tutors to educate the children. The women of this story, with one notable exception, sought out teachers to tutor their offspring in the progressive Humanist manner. The Humanist study of classical texts allowed a greater freedom for girls in the schoolroom that would have been unthinkable only decades earlier. Young women of patrician backgrounds received much the same education as their brothers. The girls quickly demonstrated that they had the ability to consider the theses of great philosophers, and that their understanding of rhetoric matched that of their brothers. They ably examined and compared the texts of Plato and Aristotle. If women could reason, they could also rule.

Beyond the schoolroom, there could be no slacking over the expected feminine accomplishments. The women stitched, sang, played an instrument and danced; they rode with a crossbow, and were as daring as any of their brothers on horseback. Caterina Sforza, another member of the sisterhood, proved particularly adept at the art of warfare, whether in one-to-one combat or the disposition of her artillery. As consorts of princes these splendid women, without excpetion, soon learned how to be able administrators, arbiters of justice and approachable figureheads to whom their husbands' subjects could appeal when bearing a grievance.

At some juncture, to complicate matters, the move from natal to marital house would almost invariably produce a conflict of interest between the neophyte regent's home territory and the dominion that the girl ruled with pride and energy in place of her husband. The near-constant state of warfare taking place somewhere on the peninsula and the consequent shifting of allegiances would one day bring sisters, cousins, mothers and daughters into direct conflict.

Significantly, whatever their husbands' or home states' political alliance, their personal relationships tended to remain their own. As their husbands collided in armed contest on the field of battle, the respective wives and sisters often found themselves sitting together, each affecting a breezy air, busy at their needlework. Or if imminent danger threatened, these intrepid creatures would walk the ramparts, often within enemy range, to put heart into the men, greeting them as though heedless of any danger. Each knowing that at any time the arrival of a courier could bring news of triumph for one and disaster for another.

During their regencies the princesses worked to bring peace and prosperity to areas of their territory famed for petty border conflicts and other vexatious quarrels. However, the rivalries and jealousies between them, including real or imagined plots, could be the cause of great embarrassment. Isabella d'Este's libidinous husband's behaviour grew quite out of hand, and it began to seem as though most of the population of Mantua under the age of fourteen had a curiously familiar look; she even remarked upon the simian trait that appeared so frequently among the children of her state. Several of the sisterhood are known to have had multiple love affairs while married, notably one with the husband of her arch-rival within the ruling female cabal. This particular liaison appears to have been covered up, as it was a perilous and sometimes fatal business if the affair was discovered.

Marriages for their children had to be prudently arranged, both according to the realities of the day and with an eye to a highly changeable future. Isabella d'Este ensured that she had forged secret alliances with the opposing forces. Her politics benefited from the speed with which she relocated her loyalties. She managed these frequent switches of fealty without the slightest blush upon her well-rounded cheeks. A true Renaissance princess, she insured and reinsured the future of her line.

In the last years of the fifteenth century, for all the exuberance, brilliance and precocity to pursue the aesthetics of ancient Rome and Greece, the loosening of old restraints, secret talks, emissaries, and spies, cardinals and kings talked in lowered voices. The fresh and joyous feeling had been replaced by a heavy atmosphere pregnant with menace. As the balls, masques, banquets and song became ever more frenetic and the festivities never-ending, so did the portentous feeling that danger lurked in the dark passages which the sunlight never touched, where killers crouched in waiting to add another life to what became terrible roll-call of death. Assassinations abounded in Italy and the peninsula acquired a sinister reputation for killing. The English playwright Thomas Nashe summed up the view of many contemporaries when he dubbed it 'the academe for man-slaughter, apothecary shoppe of poison and sporting place for mur-ther'. There were assassinations, vendettas and feuds, internecine squabbles, the origins of which had long been forgotten – but the hatred between the rival factions had not died.

Neither Isabella nor Beatrice knew why the portentous feeling prevailed, nor that they danced upon the edge of a world that was about to end and cast Italy into a fifty-year reign of bloody battles fought by foreign invaders. They were all enjoying their last carefree dance, and afterwards a new world would emerge in which those who remained of the sisterhood had matured; they were pragmatic survivors; even their triumphs could never taste the same. The joyous phase of the Renaissance ended, and a darker time lay ahead.

The women described in these pages led rich, perilous, densely entwined lives, any of which could fill a biography on its own. But their value is greater still when seen as a group. For their collective story is more than an anthology of heroic, courageous or romantic episodes – though there are plenty of those. These women were also, in many ways, the last of their kind. Living during the high days, and then the dying days, of the Renaissance, those who survived, saw that life snuffed out in 1527 with the Sack of Rome. The sixteenth century witnessed the emergence of the nation states – Spain united, and France became a cohesive single-language country, the largest in Christendom, under Francis I. These goliaths modelled their own courts on the supremely sophisticated Italian miniatures from what had become a bygone age. Life took on a stricter attitude, and as these great powers fought over and occupied the peninsula, so they crushed the living brilliance of the city states.

Perhaps, though, the deadly sisterhood triumphed after all. A surprising number of their children and grandchildren, and many generations of descendants, became some of the greatest kings, queens, popes and princes of subsequent ages. The women whose lives unfold in this book were great in their lifetimes, and proved greater still in their bloodlines. Their descendants still occupy the few thrones that remain.

PROLOGUE

She-wolf of the Romagna

14 APRIL 1488

'A Monster Disguised as a Female or La Prima Donna D'Italia'

(ANON.)

During the late afternoon of Monday, 14 April 1488, inside the ruler's palace at Forlì, a family party had just finished their *cena*.* Caterina Sforza, the twenty-five-year-old countess of the small state, rose from the table. At the same time, the tall and fashionably slender beauty, whose long, fair hair framed her renowned features, glanced at her mother and two half-sisters, recently arrived from the mighty Sforza dominion of Milan. Her expression told them to follow her lead. Upon reaching the flabby figure of Caterina's husband, Girolamo Riario, Count of Forlì, Lord of Imola and nephew of the late Pope Sixtus IV,[†] the three guests each dropped a deep curtsey taking their leave. Finally, Caterina made her usual elegant *révérence* and retired. She would not see her husband alive again.

As Caterina and her party left the Hall of Nymphs, the palazzo's shabby former showpiece where they had just dined in dismal state, a young guard on the castle's ramparts took off his small red cap and

---

* The main meal of the day in the fifteenth century, taken at different times of the afternoon or evening depending upon the time of year.

† Many believed Girolamo Riario to have been the Pope's son as well as his nephew, the second of two boys, Pietro and Girolamo, both born of an incestuous affair between the Pope when he was Friar Francesco della Rovere and his sister Bianca. The second popular theory is that the boys came from a liaison between della Rovere and an unknown woman. Adopting her nephews secretly, Bianca and her husband, Paolo Riario, a nonentity from Savona, brought the boys up as their own. Pietro, the elder, died in 1474, aged twenty-eight. At his brother's death, Girolamo took Pietro's place as the first in the Pope's affections. I shall refer to Girolamo as the Pontiff's nephew.

waved it towards the darkest corner of the main square. As he did so, he unwittingly set into motion a fatal chain of events.

Walking down the long dilapidated hallway leading to her apartments, Caterina could hardly have failed to ponder the perils she and her husband faced. Throughout his seven-year rule Girolamo Riario had managed the singular distinction of becoming the most hated prince in the mean, strategically critical Apennine mountain state's doleful litany of tyrants. The Romagnol people were a belligerent and tempestuous breed, with a brutal history, who laboured to eke a living off the largely wild and difficult terrain of north-eastern Italy. Both men and women had learned to be as dextrous with their farm tools as with their weapons, ready to spend the day either toiling over their patch of scrub, or fighting back-to-back, defending their lives and their land from the many passing opportunists wanting to make it their own. They were naturally suspicious at the arrival of any strangers.

Riario and Caterina had first arrived in Forlì with calculated splendour and in magnificent state on 15 July 1481, hailed as King Midas with his beautiful Queen Demodike riding beside him. Well might the crowds have celebrated, for on his arrival Riario, hoping to buy the love of his turbulent, ferocious people, had been rich enough to lighten considerably his subjects' heavy tax burden. Yet despite his apparent munificence, Riario had never felt entirely secure as Lord. Plots against him were rife; on the rare occasions that he appeared in the streets, he would be surrounded by a disproportionately large bodyguard.

When Riario's uncle Sixtus IV died in 1484, the count had lost his all-powerful patron and seen the folly of his generous fiscal policy exposed. Without the protection of his uncle or any revenues from his two states, Riario was broke. It had been Caterina who forced a solution, goading her husband for his senseless government and demanding that he reintroduce the previously abolished dues to rescue the duchy from total impoverishment. 'Of whom are you afraid?' she had asked Riario. 'Are the people of Forlì the only ones in the world who do not pay taxes? Shall we govern and defend them and, alone among princes, give of our own substance to our subjects, who give us nothing? Who can reproach you [for revoking

your promise]... is everyone to die of hunger because of your vow?'
Riario, realizing that he had little alternative, had enacted swingeing
new duties to refill his exchequer.

Predictably, the policy did not endear the count and – by association – Caterina to their people. Riario, a lymphatic and indolent
creature, alternated between two attitudes: he suffered both terror
over the danger to his person and paroxysms of anger at his subjects'
ingratitude. 'Are these the thanks I get for the immunities I have
given my people?' he spat, in furious self-pity. He appeared comforted only by the patrician cool of his courageous wife. Caterina
might have been weary of her husband, but they shared one single,
burning ambition: to remain the first couple of Forlì at all costs.

One chronicler wrote down his first and lasting impressions of
Caterina: 'words fail to describe her glorious beauty and graceful
manner'. Her pedigree as a Sforza princess of Milan linked the new
countess with most of the ruling dynasties in Italy, and she played
the seigniorial lady to perfection. Surrounded by maids of honour,
Caterina made daily sorties, and on the first visit to Forlì she never
appeared in the same gown twice. Each confection seemed more
brilliant than the last, though nothing outshone her feminine
beauty and youthful vigour. Beneath the courtly exterior, however,
Caterina's Romagnol roots and physical prowess lay well hidden.
She had earned a reputation as a superb equestrian and an able
practitioner both of the use of arms and of military tactics in
general.

She was also an instinctive and adept public politician. As a daughter of the Sforza house,* rulers of Milan and one of the most brilliant dynasties of *condottieri*† ever known on the Italian peninsula,
Caterina did not hide inside the palace, nor did she remove herself
from her husband's subjects. Rather, she knew she must allow herself to be seen. Latterly, despite the great danger, she had ridden out
among the people more than ever. Although she no longer appeared
in the glittering gowns of former days, her poise, stature and slim

---

* Caterina's paternal great-grandfather, founder of the house of Sforza as rulers of Milan,
  came from Cotignola, near the Romagnol domain of Imola. The Count of Cotignola in
  1488 was Guido Sforza, son of Caterina's great-uncle Bosio.
† *Condottieri* is the name given to the military commanders of mercenary soldiers.

silhouette distinguished the countess more than her rich clothes ever could. Her excursions gave her much-needed opportunities to fathom any fresh plots against Riario.

The palace seemed particularly quiet on that April evening, contrasting with the happy sounds of the boisterous throng wafting up from the piazza below. The usual household officers dining below would soon return, allowing the few left on duty to take their own dinner.

The ill-lit passages only heightened the feeling that the place had been abandoned, adding to the lugubrious atmosphere created by the palazzo's tired glamour.

At last, the party reached Caterina's rooms. During dinner the count, despite the parlous difficulties he faced, had unaccountably cast aside his habitual heavy, brooding presence. For a while he had become animated and buoyant, joshing playfully with his wife's guests, paying particular attention to Lucrezia Landriani, his mother-in-law. He also made himself unusually agreeable to Caterina's two half-sisters, Stella and Bianca.

After more than a decade of marriage to Count Girolamo Riario, Caterina, all too familiar with the uncertainties of her husband's kaleidoscopic temperament, had adroitly handled the conversation throughout dinner, fearing the wrong word might trigger an eruption from him. She knew that her union with the lumpen Riario had long since been exposed as a fantastic mismatch. The proud Sforza princess of Milan did not wish her mother or the two younger girls to witness the bleaker aspects of her marriage.

Once inside the countess's apartments, her three guests livened up the atmosphere by promising to feed Caterina's hunger for news of the large family she had left behind at the time of her marriage, aged only fourteen. They had much to tell and busied themselves with the needlework put aside before dinner. It is easy to picture Lucrezia and the girls talking all at once, their neat heads bent over their embroidery. They probably did not notice as Caterina moved away from them towards the large window overlooking Forli's central piazza.

The city square below remained a pullulating mass of people

enjoying the balmy weather, unusual for April. Happy shouts of greeting and the exchange of pleasantries carried up to Caterina who stood staring into the multitude below, particularly scrutinizing those whose faces she could make out among the mêlée nearest the palace.

Once the women had left him, the count remained in the Hall of Nymphs, where he had received two court officers in attendance that evening and a young relation to whom he had given an important post in Forlì. They were his chancellor, Girolamo Casale, Riario's young kinsman from Savona, Corradino Feo – son of Tommaso Feo, castellan of Forlì's most important fortress, the Rocca di Ravaldino, a stronghold greatly modernized and enlarged by the nervous count even before he had arrived in Forlì – and Niccolò of Cremona, who happened to be in-waiting on the count that evening. Corradino Feo had been given the post of lieutenant to his father. The small gathering gave him news and reports on diverse topics.

At the same time as Caterina stood at the window of her apartments, Riario also looked down into the square. Resting his head in his hands, he watched the pretty girls flirting with the young men below. Generally he despised the rabble, though tonight he appeared to feel a serene indifference towards them – provided they continued with their diversions and caused him no trouble. He turned to face his three companions and, leaning his elbows on the window ledge, listened to their reports, from time to time adding his own humorous assessments.

The sudden noise of the doors to the Great Hall opening silenced Riario, who appeared surprised at the lack of ceremony. He had already started scowling at the interruption, though his expression quickly changed to a smile of recognition at the sight of the unexpected caller. Francesco Orsi, known by all as Checco, one of the chief citizens of Forlì, held the dubious distinction of being the nearest the Count had to come to making a close friend. In his official capacity, Orsi received the 'gilded key', a perquisite automatically granting him access to Riario. Checco Orsi had ensured that his brother Ludovico had also become one of the count's familiars. They spent much time together, but recent arguments over taxes and money owed to Riario had caused ill-feeling on both sides. These bitter and short exchanges had included threats made by the count. The want of money in his exchequer had left him desperate and powerless.

Orsi, astonished by the count's obvious pleasure at seeing him, composed himself as Riario left the window and walked towards him with open arms in a gesture of welcome. 'How goes it, my Checco?'

Orsi bowed and mumbled that he had proof that he would be able to pay his Lord in a few days. He reached into his sleeve (often used as pockets) but, instead of a letter, Checco Orsi pulled out a dagger and plunged it into the left side of Riario's chest, exposed by his welcoming gesture. With the shout 'Ah! Traitor' the injured count instinctively tried to make his way to Caterina's rooms.

Fortunately for Checco Orsi, who stood paralysed by the horrible sensation of stabbing Riario, holding the bloody dagger aloft in what seemed an almost theatrical gesture, two experienced soldiers came in to finish the job. With them came Ludovico Panzechi and Giacomo Ronchi, who had both faithfully served the count during his uncle's papacy, when he had been all-powerful. They had been henchmen to Riario, following his orders – these usually meant aiding the abuse of every powerful position that the Holy Father had awarded him.

Now these feckless former allies dragged their victim by his hair back to where he had first been struck. There he lay, pinioned to the floor as the two soldiers, with a grim professionalism, stabbed him 'in his vital parts', then battered and smashed his lifeless face.

The first intimation of danger came to Caterina with the sound of one or more men running fast down the passage towards her apartments, followed by urgent banging upon the vast solid door into the countess's chambers. Niccolò of Cremona hurriedly broke the dread tidings and told Caterina these men certainly meant to kill her and all her children too. She must save herself and those with her.

Caterina immediately ordered the women and children to stand at the open window facing the square and shout and wail:

'Help! Help! They have murdered the count! Now they are coming to murder Madonna! Help! Help!' With the servants she pulled huge tables and chests across the doors to prevent an easy entry. She told the men carrying arms to pursue the murderers; adding the instruction to show no mercy, she declared that none of the conspirators would be allowed to live. Then she joined the terri-fied chorus by the window, including her mother, her sisters and her children, urging them to redouble their cry for help, hoping that the crowd below would feel roused by their piteous wails. But the shrill screams from Caterina's window were drowned by a louder and deeper chant of triumph – 'Liberty! Liberty! Long live the Orsi!' – as the mob slowly began to move forward towards the palace.

Within the palace, Orsi's rebels made short work of the barricade, and once in the chamber they arrested Caterina and the small group around her including two nursemaids. As Orsi demanded the coun-tess leave with them, she pulled defiantly away from the rebel's grip, saying she would go nowhere without her family. Without haste she kissed each of her children in turn before placing herself between Checco Orsi and his lieutenant. 'With measured pace she led her family as they walked out to face the mob.' The people seemed mesmerized by the appearance of the countess emerging from the palace. Without a word they parted to allow her passage, the rebel leaders flanking her as she headed the small procession of women and children.

As the bedraggled party disappeared from sight, the mob rushed into the palace to plunder what finery remained. The Orsi had given close instructions to their own men as to where they would find the choicest pickings. Only Caterina's exquisite linens remained untouched. It seemed a strange and poignant mark of respect that no one could take their Lady's most intimate personal belongings.

As the prisoners arrived at the Palazzo Orsi they could hear the shout, 'Here is the traitor who oppressed us!' Fortunately, they could not see the count's mangled body held aloft before it was cast from the palace window, striking the cobbled piazza below with a sicken-ing thud. Falling upon the unrecognizable corpse, the ravening mob stripped any remaining clothes from the count's body and mashed his flesh.

Sounds of looting filled the air as Forlì descended into a macabre feast of violence. The horrid thrill would have been somewhat muted had the Orsi known that a small group of Riario loyalists had escaped. They were led by Corradino Feo. The small group had waited for an opportune moment to make their dash for the Rocca di Ravaldino. As they reached the stronghold's massive gates, two couriers received their messages and instructions. They set off at a gallop, carrying hastily scribbled notes in Caterina's name. One headed for the Bentivoglio of Bologna and the other set out in the direction of the countess's natal state of Milan. He had been ordered to hand-deliver the note to Ludovico Sforza, Il Moro, the ducal regent of Milan, who could be relied upon to take a keen interest in his niece's imprisonment by the mob. Both missives begged for troops to restore Caterina to power in Forlì.

The miserable group of women and seven tired children at the Palazzo Orsi stood locked into a small room, unable to sit down, and guarded by men little more than criminals armed with pikes, muttering abuse at their exhausted prisoners. The terrified children held onto Caterina's gown whimpering; the two nurses could barely stand up, far less hold the infant children. Caterina cradled her two babes one at a time, and soothed their hungry wails.

At a hastily convened meeting of the town council, Checco Orsi bombastically regaled the company with interminable accounts of his leading role in the night's events. His part in freeing Forlì became nobler and more courageous at each retelling. But as the grey light of dawn filtered in, revealing the tired faces of the city fathers, the conspirators realized the enormity of their crime. The chief magistrate, Niccolò Tornielli, argued that the only possible way forward that carried a scintilla of legality would be to send for the Papal Governor and submit to him a signed act of allegiance to the pope, offering Forlì back to its ultimate sovereign as part of the Territories of St Peter.

This had not been the liberty envisaged by the Orsi, who, inebriated by their bloody deeds, suddenly found their position uncertain.

Determined to remain steady at that critical moment of shifting decisions, Checco declared that the inhabitants of Forlì deserved the freedom of home rule, and that the Holy Father should have no more than a theoretical suzerainty. Tornielli replied that 'the liberty so eulogized by the Orsi had begun in bloodshed and would not last eight days ... [making] Forlì the laughing stock of the proletariat of every other Italian city'.

He concluded with an ominous reminder to the whole council of Caterina's brother, Duke Giangaleazzo Sforza, Lord of Milan. '[Their solution must be] ... one that would not further irritate or wound the countess. That would not only be barbarous and inhuman, but would draw down fatal consequences upon the city, she being of subtle mind and of that high courage that was known to all, indomitable of spirit and inexorable in vengeance.'

Tornielli's caution offended the heroic emancipators of Forlì. Their tantalizing whiff of power had piqued their taste for more. They had not anticipated this disturbing turn of events in the council chamber. Nevertheless, the plain-speaking magistrate made his point briefly and without embellishment before sitting down to a rousing cheer from his fellow councillors, carrying the vote as he did so.

Monsignor Giovanni Battista Savelli, Apostolic Protonotary and Papal Legate in Bologna, duly arrived to a most perplexing situation. He visited the countess in her filthy chamber at the Palazzo Orsi. Her babies lay in soiled linens, screaming with hunger. Caterina listened to Savelli's attempts to console her. He promised to do all he could for the Countess and her children. He called the Orsi 'beasts in human form', and lamented that 'no Turks could have worse treated the Madonna'. He commanded that Caterina be taken away from the Orsi palace to the city gate of St Peter. There people of 'honourable disposition' would care for the 'Lady and her family'. After making a circuit around the square, denoting a papal fief being rendered back to the Pontiff, he headed for his nearby Cesena, urging his donkey to the nearest the beast could manage by way of a gallop.

Arriving back at his official residence Savelli wasted no time in recording the bloody events in Forlì. He handed his account to his fastest courier, whom he ordered to Rome with the news, then he turned around and made his way back to Forlì. As Savelli returned, he hoped that orders from the Pope would arrive without delay.

During Savelli's absence the rebels dragged the stricken and exhausted Caterina to the walls of the Rocca di Ravaldino. Standing beneath the imposing building, enlarged and reinforced by Riario, she looked up to see the figure of Tommaso Feo, the castellan.

'Surrender the fortress to these people, to save my life and those of my children!' she called.

'They can take me from here in pieces! I will not yield an inch' replied Feo, for the benefit of the crowd.

'They will murder me!'

'Whom will they murder? They have too much reason to fear the Duke of Milan,' returned Feo, who disappeared inside the fort signalling the end of the conversation.

This was exactly as Caterina had hoped. Part of her desperate instructions on the night of her arrest had been to send word to Tommaso Feo that he should not yield to her entreaties. She had known that the Orsi would do all they could to take the Rocca di Ravaldino – the hub of military power in Forlì. She had ordered that, no matter what the risk to her, the castellan must not yield unless he received word to do so.

Suspecting her duplicity, one of the Orsi rebels pulled out his dagger and placed the point at Caterina's breast. He hissed into her ear: 'O Madonna Caterina, if you chose he would give in to us, but 'tis you who will not let him surrender; I would have a mind to bore thee through and through with this dagger and to make thee fall down dead.' Caterina turned to him with slow disdain, even though the weapon was still held at her bodice. 'Do not frighten me,' she answered, 'deed canst do unto me, but canst not frighten, for I am a daughter of one who knew no fear. You have killed my Lord you might as well kill me, who am a woman.' Furious both with Caterina and their own failure to open the Rocca, the rebels began preparing to attack.

On the morning of 16 April, the rebels took Caterina to the lesser Forlivese fortress of Schiavoni. The same comedy played out there as at Ravaldino. The rebels began to grow desperate. As the days and hours passed, Savelli, having heard nothing from Rome, grew increasingly anxious. The plotters too became uncertain, wondering how long it would be before the Milanese troops appeared to liberate their duke's niece.

On the evening of 16 April the women and children left their fouled room at the Palazzo Orsi. Well guarded and led by torchlight, they reached their new prison in the city gate of St Peter, as ordered by Savelli. Savelli's carefully chosen nobles took the party into custody. Among them Caterina saw her own supporters. At last she believed she might yet carry the day.

The small cell allotted to the party was hardly an improvement in aesthetic terms, but once they had been left inside the small chamber she became visibly transformed and her spirits raised. Until then the young woman had carefully maintained an even countenance, fearing she might betray herself by showing too much good humour. Beset by practical difficulties, Caterina had plenty to concern her as a mother. The wet-nurses had no milk – the horror of the past few days had dried the last sour drop. The furious screams of baby Sforzino had faded and he lay listless and limp, his enfeebled whimpering alarming his mother more than his earlier angry cries for attention. The Countess requested food and fresh linens from her gaolers who, pitying their charge, also provided a cradle and other necessities.

Caterina then moved to rouse her mother and sisters, reassuring them that, horrid though their circumstances might seem, nothing more could touch them. She begged them to take heart and trust her. Then, clasping her little ones into her arms, the countess told them they would soon be safe, their terrifying ordeal would last but a short while longer, and they would help their mother if they did not reveal the happy knowledge. She told the children the stories her grandmother had once, long ago, told her, reminding the small, hollow-eyed children that their forefathers had been the greatest soldiers of Italy. Lost in her tale, they pushed further into their mother's sides. She drew them closer still and told them again 'fear no more'; they had left the house of the villainous traitors where they had been guarded by bad men. Those who guarded them at the city gate of St Peter had been chosen from among her own friends: men of honour, whom she knew well.

The danger had passed, she promised. They must neither have, nor show, dismay; the founder of the Sforza dynasty, Muzio Attendolo, known as Sforza, and his son Duke Francesco, had never been known to lose their fortitude, their dauntless ancestors had not known the meaning of fear … and they had always been proof against steel, fire and treason and in their day had been great princes and great *condottieri*.

A mother's understanding of her little ones can be heard in her promises that 'their uncle the duke would have already sent hundreds and hundreds of armed men, with cannon and guns and famous captains to their rescue. Her father, like theirs, had also been killed in her childhood, yet she had not lost courage … neither should they!' Caterina must have hoped that the soldiers upon whom she counted to liberate her really had set out for Forlì. She whispered stories to her small and frightened children, until eventually they fell asleep, comforted by their mother's composure, warm body, strong arms and gentle hands. Her whole being conveyed a promise that she would never let them go.

Despite her bravado, however, the countess knew that she had yet to embark on the most important step of all. She must find a way into Ravaldino. The witness to her strategy is one Andrea Bernardi, a contemporary chronicler and partisan of Catherine, who recounts that the countess confided in a loyal servant by whom she sent the crucial message to Tommaso Feo. Among her instructions, she wrote that soon the Orsi would surely be forced to bring her to the Rocca di Ravaldino, and make her beg for entry again. This time he must allow her inside.

Accordingly, when the Orsi arrived at the Rocca with Savelli at eleven o'clock the next morning, Feo delivered his conditions for a handover. If Caterina would pay his arrears and sign a document that permitted the resignation of his position with his reputation preserved, stating that he had acted faithfully and according to her will, he would yield the fastness.

On 18 April, shortly before noon, the rebels fetched Caterina. She appeared dishevelled and in a state of semi-collapse. Slowly she walked up the gentle slope above Forlì until she stood once more at the walls of Ravaldino. When Feo appeared, she begged him to hand over the fortress to Savelli, crying in apparent despair, 'Ah! If I might but enter the fortress and speak to you without witnesses, I would explain to you how things stand and persuade you to surrender.' As the rebel leaders howled out accusations of treachery, Ludovico Ercolani, one of the few partisans who had managed to escape on the night of Riario's murder, now played a masterstroke, which would allow Caterina to accomplish her entry to the fortress. He called out from the crowd:

> What are you afraid of? Have you not all her children in your hands? Do you think she would abandon them? Give her three hours with the castellan. If, when that time has elapsed, the countess does not return, do what you will to her children, her mother and sisters. Do not these hostages suffice? I offer you my children as well. If the countess is not there at the appointed time you can butcher them all together.

As the Orsi party continued to quarrel, Savelli, who must have been wondering how to save his own skin if Milanese troops did arrive to find that the rebels had countermanded his own orders, pronounced judgement. He ordered that the countess be permitted to enter the Rocca and to make her arrangements with the castellan in three hours. When this had expired, she must yield the fortress.

Caterina raised herself from the ground, where she had crumpled in a heap. She walked unsteadily at first, though her stride grew noticeably firmer and faster until she reached the gates of the fortress. As they opened to receive her, the Lady of Forlì turned towards the throng. She allowed her eyes to travel slowly across the crowd, resting deliberately on the traitors who had led the insurrection. She raised her fist defiantly, sticking her thumb between her index and forefinger. Leone Cobelli, deliciously scandalized, reported that 'Madonna went into the fortress and ... as she mounted the drawbridge she turned around and made quattro fichi at them.'

A Florentine writer recorded, 'When she entered Ravaldino she passed through the gates, and turned, making an obscene gesture to the rebel leaders.* At the same time, she 'threatened the conspirators that for the crime they had committed she would give them just punishment'. From the granddaughter of the great warlord Francesco Sforza and his warrior wife Bianca Maria Visconti, this was more than a threat. It was a promise.

The minutes, then the hours passed. Inside the fortress, Caterina first occupied herself with the disposition of artillery, ensuring that her cannon faced the centre of Forlì. Having subsisted on scraps since Riario's murder, she sat and ate heartily before lying down in an exhausted sleep.

She woke to the sound of gunfire. Rushing out in her chemise, her hair unbound, she peered over the ledge below to see of her children crying and screaming out to her in terror. The Orsi had determined they must use the last weapon they had against the countess, and threatened to cut Ottaviano, her eldest son, in pieces. One account maintains that the boy's 'shrill screams unnerved all who heard them'. All, that is, except the child's mother. Magnificently defiant, Caterina took the biggest gamble of her life. Checco Orsi had his sword in his hand. 'The spirited countess did not change expression, brazenly raised her skirts in front and with a proud look said to them, "Oh, can't you see, foolish men, *la fica mia* is full, and thank God I have the mould to make more."'

In one ingenious act, Caterina filled the rebels with terror. They had not anticipated that the countess would ever consider her children dispensable, nor can they have realized that if the Orsi killed them, she still carried a legitimate child in her body: a child who would one day avenge his father's death and that of his siblings. If she was speaking the truth, the Orsi knew that only flight could save them.

---

* Many versions exist of the obscene gesture Caterina made, but most of these were by chroniclers who were either present in Forlì but not at the scene, or by spies and representatives of various powers writing whatever they had been told. Caterina confirmed her own story to Machiavelli many years later. In the 1520s, when Clement VII (Medici) wore the papal tiara, Machiavelli had to write about the event, and asked the pope which version His Holiness wished to receive, the sober version or the real story. This demonstrates Machiavelli's enjoyment regaling those with influence with something they wished to see or hear but not necessarily the truth.

By showing her 'shameful parts', Caterina, the Sforza princess, doubled her message in a uniquely Renaissance way. Every educated person knew that the Persian men who had fled the battlefield found themselves confronted in mid-flight by a humiliating chant from their women, who sang with lifted skirts, 'Warriors and menfolk! Do you wish to crawl back from whence you first came, back into the safety of the womb?'

No familiarity with parallels from antiquity proved necessary. Soon after Caterina's debacle news arrived that Milanese troops, led by the Duke of Sanseverino, could be seen galloping towards Forlì. The Orsi fled; at the same time the many ambassadors and emissaries hurried to send reports back their masters.

One historian describes the most famous episode in the Romagnol virago's life thus: 'Caterina, stronger and wilier than all of them, had seized the fort, from whence she would bombard the whole city.' He added the telling sentence: 'All hope of frightening or touching her was at an end.'

PART ONE

1471–1484

CHAPTER I

Power from Behind the Veil

1471

'Women should be used like chamber pots: hidden away once a man has pissed in them'

MARSILIO FICINO

In later life, Caterina Sforza liked to insist that her earliest childhood memory of any significance occurred in 1471 when, during her first visit to Florence, she met Lorenzo de' Medici.

It is less likely, however, that the twenty-two-year-old *de facto* lord of Florence, and scion of Christendom's greatest banking dynasty, held more than the vaguest recollection of greeting the nine-year-old girl. Certainly, neither Lorenzo nor Caterina could have guessed that fate had already set them on a collision course that would have a devastating impact upon their lives, their houses and their states.

The purpose of the sojourn had been given as 'devotional'. Duke Galeazzo Maria Sforza, Lord of Milan, had decided to bring his young daughter with him, his second wife of nearly three years, Duchess Bona, as well as their huge entourage, to worship at his late father's favourite Florentine Church, La Santissima Annunziata. Galeazzo insisted that the entirely personal and spiritual nature of his stay amounted to no more than a private pilgrimage. Notwithstanding his pleas for privacy, Galeazzo's real reason for travelling to Florence had not been to pray, but to parade. He had secretly determined to seize this almost unparalleled and immediate opportunity to create an enduring impression of his might and his riches upon the fabled Renaissance metropolis.

Galeazzo's hopes became a reality and his stay passed into the city's history. Fortunately for the vain duke, he remained in a state of happy ignorance as to why the episode should find a place in Florentine folklore.

On Wednesday, 15 March 1471 the glint of his large, indistinct column appeared on the horizon moving towards Florence. With almost 2,000 people and 'four times as many animals', it included a bodyguard of brilliantly caparisoned nobles, knights and infantry. Litters covered in rich brocade, specially commissioned for the Tuscan promenade, carried the Sforza women, each dazzlingly adorned, on their long journey. For one making a private devotional visit, the glittering caravanserai held more than a hint of a mighty Mogul emperor arriving with his travelling city.

The fortunes of the dukes of Milan and the leading family in Florence had been intertwined for several generations, reaching back on both sides to the rise to pre-eminence of the Sforza and the Medici in their respective cities' lives.

In 1441 Galeazzo's* father, Francesco Sforza, had married Bianca Maria Visconti, the illegitimate and only child of Filippo Maria Visconti,† Duke of Milan. Last in the Visconti line of ruthless *signori* who had once ruled most of northern Italy, Filippo had been a good administrator but also a tyrannical despot who suffered from ill health exacerbated by attacks of paranoia – a combination that left him unable to command his troops in defence of the state. He had married his daughter to Francesco, who had a fearsome reputation for military brilliance, in order to make up for his defects. In his efforts to secure Francesco's loyalty and willingness to fight for him instead of against him, Filippo went further still. Not only had he given Francesco his daughter in marriage but he also proceeded to pledge the duchy of Milan to the ambitious young *condottiere*. When Filippo died in 1447, the anti-Sforza maintained that he had also bequeathed his inheritance to the King of Naples. By 1450, however,

* Henceforth I shall refer to Caterina's father as Duke Galeazzo Sforza. All the Sforza children received the baptismal name of Maria attached to their first name.
† The Visconti are believed to have received their name from their office as deputy counts (vice comiti) of Milan; and following the frequent practice of the time, it became their family name.

Francesco had fought for and taken the great northern duchy.

Francesco Sforza's military brilliance had gained him more than just a duchy. Since 1434 Sforza had received vast financial and political backing from Cosimo de' Medici, the first Medici patriarch to become *de facto* ruler of Florence. The pair created a close personal bond as Cosimo supported the duke with gold and, ever cautious, got Francesco appointed as chief *condottiere* of a league which included Florence. Cosimo desired the security afforded by Sforza's military strength to protect the mercantile city noted for 'its unwillingness to pay for war during peace'.*

Over the years, the relationship between the houses of Sforza and de' Medici flourished, and paralleled the growing affinity binding the two states, formerly traditional enemies. Their new understanding proved beneficial to both, their partnership bringing peace and stability to the habitually bickering and battling states which lasted, albeit with some notable exceptions, until 1494.

By 1471 the two visionary leaders were dead, but the alliance between both families and their states continued under their successors. In Milan, Galeazzo had proved quite unlike his father and demonstrated an 'uncertain temperament'. Immediately after Francesco's death in 1466, Galeazzo governed under the tutelage of his mother, Bianca Maria Visconti. With her demise in October 1468, and maddened by constant recitals of his father's great deeds, Milan's restless prince made his earliest sallies into the world of Italian power politics. Regrettably, Galeazzo's intemperate efforts at testing his political muscle frequently resulted in trying the forbearance of his allies rather than that of his enemies. These stormy incidents came at some cost to the hard-earned goodwill that formed a large part of his parents' legacy to their son.

In Florence, the transmission of power from Cosimo, who died in 1464, to Piero, his eldest and only surviving son, had been relatively smooth. Though the family had been in considerable jeopardy, they had survived the few serious efforts to oust them. Their salvation came from a tightly knit, pro-Medici oligarchy, supported by

---

* A wry remark made by Cosimo's grandson, Lorenzo de' Medici, about the penny-pinching Florentine mentality regarding martial matters until threatened, when the exchange of panic-stricken recriminations echoed through the city.

the people of Florence, who saw the Medici as one of their own. By this time the notion that the Medici could be treated as one of their own required quite some leap of the imagination as the family lived in their gorgeous palace on the Via Larga and had many splendid country estates. Nevertheless, any attempt at replacing them had served only to strengthen the family. They seemed an unstoppable force, and each bid against them merely tightened their constrictor's embrace around the Florentine ballot box.

When Piero died in 1469 and his son Lorenzo took his place at the head of the family, aged just twenty, he was fully aware of the responsibility that he had inherited: 'Although I, Lorenzo, was very young ... the principal citizens came to our house to comfort us ... and to ask that I take on myself the care of the City and the State as my grandfather and father had done.'* He had no option, and wrote with some truth: 'considering the burden and danger were great, I accepted unwillingly. But only because I must protect our friends and our assets; since matters fare ill in Florence with anyone who is rich but does not have a part in government.'

As his vast train approached Florence in 1471, Galeazzo would have reflected that, for all the close relations between his family and the Medici, he had not visited the city since 1459. Then he had been described as 'the most beautiful creature that was ever seen ... the son of the God Mars newly descended'. It had also been noted that the apparently well-washed lad appeared 'clean and noble'. Twelve years had passed and much had changed.

The decision to make his visit in 1471 seemed merely the latest in the growing list of Galeazzo's caprices. His plan caused immediate consternation as the proposed dates of his stay in the Tuscan republic fell during Lent, a period of fasting, penitence and contemplation in which state visits rarely took place. Princely colloquies required a lavish exchange of gifts, banquets and interminable entertainments, but after careful discussion emissaries from both sides agreed that

---

* 'Quantunque io Lorenzo fussi molto giovane, cioè di anni 21, vannono a noi a casa i Principali della Città, e dello Stato, a dolersi del caso, e conftarmi, che piliassi la curia della Città, e dello Stato, come avevano fatto l'Avolo, e il padre.' Lorenzo de' Medici, *Ricordi* .

there would be no celebrations, feasts or jousting, and that Galeazzo would maintain 'a simple and dignified form' to his stay, marked only by ceremonies appropriate to the Church calendar. Galeazzo became aware of the poor timing of his proposed visit but he did not move one jot, except for a vaguely implied irritation that Christ could surely have picked a better date for His Resurrection.

The eleven-day journey proved an immense exercise in logistics, as the route involved traversing the Apennine Mountains, forging rivers and crossing other difficult terrain. Finding lodgings, barges, fodder, building bridges and filling the myriad list of supplies from chamber pots to new liveries had kept officials busy for weeks. Galeazzo would not be thwarted. When rumours of criticism reached him, he repeated a petulant rejoinder. The journey could hardly be labelled a princely jaunt with the solemn purpose of worship at his father's favourite shrine. His true reason for coming had less to do with prayer than with taking the pulse of the alliance between the two states. Much like Lorenzo, Galeazzo had cause for consternation.

Recently, by using underhand methods, Galeazzo had gained control of the city of Imola. Although a small territory with a population of just 7,000 at the time, Imola held a strategically vital place on the eastern side of the Apennines, barely fifty miles from Florence. Since seizing the town, Galeazzo had already set about building a large and bristling stronghold with space for plenty of troops. The fortress, which remains intact today, has a sense of menacing potential. The mountain states of Imola, Forlì and Urbino also boasted impressive strongholds, and any one of them posed a potential threat – should two or three link together under one commander, the entire peninsula risked coming to a standstill. Guido da Montefeltro had held Forlì at the people's request until the Ordelaffi took the town in the early 1300s. The Montefeltro had their base in the tiny rugged dominion of Urbino: the present incumbent of this noble house of *condottieri* and friends of the Medici, Federigo da Montefeltro, frequently fought under contract to Florence.

Lorenzo and his advisers were uncomfortable living with the potential danger of Imola falling into enemy hands, as it could pose a serious threat to Florentine security.

By taking Imola, Galeazzo infuriated not only Florence but Venice and the papacy too. These two important powers both held a strategic interest in the small county's disposition. Lorenzo raved when the news reached him; he felt doubly cheated as, unbeknownst to all but a few of his closest advisers, he had been negotiating directly with Galeazzo to obtain the county of Imola for Florence. Discussions between the two leaders had reached an advanced stage and they had informally agreed a price of 100,000 ducats. Yet, presented with the fait accompli, Lorenzo could do little to oppose Galeazzo's unilateral move. This would almost certainly require military action: impossible, since Milan was the Florentine Republic's principal military ally.

Neither Lorenzo nor Galeazzo could have guessed that Imola would shortly change ownership once more – and that the hand of Caterina Sforza, the young Milanese princess awestruck by her first visit to Florence, would be part of the bargain.

The people of the city republic turned out in force to watch Galeazzo's arrival. It became immediately apparent that he had snubbed the terms of Lenten simplicity to which he had formally agreed. The baying of 500 pairs of hounds for the chase, falcons, hawks and their attendant huntsmen, infantry and running footmen, all in elaborate liveries, caused much excitement. As well as 1,000 service horses, Galeazzo had brought eighty of his finest hunters. A Sienese observer exclaimed: 'There was a livery for the greater *camerieri*,* dressed in crimson ... each one mounted on horseback, with a greyhound on a leash ... sixty pages, all dressed in green velvet, rode huge coursers, with fittings of gold and silver ... [their] saddles covered with brocade of various colours and crimson [sic]. In similar fashion they led from 65 to 70 mules with coffers and carriages, all decked with embroidered silk.' Another account describes 'twelve litters covered with gold brocade, in which the ladies of the party travelled ... fifty grooms in liveries of cloth of silver, numerous servants all clad, even the kitchen boys, in silk or velvet'.

---

* Today *cameriere* means waiter; in fifteenth-century Milan a *cameriere* was a member of the ducal household and meant anything from chamberlain to valet. In this case it implies the noble intimate who worked close to the duke. Many of these would have been his closest companions.

For Bona, Duchess of Milan, her stepdaughter Caterina and other Sforza women reclining on their litters, their first sight of Florence came as a relief. The specially crafted palanquins appeared majestic, but comprised little more than padded planks carried between two mules, every jolt tossing their occupants about during the tortuous journey. It is little wonder that the duchess and her ladies found themselves covered in painful bruises.

The ducal party were to stay at the Palazzo Medici, the rest of the vast train being assigned lodgings with rich merchant families, but at the expense of the *comune*. Waving graciously at the crowd, Galeazzo and his immediate family proceeded directly to the shrine where they made their devotions. Finally, they reached the Medici palace: an elegant, austere mansion with a solid exterior made of *bugnati* which rendered it as solid as a fortress. The Sforza party saw only a mirage of luxury and cleanliness after travelling for almost two weeks.

The next day Galeazzo, his family and most important nobles received the official civic welcome. On the Friday, Galeazzo responded by offering a similar celebration which he hosted at the Medici palace.

It is significant that, during the public state ceremonies, none of the Medici, or any other women of rank for that matter, came forward to greet the Milanese duchess formally. A Frenchman travelling through Florence wrote: 'women are more enclosed [here] than in any other part of Italy'. Upper-class women, indeed women of the city in general, led far more confined lives than their sisters at the princely courts. They did not, however, lack manner and, once out of the public gaze, the Medici women greeted their Milanese visitors with dignity and grace. One of the duke's counsellors said of Bona's arrival with her party, 'Madama was well received'. The Mantuan ambassador wrote to his master, '[at the Palazzo Medici] there were many women to greet the duchess'. Indeed, once indoors, a large party of illustrious women had gathered to greet Bona. The Medici wives and daughters might have remained partially concealed from public view, but within the palazzo their influence was not wanting.

In the Medici palace, Duchess Bona and young Caterina

encountered two contrasting visions of Florentine women in general and Renaissance women in particular. Among those who greeted the Sforza duchess would have been the Medici matriarch Contessina, now almost eighty. Cosimo's widow had always appeared uninterested while her husband and their two surviving sons, Piero and Giovanni (the latter died in 1463, Cosimo followed, dying in 1464)) increased the Medici fortune. Rather, she allowed the world to pass by outside the walls of the palazzo, happily counting buttons and pins.

As the Medici men had set out to conquer the farthest economic and political horizons, Contessina's own orbit had shrunk to enquiring whether her husband and grown sons desired capers and raisins with the rabbits she planned to send them. For the remainder of her long life the wife, then widow, of one of the richest men in Christendom became a practised scold, nagging her sons and daughters-in-law in a constant stream of hectoring missives. She seemed to find the administrators of the Medici estates lacking in almost all areas, and she incessantly reprimanded them, largely about their produce. Contessina also won a reputation for being a miser and expecting costly presents while only giving second-rate trash as wedding gifts, for instance. One bridegroom described the wife of Cosimo's wedding present as 'insignificant, cheap and of barely any value'. Contessina could not be accused of being uniquely mean. One day when Giovanni asked if he might invite a friend to eat with them that same evening, his mother told him that since she had planned to serve venison, he could bring his companion provided Giovanni could see to it that the meat be offered to them free of charge. She joyfully received a fish's tooth, a typically prized if somewhat recherché gift of their day. The ground horn of a unicorn (usually the tusk of a narwhal), supposed to counteract the effects of poison, was another appreciated offering.

Her demands regarding the wholesome farm food dovetailed nicely with her letters, which reflect an obsessive interest in the health of her adult sons (an interest with which many Italian men remain familiar today), as well as diktats regarding anything including olive oil, eczema, wine, blankets, cheese, fever and servants.

Contessina's daughter-in-law Lucrezia Tornabuoni, Piero's

wife, provided an entirely different model of a Florentine woman. Though both Medici wives came from aristocratic families, similarities ended there. Known as *grandi*, the Florentine nobles had been excluded (by the Ordinance of Justice of 1293) from a role in the executive government of Florence following years of internecine strife. By the mid-1300s the law eased, allowing the once great houses to split into several lines. Those that forfeited their family links received the right to become part of the highest governmental posts. Lucrezia's natal name of Tornaquinci hailed back to the year 1000, but by splitting away from the main branch and taking the name Tornabuoni, her sept transformed into fully enfranchised citizens of Florence, and became by far the most successful of the original Tornaquinci house.

The two matrons hailed from different eras; even their names amply reflect the seismic shift that had taken hold of the republic in a matter of decades. Contessina, born in 1392, as one of the powerful banking-feudal Bardi, recalls the medieval Countess Matilda of Tuscany; many girls born to fine houses received the name in memory of the courageous local heroine. By naming their daughter Lucrezia, by contrast, the younger woman's parents demonstrated the growing reverence for the classical world. They chose their daughter's name to celebrate Lucretia of ancient Rome, who committed suicide for shame at the loss of her virtue after being raped; only death could restore her purity, otherwise irreversibly destroyed.

Again, though for different reasons, Lucrezia suffered from the same problem as her homely, dumpling-shaped mother-in-law, who seemed to grow a notional inch or two when standing upon her honour. Lucrezia could at best be described as plain, with a long face and small mouth, myopic to the point of blindness and blessed with a long, fleshy nose that, despite its promising size, had no sense of smell. (Her son Lorenzo suffered from the same defect, later claiming it as a blessing, due to the famously putrid stink emanating from the open gutters of Florence.)

Lucrezia brought considerable property to the family, having inherited lands beyond the city limits, which probably explains one source of her later, bold attitudes. Unlike the majority of Florentine women, whose property passed into the hands of their husbands upon marriage, Lucrezia's holdings lay beyond the city's jurisdiction and she kept them within her own clever management. With geography saving Lucrezia from the republic's stifling property laws, all her life she remained a woman of independent mind as well as means.

Between 1444 and 1453 she bore Piero four surviving children: Bianca, Lucrezia (known as Nannina), Lorenzo and Giuliano, as well as raising Piero's illegitimate daughter, Maria, as was considered customary in Florentine society. She oversaw their broadly Humanist education,* and Lorenzo quickly emerged as the cleverer of her two sons.

An approachable woman when she wanted to be, and particularly as a mother to young and teenage children, Lucrezia managed not only to amuse Cosimo, Piero and his younger brother Giovanni, who died in 1463, but also to stay in touch with *l'allegra brigata* (the happy band of friends, as Lorenzo and his gang called themselves). A known writer of poetry and sacred stories, she helped her son's young friends with verses for the beauties they wished to court. Adding a word or making suggestions, Lucrezia then judged the young men's offerings and the seductive qualities of their work. Lorenzo's own efforts at writing verse in praise of nature, love and the fleet passage of youth received attention; his mother's own interests had influenced him profoundly. Later he championed the use of Tuscan Italian or *volgare*, and Lorenzo is considered by some as one of those principally responsible for Tuscan becoming the official Italian language. Lorenzo, an excellent linguist by the age of sixteen, insisted: 'Tuscan can faithfully express just as many subjects and feelings as Latin.' Another argument that favoured the *volgare* over Latin, was that boys who spoke the Tuscan tongue had far more approaches from flirtatious girls than youths who expressed themselves in Latin. Through Lucrezia's initial teaching, her elder son acquired the credentials to sit among artists, philosophers and writers as one of their number.

Yet Lucrezia Tornabuoni was more than just a poetry tutor. As the Sforza women who encountered her in 1471 would have

---

* The acclaimed Humanist Gentile Becchi served as tutor to the young Medici, and remained friends with Lorenzo for the rest of his life.

appreciated, she radiated a certain sophistication and experience quite different to the traditional Florentine ideal. A political animal, Lucrezia determined to extend her reach throughout the city the Medici dominated. Having played an important role during her husband Piero's ever-encroaching illness, she had acquired a considerable taste for power and influence in shaping Florentine policy and politics. Lorenzo might have been head of the family, but many still turned to his mother when they needed the dynasty's favour and approval.

The same young men to whom Lucrezia had once lent her skill in attracting maidens through verse, would now come to beg her assistance in far more important matters. As Lorenzo became increasingly powerful, his mother's role did not diminish. His youthful companions used their contact with Lucrezia to gain access to the Medici inner circle and favour. The educated and powerful queen mother of Florence could intercede for them with her elder son. In effect, mother and son ruled Florence jointly. Lucrezia Tornabuoni had never fallen properly into step with the stereotypical patrician role of an ideal Florentine woman. It is hard to imagine anyone following Leon Battista Alberti's ideal, and largely imaginary, Florentine woman in *Della Famiglia,* and daring to keep household accounts, papers and keys from her.

The Milanese did not make themselves popular during the 1471 visit. Galeazzo's peacock ways did not endear him to the soberminded Florentines, and matters were not helped by the sacrilegious behaviour of the Milanese. Machiavelli wrote of their 'unprecedented exhibition ... during Lent, when the Church commands us to abstain from animal food, the Milanese, without respect for either God or His Church ate of it daily'. This appalled the Florentine people, who lived regulated and largely puritanical lives, even though some are said to have partaken of meat themselves.

Galeazzo and Duchess Bona were honoured by a sacred play written to mark their visit telling the story of the Annunciation of the Holy Virgin and performed in the Piazza San Felice. Machiavelli wrote: 'Many believed that the Almighty had been offended at our misconduct.' As if proof were needed of God's wrath, the church of Santo Spirito caught fire while the descent of the Holy Ghost was being depicted. Fortunately, since neither Galeazzo nor Bona had bothered to attend the performance, they remained safe from the flames engulfing the church.

While the duke admired the beauty of Florentine art and buildings, he criticized the Florentine people for being soft and effeminate. Machiavelli scoffed in a damning postscript to the Sforza visit, 'if the said duke found the town steeped in courtly delicacies and its customs opposed to those of every well-ordered city, he left it worse than he found it'.

At last, after eight days, Galeazzo's gaudy troupe assembled itself in formation to leave Florence. Having said their farewells to the ducal party, the Medici matriarchs can only have breathed a sigh of relief. The prodigal Milanese had spent over 200,000 ducats on grotesque finery and showing-off; Galeazzo's excesses, not to mention the appalling behaviour of some among his entourage, had damaged his already flawed image before his principal allies. He seemed to have lost any sense of the impression he made upon the public. Remarking on the 'immoderate gaiety' of the Florentines, the popinjay prince had failed to understand that it had been the sybaritic antics of his own party, and in no small part his own ludicrous posturing, which had caused incredulous merriment among the citizens.

As she left with her father, young Caterina could reflect that she had witnessed at first hand how one of the great women of the early Renaissance went artfully about her business. It might not have struck the young girl at the time, but looking back she may have considered herself a privileged observer of a generation of highborn women whose way of life would very soon disappear.

CHAPTER 2

The Princess Bride

1467–1469

'Her mind was of a masculine gravity'
PAOLO GIOVIO ON LUCREZIA TORNABUONI

In the spring of 1467 Lucrezia Tornabuoni ignored chauvinistic Florentine convention and undertook an extraordinary visit to Rome. She made her journey incognito and, once there, lodged with her brother Giovanni. The use of an alias all but guaranteed that the exalted traveller's true identity would be broadcast even faster than usual. Upon her arrival in the Eternal City, Lucrezia found that her presence there had already become common knowledge.

Publicly, Lucrezia had it put about that her journey had been necessary to scrutinize a possible bride for her son Lorenzo de Medici. She had a particular interest in maidens of the powerful Orsini dynasty, and in that respect her brother was well positioned to help. Thanks to the good offices of his sister, Giovanni Tornabuoni had been given a post at the Roman branch of the family bank. He ensured accurate intelligence arrived at the bank's headquarters in Florence and his acute assessments gave the Medici more than just the latest political news from Rome.

Since late 1466 Giovanni had been recommending Clarice, a daughter of the Orsini tribe, who fulfilled the criteria set down by Piero and Lucrezia, and he energetically promoted the girl to the Medici couple. Given that Lucrezia had no sense of smell, and could see little beyond her own hand, it seems that Lorenzo's confidence in his mother's other senses did not falter, though he must have been glad indeed of his uncle's help in seeking out his future bride.

On 28 March Lucrezia wrote to her husband Piero from Rome with a description of Clarice Orsini, whom she had contrived to meet on their way to Mass:

> ... she is fairly tall, and fair, and has a nice manner, though she is not as sweet as our girls. She is very modest and will soon learn our customs ... Her face is rather round, but it does not displease me ... We could not see her bosom as it is the custom here to wear it completely covered up, but it seems promising.

A meeting followed at the Orsini palace with Clarice, her mother, Maddalena, and maternal uncle, Cardinal Latino Orsini. Fortunately the tiresome mantle which had previously covered Clarice's promising bosom had been removed; the tight robe she wore indicated that the girl, then aged about sixteen, possessed 'fine quality breasts ... of good shape'. Lucrezia also noted in her letter that the girl seemed pliable and pleasant.

But Lucrezia had not merely come to Rome to inspect her future daughter-in-law's breasts. Her visit held a further purpose. Under the pretext of obtaining the indulgences required for Lorenzo's marriage, Lucrezia met the Pope, Paul II, at the Vatican to discuss delicate and secret financial matters involving the Medici relationship to the Holy See, which had put its finances into the family's hands two generations previously.

The Pope was impressed by their meeting. Filippo Martelli, a Medici emissary living in Rome, wrote that Lucrezia's visit '[has been] most valuable, for she not only fulfilled her vow, but has acquired high favour with his [the Pope's] entire court, in such a way that even had she no more than her presence, her conversation and appearance, it would show that she was greater than her reputation. I know that the Cardinals have ... decided that no finer lady has ever visited Rome.'

However, not everyone in the Holy City felt quite as enraptured by Lucrezia's presence and appearance. The aristocrats of Rome despised the mercantile Florentines for their puritanical humbug, usury and success. Pope Paul II's predecessor, Pius II, when not in need of money, had been heard to call Florence 'that whore town'. In their disdain, the snooty aristocrats of the city enjoyed the full support of those exiles banished by both Cosimo and Lucrezia's own husband. A less flattering account of Lucrezia's visit was written by Agnolo Acciaioli, a prominent anti-Medici living in Rome, who recorded:

> She goes around with merchants, visiting each cardinal and is awaiting an audience from the Pope. She behaves like a great lady and tarts herself up like a fifteen-year-old. Here everyone laughs at her, but even more at Piero.

Piero, paralysed by illness back in Florence at the Palazzo Medici, suffered the Roman laughter in silence. He had had little choice but to send his wife and most trusted emissary to Rome, and she had achieved her aims, both familial and political. They had satisfied their most prestigious banking client, the Pope, and Lorenzo's prospective bride seemed to have passed the critical test of being approved by her potential mother-in-law.

As with most alliances between two such illustrious houses, the negotiations over the Orsini marriage dragged on through the following year. The alliance was worth the wait. The celebrated feudal clan of Orsini held three crucial attractions for the Medici. Ever bankers, rather than warriors, the Medici hoped that as one of the most important *condottieri* clans on the Italian peninsula, possessors of territories, strongholds and castles lying to the north of Rome, the Orsini could bolster their own martial weakness. Furthermore, Clarice's own house boasted two former Orsini popes, Celestine III and Nicholas III, and one living cardinal. The latter, added to their prodigious military presence in Rome, loaded them with a significant ability to sway matters within the Curia. The family's loyal soldiers and men-at-arms policed Rome in conjunction with those of their rivals the Colonna, the only other Roman feudal dynasty who could match their strengths. Beyond Rome, the Orsini held strongholds south of the Eternal City and on into Naples, whose territories occupied the entire peninsula south of Rome.

The Medici had dreamt for many years of penetrating further into the Vatican and eventually having a cardinal and, perhaps, even a pope of their own in the family. The immediate prospect suggested by Clarice and her noble blood was that the Medici would at last be able to consider themselves connected to true aristocrats and wash away the mercantile stain. Through Lorenzo's Orsini wife, the whole dynasty hoped they would finally move into the mainstream of Italian blue-bloods.

Unsurprisingly, news of Lorenzo's betrothal caused irritation at home. Many of Florence's matrons had hoped that a daughter of their own house might become Lorenzo's bride. Amid much tut-tutting about the city, and pondering upon the marriage to a foreigner, an unasked question hung in the air: had the Medici become too fine to join their elder son with one of the city's maidens? The Milanese ambassador wrote with distinct relish at the conceivable problems that a marriage to a foreigner might create for the supreme family of Florence: '[this marriage] will give the mob and the leading citizens plenty to talk about'.

The Orsini betrothal was unconventional in another, although not unknown, way: that the groom should be considerably older than his bride. Local logic held that an older husband in his late twenties or early thirties would have had time to establish himself financially and be able to support his family, while a younger bride was considered preferable, since a malleable girl could receive her education in her husband's household in the manner to best please him. Ideally a bride should be married in her mid to late teens. Lorenzo's father Piero had been twenty-seven years old and Lucrezia seventeen when they had married in 1443. Cosimo had been eleven years older than his wife Contessina de' Bardi. Now, however, the twenty-year-old scion of the house would be taking a wife only a year younger than himself. But he, like others of the ruling oligarchy, had the money to do so.

The two families set the wedding for the summer of 1469. Clarice Orsini wrote stilted letters to her betrothed revealing the uncertainty she felt about her future in a place as foreign as Florence. She received no response from the groom. This was hardly surprising as Lorenzo was all but choked with a myriad of pressing matters that both his father's health and his own approaching marriage would allow him little time to settle.

In spite of any misgivings regarding the upcoming marriage, the citizens of Florence had high expectations. Prominent families often organized public celebrations and one way to seduce the public would be for Lorenzo to hold a joust, one that surpassed anything the city had ever seen before.

Since late 1468 Clarice's family had been beseeching Lorenzo to visit them in Rome. Piero, fearful of his failing health and with much to do for his son before his diseased body finally surrendered, thanked the Orsini, but declined on Lorenzo's behalf using the approaching joust as an excuse for the young man to remain at home. Clarice's uncle Cardinal Latino invited Lorenzo for Christmas in 1468, writing that 'We should be glad to see our nephew Lorenzo ... at the feast of the Nativity. We should give a reception according to your wishes.' Lorenzo, however, did not wish to go. Instead he gave one of the only excuses that a warrior clan of feudal knights would understand. Rather than attending the Orsini Christmas, he would be holding a tournament in honour of Clarice and their forthcoming marriage.

If the Orsini were disappointed, they did their best to hide it. Clarice's mother Maddalena wrote that her daughter 'would find the waiting hard but since such a virtuous cause keeps you ... I encourage you to the joust and hope you will do yourself honour. For the women of the house of Orsini are as happy in the success and honour of their husbands as in their presence.' She added that if he could but provide the date he would be taking his place in the lists 'Clarice will fast for you in order that God will preserve you and give you victory'.

Victory was something seldom denied Lorenzo in Florence – and since he did not even bother to reply to his future mother-in-law, Clarice might well have endangered her already weak constitution by praying and fasting for too long. Fretting and fearing for the health of her betrothed, she asked God to protect her own Mars.

Had Clarice known the outcome of her prayers she might have suffered a crisis of faith. In her feudal world, jousting was a deadly serious business, which required skill as well as practice. Dangerous or mortal wounds came as part of the sport. But she need not have worried. Florentine jousting was rather more tame. The only risk to Lorenzo of being killed came from the danger that he might collapse under the weight of his gold and bejewelled costume.

The date of the jousts was fixed for 7 February 1469. On the day of the festivities, Lorenzo was in his pomp. As his brilliant banner unfurled it revealed a sun and a rainbow upon it and Lorenzo's motto 'Le Temps Revient' in gold letters. The standard had been designed by Andrea del Verrocchio and Leonardo da Vinci, a new arrival in Florence, who is also believed to have had a hand in the breathtaking appearance of the all-conquering Lorenzo. As Lorenzo knelt before the queen of the joust, the beautiful young matron Lucrezia Donati who is believed to have been his mistress and whom he certainly loved, his costume glimmered with rubies, pearls, gold brocade and gems sewn in his black velvet cap. The famous Medici diamond known as 'Il Libro' glinted from its place as the centrepiece of his shield.

The Florentines, being a people unversed in matters of martial chivalry, preferred the romantic element of the joust to the soldierly. Typical Florentine battle had therefore evolved to become a fight between show-offs and a fashion show of riches; he who wore the finest costume won. Instead of the gasp of a crowd watching horsemen charge at each other, the spectators took a collective intake of breath as they admired the young combatants in their rich costumes. Typically adept at pricing valuable objects, the audience totted up the expense of the participants' costumes.

The venue for the lists was the Piazza Santa Croce and it was here that a throng, including – unusually – many wives and daughters, gathered to watch Lorenzo show off his talent, and his costume. Luigi Pulci wrote in his *La Giostra di Lorenzo de' Medici* cxiv:

> And on the ground the youth was thrown
> And all in the field ran to help him
> But that horse through its great nobility
> Strove to do what it could not;

Now he rises, and now he falls,
Causing those admired him to sigh.

The heroics here were not Lorenzo's, but those of Falsamico, a horse given to him by King Ferrante of Naples. Pulci had not much to work with since both horse and rider fell towards the end of the day, when youthful exuberance spilled over as the young men lost control of their mounts. When Lorenzo was unseated in the mêlée, Piero and Lucrezia watched in horror as attendants hurried to remove his helmet; but Lorenzo had escaped uninjured. Remembering the joust in his *Ricordi*, Lorenzo wrote a laconic account of the day: 'To follow the custom ... I gave a tournament on the Piazza S. Croce at great cost and with much magnificence ... about ten thousand ducats were spent on it.' The champion added, 'though I am not a vigorous warrior nor a hard hitter ... the first prize was adjudged to me'.

Weeks passed, until by the spring of 1469 Clarice had to wait no more. Her proxy marriage took place in May, and the twentieth-century historian Gaetano Pierracini described the arrival in Rome of Giuliano, Lorenzo's beloved and handsome younger brother. Guiliano arrived with an escort of fifty men, their dress spangled with gorgeous gems and richly caparisoned horses. 'It is all a triumph,' wrote one spectator. The bride had been told of new Florentine dances that would take place at her wedding to Lorenzo, and had spent the last days at her Roman home learning the steps so that she would not falter at the very start of her married life – a poignant image. She knew that from the moment of her arrival all eyes would be upon her. Having captured the city's most eligible bachelor, she must prove flawless in all matters feminine and Florentine.

After the proxy wedding, Clarice moved to Florence for the religious ceremony. On Sunday morning, 4 June, she emerged in a gown of white and gold brocade with a pearl-encrusted hood. Surrounded by dancing youths all wearing fine matching silver brocade costumes, the young bride mounted Falsamico and rode in behind the vanguard of her procession. Trumpeters and fifers led the way, their joyous notes announcing the young woman's approach. Once the procession arrived at the Via Larga, an olive tree (a symbol of fertility) had to be hoisted up to the *piano nobile* and taken in through a large window before Clarice could dismount and enter her new home. At the door stood the matrons and maidens to greet the Roman girl, the *straniera* ('the foreigner' in Italian – but used by the Florentines in a derogatory manner) who, however hard she tried, would never become 'una dei nostri', or 'one of us'. The Florentines bear the same attitudes today, although sometimes with more charm. The patrician class, and not only, like to marry with 'people we know'.

After formally entering her new home, Clarice once more mounted Falsamico and, with the same party of youths who had accompanied her earlier, she returned to the Palazzo degli Alessandri. Lorenzo's young bride spent her first night as a married woman under the protection of the Alessandri, whose palace represented her father's home. This Roman custom came from antiquity and had been used symbolically to show that her husband did not hold supreme jurisdiction over his bride, and that she had not left her family completely. Clarice probably knew that, in her case, symbolism would have little bearing on reality.

Within the extensive and enthusiastic accounts of Clarice Orsini's wedding, there is a notable omission. Lorenzo de' Medici is not mentioned once. The following day, Clarice returned to the Via Larga and her new home for good. As she passed through the vast carved doors of the Medici palace and walked down the vaulted vestibule, each movement created amplified and distorted echoes. Pope Pius II had pronounced upon Cosimo's majestic palazzo, saying it resembled 'a paradise on earth'. Clarice found her strange and gilded home nothing less than a terrifying personal leap into the unknown.

The most striking condition that Clarice discovered about the Medici was the woeful state of the menfolk – her husband would be no exception. Almost every one of the males from Cosimo's line of the family suffered from gout, a deadly legacy passed from father to son. Contessina's endless admonitions and lectures to Giovanni about his overeating went unheeded and the epicurean died from over-eating, while Piero's nickname, 'the Gouty', does not include his sufferings from rheumatoid arthritis, which had been misdiagnosed at the time. One chronicler recorded paying a call upon Cosimo and seeing the dismal sight of the older man and his two sons in a row, seated in wheelchairs with their feet bound and supported on planks.

Yet Clarice would have understood that this ghastly medical curse transformed the roles of the Medici women. Within the palazzo they had access to information and influence enjoyed by no other great patrician women of the city republic. As Cosimo and, in particular, his eldest son became increasingly incapacitated, many of the levers of government were pulled by female hands; and by the time of Lorenzo's marriage the apparently private palazzo had become the unofficial seat of power, blurring the customary lines behind which Florentine women usually operated. Lucrezia – whom Cosimo, probably spuriously, is said to have once flattered with the title of 'the only man in the family' – played a crucial role during Piero's years as head of his dynasty. On days when her husband felt so ill that he could not move even his tongue without crying with pain, Lucrezia became, quite literally, his spokeswoman.

The people she received in his palace were the greatest in the Italian peninsula and abroad. Cosimo, and later Piero, entertained many distinguished guests at the palazzo, including magnates, popes and ambassadors, thereby giving the women of the Medici unrivalled privilege. They had to remain particularly careful, however, not to anger their fellow citizens by brazenly being seen stepping outside the parallel world within which even the wives of the most senior families in Florence lived. The world of women, shadowing that of their husbands, sons or brothers, provided an enormously useful conduit by which information could be passed on and exchanged, petitions and impressions made, whether true or false.

Aside from prayers or at Mass, Lucrezia Tornabuoni devoted her free hours to study and correspondence. The range of people to whom she wrote and from whom she received news demonstrates the wider sphere of her activities in comparison with her mother-in-law, and the extent of her influence beyond the palazzo. She wrote to the exiled Queen of Bosnia as well as numerous ecclesiastics and kept a correspondent in Rome, Papinio di Artimino, as a sort of private wire service for communicating vital news of Vatican intrigues in this age before newspapers. Lucrezia constantly sought intervention in matters as diverse as marital discord and property purchases, and the level at which her influence was perceived to be significant is shown in 1474, when her advice would be required as to the appointment of a new chancellor for the University of Pisa and the governorship of Vico Pisano.

Relatives, friends and business associates flooded into the palazzo with information relating to the daily conduct of their various businesses, official or informal, concerning the bank, the state and all manner of quotidian affairs and concerns. Hoping to bend the Medicean ear to their own advancement, they waited on benches set into the walls or in the *loggia*, as personal visits formed part of the duties which they owed to their patrons. Many clients wrote letters of apology if they failed to keep an appointment.

Seeing Lucrezia sweeping effortlessly through this political world, young Clarice must have expected and probably dreaded the idea that eventually she would inherit such a role for herself. Lucrezia, however, would not countenance it. Though Piero chastised her for her cool manner towards the girl, Lucrezia did nothing to include her new daughter-in-law in such activities. Indeed, her attitude to Clarice could at times be described as unpleasant. From the first, Clarice had no illusions that her primary duty would be anything other than breeding. The young bride spent the first decade of her marriage either pregnant or nursing the couple's offspring – bearing Lorenzo ten children, of whom seven survived to adulthood, between August 1470 and March 1479. At least the 'promise' of her bosom as noted by her mother-in-law on her first visit to Rome had been fulfilled, but Clarice felt frustrated at her inability to do anything for her own family and their clients. The former had begun besieging her with letters before the cloths had come off the tables of the wedding feast.

After a lifetime tortured by the agony of his many afflictions, Piero surrendered his long struggle and died on 2 December.

Following her father-in-law's death, and as consort to the new leader of Florence, Clarice became the most senior woman in the republic. Lucrezia had long been ready for this moment and, ignoring her husband's request for a simple funeral, the new *de facto* Queen Mother of Florence hurried to stake out her position to the powers that came with the place she had planned for herself beside her son.

She immediately ordered that the late Piero's obsequies be an all-male affair. As Piero finally surrendered to his many ailments Lucrezia wasted no time laying down the markers denoting her unwillingness to budge and take her place. The funeral was attended by leading male citizens, dignitaries from all over Italy and ambassadors from foreign powers. By excluding any women from taking part, Lucrezia turned a family affair into an official event. All too aware that this might prove a precarious time for their marital house, she needed all the gravitas and support she could garner to give the impression of solidity, despite Lorenzo's youth. Any doubters in the crowds could feel comfort at the splendour and importance of those attending as well as feeling affected at the sight of Lorenzo weeping openly as he walked behind his father's coffin. Significantly, Piero's cousin walked with Lorenzo. Pierfrancesco de' Medici, first cousin to Piero and head of the junior branch, had been brought up with Lorenzo after the death of his father. There had been a growing rift between the two sides of the Medici. Pierfrancesco's appearance provided additional balm to those who wanted their businesses to prosper and hoped for a trouble-free transfer of power. None of this would have been achieved by Clarice, nor had the young woman missed the implied warning from Lucrezia to keep out of any official business and to do as her mother-in-law decreed.

Lorenzo's assumption of power passed over smoothly, and unsurprisingly it was Lucrezia who handled the transition. She had no intention of retiring behind her mourning veils as Contessina de' Bardi had done at Cosimo's funeral. Rather, she now openly took up a position as Lorenzo's official hostess and adviser. Clarice remained firmly confined to the nursery, spending long and lonely periods in one or other of the Medici country houses. As a *straniera* Clarice could never hope to be considered Lucrezia's equal. Had she been a Florentine she would never have been treated so disdainfully. Clarice had few friends, poor health and a belly that swelled each time Lorenzo visited her. Worse than being hated, she was ignored.

Lucrezia's managerial capacities were not without criticism. Despite her (self-promoted) image as the pious and charitable Mother of Florence, her altruism sometimes left much to be desired. In conversation with a parish priest, she boasted of how she had given charity to a poor shoemaker who had come to the Palazzo Medici for alms, offering not only money but also two jackets and arranging for two friends to do likewise. Sycophants being as plentiful as geese at the palazzo, her bombastic self-satisfaction took a blow when the priest replied that he knew of a charity even greater than this, which was 'not to deprive others of what is theirs in the first place and not to profit from the labour and from the sweat of other men, especially those who are poor'. Nevertheless, all the sniping in Florence could not detract from Lucrezia's position at the heart of the Medici clan.

What little status Clarice Orsini had in that family was marginally improved by the birth of her first son, Piero, in February 1472. This was a cause for official as well as private rejoicing, and Clarice received the first of many 'birth trays' or *desco da parto*, three of which are listed in the Palazzo Medici inventory of 1492, one painted by Masaccio. Emboldened by the arrival of an heir, Clarice undertook an independent trip to Rome to attend her brother's marriage. She may not have counted for much in the city republic, but 'abroad' she was a Medici envoy, and the respect and honour with which she was treated came as a pleasant novelty. She entered Rome with a cavalcade of eighty horsemen and a smart company of gentlemen, though her homecoming was rather spoiled when her family complained at her lack of influence over Lorenzo. Prodded by them, she wrote several letters to her husband from there, though the response was depressingly predictable. After sending two letters recommending one Messer Alfonso from Lisbon to a post, she wearily concluded 'this is enough, I will not repeat myself'.

At the time of Caterina Sforza's first visit to Florence in 1471, Clarice had been recovering from the stillbirth of twin boys, born three months before full term. Lorenzo's anger and disappointment are evident in a brusque reassurance in his *ricordi*: 'they lived long enough to be baptized'. His wife's place within the trinity of senior Medici brides was minor; Lucrezia, not Clarice, led the chorus of women who welcomed the visiting Duke of Milan to the palazzo.

CHAPTER 3

La Dame de Petit Sens

1471–1480

'The peace of Italy is at an end'

POPE SIXTUS IV

On 26 July 1471, Pope Paul II suffered a heart attack in the private quarters of the Vatican, within which he had remained largely hidden since his ascendancy to the throne in 1464. Paul II's papacy was largely notable for self-indulgence. An enemy of learning and a committed military administrator, the sybarite burst into angry tears at the slightest provocation. Romans gossiped maliciously at the swirl of his effeminate robes and the solace he, presumably, found in the arms of his beautiful pages. Wags called him Maria Pietissima, 'Most Pious Mary'. Reports of the cause of his death vary wildly. One account claimed that he had suffered from indigestion brought on by eating a melon. His enemies, on the other hand, suggested he died while being sodomized by a pageboy. Whatever the cause of death, less than two weeks later, Cardinal Francesco della Rovere had assumed the papacy, adopting the name Sixtus IV and completing a vertiginous, hitherto virtuous ascent through the Church hierarchy. A noted theologian of humble origins, della Rovere had impressed the College of Cardinals, who hoped for a religious man rather than an aristocrat for Peter's throne. Sixtus, however, did not lack for important patrons. The Orsini – and therefore the Medici – had backed him, as had Galeazzo Sforza.

Galeazzo took especial delight in Sixtus's ascent, for he could now proceed with his plans to create stronger links between Milan and the papacy. In December 1472 the new Pope's nephew, Girolamo

Riario, arrived in Milan to conclude his betrothal to Constancia Fogliani. The young lady had excellent connections: her father was half-brother to the late Duke Francesco Sforza. Her mother Gabriella, however, a member of the Gonzaga dynasty who ruled Mantua, objected to the match on the grounds that Riario was not only unworthy of her daughter, but had also put forward absurd dowry demands. Unperturbed, Galeazzo sided with Riario. He abandoned the plan to marry Riario and Constancia and proposed his daughter Caterina, then about ten years old, as a substitute. He punished the widowed Gabriella for threatening the alliance, pursuing her with a humiliating lawsuit in which he accused her lover of stealing table silver, and refused to make another marriage for the unfortunate Constancia.

Sixtus acquiesced happily with the new arrangement. A Sforza alliance, which brought his papacy connections to a landed military dynasty, suited him very well. The Gonzaga snobbery had therefore proved Caterina Sforza's gain. A betrothal contract was concluded in February 1473 and three days later Riario's gifts were presented to Caterina. They included two dresses of brocade and velvet, three pearl necklaces, a pair of jewelled thimbles and a monumentally tasteless jewel 'in the shape of a peasant' with a pearl for a head.

As part of the complex dowry arrangements, the Pope insisted that Caterina's marriage portion of 10,000 ducats be augmented by Imola, the ever-important state whose disputed ownership had been the motivation for Galeazzo's visit to Florence two years earlier. Galeazzo consented on the condition that Imola should pass to Riario's heir, effectively retaining it as part of the Sforza appendage. The price for the cessation of Imola to the papacy was 40,000 ducats, a sum Sixtus claimed to consider excessive, but which he condescended to accept in order that Caterina should not be obliged 'to live like a simple gentlewoman'. In reality, the Pope was delighted, as he had previously tried to raise a loan from the Medici to buy back Imola – a loan which, to his tremendous displeasure, Lorenzo had refused. Through his opportune alliance with Milan, however, Sixtus now achieved a great dynastic marriage and a dominion for Girolamo. Galeazzo, meanwhile, had the satisfaction of knowing that Imola would retain its Sforza allegiance while securing his influence with the man whom he and the Orsini had promoted.

Nevertheless, Galeazzo's pleasure in the new alliance was not completely unalloyed. For some time he had been negotiating a sale of Imola to Florence, and a provisional price of 100,000 ducats had been agreed. The new situation obliged Galeazzo to write to Lorenzo, explaining that he could no longer sell Imola since it would mean countermanding the Pope's wishes. He expressed regret that he could not support his young fellow ruler in this instance, and Lorenzo concurred that papal influence seemed to be expanding ominously. Galeazzo had started to fear that Pope Sixtus, whom so many magnates had complacently felt they owned, would soon hold the peninsula tightly within his grasp. Milan, Florence, Mantua and Ferrara all had an interest in avoiding trouble in the Romagna, as each lay within a giant's reach of Rome.

A year later, however, in 1474 Duke Galeazzo of Milan had more reason to be pleased by the wedding. Girolamo Riario's brother Cardinal Pietro died on 3 January at the age of just twenty-eight – possibly poisoned by the Venetians, but more probably the result of years of overindulgence. His vast, rapidly accrued wealth had been left to Caterina Sforza's fiancé, a turn of events which cast the new alliance in a rather more lucrative light.

While Galeazzo contemplated the political consequences of his daughter's marriage and the transfer of Imola to a papal relative, he also faced other troubles. The duke was becoming increasingly paranoid about the unpopularity which his own extravagance and despotism seemed to him to provoke in Milan. His actions certainly had grown increasingly bizarre and cruel. His punishments were becoming horribly exotic, and though no one had yet dared to speak out, the city was stirring with hatred. An astrologer had predicted that Galeazzo would not survive the eleventh year of his reign, and despite having had the unfortunate seer starved to death in a dungeon, Galeazzo could not forget the warning. Following Sforza custom, he returned to Milan for Christmas 1476 with his family. His wife Duchess Bona, infected by his fear, begged her husband not to attend Mass in Santo Stefano on Christmas Day. She claimed to have dreamt, the previous night, of her husband's murdered corpse lying in the church. Galeazzo nevertheless called his children to him, said goodbye and mounted his horse, setting off over the frozen ground to the city centre.

On arrival at the church, the duke's secretary was surprised to find three members of the court already in attendance. The powerful, embittered Carlo Visconti believed that the Sforza had usurped his own family's rights and that Galeazzo had had an affair with his sister. Giovanni Andrea Lampugnani, whose family riches had been swallowed in the Sforza ascendancy, had been condemned to death by Duke Francesco and his hatred of the Sforza had not been mollified by Galeazzo having pardoned him. The third courtier, Girolamo Olgiati, had no personal enmity against the duke, but like many in the city was an ardent reader of the rhetorician Cola Montano, who had been publicly whipped for his endless seditious satires against Galeazzo.

Lampugnani and Olgiati stood at the right of the church door, along with three hired henchmen, while Visconti lurked in the shadows to the left. As Galeazzo entered and the crowd pressed forward, Lampugnani made as if to clear a passage, calling 'Make way! Make way!', then bent his knee to the duke and removed his cap respectfully. As he did so he reached into his sleeve, the classic pose of the petitioner. Predictably, he drew out a dagger, stabbing Galeazzo in the torso and again in the throat. 'A scene of indescribable violence then ensued'. Members of the duke's entourage were killed and women had jewels ripped from their throats and hands.

The plotters had come in large numbers behind the ringleaders, but it did them little good. Eleven of the conspirators were eventually overpowered by the duke's guards, and their corpses strung up on the city ramparts. Several days passed before Visconti and Olgiati were apprehended. Visconti went unrepentant to his death, declaring that, 'were I to be reborn ten times, and ten times to perish in these torments, I would give my blood and all my strength for this sacred end'. Lampugnani, meanwhile, had attempted to hide himself among the female members of the congregation of the church by covering his head with a rag. His cunning efforts failed, however, as he was pulled from the crowd and lynched, before being fed to the pigs.

'The peace of Italy is at an end,' declared Pope Sixtus portentously on hearing of the murder. Galeazzo had been loathed for his sexual rapacity, cruelty and overweening ambition, although fear of the Duke's madness had ensured a degree of stability within his lands. The young Caterina Sforza had more immediate and personal concerns. She feared that Galeazzo's death might put an end to her forthcoming nuptials. She need not have worried. If anything, Girolamo Riario was spurred on to the marriage after Galeazzo's death, his uncle hoping that papal power in Milan might thus increase. In April 1477 the fourteen-year-old Caterina married in a proxy ceremony, celebrated privately in light of her father's recent death. She then journeyed to Imola, where she received a state reception on 1 May. She was thrilled at the welcome, particularly by the crowds of people who rushed forward to claim the traditional honour of claiming the lady's horse 'with cries, blows and much tearing of hair'.

Caterina remained several days in Imola before proceeding in slow stages to Rome, where on 24 May she was received at Castelnuovo, a fief of the Colonna, fourteen miles outside the city. Next day at six in the evening she rode out into the countryside to meet her bridegroom for an idyllic picnic in the woods – the guests splendid, though possibly rather warm, in their sables, velvets and satins. They rode on to Rome, with further dignitaries joining them every quarter-mile, before being greeted by the papal court on Ponte Molle. Caterina spent the night at the Monte Mario palace, home of the Cardinal of Urbino, and set off from there next morning for St Peter's.

Dressed in 'a cloak of black damask brocaded with gold, a skirt of crimson satin and sleeves of brocade', Caterina was accompanied by members of the Orsini and Colonna dynasties. After a three-hour Mass in the Basilica, she was presented to the Pope. Her beauty as she knelt to kiss his slipper was acknowledged to be 'incomparable'. Sixtus then declared that he would marry Caterina once again, and after she and Girolamo had exchanged vows and rings, he removed a pearl necklace which she had received from her husband the previous day and replaced it with another, even more elaborate. Sixtus's evident joy at the union was remarked upon by an observer, who commented that he gave Caterina 'so many caresses that it appears to us that Her Ladyship is so well beloved by His Holiness that he makes no difference between her and my Lord the Count'.

The party then repaired through flower-strewn streets to the Orsini palace in Campo de' Fiori for a banquet for 200 guests. The customary ordeal of twenty-two elaborate courses, interspersed with orations by children costumed as angels and mythical figures, took over five hours. Many of the dishes were for display only, heavily gilded with poisonous metal dyes, which on another occasion proved the downfall of one enthusiastic though unsophisticated Sienese guest, who almost died as a result. So much did he consume that when he finally managed to evacuate the results his excrement was fought over for the gold it contained. Caterina might also have been mindful of the fate of the bridegroom of her distant cousin Violante Visconti, who so overindulged at his wedding feast that he died a week later.

When the dinner was safely concluded, Caterina received wedding gifts worth over 12,000 ducats. Duchess Bona wrote excitedly from Milan to express her 'great pleasure' on hearing of 'the honours and the gracious reception accorded to thee by His Holiness and the whole of the court of Rome ... and although we suffer from the privation of thy sweet company, nonetheless, whenever we are reminded of the happiness of thy estate we experience an incredible consolation'.

Galeazzo's death left Milan in a precarious position. His overbearing and tyrannical nature might have offended many of his subjects, but it had made him indisputable master of his duchy. Controversially, Galeazzo's will named his widow, Bona, as regent to their seven-year-old son Giangaleazzo. The ominous task of ruling one of Italy's most prestigious martial dynasties and continuing the mighty, soldierly legacy of those with Visconti blood in their veins had been left in the hands of a rather feeble woman and a boy who could not be expected to govern in his own right for a decade. The power of Galeazzo's vicious whims could easily be snatched from the kind but somewhat inane Bona.

Bona of Savoy's marriage to Galeazzo had been successful by the measures of the time. She had borne him two healthy sons early in their marriage and then two daughters, Bianca and Anna. She had followed the custom of the day by treating Caterina as a daughter, alongside her own legitimate children. Bona, one of nineteen children, had been brought up by her sister, Queen Charlotte of France. Most of her siblings had married into the ruling houses of Europe, and Bona went about with the air of a woman simply delighted to be herself. Despite the contemporary fashion for slimness, she flaunted her rotund body. This only drew attention to her plain face and unruly, frizzy hair, which she squashed under a tight headdress resembling a lid on a bucket. Nonetheless, Bona carried herself as confidently and graciously as any of the great court beauties. She was neither spiteful nor vindictive, and although she seldom restrained her tendency to beam at her own existence, she could also play a more dignified role – as she had done on the Florentine visit of 1471, where she had restricted herself to nods at the gawping populace.

Despite Bona's creditable good nature, however, it would have been hard to find a stupider woman. Less than a decade after the visit to Florence, her foolish affectations and snobbish pride in her royal ancestry imperilled not only all she valued, but also those she loved the most.

Despite his wife's royal connections and cheerful demeanour, Galeazzo had been a flamboyantly unfaithful husband even at a time when no one expected fidelity from princes: 'much subject to Venus and to filthy lust, in such a manner that his subjects felt greatly disturbed'. He had had many casual liaisons with both men and women. His greatest passion had been for Lucia Marliani, Countess of Melzo, who became not just the subject of his carnal appetites but also of a maniacal ardour that lasted until the end of his life.

Galeazzo had encountered the nineteen-year-old Lucia in 1474 and immediately began lavishing her with gifts. Initially, he tried to calm Bona's suspicions by pretending that the girl was mistress to his brother Ludovico, but he soon abandoned pretence along with reason, granting houses and lands to Lucia. Making her a countess in her own right in direct opposition to Lombard practice, he drew up an extraordinary legal document in which she was forbidden to have sexual congress with her husband without the Duke's express permission. He subsequently caused further scandal by effectively bringing Lucia into his household, declaring that she and any children they had together had the right to call themselves Visconti. Lucia gave him two sons, born in 1477.

Perhaps in retaliation, the frankly unlikely rumours circulated that Bona had gone so far as to take a lover of her own. She had been guilty of making a most inappropriate choice of confidant in the man who became her pampered favourite, Antonio Tassino, a low-born Ferrarese and meat carver to her household. The dowager duchess would not hear a word said against him – worse still, she treated his every utterance as a golden drop of wisdom that she enshrined as absolute truth. It was this handsome charlatan who came to the fore when Bona assumed her regency. Tassino was undoubtedly good-looking, but no more than a chancer and a scoundrel. If Bona's letters to her stepdaughter, Caterina, pay testimony to her best qualities, her involvement with Tassino, which caused outrage in the aftermath of Duke Galeazzo's death, served as proof of her worst. 'A woman of little sense,' observed the French chronicler Philippe de Commines.

Bona displayed her profound lack of wit throughout what she ensured would be only a short regency. The real work of governing the duchy fell to Cicco Simonetta, a trusted counsellor and former secretary to Francesco Sforza as well as serving Duke Galeazzo. It had been Simonetta who had skilfully warded off threats of insurrection in the immediate aftermath of Galeazzo's murder. Ordering city authorities to pass a number of populist measures such as the freeing of debtors, he remained unable to defuse the most serious threat to the young duke and his widowed mother. The real peril came from within the ducal family itself.

Duke Francesco and Bianca Maria Visconti had had seven children besides Galeazzo – the beautiful and highly intelligent Ippolita, who was married to Alfonso, Duke of Calabria, the heir to the throne of Naples; Elisabetta, who had died in 1472; and five younger boys. Of these, Sforza and Ludovico felt especially enraged at the provision in Galeazzo's will, believing that the regency should have passed to the senior males in the family rather than to Duchess Bona. They raised a rebellion in the spring of 1477, swiftly crushed by Simonetta, whose decisive action had saved Bona and her son. Ludovico fled via Ferrara – where he received a sympathetic welcome from Duke Ercole d'Este – and made his home for the next two years in Pisa, where he spent his time vigorously propagating the idea that Tassino, a low-born trickster, now ruled Milan, plundering the ducal coffers. Bona's indiscreet and exuberant passion illustrated his story perfectly.

Ludovico's rebellious brother, meanwhile, had been granted the duchy of Bari as part of his betrothal in 1465 to Eleonora d'Aragona, the daughter of King Ferrante of Naples. But in 1479 he died suddenly, and Ludovico saw an opportunity to change his circumstances. He hurried to Naples, to seek support from his sister Ippolita Maria and her royal father-in-law. The ruling house of Naples reeled with appropriate disgust by what Ludovico carefully portrayed of Bona's scandalous behaviour. King Ferrante granted Ludovico the late Sforza Sforza's vacant Bari dukedom, and promised troops to support him in a coup on Milan. The king saw in Ludovico's ambition a golden opportunity for detaching Milan from its alliance with Florence and Venice, then at war with the papacy and Naples as a consequence of the Pazzi conspiracy.

Bona's immoderate idiocy having been given full reign, any military measures were rendered unnecessary. Accounts vary as to Ludovico's reception upon his return to Milan – some holding that he arrived at the invitation of Bona, who had decorated the Porta Giovia castello with bunting to welcome him, others that he inveigled his way into the city through a side gate and met with the duchess in secret.

Whatever passed between them, Ludovico convinced Bona without violence or bloodshed that he should have control of the regency council. Rather than turning immediately on Tassino, he poisoned his sister-in-law's mind first against the loyal Cicco Simonetta. Simonetta warned Bona when she arrived that 'I shall lose my head and before long Your Serene Highness will lose her state'. Bona had ignored him. Almost upon his arrival Ludovico promptly accused the wretched Simonetta of treachery and embezzlement. His slander even convinced Caterina. She referred to her late father's loyal servant as 'villainous'. He did indeed lose his head, though the tough seventy-year-old refused even under torture to hand over his carefully amassed fortune which he had placed in a Florentine bank. His wife, a Visconti, went mad at the death of her husband and died.

Bona continued her feeble-minded performance. She proved utterly unable to grasp that her brother-in-law Ludovico presented the most serious threat to her position in the duchy. Her behaviour with Tassino became increasingly reckless and silly. Her favourite allowed her pampering to go to his head. With Simonetta disposed of, Tassino believed there remained no checks to his power. The favourite's conduct became absurdly grandiose. He went so far as to keep Ludovico waiting while his hairdresser pomaded him to perfection. Ludovico's patience snapped when Tassino appointed his own father to the command of Porta Giovia. Tassino found himself abruptly exiled. He scuttled out of the city, his bulging baggage clanking with the treasures he had wheedled out of Bona.

With Simonetta dead and Tassino banished, Ludovico now made his final move. He demanded that his nephew, the twelve-year-old Giangaleazzo, be formally invested as duke, depriving Bona of her nominal function as regent. Ludovico, furthermore, insisted that his sister-in-law should retire, to spend the rest of her life concentrating on absolving herself of her sexual sins with Tassino. Bona, screaming with horror, wildly declared that she intended to return to her home beyond the Alps to clear her name of the calumny Ludovico had perpetrated in accusing her of being Tassino's lover. Precisely as Ludovico intended, she abandoned her own children and placed them under his guardianship. En route for Piedmont Sforza troops apprehended her, imprisoning her in the fortress of Abbiategrasso. There she remained for some years, though she was finally permitted to travel to France in 1500 and she continued to make occasional appearances at the Milanese court.

Examination of the evidence suggests that Bona did not have a physical affair with Tassino, but her undoubted erotic obsession deprived her of the scintilla of judgement she did have. The secretary Corio reports that she became 'forgetful of her honour and dignity'. Her lack of political acumen played neatly into the trap

Ludovico had set for her, giving him control over the young Duke Giangaleazzo and his siblings. After Bona's exile, Ludovico had further housekeeping detail that demanded attention.

His own remaining brothers would pose no threat: Filippo lived quietly in the country and Ascanio had embarked upon an ecclesiastical career, for which he received Ludovico's energetic support, particularly in his bid to acquire a cardinal's hat. Ascanio, based in Rome, proved an excellent conduit for information and helping his brother devise the best strategy for their state and the Sforza dynasty. Once he had received the red hat that denoted a prince of the Church, Ascanio and his brother placed the papacy in their sights.

Ludovico, a man who heeded the dangers of illegitimate offspring and ambitious brothers, wished to avoid the risk of a fraternal stiletto being slipped between his ribs. The Renaissance was known for its lack of concern over illegitimate children. At a time when the Italian states favoured neither bastard nor legitimate child but chose the fittest, a climate of mistrust and resentment among the often numerous natural children born to the various sovereigns could hardly be avoided. With this in mind he stripped Lucia Marliani of the estates and titles given to her by the ardent Duke Galeazzo. Ludovico insisted that she make these over to her eldest son by his late brother, Giovanni Visconti, and when the boy reached the right age he came to court where he took his place but caused no fuss, despite being recognized as the late duke's son. Ludovico also ensured that Ottaviano, his younger brother, born after Galeazzo's murder, was recognized as the son of a prince. His future lay in the Church. Lucia returned to her cuckolded husband, bearing him four further children. To the end of her life she continued to clamour for the return of her titles (which in any case she carried on using, as well as the privileges she could get away with).

The new regent of Milan had dealt mercifully with her, and honoured his brother's children. With Ascanio as his eyes and ears in Rome, he set out to make his court the most brilliant on the Italian peninsula. His potential rivals from within the family removed, he could joke to his brother, 'Monseigneur, pardon me if I do not trust you although you are my brother.' For the next twenty years Ludovico, having dealt with danger from inside the family, fulfilled the promise he had shown as a young man, gifts fostered by his mother Bianca Maria Visconti, who feared the madness of the Visconti might have reappeared in Duke Galeazzo as his depravity and cruel whims seemed to suggest. At the end of his life one emissary wrote of the duke's 'acts of madness and things that cannot be written.' Ludovico proceeded to make this Milan's golden age, but he had forgotten one family member who could yet bring mischief and destruction upon the house of Sforza. He had not counted himself among those who could wreak havoc upon the ruling dynasty of Milan.

CHAPTER 4

Fair is Foul and Foul is Fair

1478–1484

'My Lords beware – for Florence is a big undertaking'
COUNT GIAN BATTISTA MONTESECCO

On 26 April 1478, the day dawned bright and sunny in Florence. As usual for the fifth and last Sunday after Easter, the faithful gathered for High Mass, quickly filling the gigantic space of the Duomo. The congregation milled about as they waited for the start of the service celebrating the Resurrection. As matters turned out on that warm April morning, there could hardly have been a more appropriate theme for the service than the bewilderment of the Apostles and their anger at betrayal by one of their own. A number of important figures were presently gathered in the city, including Lorenzo de Medici, his wife Clarice Orsini and his mother Lucrezia Tornabuoni, his principal adviser in the real seat of power, the Palazzo Medici. Lorenzo's brother Giuliano had been confined to bed for the past ten days with sciatica, and the Florentine leader hoped to see his brother improved, though his doctors had advised him to return to bed as soon as he had attended Mass, forgoing the banquet arranged by Lorenzo, and a number of dignitaries assembled in the Duomo.

The guests included Cardinal Raffaele Riario, the seventeen-year-old nephew of Caterina Sforza's husband, Girolamo Riario. With Cardinal Raffaele came his suite, the Pazzi family and their obnoxious relative Francesco Salviati, Archbishop of Pisa and nephew to Jacopo Pazzi, head of the dynasty. This ancient Florentine family of former *grandi* had built up a bank which rivalled that of the Medici in power and riches, but had never enjoyed the same popularity with the people of Florence. Curiously, Archbishop Salviati had given word that he would not attend Mass on this holy day of obligation, but would meet his family later at the feast.

Waiting for Mass to begin, Lorenzo stood chatting to friends and business associates. His brother Giuliano de' Medici arrived with their brother-in-law Guglielmo Pazzi, husband of their sister Bianca de' Medici, and Guglielmo's cousin Francesco Pazzi. The younger men were ragging as they came into the church, Francesco putting his arms around Giuliano, probing his chest and sides, asking if he had grown fat since his accident. Pazzi's embrace had a far more sinister purpose: he was checking for body armour, not fat. In fact, Guiliano was one of the best-looking men in Florence, his body one of nature's rare examples of perfect proportion, his face framed by fair brown hair and his mouth neat and beautifully shaped. His personality was as attractive as his appearance; his manner engaging, his laugh quick and his impulses generous. Even had his name not been Medici he could have had any girl in the city.

Within a few minutes the service began. The words of the priests lifted to the top of Brunelleschi's great dome through a filter of sunlight and incense. As soon as the celebrant pronounced the words 'Ite Missa Est,' the crowd started to move out of the building, their chatter mingling with the sound of footsteps. Guiliano, approaching the northern door of the cathedral, suddenly staggered backwards, a bewildered expression on his handsome face. Fingers of blood seeped in thick rivulets from his curling hair. His legs abruptly gave way and he slipped to the floor. By the time his body hit the cold stone, twenty-four-year-old Giuliano de' Medici was dead.

It had not been difficult to kill the young Medici, as their unofficial position as Florence's first family did not permit the protection of a personal bodyguard. So swiftly had the assassins entered the stuffy, crowded Cathedral, so stealthy and lupine was the strategy with which they isolated their prey, that Giuliano had been caught off guard, unaware of the mortal danger encircling him. He remained innocent of the killers' presence until the first and fatal blow had been struck. As he fell, shrieks broke out among the congregation and panic rippled through the crowd, which stampeded for the doors. Few had actually seen Giuliano fall, and many believed that the great dome above them had begun to collapse, or that the city had been hit by an earthquake.

The murderers were Francesco Pazzi and a family client, Bernardo Bandini dei Baroncelli; and their plot – known as the Pazzi conspiracy – would live long in infamy. Not content with having mortally wounded the young man, they seemed possessed by madness as they fell upon his corpse. The pair maniacally stabbed his body, slashing wildly at the mutilated remains in a fevered passion of hate. In his frenzy Pazzi even managed to harm himself in the leg, but in the first moments after the killing it was unclear who had struck Giuliano. Lorenzo stood about thirty feet away, near two priests who had been shadowing him as he moved about before the Mass began. As the Pazzi killers gave the codeword 'traitor', the two priests pulled out the daggers concealed in their surplice sleeves. More accustomed to breaking 'flesh' with their hands, the priests, for all their willing, proved inept as killers and delivered only a flesh wound to Lorenzo's neck. Fit and fast, having already survived earlier attempts on his life, Lorenzo hauled his cloak up by wrapping it around his arm, drew his sword and engaged his assailants. The clash of steel alerted those Mediceans who had not seen the attack, and they sped across the cathedral to help make good his escape. Baroncelli, having spotted a clear line to Lorenzo, had already reached him. Pulling back his blade, he prepared to kill the Medici leader. Francesco Nori, one of Lorenzo's inner circle, saw Baronecelli and deftly threw himself in front of the sword just as Baroncelli struck. The blow plunged to the hilt deep into Nori's belly, saving Lorenzo's life. The Medici leader turned and, leaping over the altar rail, made for the north sacristy.

Lorenzo's men hauled the courageous Nori with them, though he died minutes later. A relative of the Medici and member of the Cavalcanti family had also been gravely injured. The Pazzi, their murderous priests and the other mercenaries who had come disguised as friends and household attendants, realizing that Lorenzo had escaped beyond their reach, fled through a side door. They headed south, where the Pazzi properties dominated the Santa Croce quarter of Florence. A long trail of blood from Francesco Pazzi's wounded leg led straight to the imposing family palazzo, standing firmly at the centre of the Pazzi power base.

Lorenzo and his allies had bolted themselves into the cathedral and behind the sacristy door, anxiously waiting, as they believed that the enemy lurked beyond the Duomo's doors. A grotesque sucking noise intruded above their whispered questions, as one of the group had suggested that the dagger which had injured Lorenzo might have been poisoned; his friend Antonio Ridolfi pressed his lips to the cut in case any venom had been used to add a deadlier taint to the blade's sharpened steel. The company had no answer to Lorenzo's increasingly persistent questions. 'Giuliano. Where is he? Is he safe?' But no one dared to give him the terrible answer.

Cardinal Raffaele Riario had been a latecomer to the fatal devotions in the Florentine Duomo that morning. Having been presented with the coveted red hat while still a student of canon law at the University of Pisa, the Pope's young relative had been granted permission to pass through Florence and to remain there several days. Shortly before the visit, Sixtus IV had made Raffaele a papal legate; given that his own relationship with the Pontiff had become alarmingly fraught, Lorenzo de' Medici wondered whether the young man might have been sent as a possible conduit to improve relations between Florence and the Vatican. Even by the showy standards of Sixtus's relatives, Raffaele had arrived in the city republic with an impressive retinue. The cardinal and his entourage stayed at the Villa Laveggi on the slopes of Fiesole as guests of his uncle Jacopo Pazzi, close to the Villa Medici. Raffaele was acquainted with his host thanks to business dealings between the Pazzi bank and the Pope – dealings which had led to a mutually beneficial relationship between the two families.

Raffaele gave out courteously that he had a great desire to visit the Palazzo Medici, 'for he had heard of the many and incomparable treasures there and wished very much to see them'. Lorenzo de' Medici had naturally agreed, going to enormous lengths to make the best possible impression, pulling out the greatest pieces from his collection for him to admire. Statuary, sculpture and paintings were arranged for display, and the finest plate was polished up for the banquet. It was an excellent opportunity to befriend and charm the youngster as a means of improving relations with Sixtus.

Lorenzo and Sixtus had met when the former had been a member of the Florentine embassy to Rome to congratulate the latter on his election. Sixtus had singled him out for special favours, presenting him with two antique busts of Agrippa and Augustus as well as selling him pieces from Pope Paul II's collection of cameos and silver for bargain prices. The Orsini, Lorenzo's in-laws, had given their backing to Sixtus's election and in return for their support Lorenzo let it be known that he wished to give the archbishopric of Florence to Rinaldo Orsini. Sixtus agreed, in light of his debt to the great Roman dynasty. This meant, however, that Francesco Salviati, a papal favourite who had expected to receive the post, felt dispossessed by Lorenzo and bore a terrible grudge against him. Lorenzo felt no love for Salviati, despite his family's honourable Florentine connections, not the least of them his Pazzi mother. Sixtus promised Salviati that he would be compensated. Yet by the time of Orsini's appointment to the rich Florentine benefice, relations had already become strained between the Pontiff and Lorenzo, in part as Salviati had been successful in further provoking and irritating the Pope's anger against the Florentine leader. Sixtus had duly appointed Salviati Archbishop of Pisa, but Lorenzo refused to allow his passage through Florence for three years, thus depriving him of the opportunity to collect the vast revenues from his benefice until 1475. Raffaele's visit looked set to improve matters, and the Cardinal condescended so far as to use the Palazzo Medici to don his vestments before the Easter service. When the killing began, Riario was yanked unceremoniously to his feet by the canons of the Cathedral chapter. Barely able to walk, his legs trembling, they led the terrified boy away to safety. At this stage, he was unconscious of his unwitting role in the Pazzi plot.

Until the early 1470s, the Pazzi had lived uneasily under their Medici rivals. As former aristocrats who had turned to banking, the Pazzi looked down on the Medici from the lofty heights of their 500 years' history in the city, but conceded the upstart dynasty's greater financial and political influence. Guglielmo Pazzi had been a companion of Lorenzo de' Medici's early youth; in 1465 they had ridden together as part of the escort of Don Federico d'Aragona on his journey to Milan to claim Ippolita Sforza as his brother's bride.

Yet the Pazzi involvement with the papacy had created a simmer-
ing enmity between the two houses, which Lucrezia Tornabuoni
had attempted to neutralize by brokering the marriage between
Guglielmo and Bianca Maria de' Medici. Lorenzo's policies had con-
flicted with those of Sixtus in the Pope's attempt to create a state for
his degenerate nephew Girolamo Riario, who had married Caterina
Sforza in 1477. As part of Caterina's complex dowry, Sixtus arranged
the purchase of Imola from Duke Galeazzo Maria of Milan for
40,000 ducats. When the papal request for a loan of the money from
the Medici bank was declined, Sixtus turned to Francesco Pazzi. Not
only did Pazzi proffer the funds, he also gave the Pope an interest-
ing piece of information. Lorenzo had, it seemed, passed around
word that no one was to lend the money as the acquisition of Imola
would endanger Florence. Sixtus removed the Medici as papal
bankers and gave the position to the Pazzi. Francesco Pazzi and
his kinsman, the embittered Salviati, were charged with taking
the money for Imola to Galeazzo Maria in Milan. Lorenzo's spy
network in the northern duchy soon informed him of Pazzi's disobedience, but he behaved with an appearance of tact, continuing
to refer to his Pazzi 'family' while quietly ensuring that they were
unable to obtain any real influence in the Signoria, the official seat
of government.

Commenting on the Pazzis' disobedience, the Milanese ambassador wrote: 'It provoked much talk and gossip [and showed] little
regard for Lorenzo or his political establishment ... [by] stirring up
discussion of the sort intended to condemn his regime as unfree and
against liberty, indeed as princely and overbearing.' He concluded
that those intent on causing trouble for Lorenzo were reviving old
talk aimed at those who held the republic's ideals dear, dishonestly
firing them up with notions of freedom and liberty. He warned his
master: 'Unless something is done they will cause trouble.' Duke
Galeazzo also warned Lorenzo that he should seek personal protection against an assassination attempt, but Lorenzo declared that he
feared nothing so long as he retained the support of Milan and his
own key ministers of state.

Sixtus continued his machinations against Lorenzo. With no
standing army of its own, Florence had frequently relied upon

the services of the great *condottiere* Federico Montefeltro, Count of Urbino. The Pope, hoping to recruit the Montefeltro, arranged the marriage of the count's eldest daughter to one of his nephews, Giovanni della Rovere, and raised Urbino to the status of a duchy, thus depriving Florence of its traditional and most useful ally.* In response, Lorenzo called a defensive league between Milan, Venice and Florence, which the Pope declared a straightforward offensive alliance against Rome. He cunningly fanned the fears of Ferrante of Naples, who had been left out of the league because of his political meddling in southern Tuscany, as he knew the king saw the risk created by this northern bloc. Sixtus made a marriage between one of Ferrante's illegitimate daughters and one of his own useful supply of della Rovere nephews. This axis between Rome and Naples became more threatening when the murder of Galeazzo Maria at Christmas 1476 rendered Lorenzo's league all but useless.

It could only have been a matter of time before the two principal conspirators of the Pazzi plot encountered one another. Francesco Pazzi and Girolamo Riario could hardly have been less alike – the debauched and flabby Riario, a screaming statement of new money in his gold and silver brocade costumes encrusted with sparkling jewels, and the trim, *soigné* Pazzi, whose beautifully cut clothes embodied the understated style of half a millennium of self-assurance. Unfortunately he could do nothing to disguise either his diminutive stature or his fantastically haughty arrogance. Francesco had always loathed Lorenzo. At the joust preceding Lorenzo's marriage to Clarice Orsini, he had unsportingly made the star of the show his target, knocking him off his horse with such force that he felt, perhaps rightly, that he ought to have won the prize, as opposed to the man he sent flying from his saddle. Angelo Poliziano†* called him 'a bloodthirsty person, and besides, when once he desired something in his heart, he would go after it undeterred by considerations of honour, piety, fame or reputation', while in Guicciardini's opinion he was 'restless, ambitious and very spirited'. Finally, unable to watch his family humbling themselves before the gaggle of Medici

---

* The marriage took place between Giovanni della Rovere, Lord of the Papal Lands, Prefect of Rome, Senigallia and Mondavio, and Giovanna Montefeltro in 1484.

† Humanist scholar, Lorenzo's great friend and tutor to his children.

shopkeepers, Francesco had moved to Rome, which he found much more congenial to his pride, as well as to the flourishing Pazzi fortunes. Here he met Riario, the new Lord of Imola, strutting about the city with his bands of brigands. The vulgar Riario grumbled endlessly about his new dominion, declaring petulantly that it was 'not worth a bean' while the Medici held Florence. The unlikely friendship between patrician and parvenu flourished in the light of their mutual hatred for Il Magnifico. Francesco Salviati added his own loathing to their triumvirate.

Girolamo scented a means of securing the Tuscan hub of Florence to ensure the safety and enlargement of his northern-central Italian superstate, the Pazzi of displacing the Medici and taking over Florence, and Salviati the route to the long-coveted archbishopric of the city. Quite how Riario and Pazzi would resolve the issue of their mutually exclusive plans was never put to the test. The three plotters now needed to engage Messer Jacopo, the head of the Pazzi clan in Florence. Hitherto Jacopo, a shrewd businessman but a contemptible miser and niggard with a deservedly dreadful reputation for his beggarly habits, had endured his family taking second place to the Medici. Even though the honours and position accorded to the Pazzi were nominal, Jacopo was Florentine to the core and would sanction no open act of rebellion against them. Pragmatically, he observed that Francesco Pazzi had lived most of his adult life outside the city republic, while Salviati was so reviled there that Lorenzo had met no popular opposition to preventing him crossing the border to enter his see. As for Riario, he had spent half his life in Savona hawking fruit on street corners before his uncle had been elected Pope. Jacopo did not oppose the rebellion in principle, but would not discuss the notion of deposing his family's pre-eminent adversaries; the risks involved were too immense.

Undeterred, the conspirators sought an experienced military commander who could lead a force of troops to back up their plan, and found their man in the well-known *condottiere* Count Giovanni Battista da Montesecco. Over the course of several clandestine meetings they delivered a carefully glossed version of the scheme, promising Montesecco that by making their own renunciation of Lorenzo's rule visible and violent, the phlegmatic Florentines would be inspired to abandon their stoical suffering and act. Once the republic's spirit had been energized and the long habit of apathy expunged, the plotters confidently expounded upon a wronged and enslaved people ready to join in battle to resurrect their violated freedoms and avenge the offences committed by the Medici against their sacred yet long-abandoned republican values. At last the hyperbole ended and they fell silent. Expectant, they awaited the soldier's appraisal of their scheme to overthrow the Medici; indeed the scene they had so fulsomely described had almost persuaded them that they had no need of his services. Montesecco seemed equally confused, for he asked them what part they wished him to play in their plan. Salviati shot back impatiently, 'Have I not told you that we wish to change the government of Florence?'

Montesecco returned, 'Yes, you have told me, but you have not told me the means and without knowing the means I can give you no answer.' In his account, the conspirators at last articulated the words they had thus far avoided and said that there was no other way except by murdering Lorenzo and Giuliano de' Medici and to have armed men at the ready the moment this was done. Montesecco claimed that he replied, 'My Lords, beware of what you do, for Florence is a big undertaking.'

Salviati snapped, impatient with this prudent reply, 'We know the condition and state of Florentine affairs more fully than you do, and there is no more doubt that our plans will succeed than that we are all sitting here now. We have but to enlist Messer Jacopo di Poggio ... and the thing is done.' Montesecco was reluctant, and insisted on speaking to the Pope himself.

The audience took place, and Montesecco expressed his doubts, saying that it would be impossible to get rid of the Medici without killing them and that such a measure would doubtless lead to other fatalities. Sixtus's response was perfectly clear: 'In no case will I have the death of anyone, it is not my office to cause the death of a man. Lorenzo has behaved unworthily and badly towards us, but I will not hear of his death, though I wish for a revolution in the state.'

Riario interjected, 'We will do all we can to ensure there is no killing, but if it becomes unavoidable, your Holiness will pardon him through whom it happens.'

At this, Sixtus replied: 'You are an idiot, I tell you no one is to die, only the government turned out.' He continued on the theme of governing Florence without Lorenzo: 'he is a violent man who pays no regard to us. If he were expelled we could do with the republic as it seemed best and that would be very pleasing to us.'

Riario said: 'Your Holiness speaks the truth. Be then satisfied that we shall do all in our power to attain this end.' After too much of this, a satisfactory euphemism was arrived at. The conspirators asked if His Holiness was content for them to 'steer this ship' and to do so 'well'. The Pope replied that he was indeed content. Montesecco's account is drawn from his confession, that of a desperate man hoping to save his life, and was undoubtedly tampered with by the Medici after the event; but his description of Sixtus speaking according to the formality of his office while the subtext of the conversation remained explicit to all is a classic piece of Renaissance diplomacy.

Now that everyone understood one another, the coup could proceed. Sixtus called in his family connection with the new Duke of Urbino, who committed a force of 600 men which would surround the city in anticipation of the rebel signal. Riario now began to court Lorenzo to distract him from suspicion. Il Magnifico was invited to Rome to heal the rift between himself and the Holy Father, but Lorenzo refused to set foot on Sixtus's home territory, fearing for his safety. Yet he seemed oblivious to the threat converging on Florence. Montesecco met with him there several times, ostensibly bearing Riario's good wishes. He became charmed by the unaffected manners and good nature of the man he had agreed to kill, who even honoured his would-be assassin by riding with him from the country to his lodgings.

It was Raffaele Riario who unwittingly provided the ruse for the plotters to send their men into Florence without alerting the Medicis' attention. He received and accepted the invitation from the Pazzi to stay at their country villa, and the original plan was that Lorenzo would then receive an invitation for himself and Giuliano to dine with the Cardinal. Once the Medici brothers arrived at the

Pazzi residence, they could be despatched. As predicted, the invitation was accepted, but Lorenzo insisted that he should give the dinner, and when he called at Montughi, he did so without Giuliano, as the latter was bedridden with his leg injury. Giuliano obstinately remained indisposed, and the plotters seemed frustrated at every turn, until eventually Lorenzo's invitation to Raffaele to inspect the Palazzo Medici after Mass finally offered the ideal opportunity. Yet upon hearing where the murders were to take place, Montesecco claimed he withdrew his co-operation, on the grounds that he would 'not add sacrilege to murder in a place where God could see him'. Riario was safely out of harm's and presumably God's way in Rome, but the Pazzi had no chance to vent their anger on Montesecco, as two priests stepped forward as volunteers – one of them from the town of Volterra, who had rebelled against Florence in 1472 – and they didn't have time to seek out more experienced hit men.

In the sacristy, the minutes dragged past. Eventually, fists banged on the door and the voices of those who claimed to be friends could be heard, begging Lorenzo to admit them. Sigismondo della Stufa, one of the more soldierly of the small company gathered around their leader, climbed the stairs leading to the organ gallery and looked out. He saw that the men hammering on the door were indeed who they claimed to be, the staunchest of Lorenzo's allies and family, among them the Tornabuoni. They carried arms to take the fight back to the palazzo. Della Stufa surveyed the scene below him once more and at last saw the man he believed to be Giuliano. Lorenzo had understood that his brother must be dead, but the fact that his own life and that of his entire family were at risk now made a quick escape imperative. If he survived, there would be time enough to deal thoroughly with the murderers.

When physicians examined Giuliano Medici's remains in the late nineteenth century, they found evidence of at least nineteen wounds, any one of which could have proved fatal. These spoke as loud as any living witness of the assassins' brutality, of their bitter hatred and determination to achieve their ghastly intent. Many of the stab wounds had left deep cuts and marks in the bones, while one blow, probably the first, had split the skull almost in two and another particularly vicious thrust had cut through the backbone and severed the spinal cord. While the body still lay on the floor of the Duomo in a pool of blood, the partly eviscerated stomach emerged through the slashes in Giuliano's costume, until moments before so fine and clean. Angelo Poliziano, a witness to the terrible events in the Duomo, glimpsed the corpse as he and Lorenzo's small band of supporters hurried their master from the sacristy door to the safety of the Palazzo Medici just a few hundred yards away. The horrific memory haunted him, and he later expressed his regret that there had not been a moment respectfully to cover the flesh of the man he professed to have loved almost as much as Lorenzo.

During the next hour it became clear than an anti-Medici coup had begun. Many of the congregation had fled to their homes, but not before spreading the rumour that both Medici brothers had been killed. Though at first few people appeared in the streets, those closest to Lorenzo felt certain that the plan to undo the leading Florentine family had not yet been achieved. The enemy had failed to kill Lorenzo, a blow from which they would require a near-miracle to recover. In the palazzo, Lorenzo's companions tried to piece together what each had seen in the Duomo, and any other strange occurrences leading up to Giuliano's killing. The guilt of the Pazzi they pronounced unanimously, but could not fathom the number or identity of those working with them.

The rebel action had also struck the Signoria. According to plan, Archbishop Salviati walked the short distance to the Palazzo Vecchio with his attendants and announced confidently that he carried an important message from the Pope which must be delivered in person to Cesare Petrucci, the current *Gonfaloniere*. Petrucci happened to be dining when Salviati arrived. The message struck him as odd, so he sent a messenger to see whether the streets outside were orderly and to try to detect any clue as to whether something untoward was happening. The guard asked Salviati to wait, and offered more comfortable seating for his retinue in an adjoining room. In reality, the 'clerics' in the Archbishop's train were mercenaries from Perugia. Petrucci received Salviati, but the Archbishop was now so nervous that he mumbled the message, glancing round anxiously and flushing. Petrucci, unconvinced, called for his guard, upon which Salviati rushed from the room, calling for his mercenaries to strike. It would have been better for the plotters had any of them spent enough time in Florence to learn that Petrucci had had the door of the Signoria fitted with catches which did not open from the inside. The mercenaries were trapped, and useless. Yelling for the warning bell, the *Vacca*, to be rung, Petrucci grabbed a *spiedo* (short spear) and set upon Salviati. As the great bell sounded, Pazzi supporters could be heard in the streets crying 'Down with the Medici! Liberty!', though they were met with the Medici rallying cry 'Palle, palle!' Medici supporters now entered the Signoria and assisted the *Gonfaloniere* and his guard in despatching the Perugians. Their heads were plopped on lances and swords and paraded through the piazza.

The ringleaders had now been rounded up in the Palazzo Vecchio. Jacopo Pazzi, Salviati and Francesco Pazzi were stripped, tied and hanged from the windows, along with two more of Salviati's companions. Angelo Poliziano saw Salviati desperately trying to gain some purchase as he swung by tearing at Pazzi's naked body with his teeth. Lorenzo appeared at the windows of the Palazzo Medici to beseech the crowds to calm themselves, but Florence now erupted with bloodlust and for several days the people, 'driven by the Furies' in Poliziano's words, rioted, attacking anyone whom they believed to be associated with the conspiracy. By the time the corpses dangling from the Palazzo Vecchio began to putrefy, another eighty people had died. Cardinal Riario was kept in custody by the Florentine authorities – allegedly for his own safety – until diplomatic pressure forced his release a few weeks later, being led out of the city and escorted in disguise to Rome, where it was said that his young face never lost the whiteness it had acquired at the ghastly shock of the murders.

Giuliano's body had been returned to the palazzo. After the physicians had stitched the corpse back together they performed the ritual. Staggering in horror, supported by her women, Lucrezia Tornabuoni demanded to see her son, despite the pitiful condition of the body. Lorenzo knew his mother too well to argue. As Lucrezia approached the mutilated body, keening piteously, she had to be restrained from flinging herself upon her son. Wails of sorrow and disbelief broke from her lips. Yet her incoherent words also signalled her battle cry, a demand for revenge for young Giuliano, brought down in all the gifts of his birth, youth and beauty. The whole of Florence mourned with her. When Giuliano's funeral was held, the public clamoured to show their grief and pity for their first family. The burial demonstrated clearly the level of Medici sway over the city, and this time, unlike Piero's funeral, the women of the family attended, as did those of other magnate houses. Lorenzo asked that space be left him to lie beside his brother when his own time came.

Lorenzo's vengeance proved swift. The Pazzi were exiled and dispossessed, their name and coat of arms suppressed by the Signoria. According to custom, portraits of the conspirators were painted on the walls of the Bargello, with rope around their necks, though posthumous infamy may have been soothed somewhat by the fact that the painter of the family's disgrace was Botticelli. In celebration of his survival, Lorenzo commissioned three images of himself from Verocchio, which were set up in the churches of Chiarito, Santissima Annunziata and Santa Maria degli Angeli. His next concern was the safety of his family. Clarice and the children were sent first to friends at Pistoia and then to the fortified house at Cafaggiolo, where they lived, heavily guarded and in isolation. The family tutor, Poliziano, chafed at being absent from his beloved Florence, but Clarice was touched by the loyalty of the country people. 'She rarely goes out,' reported Poliziano. 'We want for nothing. Presents we refuse, except for salad, figs and a few flasks of wine ... These citizens would bring us water in their ears. We keep good watch and have begun to put a guard on the gates.'

Lucrezia Tornabuoni had no intention of being shuffled off into rustic exile. Besides, she had urgent family matters to deal with. Soon after Giuliano's murder, it was revealed that he had fathered an illegitimate son, Giulio, by a girl from a modest family, Fioretta di Antonio Gorini. Lucrezia insisted that the child be raised as a Medici, and persuaded Lorenzo that he should be brought up in the palazzo, though he was educated for a time at the monastery of the Carmine. Lucrezia clearly had to overcome opposition from within her family, as the writer Nardi – admittedly a committed anti-Medici – observed: 'if it had not been for the prayers and authority of his grandmother, Lucrezia de Tornabuoni, deeply attached to her own blood ... it is likely that this child would not have been accepted in the family and raised as Giuliano's son'.

The repercussions of the Pazzi conspiracy spread beyond Florence. Sixtus raged when he heard the news of its failure and, forgetting his own part in the proceedings, declared that the Florentines had committed sacrilege by hanging an archbishop. As a result he issued a bull excommunicating Lorenzo de' Medici and placing Florence under an interdict. For Lucrezia and the other women of the Medici family, whose piety was not only personally essential to them but, as Lorenzo's erection of the images had shown, an essential means of manifesting Medici power, this was unbearably upsetting. Religious from beyond the city severed communications with the Medici, fearful of offending the Pope and incurring the interdict; as the Prior of Serviti wrote to Lucrezia, 'I would have liked to have come just for a few days, but if we, members of religious orders, do not obey the Pope's command, the punishment will be very severe'.

Girolamo Riario attacked the Florentine embassy in Rome with 300 papal soldiers and imprisoned the ambassador, while his uncle sent a delegation to Florence insisting that the 'culpable, sacrilegious, excommunicated, anathematized, infamous, unworthy of all trust and spiritually disqualified' Lorenzo de' Medici be sent to Rome to be tried for sacrilege and blasphemy. Everlasting ruin and eternal disgrace were similarly pronounced on the Signoria of Florence. Sixtus declared their property forfeit and commandeered the assets of the Medici bank at Rome. Initially, the Florentines demonstrated some of the independence and pride which the Pazzi had claimed was crushed by the Medici and defied the bull, going so far as to issue a counter-version excommunicating Sixtus. Their bravado was punctured when Sixtus declared war on Florence. The Milanese were preoccupied with Ludovico Il Moro's coup following the murder of his brother, besides having to deal with a rebellion in Genoa and a Swiss inroad into the duchy. They sent only token forces in their ally's defence. The Venetians had their hands tied by their war with the Ottomans. Lorenzo's Orsini in-laws mustered their own private troops and the Duke of Ferrara promised a small force. None of this would avail much against the full might of the papal armies under their brilliant commander the Duke of

Urbino, particularly as Sixtus had formed an alliance with Ferrante of Naples. By the end of the year the Neapolitans, using their protectorate of Siena as a base, had ravaged large swathes of Florentine territory, while the republic commander Ercole d'Este proved too prudent to act forcefully. Matters only became worse the following year, the Florentines, despite Venetian aid, suffering defeat in battle and the loss of the important town of Colle Val d'Elsa.

This was the greatest crisis of Lorenzo de' Medici's career. Tuscany was in a state of grave unrest, armed bandits were preying on country villages while in Florence famine threatened and the citizens were increasingly resentful of the taxes which were being levied to pay for the war. Outbreaks of plague in the summers of 1478 and 1479 left the hospitals and streets filled with corpses, the Arno broke its banks and flooded much of the city, and a peculiar combination of savagery and lassitude became the prevailing mood. It did seem as though the proud city republic had been abandoned by God.

Lorenzo was desperate for money. Despite his enormous personal wealth, the declining condition of the Medici bank coupled with the costs of the war necessitated huge loans. He borrowed over 50,000 florins from his cousins Lorenzo and Giovanni, a loan which was secured in great part with the possessions of his wife and mother. Clarice and Lucrezia pledged jewellery, silver and objets d'art, listed in the *Inventario di Gioie* of 1481 as being of the value of 18,148 florins still outstanding on the loan, though it is impossible to ascertain which woman gave what as the value, but not the owner, of the goods is recorded. Lucrezia's exceptional position on the board of the Florentine *monte delle doti* was also of crucial importance at this time. This was one of the most impressive innovations of the Florentine banking system, established in 1425 as an investment fund for girls' dowries. Fixed sums could be deposited during a girl's childhood to guarantee an increased return when she married, though if she died or did not marry the money reverted to the *comune*. In the fifteenth and sixteenth centuries, 20,000 women are recorded as using the dowry fund, which also functioned as a bank, making loans and investments to other houses in the city.

Lucrezia Tornabuoni was among them, and was later appointed as one of the directors of the fund. Here, the 'porous' relationship between the Medici family's personal funds and those of the city becomes contentious. Given that the Medici had no official status as governors of Florence, there were no ratified distinctions between their wealth and that of the city. Lorenzo and Lucrezia have been accused by contemporary and subsequent writers of plundering Florence's coffers for their own purposes, but this must be set against the enormous sums they were obliged to disburse privately for the support of the government. Precisely how much was appropriated from the *monte delle doti* and even more from the *monte* tout-court (Florence's public debt institution) in the aftermath of the Pazzi conspiracy is not recorded; but, given that the fund continued to flourish, it could not have been entirely detrimental, and, arguably, whatever further 'loans' the Medici took from it, their end after all was the preservation of the city.

Lorenzo himself was acutely conscious of the threat to which his continuing presence exposed Florence. In December 1479 he left the city in secret. He explained his actions in a letter to the Signoria:

> I am convinced that the action of our enemies is mainly directed by
> hatred against me and that by giving myself up to them I may be
> able to restore peace to our city … Because it has been chosen that
> I have greater honour and responsibility than other private citizens,
> I feel more bound to serve our country, even if it means risking my
> life … I desire that by my life or my death, my fate or my fortune I
> may contribute to the welfare of our city.

At Pisa, Lorenzo took ship for Naples.

The mission was not perhaps quite so heroic as it first appeared, as Lorenzo had been corresponding with Ferrante and was given a warm welcome in Naples, where he stayed at the headquarters of the Medici bank. Ferrante was a notoriously volatile and deceitful character, but despite the commonly held belief that 'there is no doubting that Lorenzo was in real danger', Lorenzo had little to fear. For sure, the wily Ferrante (who on the eve of the Pazzi conspiracy had warned Lorenzo about possible plots against him) kept every option open, including the prospect of the Medici regime imploding. Yet the king preferred a diminished Lorenzo as a friend, rather than a 'free' Florence under papal control. Besides, Ferrante benefited from Florence's banking activities and not perchance one of the chief informal Florentine negotiators had been Giuliano Gondi, one of Ferrante's most important creditors. In true Medici style, Il Magnifico set about spending his way out of trouble, buying his way into the Neapolitans' good graces with gifts of dowry money, impressive entertainments and generous charitable donations. He even purchased the freedom of the 100 galley slaves who rowed him from Pisa to Naples. Ferrante was also charmed by his scholarly and enlightened conversation.

Yet perhaps Lorenzo's most significant ally at the Aragonese court was Ippolita Sforza (wife of Alfonso, Duke of Calabria, Ferrante's eldest son), his friend since their first meeting in Milan when Lorenzo was just sixteen. 'That the Duchess of Calabria was a significant contributor to the positive outcome of the peace negotiations in Naples is fairly well attested.' Ippolita was an essential point of contact for Lorenzo in the initially precarious environment of a hostile foreign court. An indication of her importance as a link between the governments of Florence and Naples is provided by a letter of July 1480, soon after Lorenzo had returned to the republic, in which Ippolita notes that her father-in-law the king is keen to know 'como sto con lo mio colligiato, cioe con vui' ('how I stand with you'). Ippolita reminds Lorenzo of the time they spent together in Naples, particularly a walk they enjoyed, which is now blooming with summer flowers, a probable reference to the garden of her home at the Castel Capuano. Ippolita's activities on Lorenzo's behalf extended much further than charming sightseeing. In December 1479 the Milanese ambassadors to Naples reported that Ippolita, after meetings with Lorenzo, had proposed a favourable compromise to King Ferrante regarding territories in Tuscany and the position of the lords of the Romagna, a compromise to which Ferrante ultimately acceded. Lorenzo himself reported favourably of the intercession of the 'generossissima Madonna' in the matter. On 6 March 1480 Ippolita was appointed Lorenzo's representative, and on the 13th she was, in this capacity, one of the witnesses and signatories to the peace treaty between Naples and Florence which she had helped to achieve. For Isabella, this was particularly gratifying, since peace between the kingdom and the republic also meant peace between her marital and natal families, as Milan was allied with Florence. The betrothal of her daughter Isabella d'Aragona to Giangaleazzo Sforza, Duke of Milan (Lorenzo's godson), the same year furthered the promise of peace on the peninsula – a peace which, after Sixtus IV's death, would endure for the remainder of Lorenzo de' Medici's life.

CHAPTER 5

Mistress of the Revels in Rome

1477–1484

'Caterina if you make the dance go thus, Atlas will find the
world a lighter burden.'

RENE DE MAULDE LA CLAVIÈRE.

Until the Pazzi conspiracy, Caterina Sforza appeared to have led
a charmed life. Her marriage to Girolamo Riario had begun brilliantly in St Peter's itself in 1477, and the following year, aged fifteen, she gave birth to a daughter, Bianca, the first of the six children
she would give her husband. The young family lived at the Palazzo
Riario (now Corsini) in Rome, overlooking the Farnese Gardens on
the banks of the Tiber. Bedecked in a privateer's haul of treasure,
Caterina soon became one of Rome's most stylish and sought-after
hostesses. One commentator who spied her stepping down from a
litter gushed:

> . . . it was as if the sun had emerged, so gorgeously beautiful did she
> appear, laden with silver, and gold and jewels, but still she was all
> the more striking thanks to her natural charms. Her hair, wreathed
> in the manner of a coronet, seemed brighter than the gold with
> which it was entwined. Her forehead was of burnished ivory and
> her eyes sparkled as morning stars behind the mantling crimson of
> her cheeks.

During the early years of her marriage, the young bride lost herself in the sophisticated pleasures of Rome, where she often led the
dance. The manuals carrying instructions for the latest steps could
be seen grasped by dance masters hurrying to the Palazzo Riario

where Caterina, eager to show off her talents, waited, impatient to learn any new or innovative steps. She excelled at the energetic Lavolta, as her partner lifted her up high in his arms while turning quickly in half-circles with a flourish. The slow and stately Pavane or Almain illustrated Caterina's lithe elegance. The historian René de Maulde la Clavière described the Sforza princess as the effortless leader, usually at the forefront of all festivities. 'Caterina, if you make the dance go thus,' he trilled, 'Atlas will find the world a lighter burden.' When the heat and dust of the city became intolerable she bought a Sylvian escape in the country outside Rome. There she introduced new breeds of cattle and the farm produced great cheeses, cured meats, curd and other produce. Their rustic simplicity evoked yet more rapture and praise. Another bewitched admirer observed 'how well she knew, in the intervals of her frenzied existence, to enjoy life, when she gave herself up to the beauty of her flowers, the charm of her gardens and the delight of seeing her splendid herds of cattle peacefully grazing in her parks'.

Riario's young bride grew accustomed to being mobbed in the streets, the crowds pushing forward to surround her, anxious to catch a glimpse of her glorious face and the richness of her dress. Roman aristocrats and visiting princes filled the stately rooms of the Palazzo, quickly making their residence a centre for entertainments, planned expeditions and feasts of all sorts. In their midst stood Caterina, queen of festivities, even, much later, while organizing military enterprises.

The Pope's favour further contributed to Caterina's popularity. Sixtus considered her a splendid catch for his nephew Riario, even if he was somewhat taken aback by her strong will, independent spirit and the self-assuredness of rank and breeding. In the company of great princes, she could answer any question or compliment with the requisite wit and grace; in the presence of famous churchmen or visiting diplomats, Caterina behaved with the appropriate show of grace and humility. This highly nuanced courtly language that combined ritualized questions and replies was not just a display of etiquette: it was a means to power. Through Riario, Caterina could secure her own ambitions. From their earliest days together, she had determined to seize every available opportunity to raise her own status through her husband's powerful connections. By receiving petitions to intervene with her husband on behalf of supplicants or to pass on to Sixtus, she reinforced her own growing stature within the peninsula's power politics, and the importance of acquiring her own clients.

Caterina did not love Riario, a bully and a coward surrounded by his villainous gang of thugs who kept him company while acting both as his bodyguards and enforcers. As the putative son of a lower-middle-class man from Savona, Riario was hardly one to tutor his sons in the martial skills upon which nobles relied to refine their technique for warfare. Almost immediately after his uncle Francesco had been crowned Pope, Riario, who had never held a sword in his life, had been created Captain-General of the Church, commander of the papal forces and charged with all military matters relating to the papacy. A notoriously gutless invertebrate with little more than the basic knowledge of how to ride a horse, not to mention the disposition of artillery, he could hardly have been a less appropriate choice. As the descendant of celebrated Sforza soldiers, Caterina despised her porcine thirty-four-year-old husband for not even attempting to learn the essentials required of him in his new role. The only interest he took in weapons and their tactical uses related to his craven terror of assassination.

Caterina's relationship with Sixtus proved far more complex. The Pope, a curious, morally mangled creature, was gripped by an obsession to create an enduring dynasty. Few pontiffs illustrate the overriding paradox of the Renaissance so well. A genuinely pious and aesthetic man, his reign produced works of artistic and architectural beauty, creating the foundations for the re-establishment of Rome as the eternal home of the Catholic Church. Yet at the same time an unprecedented climate of depravity and cruelty characterized the city. His own corruption decayed its moral heart. Still, Sixtus viewed Caterina as a valuable asset, and underscored his evident delight at the birth of her first son, Ottaviano, in 1479, by granting a number of her innocuous requests. Some historians have suggested that Caterina became the papal confidante; although the Pontiff felt an affection for Riario's exalted bride this did not mean that they kept one another's counsel.

Sixtus is credited with bringing the early Renaissance to Rome: gathering artists, architects and sculptors there. He also built the Sistine Chapel, the Ponte Sisto (the first bridge to span the Tiber since ancient times), as well as restoring over thirty half-ruined churches. He created the Vatican library and the Capitoline museums. As a scientist and man who had acquired a fine taste in music, he also enlarged the choir and brought some of the greatest singers in Christendom to the city, as well as northern composers such as Gaspar van Weerbeke and Mabrianus de Orto.

Despite the grandeur of his artistic programmes, Sixtus (fittingly, considering his future role as Holy Father) had been born the son of a fisherman so lowly he lacked a family name, taking that of della Rovere (meaning of the oak), even though a noble family already existed with the same name. Acutely aware of his own uncouth manners, he had never felt entirely at ease among the Roman aristocracy. Within a social gathering Sixtus would often fall silent and shift about uneasily, as though others could see him as he saw himself in occasional flashes of truthful self-appraisal. Much as he admired Caterina's fluid and flawless comportment, so too did he fear that it accentuated his coarseness and all that betrayed his lack of breeding.

Sixtus squirmed self-consciously at exquisite courtly manners and thought nothing of betrayals, lies and crimes, all committed as part of his urgent ambition to create a Riario-della Rovere dynasty. He exploited the papacy and the Church's immense riches and the possibilities these created for him to benefit his family. The former simple Franciscan friar became the first modern Pontiff to abuse his position in an analytical and orderly manner. He worked his mischief brazenly, vandalizing the Church for the benefit of his family. Having plundered her riches systematically, milking the obvious avenues for personal gain, the Pope unearthed ancient rules and laws allowing him to commit further outrage. Nor did he restrain his earthly appetites at the same time as he pursued the promotion of his family. He often resorted to violence and murder to achieve his aim for the Riario, the cynosure of his secular, dynastic focus. The unsavoury methods he employed to further his aims brought no blush to his waxen old cheeks. It is hardly surprising that Sixtus IV is given the hotly contested distinction of being the most corrupt and nepotistic pope of early modern Christendom.

Following the fearsome aftermath of the Pazzi conspiracy, 1480 would prove to be a momentous year for Caterina. As her uncle Ludovico Sforza assumed regency powers in Milan, Sixtus invested Riario with the county of Forlì. The head of the ruling family, Pino degli Ordelaffi, had died that year, and fighting between rival factions resulted in the poisoning of his infant heir Sinibaldo. The Pontiff, in his dual and conflicting roles as temporal monarch and spiritual Father, promptly confiscated Forlì, since it formed part of the Territories of St Peter. He issued the disingenuous statement that the Ordelaffi had forfeited their domain for 'having used violence, killed and wounded the soldiers of the Church and attacked the fortress with trebuchets and bombards'.

In handing Riario and Caterina control of Forlì, Sixtus placed a strategically vital part of the Romagna under their command. Riario already held Imola as Caterina's dowry. Adding Forlì to create a joint lordship put him in control of the gateway to the Romagna, with great redoubts to protect his dominions on the eastern slopes of the Appenine hills, in which he could hide an army of 10,000 men and control the main routes north to south and east to west of the peninsula. Sixtus's dream of leaving his family as a great dynasty seemed promising as Riario, the young thug and alleged former street vendor, had became one of the most strategically placed magnates on the peninsula. The mere thought of his potential power terrified him.

As Riario's investiture took place on 31 May 1480, Caterina provided a felicitous and personal oblation on the altar of the Pope's dynastic ambitions by giving birth to her third child, a son, Cesare. At the same time, the first stone was laid at the Rocca di Ravaldino, the giant fortress built above the centre of Forlì's piazza, which boasted the latest in technical and mechanical innovations. The project occupied much of Riario's attention: always fearful for his own safety, he became animated at the slightest improvement that could

be added to the vastly increased and modern fortress. Riario claimed
he wished to ensure that the entire population could fit into the fortress, and find safety with him there should they come under attack.
He pored over the plans with the best engineers in fortification, and
at the same time renovated the dingy ruler's palace. Ensuring that
churches, schools, hospitals and civic buildings received his generous investment, Riario felt cautious optimism about his prospects of
survival as the new ruler of Forlì.

The Count and Countess of Forlì had to remain with the Pope
until a year after their investiture. Sixtus had been beset by troubles:
war with Naples combined with the threat of an imminent Turkish
invasion. Only when the Sultan died were the Riarios free to travel
to their new dominions. They finally arrived at Forlì in July 1481, celebrating with seven days of feasting and dancing. Caterina dazzled
the guests with her astonishing jewels and a turban headdress, her
veil embroidered with a rising sun motif in silver and pearls and the
motto *Diversorum operum* ('opposite powers', a reference to Cupid's
arrows lifted from Ovid). Caterina's clothes formed a significant part
of Riario's plan to convince his new subjects of his wealth. She wore
a new dress every day of her stay in Forlì, and her ladies wore gowns
almost as magnificent as the glorious creation worn by the new
countess herself. The citizens received an invitation to view the display of hastily installed plate and china, valued at 100,000 ducats, in
the palace.

From Forlì the couple moved on to Imola, where Riario repaved
the streets, building towers in the city walls and pulling down ram-
shackle buildings. Philip of Bergamo commented that Riario had
transformed 'the dregs of Romagna into one of its most beautiful
cities'.

Caterina's undoubted ambition might have been satisfied by her
husband's political success in the early 1480s, but not by his treatment
of her. There is considerable evidence to suggest that he became
physically violent towards her, and that in this period of her life,
while she was often pregnant or nursing, she feared her husband.
Despite all that he had done and all that he had spent, Girolamo
could hardly fail to grasp that he lacked any popularity as a prince;
he found himself equally unbeloved in his own dominions, and

vented his fear and increasing paranoia on his wife. The Milanese ambassador reported that he had approached Caterina with a view to her visiting her home city, but that she had begged him not to make the invitation as 'My Lord the Count, her Consort, had refused it, not without some anger … this would make a breach between herself and My Lord, who would believe that she had been the cause of my coming.' Caterina always behaved graciously towards her husband, maintaining her reputation for manners and bearing, but on another occasion Caterina confided to an envoy that 'she envied those who died' at their husbands' hands – a fate she considered preferable to enduring his treatment of her.

In September the Riario couple left Imola for Venice. Ostensibly, Sixtus had ordered their mission to discuss a political alliance with the Venetians. The Pazzi war between Florence and the papacy had caused Ercole d'Este, Duke of Ferrara, to ally himself with Florence, even though Sixtus claimed Ferrara as a papal fief. The Pope had furiously declared Ercole excommunicate and deposed him from Ferrara, gestures which Ercole greeted with scorn. Venice had been antagonistic towards Ferrara since Ercole's marriage with the Neapolitan princess Eleonora d'Aragona in 1473, and planned to overwhelm the duchy, thus extending their own territories to the borders of the Florentine republic, in the process acquiring the strategically important Polesine salt-mines. Sixtus hoped to obtain the help of Venice in his own war against Naples, in return for a grant of territories in Ferrara. Sixtus hid his real intention to carve up the duchy and bestow it upon Girolamo Riario.

Initially, the visit went well. Caterina and Riario received a warm welcome from the Doge, who gave the couple a personal tour of the city, while 115 Venetian ladies were conscripted for attendance on the Countess of Imola and Forlì. Nevertheless, however courteously they received the count and countess, the Venetians did not believe Sixtus sufficiently powerful to take Ferrara, and saw little benefit in the alliance. The Archdeacon of Forlì wrote to Lorenzo de' Medici claiming that despite the glamour and flattery the leaders of Venice laid on to dazzle their guests, the neophyte diplomats usually did not realize they had received no firm commitment from the maritime republic, only ephemeral half-promises. 'When all is said and done, his [Riario's] journey has not produced anything that can be displeasing to His Magnificence'.

As Caterina and Riario returned via Ravenna to the Romagna, they received worrying news: two plots against them had been put down at Imola, and rumours abounded of another conspiracy to murder the count at Forlì. Riding so closely among their guards that they seemed to be travelling in a mobile fortress, the couple arrived to see the bodies of their enemies hanging from the palace windows. Caterina felt all too aware of the threat of assassination, and although she maintained her composure, attributed by her companions to her youth and lack of experience, she must have been worried. Even as they left Forlì for the safety of Rome, taking their children and valuables with them, the countess began to contemplate a future without her husband.

In May 1482, the War of Ferrara broke out. Notwithstanding their initial coolness towards Sixtus's plans, the Venetians attacked and occupied the Polesine territories* of the Ferrarese. Now, all the alliances built up in previous years were triggered. Milan, Florence and Naples quickly mobilized in support of Ferrara. When Sixtus refused permission for Neapolitan troops to pass through the Papal States en route to confront the Venetians, the King of Naples responded by sending the Duke of Calabria to invade the papal territories. Riario led papal troops against the duke, but halted at San Giovanni in Laterano, not far from where Calabria was encamped. Instead of engaging the enemy, Riario passed his time by gambling the money with which the Pope had entrusted him, playing dice on the very altar of the church, much to the horror of the local citizens. Soon he had nothing left to pay the men, who took to looting. The Pope was obliged to call on the Venetians, who sent a party commanded by the famous general Roberto Malatesta which routed the Duke of Calabria at Campo Morto on 21 August 1482. Riario

---

* Polesine territories refer to the wetlands between the River Po and the River Adige, the first and third largest rivers of the Italian peninsula. Important towns lay in the area belonging to Ferrara.

meanwhile drank himself into a stupor, too inebriated to know the outcome.

In Rome, Caterina felt haunted by the consequences of her husband's cowardice. As she awaited the outcome of the confrontation, she spent her time dressed as a penitent, fasting herself to emaciation and spending hours in front of the tombs of the Apostles. Caterina wrote that she hoped by these means to compensate for the wrongs perpetrated by Riario and that by making sacrifices in God's name her husband might be granted victory. Her vigils proved effective and Malatesta won the day, but Riario was spotted ignominiously retiring to his tent before Calabria's attack. Even this did nothing to diminish Sixtus's obsession with his nephew's legacy: 'the Pope has given up the government, both temporal and spiritual, and moneys and everything else, to the Count ... and there are not wanting judges who give sentences according to their pleasure,' reported the Sienese orator Landi.

Caterina's complicity in the next phase of Riario's career is as dubious as her involvement in the Pazzi conspiracy, both assertions being based on the exaggeration of her intimacy with Sixtus. Caterina shared her husband's hunger for power, but she was not prepared to go to the same lengths to obtain it. Virginio Orsini, commander of the Pope's troops, may have been Riario's drinking and gambling partner but in truth he despised Riario and hoped only to receive the benefits he could in the Orsini-Colonna feud. Orsini's family had long been enemies of the equally powerful Colonna clan, doubtless delighted in the designs Sixtus had on the Colonna properties, and allowed his mercenaries to sack the districts of Rome in which they lay. Riario, however, refused to consent to a truce between the papacy and the and had the messenger who carried the proposal murdered. He insisted that Sixtus consent to a special tribunal to try the proto-notary, Lorenzo, whom he had tortured and executed after receiving his surrender to Orsini. This caused outrage in Rome, but the people were too afraid of Riario to do more than mutter. Caterina made her feelings clear by avoiding entertainments which her husband also attended, doing her best to disassociate herself from him.

Having failed in his attempt to enlist Venetian help in a papal conquest of Ferrara, by the end of 1482 Sixtus had grown concerned that Venice would act unilaterally to conquer Ferrara for itself. Sixtus therefore abandoned his onetime ally and, in early 1483, created a league against Venice at the Conference of Cremona, where he sent Riario to represent him. Florence, Milan, Ferrara and Naples united against the Venetians. Fifteen months of desultory warfare ensued, until the Venetians raised the stakes by appealing to international powers. Spain had declared for the Aragonese King of Naples, and Venice proposed that the French should join them in attacking the Neapolitans in the name of their ancient Angevin claim to the Kingdom, as well as the Milanese in the name of their Orléans claim. The peninsula looked set to descend into chaos, and the War of Ferrara became known as the Diplomats' War for the battling envoys who now struggled to undo the confusion created by their masters' destructive ambitions.

Sixtus's intrigues in the Ferrara conflict came to nothing. In the summer of 1484, his ambitions for Riario were put to a decisive end. At Bagnolo, on 7 August, a peace treaty found swift conclusion between the opposing factions, all of whom recognized that international conflict threatened if they did not come to terms. Ludovico Sforza had pulled out of the papal league against Venice and the treaty proved favourable to Sixtus's enemies, despite the papacy's potential gains. Sixtus had long been growing sick from gout, and the terms of Bagnolo struck him a fatal blow. When she could, Caterina would visit Sixtus and place clean bandages on the suppurating sores on his hands.

On 12 August the emissaries arrived to deliver the terms of the Peace of Bagnolo personally. While listening to the conditions of the treaty, Sixtus turned a livid colour and cried that he would give neither his sanction nor blessing to this 'ignominious' peace. Having made the exclamation, he withdrew his right hand from its soiled and stinking bandages. Once the foul rags fell off he made a gesture that nobody could decipher. It was uncertain whether he wished to curse or bless the messengers; but in the event, he had time to do neither. The old man became insensible, babbling incoherently until at last he could make no further sound. He had suffered a seizure, probably brought on by his fury. The emissaries wished His Holiness a quick return to health, but it was a futile hope. The Pope would not live through the night. Roman wags circulated an apt analysis of his death: 'Nothing could daunt the ferocious Sixtus, but as soon as he heard the word of peace, he died.'

When Sixtus breathed his last, Caterina, having released herself from the Pontiff's gouty grip, had arrived at her husband's military encampment, taking the children with her to play the martial wife living under canvas. She had known better than anyone that the Pope was on the verge of death. Caterina had spent the most time with him and knew the old man almost longed to be freed from his own follies, from the agony of his gout and the ultimate disappointment that power had brought him.

Anticipating the old Pope's death and dealing with its consequences, however, were two different matters. Caterina had a clear idea of how violently hatred had grown for those close to the Pope. Now that he was gone, her future was in jeopardy. There was no question that her husband would be the clearest target for retribution against the old Pope's party. Riario, known to many as the 'Arch-Pope', was marked out for death. Few had become as rich as he under Sixtus; fewer still had been honoured with such power under the late Pontiff, and no one had abused it as conspicuously. It would be fair to say that of Sixtus's favourites and allies, no one had been more hated than the Count of Forlì. His wife knew that if any salvation were possible for her husband and family, then she must return to Rome before matters spun out of control. It would be a perilous undertaking, for Caterina herself was tarred by her association with Sixtus and Riario. But as a dutiful wife and fiercely protective mother, Caterina depended upon her husband remaining alive, and in some authority.

The reign of Sixtus had been marked by a rotten opulence, orgies of bloodletting, as well as splendour and huge strides in the rebuilding of the Eternal City. His pitiful and lonely end without any family at his side provided a stark contrast to his early days as Pope when he had summoned his nephews and nieces and sat surrounded by

98 THE DEADLY SISTERHOOD

them. Although a few had done well and climbed high through his nepotistic promotions, most of them had quickly become incontinent and greedy creatures, loved by their uncle who watched benevolently over them and their careless gorging.

CHAPTER 6

The Virago Holds The Holy City Hostage

AUGUST–SEPTEMBER 1484

Sixtus at last you're dead: and Rome is happy,
for, when you reigned, so did famine, slaughter and sin.
Sixtus at last you're dead, eternal engine of discord
even against God Himself, now go to dark Hell

ANONYMOUS VERSE ON THE DEATH OF SIXTUS IV.

On the morning of 14 August 1484, a special courier brought the unwelcome news of the Holy Father's death to his nephew, Girolamo Riario. As Captain-General of the Papal Armies, Riario and his men were encamped alongside the troops of his ever-present companion, Virginio Orsini, laying siege to Paliano, deep in Colonna territory south-east of Rome. Caterina, seven months pregnant, had arrived a few weeks earlier bringing the couple's daughter and two sons, hoping to avoid the fevers and outbreaks of plague that arrived annually as deadly companions to the summer heat of Rome.

Riario generally allowed others to take risks for him in hazardous situations, but this most troubling development prevailed over his cowardice. With Sixtus dead it was clear that he and his wife must act together. Her powerful family could prove invaluable to him now, but he had to play his part in the dangerous days ahead. If he were to hide himself away the couple had little hope of retaining the dominions, assets, offices, powers, stipends and other incalculable benefits accrued under the pontificate of his doting uncle.

Orders recalling Riario and his men had arrived at the same time as the news of the Pontiff's death. The Sacred College of Cardinals commanded the Captain-General to proceed as far as Rome with his men, but to stop at the far end of the Ponte Molle. Ostensibly they had been ordered there to prevent trouble by blocking the bridge, though many considered that the danger might well be Riario himself, sitting in a predatory position with his own and Orsini's men. With no time to lose, Caterina contrived a basic scheme. What passed between the count and countess is not known, but they had certainly formulated a plan as they prepared to head north for Rome with Orsini and their combined troops.

Following his orders, Riario raised the siege at once, citing the will of Rome as his excuse for the speed with which he prepared to depart. Behind him he left injured men, materiel, horses and provisions. To the casual and uninformed onlooker the Captain-General's disorderly withdrawal appeared much like a craven flight made in panic.

In truth, the Sacred College felt equally panicked. During Sixtus's last months Rome had become a battleground between the two central factions who would vie to fill his place. In the weeks following the Pope's demise, the situation deteriorated further. Many of the cardinals feared Riario – not only because he had the support of the Orsini and an army under his command, but also because stooges of his own family, both della Rovere and Riario, peppered the College. The cardinals hoped that by keeping the late Pontiff's nephew close, they would be forewarned if he attempted to force the outcome of the papal election. At the same time detachments of soldiers had been assigned places of importance for the restoration and maintenance of civil order in Rome.

Riario had one further advantage: his wife. As Caterina prepared to join her husband in departing for Rome, she hurriedly gathered up the few possessions she needed and gave orders for those left behind. The heavily pregnant Countess of Forlì appeared revitalized, excited by the danger that lay ahead, and ready to fight for her family's survival.

Certainly Caterina had lost neither beauty nor charisma, but the vigour she radiated after the arrival of the courier made her seem to be made of a different mettle. Her desperate attempts to atone for her own sins and to protect her husband had given little comfort. For too long Caterina had been the unwilling witness to a code that breached all her beliefs. A girl of strong spiritual habits, she had breathed a corruption so foul that it had filled her heart and lungs. The careless observer could not see that Caterina hid within her the courage for the day she would need it. Though her bold spirit had been reduced to a fragment of its former strength, she had kept it alive.

Caterina set out from Paliano with Paolo Orsini while Riario and Virginio Orsini rode together, spurring their horses with the intention of reaching Rome before nightfall. Orsini may now have wished that he had had time to distance himself from Riario and the Sistine papacy. But it was too late. As they arrived he could hear for himself the shouts in the street of 'Colonna! Colonna!'

Riario, meanwhile, recognized the threat to his immense power, although he showed no signs of sadness for his uncle. While he is said to have responded decently to expressions of sympathy during the immediate aftermath of the Pope's death, there is no recorded act, expression or utterance where Riario showed grief for Sixtus's demise.

As hoped, Riario and Caterina reached Rome in the early evening of 14 August and Caterina left her husband following instructions and deploying his troops on the Ponte Molle. Taking Paolo Orsini, the countess rode on imperiously towards the Castel Sant'Angelo, the great round castle that loomed over the city from the northwest. Originally built by Hadrian in the second century AD as a mausoleum, the huge cylindrical building had long since been converted into a papal fortress. In times of peril it allowed its holders to maintain the military advantage over the Holy City. In the chaotic aftermath of Sixtus's death, Caterina knew that possession of the castle – whose guns could quite easily be turned upon enemies within the city – could mean the difference between survival and slaughter.

As Caterina rode for the fortress, a great change seemed to come over her. Divested of the muted and carefully adapted personality she had presented in her role as dutiful wife, she now emanated the charisma and power expected of an exalted person of ancient lineage. People hailed the Sforza princess as she passed, her appearance being so striking that people crowded around her shouting 'Duca!' 'Duca!' 'Il Duca!' Caterina required no gems or fine brocades to attract attention as she rode past with a demeanour of both warrior and empress. For all that she had clad herself as a Riario, the crowd recognized, as she hoped, the Sforza blood that had given her fortitude and courage.

The lieutenant-governor of the castle must have heard the noise of Caterina's approach, but by the time she reached the entrance to the fortress she had become an unstoppable force. As the way cleared before her, guards and others in authority seemed impelled to allow her to pass, despite almost certainly knowing that she had got the better of them. At last Caterina turned and announced that she had come in the name of her husband, the Captain-General and Governor of Castel Sant'Angelo. Her orders were to hold the fortress, quell any trouble in the city and to give up the stronghold only upon the election of a new pope. All resistance melted before her. She entered the Castel Sant'Angelo without a single drop of blood being shed.

Once inside, she went to work. The countess knew that a lack of common sense often proved the undoing of so many great men and women. To avoid tripping up on an obvious threat she called the men-at-arms and issued her first orders to them. The entrance and staircase leading to and from the Vatican should be well barricaded and they must start immediately.

It is here that Cerratini describes Caterina, the Lady of Forlì, as 'Wise, brave, great, with a full, beautiful face; speaking little. She wore ... a man's belt whence hung a bag of gold ducats and a curved sword.' Presumably Caterina employed the scimitar, her preferred weapon, and the gold in the pouch hanging from the belt around her waist was to appeal when necessary to the pragmatic side of human nature. Cerratini added that 'among the soldiers, both horse and foot, she was much feared, for that armed lady was fierce and cruel'.

The account of how Caterina Sforza took the Castel Sant'Angelo, during the hot days of August 1484, and her subsequent dauntless dealings with the great men of the city became the genesis of the legendary Lady of Forlì. Within days she proved a sensation throughout Italy, a woman who is remembered with pride in Italian history. She did not act out of heroism to save others, but from a genetic

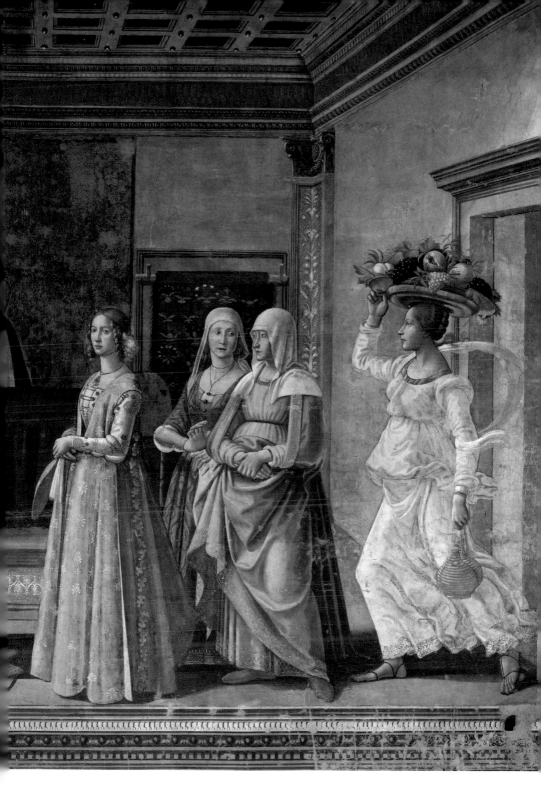

Lucrezia Tornabuoni (third from the left, with hands folded on her stomach) more than compensated for her short-sightedness with an extremely sharp eye for power.

Although no fool, Piero ('the Gouty') de' Medici's chronic illness caused him to devolve the handling of his political affairs to his wife Lucrezia Tornabuoni – probably the best decision he ever made.

The Blessed Virgin with Jesus and Angels by Botticelli. The Florentine youths here depicted, so cherished by nineteenth-century Romantics, often combined exquisite finesse with gory savagery.

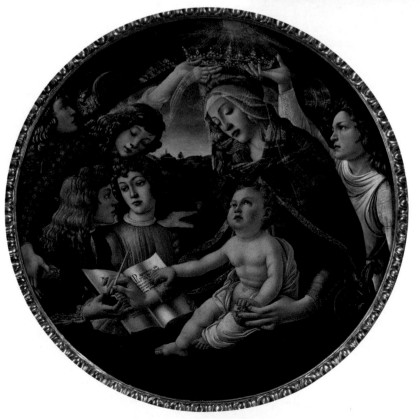

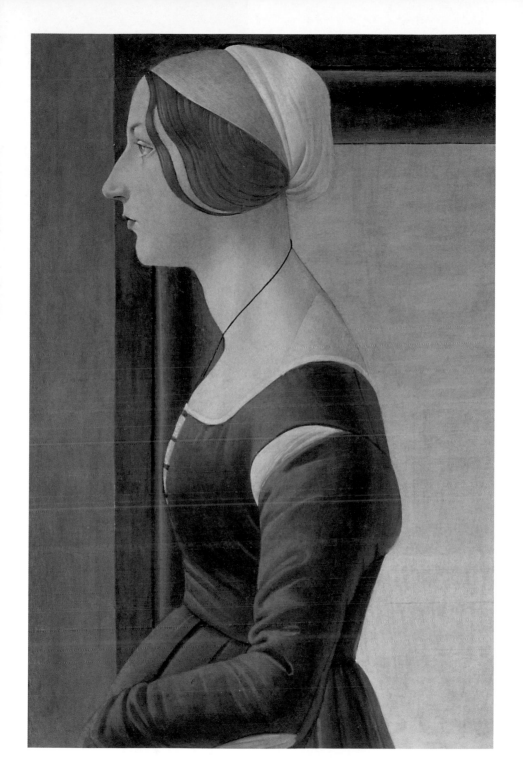

Clarice Orsini, the long-suffering wife of Lorenzo de' Medici, would prove crucial in advancing her husband's social and political ambitions.

Often described as the epitome of ugliness, Lorenzo de' Medici, though a man of considerable ability, owed his power to Lucrezia Tornabuoni's business acumen and political networking.

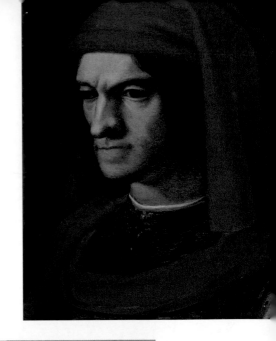

Lorenzo de' Medici's friend and ally, Ippolita Maria Sforza avidly cultivated learning – a quality wasted on her uninterested husband Alfonso of Naples.

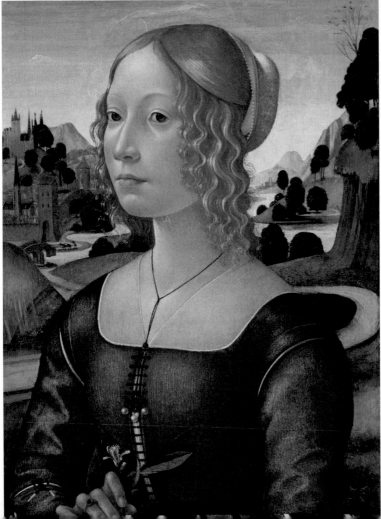

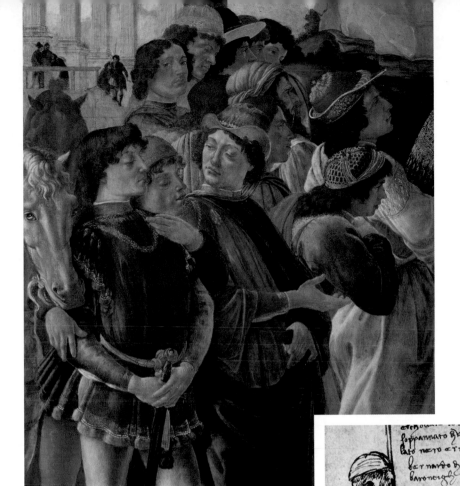

Giuliano de' Medici (left), with Agnolo
Poliziano and Pico della Mirandola. The
finery worn by the young Medici and his
humanist friends hides the bloody reality
of their lives – and the death blows
Giuliano would receive but three years
after the completion of this painting.

The hanging of Bernardo
Baroncelli by Leonardo
da Vinci. 'Those who deal
with the powerful are last
at the table and first on the
gallows,' goes a Florentine
saying. Baroncelli might
have known that before
joining the Pazzi conspiracy.

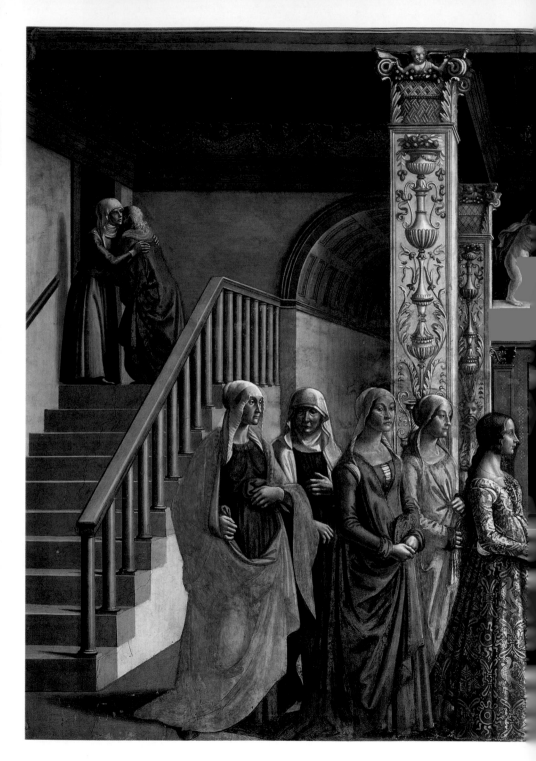

Tightly-knit, caustic and generally bornée, the ladies
of Florence's upper crust never accepted Clarice Orsini,
'a foreigner' and, by their exacting standards, a boor.

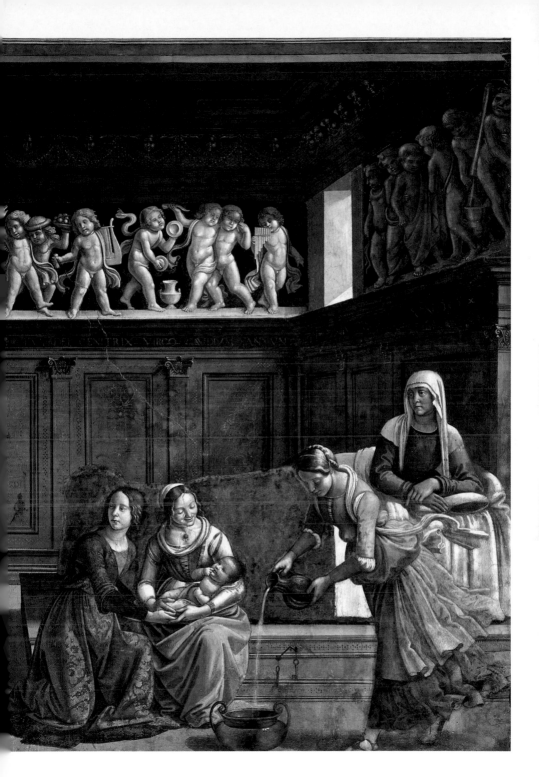

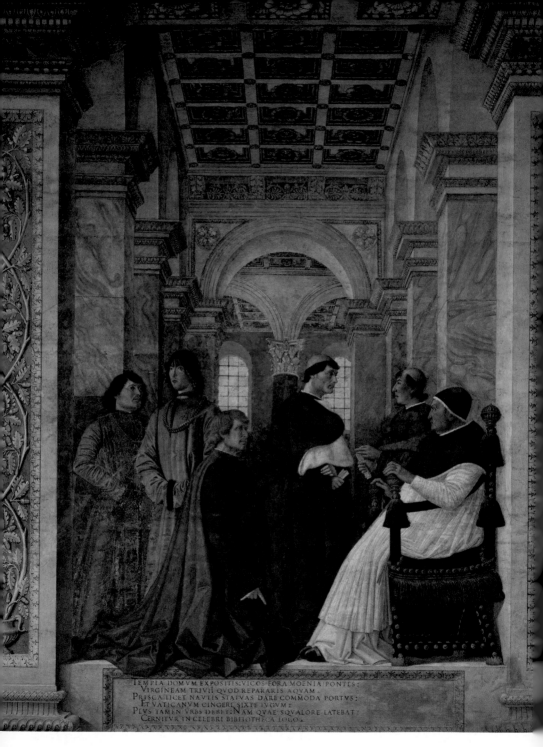

Within the painting:

TEMPLA DOMVM EXPOSITIS VICOS FORA MOENIA PONTES:
VIRGINEAM TRIVII QVOD REPARARIS AQVAM.
PRISCA LICET NAVTIS STATVAS DARE COMMODA PORTVS:
ET VATICANVM CINGERE SIXTE IVGVM:
PLVS TAMEN VRBS DEBET: NAM QVAE SQVALORE LATEBAT:
CERNITVR IN CELEBRI BIBLIOTHECA LOCO.

Sixtus IV is seen here receiving the Vatican librarian Bartolomeo Platina (suitably, on his knees). The violently nepotistic pontiff is surrounded by his kin, including the steamrolling cardinal (and future pope Julius II), Giuliano della Rovere (standing, in front of the pope), and Caterina Sforza's husband, the cowardly bully Girolamo Riario (in blue, second from the left).

imperative compelling her to claim all that she considered rightfully to belong to her husband and their house.

When the cardinals heard that they had been trumped by a twenty-one-year-old woman, and by the wife of Riario, they could hardly contain their anger. A group of them hurried to the palazzo of Riario's nephew, Cardinal Raffaele Riario, a Sistine loyalist who they hoped would be able to persuade Caterina to leave Rome. After listening to his fellow cardinals' shrill protests, Raffaele Riario despatched a messenger to see the countess. The prospects did not seem promising. Far from appearing ready to listen to entreaties of peace, Caterina was busily ejecting from the fortress all those whom she considered injurious to her interests.

The vice-governor of the Castel Sant'Angelo was among the first to be thrown out. A native of Imola named Innocenzo Cordrochi, he was technically one of Riario's subjects. But Caterina had seen enough evidence of plots against Riario from his own people to find Cordrochi's particular brand of loyalty less than appealing. She had no confidence in those who professed allegiance by geography rather than deed, and at his release she ensured that all other Imolese be sent away at the same time. Riario, for his part, began testing the waters. He opened with a gutsy note, stating that he wanted to let his wishes regarding a suitable pope to follow his uncle be known.

Raffaele's envoy arrived at the Castel Sant'Angelo to find the countess in frosty mood. He high-handedly announced that his master wished to see her; but when the haughty demand had been repeated to Caterina, she decided to remind the spoiled boy of her Sforza blood. She responded crisply that neither cardinals nor family inspired her with any confidence at present. She returned Raffaele's lackey to his master with the imperious message that on no account would she allow the young cardinal access to the Castel Sant'Angelo 'at his pleasure'. She stated, rather, that she would permit the cardinal to speak to her in person only provided that he came escorted, while she would have a witness present at their interview. The flunkey fell into a rage at this response and was dragged away. When Caterina was told she cried out: 'Ah! This man would match his wits with mine! Does he not know that I have the brain of Duke Galeazzo, and am as headstrong as he?'

As Rome descended into popeless chaos, held hostage by Caterina in the Castel Sant'Angelo, the great men and women of the peninsula watched with interest and alarm. Battles between the Colonna and Sixtus's loyalists, the Orsini, were becoming more intense, and the cardinals of the Holy City lived in fear for their lives. Rather than the election of another pope, it seemed very possible that the height of summer 1484 would see Rome erupt into all-out civil war.

One particularly keen observer was Lorenzo de' Medici, who kept open a diplomatic channel through the Florentine orator Guidantonio Vespucci, who visited Riario at the Ponte Molle, where he waited with his troops and the omnipresent Orsini. The Florentine emissary received a gracious welcome but had little time to make himself comfortable before Riario delivered a stream of demands. Reporting back to Lorenzo, Vespucci informed his master that 'on no account would he [Riario] suffer the election of the following cardinals, Giovanni Battista Cibo, Cardinal of S. Cecilia and Bishop of Molfetta, San Marco nor Savelli'. Vespucci noted Riario's threat that 'he should keep on his guard, for if it happened that one of these were elected he would have recourse to arms, and give a turn that suited him to the affair'.

The report ended with Vespucci describing Riario's feeble gratitude when the orator 'tendered the offices of Lorenzo to him, in the protection of the latter's State in such wise as to bring tears to the count'. Riario cannot have believed these soothing words, being at least partially aware that Lorenzo's interests in the Romagna could spell Riario's total obliteration, and that if he should bestir himself in the case of the count's dominions it would be to snatch them for Florence. Equally, the Medici statesman knew Riario's tears were nothing more than those of affected sorrow.

Rome continued in uproar and the terrified cardinals locked themselves up in the secure splendour of their palazzi. Like Cardinal Borgia, who happened to be the Riario candidate, as well as Ludovico Sforza and Cardinal Giuliano della Rovere (another of

Sixtus's nephews), they had turned their palazzi into fortified dwellings, bristling with unpleasant surprises for anyone who might attempt to attack – not only fortified with outworks and artillery, but filled to the rafters with troops.

No such protections were in place at properties belonging to Riario and Caterina. On 13 August a mob shouting 'Colonna!' 'Colonna!' had arrived at the Riario palazzo, broken in and stolen whatever they could, as well as smashing precious carvings or inlaid floors that could not be moved. They chopped down the beautiful old trees that had stood in the gardens, and when the last loot had been carried off, and the stables ruined to the extent that no horse could stand there, the ringleaders prepared to put a torch to the palazzo. At that moment armed officials arrived and prevented the fire, but little remained of the once glorious Palazzo Riario. The spoils must have disappointed the looters, for Caterina had taken the precaution some time before of removing most of the valuables and hiding them far outside Rome. The farm Caterina owned in the Roman Campagna, Castel Giubileo, fared as badly as the palazzo. The locals stole the livestock, wrecked the buildings and even rolled away large cheeses and any hanging meat or game they could find. Nobody with a connection to the late Pope's Ligurian homeland considered themselves safe.

Sixtus's funeral began on 17 August and continued for eight days. St Peter's, however, had rarely seen such a meagre turnout. Only eleven cardinals appeared, a fact reported by the various spies and ambassadors of the Italian states. Giuliano della Rovere's absence from his uncle's obsequies was also noted. He would not budge from his safe house. And none of the cardinals could be persuaded to attend the conclave at the Vatican.

Gradually, however, through the good offices of the wise Venetian Cardinal Marco Barbo, the first steps were made towards peace. After much violence, the Orsini and the Colonna finally agreed to withdraw to their respective territories at Viterbo and Lazio, and agree to a truce that would last until a month after the coronation of the new pope – whoever it might be. Meanwhile, the cardinals began to treat with Riario in order to get rid of 'that woman' who was holding Rome hostage.

'That woman', however, would not easily be moved. Caterina had long been sensible of the dangers to her husband and children, and the threat to their interests once Sixtus died. Riario's main problem was lack of funds, as he could no longer regard the papal treasury as his personal money box. This in turn reawakened a series of spectres from the past, and if she did not keep alert, she might well find herself a co-victim of *vendette* arising from his failed ventures, military incompetence, poor decisions and craven betrayals.

In such a circumstance, it paid to have powerful backing. The countess had already called upon her uncle Ludovico for help. Lanti, the Sienese orator, wrote: 'I know from a good source that the State of Milan is protecting the States of the Count, and has furnished him with soldiers for his safety. Whether or not it has intervened in the affairs of Rome, I do not understand. Every one's procedure is underhanded and silent. If treason, dissimulation and treachery were lost arts, they might be re-discovered here in these days.' In a further report he added, 'God grant us a good change for we cannot do worse then heretofore.'

As Caterina assured herself of support from Milan, Riario was presenting his demands for her withdrawal to the cardinals. He asked for 8,000 ducats (needed largely to settle the arrears due to his troops), compensation to him for his losses over the Palazzo Riario in Rome, and a safe conduct out of the city for him and his family. The cardinals, willing to pay virtually any price to be rid of the Riarios, agreed. They also vouched for the continuation of the stipends he had received under Sixtus, as well as his title of Captain-General of the Church – and, most importantly, that he be reconfirmed as Lord of Imola and Count of Forlì. Nor was this all. Riario prepared a full set of accounts that listed vast amounts owed to him in the service of the late Pope. In rendering these to the Apostolic Chamber, he unwittingly provided for the future of his wife and children. In return the cardinals asked Riario to leave Rome immediately and surrender the Castel Sant'Angelo on 24 August. By 22 August Riario had received 7,000 of the 8,000 ducats for payment of his troops, the cardinals having taken silver and other valuables belonging to the late Pope as their security. His withdrawal appeared to have been secured.

Caterina, however, had no intention of allowing herself to take satisfaction or comfort from promises made on behalf of a pope as yet unelected. The situation could still fluctuate wildly; for some cardinals supported the Riario, while others wished for nothing more than their downfall, death and total obliteration. She had not come this far to accept undertakings that might only appear good. Considering their precarious circumstances, Caterina felt that they should wait out the elections before accepting that the pledges made to them had truly been secured. Unfortunately, the countess knew her husband too well and feared that he would prove far more ame- nable to the syrupy proposals he wished to hear.

August 24 – the day Riario agreed to his wife's departure – came and went without any sign of Caterina leaving the Castel Sant'Angelo. In his next dispatch Lanti wrote: 'The Countess is reported to be ill and therefore her departure is to be postponed.' Caterina's advanced pregnancy had indeed laid her low, and the strain of the last ten days had left her tired and feverish. The announcement made on her behalf that she felt indisposed had those anxious to be rid of the 'energetic' Sforza woman half-believing her. Had the indomitable Countess of Forlì fallen prey to the sultry, sickly heat and, aggravated by her condition, been sapped of her redoubtable energy? This was plausible, given the heavy atmosphere of a Roman August; but most knew better than to rely on the word of the Sforza virago.

Caterina now proceeded to misjudge matters, and overplayed her hand. Instead of leaving Rome, in the early hours of 25 August she smuggled 150 loyal soldiers into the castle. Outside, Riario cringed, as the incandescent churchmen blazed and thundered threats that they would revoke their pledges. They told him that as he had taken their down-payment and guarantees, he would be ill-advised to back out of the arrangement with them.

On 25 August Caterina, realizing that she would be forced to negotiate, allowed eight of their number (including her uncle Ascanio Sforza, a powerful cardinal who had the full confidence of his brother Ludovico) to enter the castle. The eight delegates issued promises during the calm discussion that ensued. Caterina now learned that her husband had sold himself during her courageous efforts to have their position legalized and understood that she had no choice but to leave. It mattered little whether her husband had accepted one denaro or 7,000 ducats from the Sacred College; by taking the money he had broken faith with his own wife, and had become a man under oath to the very men whom she feared might prove his, and therefore her own, undoing.

The churchmen, particularly Ascanio Sforza, who had a strong influence upon her decision, gave the Countess their guarantee that if she gave up the stronghold without further delay she would receive safe conduct out of the city for herself and her family. The orator Lanti hurried up to the Castel Sant'Angelo to witness Caterina's departure for his Sienese masters. Late on the evening of 26 August the great gates opened for the Countess of Forlì, accompanied by her men-at arms, some with pikes, as well as halberdiers in a protective phalanx around their lady as her other attendants brought up the rear. The proud daughter of the Sforza house appeared with dignity and authority on her fine palfrey. Although riding at the centre of her heavily armed men, she was easily visible, with her head held high and her back straight. In sorry contrast to the radiant young woman who had arrived thirteen days before, an unusual pallor tinged the countess's face, with dark circles under her wide-set, pale grey eyes.

Caterina Sforza's twelve days holding Castel Sant'Angelo eerily adumbrated future events at the Rocca di Ravaldino at Forlì, which would ensure her place in Italian history. For the moment, her courage and heroics sent a clear message to the princes and prelates ruling the peninsula. In future, anyone who underestimated the young Sforza princess did so at their peril.

Finally, with the poorly attended obsequies of Sixtus at an end and Caterina Sforza's surrender complete, the Sacred College of Cardinals agreed to go into conclave. They met on 26 August at what a great historian of the papacy has called one of the two 'most deplorable [conclaves] in the annals of Church history'. After the calamitous thirteen-year tenure of the late Pontiff, the whole edifice of the Catholic Church screamed for reform. Alas, only further corruption followed.

Twenty-four princes of the church attended the conclave: twenty Italians, two Spaniards, one Portuguese and a Frenchman.* Many of them had not taken part in a papal election before, and most had determined that the disorder that had detained their business should now benefit them. They prepared to wring the Holy Mother Church for as much as they could, while they could. Any cardinal who did not receive a minimum of 4,000 ducats from his own benefices would henceforth receive 100 ducats per month from the Church's coffers. They carefully included legislation to protect themselves with 'a complete indemnification for those among their number who might be punished for their vote by secular princes, with the confiscation of revenues'. Before electing a new pope, they considerably enhanced their own powers and dramatically changed the constitution of the Church from monarchical to aristocratic, a system far more in sympathy with their own interests than those of the pontiff they would shortly elect. The company heedlessly cast aside important Church matters until their greed had been satiated.

At last the real reason for their assembly took precedence and the election got underway. 'He who goes enters the conclave a Pope, leaves it a Cardinal,' wrote the Florentine envoy, quoting an old Roman proverb that circulated at the time of papal elections; and he referred particularly to Rodrigo Borgia. Borgia had been Vice-Chancellor of the Church (the second most senior office to the pontiff) during the past four papacies, and would have stood in direct competition against Riario's cousin, Cardinal Giuliano della Rovere. Two of the most cunning political animals of the cardinalcy, Borgia and della Rovere, realized that their time had not yet come. The adversaries buried their mutual dislike, and met in secret dressed as their own servants to ensure the election of a man they both considered would be a tame pope for both of them – Giovanni Battista Cibo, the man Riario had blustered he would on no account accept as pope.

* Eighteen cardinals had attended the conclaves for Nicholas V, Pius II and Sixtus IV; only fifteen had been present for the election of Callixtus III, formerly Alonso Borja (later Italianized to Borgia from Spanish by his nephew Rodrigo, far better known to history as Alexander VI). Some accounts have fifty-six, others ninety-two and 103 cardinals though Pastor cites the Vatican Secret Archives, as well as other reliable contemporary sources, as giving the number of electors as twenty-five.

Born in Genoa in 1432, the fifty-two-year-old Cibo descended from the Doria, 'the richest family in Genoa'. His mother was the well-born Teodorina de' Mari of Genoa; his father, Arano, had been a senator in Rome. Cibo seemed a safe and malleable choice for the two puppeteers, della Rovere having made the new Pope by convincing his uncle Sixtus to raise Cibo to the cardinalcy. The tall, bulky, fair-haired Cibo, who could barely formulate a thought without della Rovere articulating it for him first, was also favoured by Borgia. The two cemented their truce and, during the night of 28 August, roused their fellow cardinals by announcing Cibo as the next Pope. Some of their number required persuasion and the pair duly negotiated on their candidate's behalf using all the inducements the Church could offer. Although not illegal at the time, this mercenary election could hardly have been considered an auspicious start to the largely ineffectual, though generally good-natured, Cibo's tenure.

At nine o'clock on the morning of 29 August 1484, Cardinal Piccolomini emerged before the crowd waiting outside the Vatican to declare that Cardinal Giovanni Battista Cibo had been elected to the throne of St Peter and had taken the name Innocent VIII. The crowd cheered, accompanied by the sound of church bells ringing throughout the Eternal City.

Lorenzo de' Medici learned of the election with satisfaction. Whereas Sixtus had been the bitterest enemy of the Medici, Innocent was a worldly fellow, mightily impressed by the princely Lorenzo, who by 1484 was reaching the zenith of his active and prestigious political life, particularly abroad. The new Pope also nursed a warm regard for those with money, and he felt a blazing desire to please one as rich and powerful as Lorenzo de' Medici. Almost as soon as he became Pope, Innocent wrote to Pandolfini, the Florentine papal legate: 'Lorenzo shall learn, that never was a pontiff who loved him and his house as I do. And having learnt by experience the extent of his faith, integrity and prudence, I shall be governed by his memory and opinion.'

For the Florentine ruler's part he felt reassured that, unlike Sixtus, who had seemed an austere-living churchman until elected Pope, the new Pontiff had at least enjoyed the usual sins that could be attributed to most popes. As Bishop of Savona and then cardinal,

Innocent had been popular, considered a sympathetic and comfortingly earthy churchman. He had felt no particular calling for a life in the Church, to the extent that there was an inaccurate rumour that he had been married, but there is no argument about the fact that he had enjoyed many affairs by the time of his election. He had produced at least two children while still a teenager, both of whom enjoyed the status of being fully and unashamedly acknowledged as the Pope's own offspring.* Innocent's eldest child, a son named Francesco (known as Franceschetto), had little if anything but his connections to recommend him. Spoiled by his father, Franceschetto enjoyed a glorious career as a violent drunkard and compulsive gambler, who in one memorable night lost a sum so vast to Cardinal Raffaele Riario that this brat, equally spoiled by a pontiff, had the means to build himself a palace, the Palazzo Camerlengo, on the proceeds. Teodorina, the pope's daughter, seems to have been a paragon of modesty compared to her brother.

By the time of his election, however, Innocent had given up the sin of lust for those of gluttony and sloth. The new Pope consumed incredible amounts of food and slept for most of the day. Always used to living beyond his means, he also had the reputation for enjoying the rewards that came with his position. He could be described as an amiable but bone-idle bear, perambulating through life as slowly as possible, with a taste for luxuries and comforts that cost far more than he could pay.

Fortunately a near-narcoleptic Pope mattered little at this time when it came to the daily business of running the Catholic Church; the brilliant administrator Borgia and the politically crafty della Rovere carved it up between them. The pair barely needed to bother Innocent with papal business, and for most of his reign he merely had to attach his stamp to the orders drawn up on his behalf. It has been said that the Pope's post-prandial stupors could only be dispelled by the mention of witches. The pontiff has been accused of starting witch-hunts by the concession of the bull *Summis desiderantes*

---

* Some commentators attributed many more children to Cibo, the numbers varying between seven and sixteen. It is possible that further children had been born to the Pontiff before his election, for there are many accounts of numerous papal 'nieces and nephews' staying at the Vatican; but sixteen is a literal translation of a piece of doggerel.

affectibus ('We desire intensely') to two crazed German Dominican friars, the 'two savage misogynists' Heinrich Kramer and James Sprenger, whose personal crusade against witchcraft in lower Germany had produced few results. They included the bull in their treatise *Malleus Maleficarum*, 'The Witches' Hammer', destined to become the witch-hunters handbook in the sixteenth century. The bull was more political than doctrinal – landing in the middle of a fight within the Church in Germany – and its similarities with previous documents could be yet another example of papal apathy. In general, inquisitors in Italy took a rather pragmatic approach to witchcraft, even during the Counter-Reformation, treating the claims of women to be witches as delusions. Unfortunately witch-hunts became a tool in the struggles between Catholics and Protestants north of the Alps in the following century, and for this Innocent must also share the blame.

Witchcraft was not, thankfully, a threat facing Caterina Sforza. But Innocent's elevation was troubling to her and her family all the same. Riario's melancholy caravan received the news of the election on their way to the dominions with which they hoped they would remain invested by the new Pontiff. Caterina's anxiety that her husband's weakness had led to her surrendering the Castel Sant'Angelo weighed heavily upon her, for she knew well, as did Riario, that Innocent had clashed with the count. Her greatest hope was that the presence of Cardinal della Rovere behind the papal throne would ensure that she and her husband remained in favour. For, as Vespucci wrote to Lorenzo de Medici, '[della Rovere] may now be looked upon as Pope and he will maintain his influence better than under Sixtus'.

The couple arrived in Forlì on 4 September, tired and dispirited, but could not allow anyone to see their anxiety. They ordered the bells to be rung and celebrations held for the election of their enemy Innocent. At last, on 7 September, Caterina could celebrate, if somewhat tentatively, when news arrived that the Pope had invested the count with his previous domains of Imola and Forlì. The couple again set about winning the hearts of their subjects, not comprehending the numbers and extent of Riario's implacable and deadly enemies. Yet Caterina soon began to wonder how long they would have before the full force of those who hated her husband, whether peasant or prince, would render their present efforts useless. For once, the Countess of Forlì had not guessed that the hearts of those they now tried to win with tax cuts, buildings and favours had already been bought, acquired by those whom Riario had harmed. The countess could feel the spectre that menaced them, though knew not whence it came. The indomitable woman would have been gripped with fear had she realized the ill-wishers had already surrounded her husband, waiting for a propitious moment. They had ensured Count Girolamo Riario had no means of escaping the fate that awaited him.

Less than four years later Riario would be dead, stabbed to death and thrown from the window of his own palazzo; and Caterina Sforza would be further embellishing her reputation as the most fearless woman in the Italian peninsula.

PART TWO

1477–1503

CHAPTER 7

From Kissing Cousins to Killing Cousins

1477–1493

'Born for the ruin of Italy'
PAOLO GIOVIO ON LUDOVICO IL MORO

In the middle of May 1477, just as the heat of early summer began to warm the pink stones of the great castello dominating the centre of Ferrara, the duchess, Eleonora d'Aragona, wife of Duke Ercole I d'Este, bade farewell to her husband. She had a long journey ahead of her as she set out for an extended stay with her father, King Ferrante of Naples. Ferrante had been a widower for almost twelve years and had expressed a particular wish that his strong-minded, intelligent daughter should be present to celebrate his second marriage, which would be to his first cousin, the twenty-two-year-old Princess Joan of Aragon.

King Ferrante wished to make his forthcoming marriage a family affair as well as a royal occasion. Princess Joan's brother was King Ferdinand 'the Catholic' of Aragon, the husband of Queen Isabella I of the mighty state of Castile. The couple had twinned their crowns following their marriage in 1469 and by 1492, after a lengthy war, they had finally succeeded in ejecting the Moors from the Iberian peninsula, laying the foundations for a united Spain, one of the most powerful nation states in Christendom. Ferdinand and Isabella each held the title 'Most Catholic Kings'* irrespective of gender, an appellation given in the plural even when referring to only one of the Spanish monarchs. This was a powerful connection for the King of

---

* An honorific which they received from Sixtus for their crusade against heretics.

Naples to make, and it was only natural that he should have as many as possible of his own illustrious family around him.

Duchess Eleonora, a plain woman who lacked beauty but projected a somewhat majestic persona, had never been one to gloss over matters concerning her own royal lineage. She all but quivered with ecstasy over her father's nuptials with the young Aragonese princess. The union gave Eleonora particular reason to feel puffed with pride, as it amplified the pre-existing connection with her paternal family of Aragona and the Spanish monarchs. King Ferrante rejoiced that his daughter and grandchildren could attend the wedding and be at his side to help him welcome the bride-to-be.

Thus, the duchess and her daughters Isabella and Beatrice travelled overland to Pisa, where galleons flying her father's flag on their masts awaited to transport them down the long Mediterranean coast to Naples. On 1 June, the stately cortège arrived in Naples to great splash and fanfare. Ferrante had ordered that brilliant pageantry should welcome his daughter and grandchildren, as well as various members of the d'Este household. The colours flew while the flourish of trumpets and banging of drums made a happy, discordant noise. To the little minds of Eleonora's children, the boisterous joy signalled their arrival in a new world.

Isabella, aged three, and her sister Beatrice, her junior by one year, had been too young to understand their mother's wistful descriptions, pining for her sun-drenched homeland, which contrasted so sharply with her husband's northern duchy of Ferrara, over which lay an almost permanent hovering mist. Perhaps they missed the finer points of their mama's reminiscences, but once they arrived at Naples the little girls soon grasped the delightful change in the way of life at their grandfather's royal court.

Eleonora had not only brought her two daughters with her, but also the infant heir to the Ferrarese dukedom, her one-year-old son Alfonso. (The longed-for male Este heir had been baptized in honour of his uncle Alfonso, Duke of Calabria, the title held by the heir to the Neapolitan throne.)

During their long summer stay in the Kingdom, the two small girls' different personalities became apparent. Isabella, the elder, was a curious, clever child who, despite her puppy fat, already felt able to stand upon her honour and often behaved in a comically grown-up, if somewhat imposing, manner for a child of her age and height. Beatrice, meanwhile, revealed a daredevil streak that ignored ceremony; she preferred climbing up on anything that posed a challenge or provided a platform.

Ippolita Sforza of Milan, who had become Duchess of Calabria at her marriage to the Estense children's uncle Alfonso, ensured that her young visitors enjoyed an unforgettable stay. She had two children of her own, who provided excellent playmates for their d'Este cousins. The seven-year-old Isabella d'Aragona delighted in her two guests. Her brother Ferrante, aged eight, occasionally joined in with the girls' games, and found his two cousins a happy addition to their company, though the three little girls became an inseparable trio. Running through the cool rooms of the palace or exploring exotic gardens, the princesses played games of make-believe, until they hurried to their uncle's many pools, fountains and ponds for more fun as they splashed the refreshing water over each other.

In the years ahead, the young women would have many opportunities to look back and mourn the bygone idyll of 1477, each reflecting bitterly upon how their entwined destinies and opposing fortunes had doomed their feelings for each other.

In September 1477, while still at Naples, Eleonora gave birth to a second son. The child's arrival further secured the Estense line, and marked the occasion of further rounds of festivities. The infant boy received the name Ferrante, in honour of his jubilant grandfather. Delight, however, was to be short-lived, as some months later disturbing word filtered south from the duchy of Ferrara. Duke Ercole was facing political strife, and he needed his wife to break off the idyllic sojourn in her home kingdom and rejoin him as soon as possible. War had broken out in the north, and the duke required Eleonora to serve as regent of Ferrara while he led troops into battle in his appointed role as Captain-General of the Florentine armies with whom he was allied.

That Duke Ercole put such faith in his wife was testament to her robust political temperament and immense personal bravery. The previous year, shortly after Duchess Eleonora had given birth to Alfonso, an illegitimate nephew of Duke Ercole had attempted to oust him from the throne. The conspirators had stumbled upon added resistance during their hitherto silent and successful approach to the duchess's apartments. Hearing the disturbance, Eleonora showed her mettle. Picking up her infant son and two daughters, she had run across the covered passage joining the d'Este palace (where the ducal couple lived) to the Castello Rosso and safety. Moments after Eleonora's escape, the conspirators broke down the door and found their hopes to kill the duchess and her three children had been confounded. Her courage and quick thinking then had saved the d'Este line from destruction (Duke Ercole had subsequently condemned 200 rebels, including Niccolò d'Este,* to death).

Eleonora did not shirk her duties. She told her father with some regret that it was time for her to depart. But her father requested that she grant him a special favour. Both King Ferrante and Queen Joan felt deeply attached to little Beatrice. They asked the duchess to leave the child to live with them. Ferrante told Eleonora that neither he nor his young wife could bear to part with the mischievous little girl.

Not insensible to the many advantages her younger daughter might enjoy living as an adopted child to the King of Naples, Eleonora agreed. Due to the grave situation in the north, she also left her newborn son behind until the perils there had ceased. After making their hasty farewells, the duchess and her entourage set out on the long journey to Ferrara, taking only her one-year-old son, Alfonso, and her elder daughter Isabella with her.

Beatrice spent the next eight years of her life at the court of Naples separated from her immediate family. She would return to Ferrara as a ten-year-old girl betrothed to the man destined to dominate Italian politics for the last decade of the fifteenth century.

As she grew up in Naples, Beatrice d'Este enjoyed the life of a Neapolitan princess – a privilege that had been accorded to her

---

* Niccolò d'Este was the illegitimate son of Leonello d'Este, ruler of Ferrara. Leonello's half-brother Borso d'Este succeeded him and raised Ferrara to a duchy. Illegitimacy was the norm among the rulers of Ferrara; Ercole proved the rare exception, born as the legitimate heir, and the heirs that followed him were also born within wedlock.

mother, and to which she took with obvious relish. Her aunt Ippolita was responsible for the child's upbringing and education, and was therefore the formative influence on Beatrice's life.

Ippolita was the Milanese daughter of Francesco Sforza and his wife Bianca Maria Visconti. Growing up during what is often called 'the Golden Age of Bastards', she had at least twenty-one siblings, legitimate and illegitimate, by numerous other mothers; the legitimate children included Galeazzo Sforza, who once confessed that his sister stood alone as the one person he completely trusted.

Ippolita had been a precociously intelligent young girl, who at fourteen years old had delivered a Latin oration to Pope Pius II and, later, had engaged in spirited competition with a young Lorenzo de' Medici to prove who had the better knowledge of classical texts. She had grown up to become a slim and attractive woman. She had a high forehead and almost translucent white skin, which showed off her raised cheekbones, as well as a beaky nose – both genetic footprints she shared with her brother Galeazzo. A high forehead was a hugely admired feature among women at the time, though Ippolita needed no recourse to the effective though deadly depilatory treatments of the day, most of which contained arsenic among their ingredients. Her blue eyes, naturally wavy long blonde hair, small, well-shaped mouth and smooth white skin should have made her a beauty, were it not for her unhappiness and isolation in a country far from her home.

Ippolita's intellectual precocity had enabled her to profit from the cultural atmosphere of King Ferrante's court as Naples reached its apogee as one of the great artistic capitals of Europe. Ippolita enjoyed the Moorish and Andalusian-style gardens with long walkways, shaded by the broad panoply of tree-lined avenues. Formally laid out pools, as well as fountains, fishponds and baths, gave a unique beauty to the gardens. Classically inspired columns, temples, ruins, grottoes and follies stood waiting to enchant those turning off a formal avenue or sun-dappled grove. Her husband had demonstrated his own typically basic sense of humour, shared by many of that time, by his use of the ingenious hydraulics he had installed for the garden pools. During dinner al fresco in one of the sunken gardens, a discreet signal from Alfonso sent jets of water up through the guests' seats, as the garden quickly flooded to become a large pool.

Alfonso and Ippolita's palazzo was held to be the finest in the region, attracting many visitors while under the Duchess of Calabria's tenure. Many of the pilgrims came for philosophical debate, to escape from the hot city and to benefit from an atmosphere of calm and serenity, particularly of the palazzo gardens. On one of her many walks at La Duchesca, the otherwise lonely duchess availed herself of the opportunity to talk with a member of the Humanist Academy of Naples and discuss the finer points of classical scholarship. She enjoyed the company of scholars such as Giovanni Pontano, who had founded the academy and wrote *De splendore,* a treatise on how to be a great prince.

Despite the 'strange medley of luxury and vice, of refinement and cruelty' which characterized the court of Naples, Ippolita herself had simple, even austere tastes.

She disliked people who dressed with excessive ostentation and preferred to give away her valuable gowns. She also gave up a number of her personal jewels for the benefit of charitable works, which along with scholarship were one of her main occupations. As the years passed, Ippolita tired of frivolity and the greed at court, and if a petitioner's case began to resemble a long complaint about some trifle, she closed her fan with a snap and then tapped it against her arm or bodice, a signal that the audience had ended.

The Duchess of Calabria, in common with most noblewomen, found solace in her love of the chase. Despite financial difficulties she managed to keep her falcons and hounds. This provided a shared interest for the d'Este sisters, though out of the siblings' mutual passion grew a determined rivalry that spread into almost every area of their later lives. Ippolita showed a great fascination and gift for a wide range of interests, including an impressive knowledge of agricultural matters, warfare and weaponry.

Despite the sophistication of her world and her own wide-ranging interests and knowledge, however, Ippolita was not content. As she carried out her surrogate parental duties, she would have hoped for Beatrice to grow up to a more satisfying marriage than she herself had. Her relationship with her husband Alfonso d'Aragona,

Duke of Calabria and Crown Prince of Naples, was not an easy one. Ippolita had known few happy days since she had arrived as Duchess of Calabria in the kingdom her husband, heir to the throne, had been born to rule.

Alfonso was not blessed with the same refined features as his wife. He had bulbous eyes, a hooked nose and long, unkempt hair. He enjoyed soldiering and proved a courageous commander in the field: as a young boy of fifteen he had helped his father in the ruthless despatch of the unruly barons who rose up against the Neapolitan crown. Both the duke and duchess loved culture and learning, though he had determined to find no common ground with his wife. Instead, intimidated by her natural self-possession and education, he kept her woefully short of money, and embarrassed by his open philandering. Ippolita was forced to sell or pawn much of her magnificent trousseau, including a mirror worth 10,000 ducats. Upon becoming a widow, her mother, Bianca Maria Visconti, had presented her eldest daughter with a valuable necklace given to her by Duke Francesco. Due to Alfonso's spendthrift habits, his wife found herself in almost permanent want of money and circumstances forced her to swap the gem for 30,000 ducats (well below its market value) in order to support her household.

As his wife sold jewels to stay solvent, Alfonso took a mistress, as well as many lovers of a more fleeting nature. He largely abandoned Ippolita and their children, eventually living all but openly with his mistress of many years, Truzia Gazela.* Although he never managed to marry Truzia, he legitimized Sancia d'Aragona and Alfonso, created Duke of Bisceglie,† the two children she had borne him during his marriage to Ipoolita. Sancia and her brother would soon have an important impact on the history of the peninsula.

With Eleonora in Ferrara, Ippolita took her maternal obligations towards Beatrice very seriously. That extended to organizing the

---

* Some spell Truzia Gazela as Trogia Gazzela.
† Sancia d'Aragona, Princess Squillace, born 1478. Alfonso d'Aragona, Duke of Bisceglie and Prince of Salerno, born 1481.

young girl's wedding to Ippolita's esteemed elder brother. In 1480, Ludovico Sforza had received permission from Duke Ercole to take Beatrice d'Este as his wife, deepening the connections between the houses of Sforza and d'Este. (Earlier, in 1477, the engagement had been announced between the Milanese princess Anna Sforza and Alfonso d'Este, Beatrice's younger brother and heir to Ferrara. Anna, the youngest daughter of the late Duke Galeazzo and the Dowager Duchess Bona of Savoy, was also Ippolita and Ludovico's niece.) Ippolita took care of many of the details concerning the couple's betrothal, even if the age difference between them seemed somewhat alarming, as she prepared for the formal engagement between her little five-year-old charge and her twenty-nine-year-old brother.

Beatrice was not Ludovico's first choice as bride. In fact, he had originally approached Duke Ercole with a view to taking Beatrice's elder sister Isabella as his wife. The duke replied that he had already promised Isabella to Francesco Gonzaga, heir to the marquisate of Mantua. Ercole casually suggested that in view of the prior commitment, perhaps his younger daughter would do just as well as a substitute. He wrote to inform Isabella's future father-in-law Federico Gonzaga in Mantua:

> The most illustrious Madonna Duchess of Milan and His Illustrious Highness Ludovico Sforza have sent their ambassador ... to ask for our daughter Madonna Isabella on behalf of Signor Ludovico. We have replied that to our regret this marriage was no longer possible, since we had already entered into negotiations on the subject with your Highness and your eldest son. But since we have another daughter at Naples, who is only about a year younger, and who has been adopted by His Majesty the King of Naples as his own child, we have written to acquaint his Serene Majesty with the wish of these illustrious persons, and have asked him if he will consent to accept the said Signor Ludovico as his kinsman.

His Serene Majesty was amenable, and Beatrice returned to her family in Ferrara in 1485, now using the title of Duchess of Bari in accordance with the terms of her betrothal.

She came back to a court just as culturally sophisticated as the one she had left behind in Naples. Despite its size, Ferrara had a tradition of cultural patronage to rival that of Naples. Giotto and Petrarch had been received there and Pisanello, Piero della Francesca and Jacopo Bellini been given commissions by the Este dukes. Ercole had the plays of Plautus and Terence translated for performance at Ferrara; Xenophon, Euripides and Seneca were among his favourite authors. The duke himself translated Plautus's greatest comedy *Menaechmi* from Latin to the *volgare*, and in order to stage the latter as well as the pastoral comedies of the ducal cousin, Niccolò da Correggio, Ercole ordered that a fine new stage be built at the Palazzo della Ragione.

Beatrice's mother Eleonora established her own library, which included translations of the romance poets, later favourite works of both her daughters. The library comprised a huge variety that also contained Pliny's letters and philosophical works such as the *De Consolatione* of Boethius. Duke Ercole had a similarly passionate interest in architecture. The family seats of Schifanoia and Belriguardo seemed under constant renewal, modernization and improvement.

Cosimo Tura decorated the chapel at the castello of Ferrara and the hall at Schifanoia with frescoes of hunting scenes, also producing portraits for the young princesses of their betrothed husbands. Tapestries were considered by contemporaries to be as significant as, if not more important than, paintings, and Duchess Eleonora bought works from Urbino and Faenza to add to those of the Spanish embroiderers whom she kept at court.

Alongside her sister Isabella, Beatrice could now complete the education she had begun under the supervision of Ippolita. Overseen by Duchess Eleonora, it would concentrate on teaching the sisters how to grow up to be wives, regents and players in the dynastic politics of the peninsula. As in all things, Duchess Eleonora ensured that the pair received a meticulous preparation for their future lives. They studied the classics, as well as French and the Provençal dialect (the language of troubadour literature). Isabella's intelligence had been already remarked upon at the age of five by the Marquis of Mantua's emissary, who had come to inspect the prospective Gonzaga bride and wrote with the hyperbole expected at the time:

> Madonna Isabella was led in to see me and I questioned her on many subjects to all of which she replied with rare good sense and quickness. Her answers seemed truly miraculous in a child of six [sic] and although I have already heard much of her singular intelligence, I could never have imagined such a thing to be possible.

The d'Este daughters received the same rigorous education as the sons, as well as learning the feminine accomplishments expected of aristocratic women at the time. Isabella's tutor Giovanni Martino, a German priest from Constance and choral master of the ducal chapel, taught the children music. Isabella learned to sing and played the lute, while young Alfonso acquired a deft hand playing the violin. The whole family had a bent for music and they received some renown for performing for the Ferrarese people, each member of the family playing an instrument. The ordinary public attended these shows with great enthusiasm, though it is difficult to know how much their cheers could be put down to their love of liberty by pleasing the duke, and how much their wild shouts of joy arose from genuine appreciation of the music.

Isabella continued a Humanist education throughout her life. This might have fuelled her love of owning outstanding pieces from antiquity, unusual sculptures, gems and all manner of artefacts. Isabella was to earn a reputation as much for her acquisitions as for the methods she used in gathering her store of treasures. Certainly, her considerable powers of persuasion – indeed, some might say extortion – later played a huge part in her famed collections that included the great artists of her time.

The family shared a passion for hunting. The two sisters vied with each other to be seen as the bravest, often shocking their companions by their recklessness as they pursued wild boar, wolves and other quarry. They learned to ride with speed and skill mounted on one of their father's famed prize-winning Barbary horses.

A letter from Caterina Sforza to the Duchess Eleonora begs

her for two of the famous greyhounds she bred in her own kennels:

> I know that the most illustrious lord your spouse and your most illustrious ladyship adore hunting and birds and that you have always an abundance of dogs, excellent, perfect. I beseech Your Excellency, very earnestly, that you would deign to make me a very beautiful and a very precious present, namely a pair of greyhounds. Well trained and fleet-foot for the deer of Campagna are very swift.

Beatrice herself mentions hunting frequently in her correspondence with Isabella, as here:

> ... every day we go out riding with the dogs and falcons and ... I never come home without having enjoyed myself exceedingly in hunting herons and other water fowl ... Game is so plentiful here that hares are to be seen jumping out at every corner. Indeed the eye cannot take in all that one desires to see, and it is scarcely possible to count up the number of animals which are to be found in this neighbourhood.

It was just as well that Isabella adored hunting, as her future husband, Francesco Gonzaga of Mantua, could hardly be called an intellectual. Horses, rather than Humanism, were his passion, and his childhood tutors complained that he rarely concentrated on his books. Yet he grasped the principles, if not the pleasures, of artistic patronage as an instrument of princely power, and continued a tradition in which Mantua, though smaller still than Ferrara, was nevertheless an impressive competitor.

The Gonzaga dynasty had ruled there since 1328, and the marquisate had achieved a good deal of political significance under their authority. The city centre had been greatly enhanced in the late fourteenth century, while in 1432 and 1436 Brunelleschi had visited to advise Gianfrancesco Gonzaga I on the construction of dykes to aid the agriculture and cloth manufacture that provided Mantua's main sources of revenue. Gianfrancesco and his wife Paola Malatesta selected the distinguished Humanist Vittorino da Feltre as tutor to the Gonzaga princes; he eventually established a mixed-sex school, where he took in students who had difficulties with their studies, as well as others with great promise whose families had not means to pay for such an education. The school was opened in Mantua in 1424, at the somewhat unfortunately named Casa Zioiosa (meaning 'the House of Joy'), having once been just the sort of place the ascetic da Feltre disapproved of; he quickly changed the spelling to Casa Zioisca. Interested in the best methods of teaching, he cast aside many of the old habits. An advocate of 'a healthy body and a healthy mind', the pedagogue taught his pupils in an environment with greater freedoms, both mental and physical. He advised his charges not to pronounce on matters unless they had something to say. If they did then he would teach them how to deliver their message plainly. He explained the sophistry used to twist a meaning by 'sleight of mouth', and the various philosophical disciplines fashionable among Humanists in their verbal duelling.

Da Feltre stated: 'I wish to teach them to think, not to split hairs.' The word 'sophist' originally meant 'wise' but garnered a pejorative meaning as 'itinerant intellectuals' received large sums to use their verbal acrobatics and spin out a line of rhetoric in any desired direction by their adroit use of language. Aristotle called sophistry 'specious arguments used for deception' and it became an art form in itself. It will surprise few that many of these men were the first lawyers in the modern sense of the word; they also worked in politics and what we would call public relations today.

During the summer months da Feltre would take his pupils to the house high in the hills at Pietola, the birthplace of Virgil. There the master would send his young scholars to play games. Once thoroughly exercised, they grouped around their teacher, sitting on the grass slopes, perhaps taking shade under the trees. In the groves once walked by Virgil, da Feltre held his students in a state of rapture as they listened to the great tales of Perseus and Hercules. Castiglione's 'model prince', Federico da Montefeltro, the first Duke of Urbino, counted among the school's many distinguished alumni, and hung da Feltre's portrait in the place of honour at his palace, with an honourable inscription and dedication. The Marquis Ludovico Gonzaga, Francesco's grandfather, would not sit down in the presence of his former master, da Feltre.

During the 1470s Isabella d'Este's future father-in-law, Marquis Federico Gonzaga, welcomed Leon Battista Alberti to Mantua. His views on architecture proved considerably sounder than his thesis on the ideal Florentine woman. He believed that the female sex, as the daughters of Eve, had an inherent wickedness. He instructed that the seductive sirens needed a firm hand, and constant occupation, working hard as semi-prisoners within their own homes. He hoped his suggested precautions would stymie women who exercised their cunning wiles to corrupt foolish and innocent men, and lead them direct to the devil himself.

It is the state's court painter, Andrea Mantegna, however, who must receive the laurels as the most famous figure associated with Mantua and the arts during this period. His painting of Cardinal Gonzaga returning to the court of his father Marquis Ludovico is one of the pinnacles of Renaissance art. The frescoes in the Camera degli Sposi, completed in 1474, perfectly evoke the transition from the austere, martial medieval world to the clarity and grace of the Quattrocento.

On 23 February 1483, Isabella d'Este's future husband, Francesco Gonzaga, welcomed Lorenzo de' Medici to Mantua. The role of entertaining the peninsula's most famous patron of Humanism, fêted political celebrity and ruler had fallen to young Francesco due to his father's absence. Francesco adored his sisters, though the eldest of his siblings, Chiara Gonzaga, had already left Mantua upon her splendid marriage two years earlier to Gilbert de Bourbon, Court de Montpensier, a cousin of the French King. Elisabetta and her younger sister Maddalena had suffered from poor health since their birth and caused their father and Francesco real worries, especially since their mother's death two years earlier. Word had been sent up to the girls from Il Magnifico that he should like to pay the young princesses a visit after he had dined. Lorenzo particularly enjoyed the company of young children, and would spend hours at a time with his own offspring. He behaved more in the manner of a modern father than a Renaissance prince, and when in their company he became playful and treated them as equals. The two Gonzaga girls came to greet the mighty Medici prince, each taking him by the hand and leading him up to their rooms. There he sat on one of the beds and engaged in attentive conversation; their governess overheard him asking the girls questions, joking and playing with them. Before leaving them to sleep, he said that their father was probably the richest prince in all Italy having two such daughters, who were more valuable than the largest jewels he had ever seen. To Lorenzo they must have seemed a fount of innocent reason, and he returned to Francesco, pronouncing himself enchanted with his sisters' company. The next day young Francesco toured the city with Lorenzo, reporting proudly to his father that he had shown off Mantegna's house, where their guest 'greatly admired some of Master Andrea's paintings, as well as certain heads in high relief and other antiques in which he seemed to take great delight'. Mantegna proved an awkward genius. He lived in hope of receiving the title of count; when not importuning the late Ludovico or his son for the title he desperately desired, he behaved in a penny-pinching and disagreeable way.

The family had come to dread a courier bringing word from the Master. The letters usually consisted of little more than an interminable grumble about his neighbours' thoughtless behaviour, apples being stolen from his orchard, or the incompetence of his tailor. The correspondence usually ended with a reminder that lacked any subtlety. Perhaps 'His Most Illustrious Prince and excellent Lord Marquis had overlooked the matter of the payment that had recently arrived from His Excellency, but the amount had been short by ten ducats.' With infinite patience Francesco penned a reply to the ungracious genius.

Even in times of war or plague, when the ruling marquis had little in his coffers, Mantegna would grind on and on, and yet as soon as the money arrived his apparent state of starvation would transform, and finally the Master built himself a large palazzo in the centre of Mantua. The marquis even intervened and ensured that Andrea Mantegna of Padua received a Palatinate countship. The indulged court painter lived in a state of ecstasy although, as ever, he complained about money; but his work brought an aura of glory to the Gonzaga. His joy might have been cut short for good reason had he realized he would soon have Isabella d'Este to deal with, and would find himself quite outclassed when it came to scrapping over money and favours from the ruling family.

Francesco would soon become used to entertaining such grandees as Lorenzo as one year later, in 1484, his father Marquis Federico Gonzaga of Mantua died, and Francesco succeeded to the title. One of the first commissions of his reign went to Mantegna, who painted a series of triumphal frescoes for the castello. The prince and the painter continued in their friendship for the remainder of Mantegna's life. The warm and lasting ties between them could perhaps be attributed to the marquis's relatively philistine attitude to art compared to his forefathers' inestimable taste and his willingness to spend money hard earned as a *condottiere*.

Francesco also arranged glowing alliances for both his young sisters. In 1486 he betrothed Elisabetta to Guidobaldo da Montefeltro, the son of Federico, Duke of Urbino, and Maddalena to Ludovico Sforza's nephew Giovanni of the junior branch of the Sforza dynasty. Giovanni Sforza, the most senior Sforza apart from those of Milan, ruled Pesaro, a small but not insignificant state on the Adriatic coast.

Two years later, the seventeen-year-old Elisabetta set out for the Montefeltro court at Urbino. Elisabetta was something of an invalid, and she found the journey in the harsh February weather a great trial; but when her party paused at Ferrara she was introduced to Isabella d'Este. The two embarked on a friendship that would blossom after Isabella's marriage to Elisabetta's brother Francesco in 1490 and her subsequent arrival in Mantua. In the early months following their wedding, Isabella's husband was often absent in Venice, and Elisabetta proved the perfect companion, sharing a taste for music and romance poems and accompanying her on excursions. Isabella describes one of these trips in a letter to Francesco:

> The Duchess of Urbino and I ... went to dine at Desenzano and to supper at Tuscullano, where we spent the night and greatly enjoyed the sight of this Riviera. On Friday we returned by boat to Sermione and rode here on horseback. Wherever we went we were warmly welcomed and treated with the greatest attention, most of all by the captain of the lake, who gave us fish and other things, and by the people of Salo, who sent us a fine present.

An observer described the two young women as 'indefatigable in making excursions by boat and on horseback and [they] have seen all the gardens on the lake with the greatest delight. The inhabitants have vied with each other in doing them honour and one Fermo of Caravazzo caused his garden to be stripped for the Marchesana and her party and loaded them with lemons and pomegranates.' Isabella's evident relish for the culinary part of the proceedings no doubt contributed to the already visible rotundity of her figure, which was later to become truly remarkable. 'There is no one I love like you,' Isabella wrote to her new friend, 'excepting my only sister [Beatrice] the Duchess of Bari.'

In summer 1490, Beatrice's title remained no more than a courtesy. It had been hoped that her wedding would be celebrated at the same time as that of her sister, but Ludovico Sforza was proving something of a reluctant bridegroom. The Ferrara archives contain a receipt of 1485 for four gold florins from Cosimo Tura for a bust-length portrait of the ten-year-old Beatrice to be sent to her 'consort'. For the next five years, Ludovico had been partially occupied with consolidating his power in Milan and a great deal taken up with his mistress Cecilia Gallerani. He found himself quite ensorcelled by the beauty, giving her rooms in the castello of Milan, and commissioning her portrait by da Vinci himself. It was not until King Ferrante began to pressure him that Ludovico sent a necklace of pearls, emeralds and rubies to Beatrice and arranged with the Duke and Duchess of Ferrara that she should travel up to Milan with her brother Alfonso, who would return to the duchy with his own betrothed, Ludovico's niece, and yet another half-sibling to Caterina, Anna Sforza.

On 29 December Beatrice set out on an appalling voyage even by the standards of the average contemporary bridal journey. Isabella had already come from Mantua to join her sister, and along with Duchess Eleonora they embarked on the Po in a small fleet of galleys. The provisions were held up by the bad weather and until they arrived in Piacenza on 12 January 1491 they had practically nothing to eat, which Isabella must have found particularly hard to bear. They hardly had time to recover before they pushed on through heavy snow and the freezing Lombard mists, where at last they saw

Pavia, an oasis of warmth and shelter. Ludovico had come to meet them.

The wedding was celebrated there in the Visconti chapel on 17 January. The following Sunday, the Duchess of Bari made her entry into Milan through streets 'hung with costly brocades and wreathed with ivy'. Bona of Savoy reappeared for the occasion, and Beatrice was met by the young man who in theory ruled her husband's duchy, Duke Giangaleazzo Sforza, Lord of Milan. Of the three little girls who had played together in the palace at Naples, Beatrice was the last to marry.

The previous year, Isabella d'Aragona had endured her own winter journey along the coast to Genoa to take up her title of Duchess of Milan as her cousin's bride. Giangaleazzo may have been called the duke, but his inadequacies when compared with his uncle Ludovico were painfully apparent. As he grew into his teenage years, he manifested many of the disquieting signs of the insanity within the Visconti genes. Put simply, Galeazzo's son, at whose birth he had been so proud, grew into a cruel half-wit. He proved quite incapable of making any sound political judgement, much less participating in the general running of the huge duchy, one of the few Italian states that had vast riches at its disposal. He liked to live a life without any responsibilities. The simpleton preferred to play while Ludovico governed. This arrangement naturally suited the latter very well, but was an immediate source of frustration for his wife, and of tension in her relationship with her old friend Beatrice.

Initially, however, the two girls fell comfortably back into their old understanding, having shared a large part of their early years as siblings. They hunted together, played endless games of *palla* and sat chatting and sketching dresses they wanted to have made. Beatrice, always the naughtier of the two, continuously cajoled her cousin Isabella to do something more fun; she begged and pleaded until the sweet Isabella felt she must please her, and agreed to whatever plan she had in mind. Often the two of them would set out for the market place dressed in disguise, with neither guards nor chaperones. But when they became mothers the real differences in their status swiftly emerged as a cause of dissent. Isabella gave Giangaleazzo a son, Francesco, the Count of Pavia, in 1491, and Beatrice's own boy

Massimiliano was born the next year, at the same time as Isabella gave birth to a daughter. When the women processed to Santa Maria for their 'churching' (the purification ceremony performed for new mothers), Beatrice's outfit of gold brocade embroidered with blue and red silk under a fur cape caused comment. The splendour of her clothes reflected the honours Ludovico was determined to do for his own son, honours which had conspicuously not been paid to the rightful heir to Milan, the Count of Pavia. The church bells were rung for a week, thanksgiving Masses were heard in the Duomo and food distributed to the people. Isabella d'Aragona was furious and wrote to her father Alfonso to complain of this disparaging treatment.

Isabella's misgivings were well founded. Ludovico Sforza was scheming to have himself invested as Duke of Milan. This meant the all-important recognition by the Holy Roman Emperor. The Visconti had received their dukedom from the Emperor, though the Sforza had not yet managed this not inconsiderable accomplishment.

If, however, the Holy Roman Emperor bestowed the coronet on Ludovico, this would disinherit Giangaleazzo and establish Beatrice's son, rather than Isabella's, as the next in line. While maintaining a show of cordiality with his former ally the King of Naples, Ludovico was cultivating Maximilian, the heir to Emperor Frederick III, with the prospect of a betrothal to his niece Bianca Sforza. Simultaneously he wished to establish a new league of alliances which was to range Milan with the papacy, Venice, Mantua and Ferrara, while Maximilian (and, in secret, Ludovico) would ally himself with the King of France in support of his claim against Naples. The Milanese envoy Belgioioso warned Ludovico that such an alliance with the French was potentially catastrophic, but Ludovico was too busy securing Venice as his ally to pay attention.

Beatrice had her own role in the plot. She and Ludovico were returning with their son from a visit to her parents in Ferrara when Ludovico received the news that Maximilian and Charles VIII of France had come to terms in the Treaty of Senlis. Extreme caution was now necessary. Ludovico rightly believed that every spy, envoy, ambassador and opportunist who had information to sell would broadcast the news of any visit Ludovico paid to the Doge of Venice and it would echo down the peninsula to Naples in a matter of days.

Ludovico decided to send his dizzy young wife Beatrice to Venice under the guise of a pleasure trip with her mother Duchess Eleonora in order to further negotiations for the new league. One of Beatrice's ladies-in-waiting termed the excursion 'the war of the two duchesses' – certainly the d'Este ladies had armed themselves down to their last diamond. Beatrice was evidently thrilled to be included in her husband's most important career move to date, and she and Ludovico tried to determine how to strike precisely the right note with the mercantile Venetians. Splendid, regal and confident, the eighteen-year-old duchess's magnificence should be unmistakable, even to the beady eyes of her hosts. Nothing could be permitted to disturb the impression of Ludovico's wealth and power.

The Venetians seemed gratifyingly awestruck. Beatrice's sumptuous procession of brilliantly caparisoned horses, their trappings sparkling with gems, her liveried servants and her own gowns and jewels had the crowds cheering and exclaiming at what appeared a heavenly apparition. Beatrice wrote a jubilant letter to her husband, imitating the cries which swirled around her as she paraded through the streets; 'Look! This is the wife of Ludovico Sforza – see what fine jewels she has, the splendid rubies and diamonds.'

As Beatrice's flotilla of bucenteurs passed San Clemente, a volley of cannon fired a deafening salvo from galleys on either side. Travelling down the Grand Canal the party found a swarm of multi-coloured gondolas crammed with crowds swaying wildly in the desperation to catch just one glimpse of the shimmering figure of the duchess.

Beatrice held her first reception in her father's Palazzo d'Este – Ercole and her mother had ensured that their palace had been gorgeously refitted for the occasion. The Doge and the Signoria wore their finest robes. Beatrice comported herself with a disingenuous blend of great charm and blushing inexperience; aware of her reputation as a pleasure-seeker, caring only for distraction, she knew that it disarmed her interlocutors, and made her first foray into the delicate world of high diplomacy easier to achieve. The next day Beatrice and her most senior attendants went to the first of two meetings in the Doge's Sala del Collegio. There the young Duchess of Bari made a speech. Her childhood training in classical rhetoric proved useful as she intimated, without being explicit, that her husband felt nothing but goodwill towards Venice, and that as *de facto* ruler of Milan, he was held in similar esteem by the Emperor and Charles VIII of France.

She continued by imparting what can best be described as stagey confidences. Her husband, she said, had been apprised by the French King of his plans with regard to Naples. Carefully she emphasized that while Ludovico was possessed of all the military and material might of Milan, he nevertheless wished to consult the Venetians as to how he might proceed.

Beatrice described the event in a letter, reporting that she had explained to Doge Barbarigo: 'my husband has money and enough fortresses that he could consider himself the only Lord in Lombardy' and emphasized that he required recognition from the Venetians. A pronouncement upon the duke being the one and only rightful Lord of Milan would carry the implicit message that the Venetians opposed the rightful ruler, Giangaleazzo. Beatrice's enthusiasm for the wonders of Venice, and her own amazing diplomatic prowess, allowed her to believe she had brought her husband success.

Her visit lacked diplomatic finesse and, with a race as canny as those of La Serenissima, the requisite sure hand of a professional. Due to her inexperience, she mistook her hosts' hot air for substance, and their assurances of goodwill seemed to her as much as signed agreements. The seasoned Venetians must have sniggered into their capacious sleeves. They had committed themselves to nothing and that little slip of a girl had given away a great deal more than she knew.

It provided an intoxicating taste of intrigue for Beatrice. Unfortunately, any peasant vendor at the market place possessed of their wits could have told her that the visit had been a fool's errand. She had achieved nothing; worse still, everything about her supposed shopping jaunt with her mother all but announced that Ludovico plotted something, and fooled few as to what that might be.

Isabella d'Aragona, the Sforza duchess and wife to the Lord of Milan, tried hard to make the dribbling hysteric she had married understand his perilous situation. The daughter of two highly intelligent parents, she cared for Giangaleazzo and feared for him and for their children. She wept bitter tears of fury and exasperation when the poor fool, desperate for Ludovico's love and approval, hurried to tell him what his wife had said, repeating her bitter remarks about Ludovico and Beatrice. Isolated and friendless, Isabella could only watch in despair as their uncle prepared to usurp both her husband's position and their son's birthright – a move that would bring catastrophe to the peninsula and expose the ugly underbelly of the Renaissance.

CHAPTER 8

Queen Mother of Florence and the Princess Brides

1475–1492

'The like of whom cannot be reproduced'
CATERINA SFORZA ON LORENZO

Lucrezia Tornabuoni appeared determined to consign Clarice Orsini to obscurity. As she had demonstrated during the Pazzi conspiracy and the war of the same name, there was no place for Clarice anywhere but Lorenzo's bed. Clarice had been perpetually pregnant for the first decade of her marriage, and had six living children at the time of the Pazzi murders: Lucrezia, born 1470, Piero, born 1471, Maddalena, born 1473, Giovanni, born 1475, Contessina, born 1476 and Luisa, born 1477. Her last child, Giuliano, named after his murdered uncle, appeared in 1479. Clarice spent the best part of her time either giving birth or recovering from it in one of the Medici properties in the Tuscan countryside, effectively returning to Florence only to be impregnated. Her strongest link to her husband was the scholar Poliziano, who rather touchingly tried to keep her abreast of her husband's doings, as Lorenzo could hardly be bothered to write to her. In 1475, for example, Poliziano was at Pisa with Lorenzo, and wrote to Clarice, who was about to give birth to Giovanni:

I did not write to your Magnificence yesterday because Lorenzo sent me to Lucca ... I at once take up my pen so as to keep my promise. Lorenzo is well and of good cheer [here follows an anecdote about Lorenzo having lost his favourite falcon on a hawking expedition] ... just now we do nothing else either in the morning or the afternoon. This evening I hear that on Monday Lorenzo intends to hunt the roe deer and then to return at once to Florence. Pray God we may find you with a boy in your arms.

Given that Pisa lay five hours' ride away from Florence, it can hardly have been comforting to Clarice, preparing yet again to undergo the perilous agony of childbirth, that her husband was too taken up with his hunting to return to her.

The following summer, Clarice was at the family villa at Cafaggiolo while Lorenzo remained in the city transacting business with his mother. Clarice wrote plaintively

> We have expected you for the last three evenings ... and were very surprised you did not come. I am afraid something out of the ordinary must have detained you. If there is anything new, please let me know for in any case it would be better to be together rather than one in Florence and the other in Lombardy. We expect you tomorrow in any case, so please do not let us wait in vain.

If Lucrezia Tornabuoni had considered invisibility suitable for her daughter-in–law Clarice Orsini, she certainly had no intention of remaining in docile sequestration herself. After her own husband Piero de' Medici's death in 1469, she had effectively taken charge of the Medici property holdings at Cafaggiolo, Careggi, Fiesole, Mugello and Casentino, hoping to give Lorenzo time to concentrate on politics, or, for that matter, hunting. By 1480 Piero's *castasto*, or tax return, showed that Lucrezia had added to Medici purchases a palazzo and farm at Pisa with a house and several commercial properties, *botteghe*,* bought in her own name, as well as farmland and a dairy herd. For her agricultural properties, Lucrezia used a contract known as a *mezzadria*, which gave her the right to half of the harvest, or half of the profits from it, in rent. In Florence, she bought a house near the tower of San Pier Maggiore, a *bottega* and a third of a farm outside the city. For all her property dealings Lucrezia employed her own managers, who reported to her overseer, Rinaldo da Panzano. In 1475, she wrote to her notary Francesco d'Antonio Dovizi about a

* Shops, stores or businesses.

project to turn the river at the Medici property near Bibbiena into a lake, but despite the lawyer's promises that it could be well stocked with trout and crabs, Lucrezia became quite distracted by her most daring business venture yet: the spa of Bagno a Morba near Volterra.

The waters at Bagno had been popular with Florentines for over a century and were reputed to be excellent in easing arthritis and rheumatism. A lease had been bought from the *comune* of Volterra in 1389, but the baths had fallen into disrepair, so that when Lucrezia visited she found small, dirty, cell-like rooms swarming with bugs which, she reported in disgust to Lorenzo, were the size of capers. In 1478, Lucrezia signed a lease for the property in perpetuity for an annual sum of fifteen ducats. She supervised much of the renovation personally. With the advice of engineers, Lucrezia installed a hydraulic system to run water into baths and showers, and Bagno a Morba became the fashionable resort for Florentines in the spring, with private treatment rooms and accommodation for guests.

There were no such distractions for Clarice at Cafaggiolo during the early days of the Pazzi War. A letter from Poliziano to Lucrezia of December 1478 positively drips with dyspeptic boredom: 'The rain is so heavy and continuous that we cannot leave the house … we have exchanged hunting for playing at ball so that the children should have exercise … I have no other news to give you, I remain in the house at the fireside in slippers and a greatcoat … I declare to you that I am drowned in weary sloth, such is my solitude.' Poliziano evidently felt that Clarice's company was a feeble substitute for Lucrezia's, with whom the tutor could 'air his fantasies'. This despite the fact that the previous month Clarice had been involved in a kidnap plot. With anti-Medici feeling smouldering after the Pazzi conspiracy, Piero Baldinotti of Pistoia had corresponded with the Neapolitans, who had agreed to land boats at the Tyrrhenian port of Pietra Santa near Lucca and then travel inland to capture Clarice and her children. Baldinotti was executed at the time that Poliziano was writing to Lucrezia, and though he speaks of the 'perpetual anxiety' of the household, the atmosphere he evokes of Clarice's country retreat is one of dreary lassitude.

Clarice spent fourteen months after the Pazzi conspiracy holed up in the country with Poliziano. The Baldinotti plot had shown the necessity for this, but she felt increasingly embittered and melancholy, particularly when Poliziano, whom she had believed to be a friend, began to turn against her. Poliziano had written to Lucrezia and Lorenzo complaining that Clarice was interfering in his teaching of young Piero. It is easy to imagine that a brilliant man like Poliziano, a true Humanist scholar, would have been bored at the best of times trying to inculcate the fruits of a lifetime's study into a not particularly apt pupil, and the lack of the congenial circle of male companions to which he had been accustomed in Florence could only have irritated him still more.

Clarice was aware that she was not Lorenzo's intellectual equal, that she could not speak the witty language in which his friends bantered among themselves nor share their appreciation for exquisite paintings or eloquent poetry, yet she presented a proud face. She was an Orsini, greater than her husband by birth if not brains, and she knew that it suited her mother-in-law to keep her a-breeding in the country while she monopolized Lorenzo. Slowly, her loneliness simmered into anger. Poliziano made no secret of his longing for sophisticated city life and offended Clarice with his ever more pointed hints that rustication bored him.

In April 1479, Clarice dismissed Poliziano. No evidence exists as to the exact pretext upon which she did so, though some writers have gone so far as to suggest he was corrupting little Piero's body as well as his mind. Clarice possibly believed this. There are grounds to suspect that her reaction was hysterical enough even the *idea* that Poliziano might be homosexual. Lorenzo wrote to her instructing her to take back the tutor. Clarice had thrown him out on the road without even his books; as she grew more incensed when she discovered that Poliziano was being housed in a Medici property at Fiesole at her husband's and mother-in-law's invitation. 'I have endured a thousand insults,' she wrote to Lorenzo, but it was painfully clear that Lorenzo and Lucrezia took no account of her suffering at Poliziano's ridicule, and that the place of the Orsini bride was the nursery.

Even more galling was Lucrezia's prominent place among the intellectual stars of Florence for her poetry, having completed several works by 1479, although to our contemporary tastes it takes some imagination to describe Lucrezia as an original or particularly talented writer. Perhaps the most that can be said of her work is that it recalls Dr Johnson and the walking dog. This, however, should not entirely negate her achievement, which was to demonstrate that women were as capable as men of participating fully in every aspect of social, financial, political and cultural life.

Despite the dismissive attitudes of her husband and mother-in-law, Clarice was not uninterested in cultural matters, though the works she patronized tended towards a more traditional Christian model. As well as making rich gifts to churches and convents including the Duomo of Florence, for which she commissioned a pair of gold brocade vestments, Clarice herself was a patron of the Humanist philosopher Marcilio Ficino, funding a translation of St Jerome's Latin Psalter, while the Humanist book-dealer and biographer of Cosimo de Medici Vespasiano da Bisticci dedicated a preface of his life of St Paula, a follower of St Jerome, to Clarice. By 1480, Poliziano was back in his post, and remained Piero de' Medici's beloved and best-trusted confidant until after Lorenzo's death. Posterity, however, gives the argument to Clarice, as Piero, the prize pupil of the great Humanist, managed to have the Medici dynasty thrown out of Florence for eighteen years, while Giovanni, whose education had been entrusted to his mother as a sop to her pride, became Pope. It is hard not to see Clarice's point.

March 25 1482 proved a sad day for the Medici and Florence, but not, it might be suspected, for Clarice Orsini. Lucrezia Tornabuoni, the *Magnifica Madonna*, a woman who brought 'glory, fame and honour to the female sex', died and was buried the following day in San Lorenzo, according to her eulogist Francesco de Castiglione. Lorenzo de Medici wrote to Eleonora d'Aragona, his royal guest, that 'I have lost not only a mother, but the only person I could turn to in many vexations and who aided me in many troubles.' To Eleonora's husband, Duke Ercole of Ferrara, he mourned, 'Even still in tears and anguish, I cannot but tell you of the sad event of my dearest mother, who today passed from this life. Words cannot express the depths of my unhappiness.'

With Lucrezia dead, Clarice finally had the space to take a more prominent role as Lorenzo's proxy. She had travelled more frequently than other Florentine women, often returning to her natal family in Rome, where at least she was welcomed and lauded, if only for being the wife of the magnificent Lorenzo. Her husband may have been indifferent to her, but outside Florence she was greeted with respect as the representative of the Medici leader. In 1485, for instance, when returning to Florence from Volterra, she met the Sienese ambassador to discuss business between the two cities. While such activities remained informal (Clarice was not there the next day to be presented to the council of Colle), she proved extremely popular among the wives of other influential men, as demonstrated on the occasion when she had the female relatives of the prefect of Colle Val d'Elsa presented to her. The women were so thrilled to meet a Medici that they mobbed her and she had to be rescued by her travelling companion, her chaplain Matteo Franco. And whatever her views on their education, there is no doubt that Clarice was a loving and attentive mother to her children. On the same visit, Clarice and Franco stopped at the Certosa del Galluzzo, three miles from Florence's Porta Romana gate, and Franco described the reunion:

> Then we met paradise full of festive and joyous angels, that is to say Messere Giovanni and Piero, Giuliano and Giulio on pillion with all their attendants and as soon as they saw their mother, they leaped from their horse, some without help ... and ran forward into the arms of Madonna Clarice with such joy and kisses and delight that a hundred letters could not describe it.

Public emphasis on the maternal virtues of the Medici women formed a crucial source of ceremonial power, associating them with the Virgin Mary. The numerous Medici clients who had appealed to Lucrezia Tornabuoni to intercede for them at the Palazzo Medici, to resolve disputes or bestow charity, had often addressed her in Marian terms. The Captain of Pisa described her as 'Magnificent and generous, honoured as a mother,' while Lotto Mancini of Pistoia wrote: 'Most reverend as a mother ... because of your great human kindness, I am sending you a gift of trout.'

After Lucrezia's death, Clarice spent more time in Florence and

received such petitions in greater number, having similar reveren-
tial terminology applied to her; Matteo Bonaccorsi thanked her for
aiding him, adding, 'I have no other refuge than this Magnificent
House, through your Magnificence,' while a poor widow thanked
her for relief from taxes, repeating, 'I have no other refuge besides
Your Magnificence'. Much in the manner of the d'Este sisters,
Ippolita Sforza and Caterina Countess of Forlì, Clarice's participa-
tion in charitable intercession, for both lay people and religious,
provided not only a means of performing her Christian duty to the
poor – it was also an advertisement for the compassionate side of
her marital family's power, a means of securing loyalty and support
among all classes.

Clarice's influence in Florence was far more covert than
Lucrezia's, but to some extent she was able to involve herself in
Lorenzo's project of expanding Medici alliances with Naples, Rome
and the peninsula as a whole while securing a consistent power base
within Florence itself, as her children were the tools of that strategy. In February 1487 her daughter Maddalena married Francesco
(Franceschetto) Cibo, the illegitimate son of Pope Innocent VIII.
The marriage had been postponed as the bride was only thirteen
years old. While Franceschetto had little to recommend him personally, being a drunkard and a compulsive gambler, he provided
an essential ingredient in binding the Medici and the papacy closer
together. In February of the same year an equally grand match
was made for Piero II de Medici, Clarice's eldest son, later known
as Piero the Unfortunate. His bride, Alfonsina, another Orsini,
though from the senior branch of the line, daughter of Roberto,
Count of Tagliacozzo and Alba, and Caterina di Sanseverino provides further proof of how Medici status had not just increased but
changed in character in one generation. The bride was not subjected
to the minute physical inspection which Clarice had undergone at
the hands of her mother-in-law. She was pronounced as being of
mediocre appearance by the aristocrat Bernardo Rucellai, his only
complaint being that her throat seemed a little thick, while Clarice
herself claimed she was satisfied.

The wedding was celebrated with maximum Medici pomp in
the presence of the Neapolitan royal family, as Alfonsina, named

for Alfonso of Naples, had close links with the house through her father's vassalage to King Ferrante. Clarice's other children had their marriages negotiated with a view to maintaining Medici relations closer to home. In 1481, Lucrezia was betrothed to Jacopo di Giovanni Salviati, with the wedding celebrated in 1486. The Salviati had been involved in the anti-Medicean party after the Pazzi conspiracy, and the wedding was part of a strategy of rehabilitation. Her younger sister Luisa was betrothed to Giovanni di Pierfrancesco de' Medici, in an attempt to restore cordiality between the senior and junior branches of the family, but she died only a few years later. Her younger sister, Contessina, would later marry Piero Ridolfi.

In November 1487, Clarice and Maddalena had set out for Rome. 'My wife Clarice,' wrote Lorenzo to his Roman agent Giovanni Lanfredini, 'has decided to visit her relations to see what effect the Roman air will have … a short time ago you spoke of a wish that Maddalena should come there. If this is still the case she could conveniently accompany her mother.' The business aspects of the marriage had already been arranged, after considerable haggling. Maddalena's dowry was 4,000 ducats, as well as the former Palazzo Pazzi in Florence, their Pazzi villa at Montughi and a country estate near Spedaletto. (This compared to the average elite Florentine dowry of 1,400 ducats.) Shamefacedly, Lorenzo had had to grovel to the Pope, who was reluctant to part with a single gold piece, for some sort of arrangement for Franceschetto: 'it seems to me unlike your innate goodness and kindness not to provide him with means to keep up his position'. Lorenzo felt somewhat mollified at the presentation to Maddalena of jewellery worth 10,000 ducats at her wedding banquet. Clarice and her daughter had been met at the city gates by a huge retinue of papal servants and Florentines, members of the merchant community who had turned out to see 'their Princess' and the 'Orsini foreigner', who was returning to her home for the last time. They remained in Rome over the winter, but almost immediately the marriage began to go wrong.

Lorenzo, a fond father, had misgivings about handing over his daughter so young, and wrote to her tenderly, urging her to: 'Remember the sacredness of the place where you are and what the Roman people expect of you. Consider that, while it is shameful to neglect your duties, it is honourable to perform them well and do not forget that it is your first duty to please the Pope and to cherish your husband.'

Maddalena tried to follow her father's bidding, but Franceschetto had no interest in his wife, staying out all night while she waited patiently at home. Clarice's chaplain Franco, whom she trusted greatly, both with her money and her person, writing, 'I will not allow any man to have the spending of my money but Franco and I will eat nothing but what has passed through his hands' – wrote back to Florence that both Clarice, who was frequently unwell, and Maddalena, had fallen ill. She had 'lost her sleep and appetite, becoming like a glow-worm'. Although she had become swollen due to acute constipation, she refused all treatments such as enemas 'so as not to stink her husband's bed', in Franco's view so that he would not say 'go and sleep alone'. Lorenzo replied that he wished Clarice and Maddalena to return to Florence, as 'she is but a girl, the house of Messer Francesco is in disarray, and for Clarice's happiness'. Cruelly, Maddalena's husband would not allow Franco, who had volunteered to become part of Maddalena's household, to return with them, insisting that he travel instead to Stigliano, where he possessed a spa which he wished to refurbish. Disgusted, the chaplain reported that 'the place is filthy ... Bagno da Morba is a Careggi in comparison. The air is accursed. The men are Turks and everything is of the worst quality. Day and night I struggle with bandits and soldiers and thieves with poisonous dogs, lepers, Jews, madmen, fools and Romans.' To a business-minded Florentine the squalor of Stigliano, and Francesco's refusal to invest in repairs, was shocking.

Franceschetto found Florentine frugality equally outrageous. In June 1488, he arrived in Florence with a huge retinue of Roman gentlemen. Lorenzo had his son-in-law to dine every evening in an informal atmosphere, but Franceschetto interpreted this as meanness, and became anxious that once the Pope died he would be reduced to living in Tuscan simplicity. He complained to a more sophisticated member of his suite that he was being treated in a manner likely to expose him to ridicule back in Rome, but his companion explained that Lorenzo receiving him *en famille* was an honour, an interpretation with which Innocent VIII concurred. Ever conscious of her duty to further the family goals, Maddalena returned to Rome with her husband that year.

Despite the unhappiness of their marriage, and the deleterious effect Franceschetto's lifestyle had upon Maddalena's health, they nevertheless managed to produce seven children, numbering a cardinal, a marchioness and a duchess among them.

Franceschetto provided a constant source of shame to the prudent Medici daughter, modestly educated in the virtues of *masserizia*, as when in 1490, amid rumours of Innocent's death, he attempted to seize the papal treasury and was only prevented from doing so by the cardinals, Maddalena's brother among them. She was often to be found writing to her brother Piero II de' Medici bemoaning the fecklessness of her husband: 'I see the Lord with little or no income, spending much of his capital without profit and not knowing what to do, or should be done with his possessions.' Piero, she explained, would have to have the brains for both of them, since her husband's character would not allow him to behave any other way. If Franceschetto were not enough to tolerate, Maddalena's deeply sinister father-in-law could not have differed more to her own loving, brilliant father Lorenzo.

Obese and dissipated, Innocent VIII also suffered from acute hypochondria. His 'treatments' included drinking fresh breast milk at the source and contingents of dwarves, idiots and freaks who were invited to disport themselves in the apartments of the Vatican to relieve the papal melancholy. According to an unconfirmed and probably malicious story, in 1492 it was determined that Innocent's 'humours' would be improved by a blood transfusion. Three young boys were offered a ducat apiece if they would give His Holiness some of their blood. The effort, the first operation of its type to be recorded, predictably went horribly wrong, and an example of the prevailing spirit in the Vatican of the time was provided by Innocent's attendants, who wrenched back the ducats from the pathetically clenched hands of the dying children. Maddalena received some comfort in Rome from her mother's Orsini kinsmen, but this could hardly compensate for the fact that after her return to the Holy City she would never see her mother again. Maddalena died in 1528, nine years after Franceschetto, who, for all his debauchery, survived until the age of sixty-nine.

Clarice, whose health had never been strong, died aged thirty-five in July 1488. Thin and weak, she had struggled through Maddalena's wedding party and the marriages of her other children with little regard for her own wellbeing. Lorenzo's neglect of her throughout their marriage has been read into his refusal to attend her funeral, though in fact this is a misinterpretation of contemporary etiquette. His protestations to the Pope that the loss of the 'sweet manner and company' of his 'most dear and beloved wife' had left him 'unable to find peace' have equally been read as merely conventional phrases, but despite the intellectual distance between husband and wife, there is no reason to assume Lorenzo did not care for Clarice. Certainly their sexual relationship had been successful, but as a result she was unable to be the help to him that his mother had been. Lorenzo had been too busy to spend much time with his wife, and there is something poignant about her obvious love for him; in any event their marriage had, by contemporary standards, achieved its ends.

Nowhere was this more evident than in the Medici's plans to gain a place in the Curia. Maddalena's marriage secured the relationship with the Pope which provided Lorenzo with his greatest ambition, a cardinal's hat for his second son, Giovanni. Giovanni had been tonsured at thirteen in preparation for his elevation, and in March 1489 Lorenzo was able to write to his ambassador in Rome of 'the greatest honour that has ever fallen to our house'. Disingenuously, Lorenzo did all he could to publicize the news, to the fury of Innocent, who wished to keep this particular piece of nepotism as quiet as possible due to the candidate's young age. Given that one of the chief reasons for his marriage with Clarice had been to produce a family cardinal, Lorenzo was beside himself with glee and terror simultaneously. Brimming with satisfaction that the Medici were now members of the most exclusive society in Europe, he felt extreme anxiety that the Pope might die before his promise was fulfilled, and broadcast the appointment as one way of ensuring Innocent did not renege on his promise. Sadly for Lorenzo, with his own health deteriorating, he had to be carried in a litter to witness his son's investiture at the Badia of Fiesole. Shortly afterwards, the new Cardinal de' Medici left for Rome.

Clarice Orsini left another legacy, one which was ultimately to guarantee not only the survival of the Medici dynasty, but their ascent into the monarchies of Europe. Clarice had been ridiculed for her old-fashioned attitudes by the sophisticated Humanists of Florence, but her consciousness of the ethos of an earlier age proved a greater investment for her marital family than anything deposited in their bank. During her long periods of maternal exile in the countryside, Clarice had continued to perform the functions of a great feudal lady, inspiring an enduring loyalty among the *contadini* whom the forward-looking Humanists of Florence despised as country bumpkins. Clarice felt true patrician responsibility for the Tuscan peasants, recalling her own Orsini origins in the land, rather than in finance, and when the two great crises of the Medici family came, in 1494 and again in 1527, it was among these simple people that the noble Medici scions found shelter, refuge and support.

Lorenzo knew that his death must be imminent, and wrote a long letter to his son Giovanni. He explained the boy's duties in what can be read as a manifesto for the personal philosophy of this greatest of Renaissance princes. Recalling his own assumption of Medici rule at a young age, he advised: 'as the youngest cardinal that there had ever been hitherto, therefore it is necessary that when you take part in any assembly of them [to] be the most unassuming and humble'. Intimate topics of conversation should be avoided, but general subjects should be pleasantly and graciously aired. Lorenzo recommended a simple style of entertainment: 'I should prefer a fine house and a well-ordered household to one extravagant and ostentatious.' Rather than spending lavishly on showy clothes, Lorenzo saw the true manner of a prince revealed in his acquisition of 'antique things and beautiful books'. Plain food, plenty of exercise and early rising were essential to maintaining a body and mind fit for government. He urged Giovanni to think over the duties of the following day 'that nothing may come at you unprepared'. Intercessions with superiors should be limited and confined so far as possible to pleasing requests, made with 'humility and modesty'. Works such as Machiavelli's *Il Principe* and Baldassare Castiglione's *Il Cortegiano*, based upon Urbino, are often taken as the definitive manifestos of Renaissance princely practice, but many of their elements are already contained in this, Il Magnifico's last letter to his son.

On 9 April 1492 Lorenzo died at Careggi. At his bedside were Poliziano and the philosopher Pico della Mirandola, as well as the adamantine friar Girolamo Savonarola. His legacy has been disputed by historians ever since. For some, Lorenzo remains the paradigmatic Renaissance prince who raised Florence to commercial prosperity and political might, who maintained the peace in Italy by converting chronic enmities into loyal friendships, who carried forward the resuscitation of learning and the arts to produce a conglomeration of brilliance which had never been paralleled in Europe. For others, he will always be a power-crazed tyrant, the brutal despot who ordered the massacre at Volterra and who destroyed the republican dream of Florence. Caterina Sforza, lamenting his death, described him as 'the like of whom cannot be reproduced'.

In Italy, the death of Lorenzo de' Medici, Il Magnifico, represented the end of an age.

CHAPTER 9

A Wonderful Family Man

1492–1494

'Do people say that I am both your father and your lover? Let the world ... believe the most absurd tales about the mighty ... for those destined to dominate others, the rules of life are turned upside down and duty acquires an entirely new meaning. Good and evil are carried off onto an entirely different plane.'
POPE ALEXANDER VI TO HIS DAUGHTER LUCREZIA BORGIA

On 12 August 1492, after almost three weeks of waiting for a decision from the conclave of cardinals, the bells of the Vatican sang out over Rome, the traditional signal that it had elected a new pope. After bitter disputes between the princes of the Church, a compromise candidate had been chosen: Cardinal Rodrigo Borgia. Christ's new Vicar on Earth announced that he would take the name of Alexander VI.

For months, the population of Rome had increased substantially with additional ambassadors, emissaries extraordinary, spies, chroniclers and opportunists. The gathering of pilgrims, both the political and the faithful, had started early in July. Innocent VIII had not long to live and he obliged those waiting in the heat by dying on 25 July. His death had caused a further influx to the city; representatives of those with vested interests in the outcome had waited in suspense as the cardinals withdrew. Once the result had been declared, couriers on their fast horses galloped to all parts of the Italian peninsula taking the news to their masters. The election would be a blow to some and a reason for the gleeful rubbing of hands to others. It also proved that people had short memories, for the newly elected Pope came from Valencia in Spain. Just over three decades earlier, in 1458, upon the death of Alexander VI's uncle, Pope Calixtus III (Alonso Borgia, or Borja in the original spelling), the Church and those in power throughout Italy had sworn never to elect another non-Italian pope, with a particular emphasis on the exclusion of Catalans. The cause for this xenophobic reaction provides an important insight into why the Borgias felt the need to cleave unto each other, and helps explain their clannish loyalty. It is also part of the reason that the Borgia name has been unfairly ascribed the bloodiest, most immoral and sexually deviant legacy. The verdict came from Italian contemporaries of the Borgias and those who followed shortly after, crystallizing as later historians picked up descriptions, many of which are falsehoods and fantasy. The Borgia popes were no more (and often far less) guilty than many pontiffs, before and after Alexander VI. Nevertheless, their name remains tarred and conjures up images of the most violent and horrid scenes of the Renaissance papacies.

As descendants of the ancient Romans, fifteenth- and sixteenth-century Italians knew that their early ancestors had experienced long, difficult campaigns to take Spain. Most Renaissance Italians qualified as snobbish xenophobes. They feared and despised the German nations, they hated the French, and the Spaniards fell into a category politely described as 'uncivilized'. Furthermore, the Catalans could be considered as a species of lower beings, thanks to their physical proximity to the infidel, as well as their blend of Moorish, Jewish and Christian Aragonese blood. The Italian heirs of Caesar's Rome smugly regarded themselves as keepers of the flame of civilization, and relegated the Catalans to the *ordure* of Christendom – indeed they felt unconvinced that the band of southern barbarians belonged to Christendom at all.

The Aragonese Borgias had moved south to Valencia, where the Moors had once ruled their own kingdom. The Borgias had lived in this land tainted by the infidel for over 200 years. Calixtus had not helped matters by bringing a huge train of his compatriots with him to Rome, among them Rodrigo Borgia, who had been given offices and benefices from an early age, and received his cardinal's hat aged only twenty-four. Throughout Calixtus's papacy of only three years, he carefully surrounded himself with a *cordon sanitaire* of his own countrymen, especially members of his family, who received great favours and offices.

No one had been more surprised than Calixtus at his elevation.

The election had arisen as the result of a deadlocked conclave which considered his extreme old age made him an acceptable compromise candidate. Upon his death, the Romans fell upon the Spaniards as though on a holy mission in a manner that could well have been mistaken for rage. They unceremoniously cleansed the Church of Calixtus's creatures. Not only did they boot the half-breed *marranos** (as they were known) out of their comfortable papal offices, bishoprics and other soft spots within the Curia; they also saw them off Italian soil. Rodrigo Borgia proved a notable exception as the next Pope, Pius II, had seen young Rodrigo's loyalty in nursing his dying uncle while other family members fled. He also spotted the rare abilities of the young Borgia. The juvenile cardinal had further assured his position by his vocal support for Pius during the highly contentious conclave of 1458.

Alexander VI had been born in Valencia in 1431, to a family of insignificant backwoodsmen and minor nobles. He had profited greatly from his uncle's elevation within the Church and earned himself a reputation for being a clever, able and libidinous man with a large measure of genuine piety, not considered incongruous at the time.

The new Pope had probably fathered seven or eight children by the time of his election, and at least one more son followed later on in his papacy. Three of his children lived in Spain, but those whom he held by far dearest to him were the product of a long union with Vannozza Cattanei, his mistress in Rome. Vannozza had most probably lived in the Eternal City for most of her life, though she is believed to have come originally from Mantua, possibly the daughter of Jaicoppo Pincturis, a painter as his name suggests. The fine-looking woman with a high forehead, thick auburn hair, a strong though fine-boned face and beautifully arched eyebrows had kept the cardinal captivated for many years. Alexander, meanwhile, consistently ensured that she had good husbands, and as each one died, Borgia found another respectable victim to marry Vannozza. She wore out at least three.

Vannozza's loveliness and sensuality belied her foremost character

---

* *Marrano* was the highly derogatory, largely anti-Semitic term used to describe the Valencian people.

trait: avarice. Her rapaciousness and cupidity seemed the more repulsive for her small-mindedness. Perhaps her scrabbling for the smaller coins took her eye off the truly great fortune she might have amassed through her connection with Alexander VI as mother (if no longer his lover) of his favourite offspring, the pope could hand out staggering sums of money and estates of high value to them. Whatever the reason, Vannozza set her sights too low and while she owned a number of properties accumulated over the years – all gifts from Borgia – she did not possess a great fortune. Many of the properties were in respectable areas of the city while others stood, for the most part, in the squalid districts frequented by prostitutes, to whom she had no trouble renting them. Woe betide those who did not pay their rents on time. No amount seemed too small for her to pursue. No wonder she was described as a 'woman possessed of the devil' when crossed over money. Although she whined to her patron and asked for his support, her star had waned.

Borgia must have seen what a poor mother she made to the four children that she called her own. Cesare was born in 1476, before a second, most beloved son, named Juan in 1478. In 1480, Borgia delighted at the arrival of a girl, naming her Lucrezia and in 1482 Vannozza gave birth to a fourth child, another son, named Joffre. Borgia hotly contested fathering the boy, and accused his mistress of infidelity with her husband and then trying to pass the boy off as a Borgia. Ultimately the cardinal took the feeble, vain and spoiled Joffre as his own. However, long after his ardour had cooled for the vulgar Cattanei, the cardinal continued to protect the mother of his dearest offspring, and did not cease his goodness to her when he became Pope.

By the early 1480s, Cardinal Borgia, by now one of the most powerful men in the Church, decided to remove the four children from their mother's care. He nursed great hopes for them, but felt the frankly common Cattanei would not be able to make young gentlemen out of their sons, nor a lady of Lucrezia. The boys lived in the style befitting sons of a nobleman, supervised by tutors and guardians, in their own house with the usual attendants expected for young men of rank. Lucrezia, whom Alexander loved 'superlatively', needed a woman of discretion as well as suitability to oversee her upbringing and he had in mind the ideal candidate to care for the smiling, golden-haired cynosure of his eyes. Adriana de Mila, Borgia's Catalan cousin and member of the Orsini dynasty by marriage, would be the matron Lucrezia needed.

It seems that none of the Borgia children had close relations with their mother except for Cesare, who adored her throughout his life. While his siblings barely communicated with Vannozza, he admitted to having only ever admired three women: his mother, his sister Lucrezia and Caterina Sforza.

Reports of Cesare and his masculine beauty abound from the time of his father's election to the papacy. Portraits and detailed descriptions of the young man are loud in his praise. Dark and handsome, with a well-proportioned figure, he had rich brown hair and eyes. At seventeen, good humour, high spirits and modesty seem to have been his predominant characteristics, while his good looks grew better with age. Lucrezia's brother loved to hunt, was an excellent horseman, a fine shot and sportsman. He also had a formidable, if not outstanding, intelligence, for he excelled at his studies at the universities of both Pisa and Perugia. He and Giovanni de' Medici, the son of Lorenzo and Clarice, had attended Pisa University at the same time in 1491. Giovanni turned out to be one of the few whose hatred for *marranos* predicated a negative opinion of Cesare.

In 1493, when the Estense ambassador, Giovanni Andrea Boccaccio, reported to Duke Ercole d'Este on the closeness of Giovanni's friendship with Cesare, he added: 'he possesses marked genius and a charming personality ... [Cesare has] the manners of a son of a great prince ... Above all he is lively and merry and fond of society; being very modest, his bearing is much better than that of the Duke of Gandia, his brother'.

Boccaccio also commented upon the priest's tonsure worn by Cesare, the only visible sign that Alexander had marked him for a brilliant career in the Church – a career ill-suited to a young man who believed in the philosopher's credo 'a man can do anything he wishes', far more than in the credo of the Catholic Church.

Juan, Duke of Gandia, Cesare's younger brother, upon whom Alexander placed great hopes, could hardly have contrasted more.

His father treated him with obvious favouritism and, thanks to his close relationship with King Ferdinand of Aragon, had managed to have the boy made a grandee of Spain, with the title Duke of Gandia. The dukedom had originally been bestowed upon the Pope's eldest son Pedro Luis, born in Spain of another mother, and guardian to his half-brother. In 1488 Pedro died, leaving to Juan not only the dukedom, but also his semi-royal fiancée, Maria Enríquez, niece to the Aragonese King.

By the year of her father's election Lucrezia had grown into a tall girl for her time, with a promising face for the beauty to come: clear eyes under well-defined brows, a pretty mouth and white teeth, and a long, slim neck almost hidden by her thick blonde hair. She is often described as laughing and high-spirited, good-humoured and elegant, fine in her movements, with a slender body and delicate feminine gestures. No wonder her father already had schemes for her future. These stood closer to Lucrezia and her innocent gaiety than she could have guessed.

At the age of twelve, Lucrezia Borgia had already been betrothed to two different bridegrooms: in 1491 to Querubi de Centelles, heir to the Count of Oliva, and two months later to Don Gaspar de Procida, the son of the Count of Almenara and Aversa. Rodrigo quickly broke this contract when it became apparent that there was more to be gained by an Italian marriage. Thus in February 1493, a contract was signed with Giovanni Sforza, Lord of Pesaro. In some ways it was a surprisingly modest match for a girl who was, effectively, a princess of the Church; but Rodrigo was using Lucrezia to pay off an essential ally, Ascanio Sforza, who had, it was widely believed, assisted his election. Ascanio, the brother of Ludovico Il Moro, was an insinuating tentacle of Milanese power in the Holy City, and had himself been mooted for the papacy. When it became clear that he could not carry the election, he devolved his supporters onto Rodrigo, in return for Rodrigo's former position of Vice-Chancellor of the Church, numerous palazzi and benefices and, it was rumoured, a mule train of silver which had been spied passing between the Sforza and Borgia residences. Rodrigo's election was certainly unanimous, and, it appears, merited. Nevertheless he was grateful to Ascanio, and in turn the Sforza were greatly relieved by the match. 'The Pope being a carnal man,' wrote Ascanio to Ludovico, 'and very loving of his flesh and blood, this will so establish the love of His Beatitude towards our house that no one shall have the opportunity to divert him from us and divert him towards themselves.'

The twenty-six-year-old Giovanni Sforza had very little say in the matter, even had his opinion been asked. As ever with Rodrigo and his multi-layered politicking the betrothal also provided a means of snubbing King Ferrante of Naples, who in an attempt to limit Borgia power in Rome, had conspired with the Orsini family to finance the purchase of two fortresses near the city just prior to the election. Ferrante proposed his grandson, Ippolita Sforza's son, but Rodrigo had a proxy ceremony performed in private, with only eleven men present, in order to thwart him.

The absent bridegroom had been Lord of Pesaro since 1483, when, although illegitimate, he succeeded his father Costanzo. The Sforza of Pesaro were descended from a collateral branch of the great Sforza line of Milan, sharing a common ancestry in the original Counts of Cotignola. Unlike their relatives further north in Milan, they ruled a small and charming city that lay on the east coast of the peninsula. The Sforza of Pesaro patronized poets and artists on a minor but sophisticated scale and rented themselves out as *condottieri* to keep the family coffers supplied. With an income of 12,000 ducats a year, Lucrezia's dowry of 31,000 ducats would have been welcome. Still, Giovanni could boast some connections among the *elite* of the peninsula, as his first wife had been Maddalena Gonzaga, sister to the Duchess of Urbino and sister-in-law to Isabella d'Este.

From the beginning, however, Lucrezia's marriage held a taint of a shabby, hole-in-the-corner affair. Though Rodrigo had determined upon secrecy, the Mantuan ambassador was able to report by 4 November 1492 that Giovanni Sforza had arrived in Rome, his arrival being lent a delicious air of scandal. Lucrezia's second fiancé, Procida, had turned up in Rome and was carrying on in a most quixotic fashion. He raised 'a great hue and cry, as a Catalan,' according to the Ferrarese ambassador, and proclaimed to anyone who would listen that his marriage had been validated by the King of Spain and that he had been cheated of his rights. Ludovico Sforza and Rodrigo eventually bought off Procida between them, but 'there was much gossip about Pesaro's marriage'. Rather shamefully, Giovanni had plundered the jewel-boxes of his former in-laws, the Gonzaga, so as to appear in suitable magnificence, but most recognized the thick gold chain around his neck as Gonzaga property.

Lucrezia herself appeared far more splendid, though witnesses agreed that her pubescent good looks could not match those of her father's luscious mistress, Giulia Farnese, married to an Orsini step-son of Adriana's, who acted as bridesmaid along with another Orsini wife. Her trousseau included a fabulous dress reportedly worth 15,000 ducats, while her wedding dress and jewellery were at least her own. Both the groom and Lucrezia's brother Juan Gandia had opted for the fashionable 'turcha' style, with long robes and curled gold trains, though Juan was absurdly splendid, wearing a jewelled cap worth 150,000 ducats with pearls embroidering his sleeves.

Lucrezia and Giovanni were married in the Vatican on 12 June 1493, kneeling at the Pope's feet beneath an unsheathed sword. The party then repaired for entertainments consisting of a pastoral eclogue by Serafino and Plautus's comedy *The Menaechmi*, which His Holiness found so dreary that he had the performance cut short. Unlike Caterina Sforza, Lucrezia did not have to endure a lengthy wedding banquet, as her father gave a men-only dinner that night at Lucrezia's home at the newly built Palazzo Santa Maria. Nor was Lucrezia expected to go through the traditional bedding ceremony where the newlyweds were tucked up together for the first time. This was conventional enough, as though the canonical age of consent for matrimony was twelve, it was not uncommon for careful parents to insist on delaying consummation for several years. The Pope's neglect of this aspect of the proceedings may have been as much concerned with politics as with his daughter's health. If the marriage were not consummated, it could easily be annulled, and Alexander was aware that while the Pesaro marriage might serve for the present, Lucrezia's diplomatic value should not be immediately squandered.

Was the boys-only entertainment also a sop to Lucrezia's pride? Witnesses had remarked that the bride had been outshone by Giulia Farnese at her own wedding, and some evidence suggests that there was a rivalry between the two young women and best friends, who had been brought up in such curious proximity. They were connected through Adriana de Mila, who by 1489 had been widowed of Ludovico Orsini of the powerful Roman clan and who superintended Lucrezia's education. Initially, Adriana looked after her at the Orsini palace of Montegiordano, and Lucrezia also spent time at the Dominican convent of San Sisto on the Appian Way, a place which retained a great deal of spiritual significance for her and to which she was frequently to take refuge during the more stormy periods of her life. Lucrezia received an education suited to a Renaissance princess, speaking Latin, Italian, French, Catalan (the family language of the Borgias) and a little Greek. Adriana also ensured her charge was instructed in the graceful conduct necessary to appear well in court life, and Lucrezia's carriage was to be particularly admired, as she walked so fluidly that she barely appeared to be in motion. When Adriana and Lucrezia repaired to the Palazzo Santa Maria in Portico, near the Vatican, after Rodrigo's successful election, they were joined by Adriana's daughter-in-law, Giulia, six years Lucrezia's senior.

Giulia Farnese's family had been Lords of their domains near Capodimonte for centuries, although the grandeur of the family name was not matched by any political clout. In Giulia, the most beautiful woman of her generation, they found their ticket to wealth and influence. Her marriage to Adriana's stepson Orsino Orsini (known as Monoculus for his unfortunate but pronounced squint) was celebrated in 1489, when the bride was fifteen. Initially the marriage appeared genuine, and not a front for an illicit relationship with the then Cardinal Borgia, it was not long before the two, meeting frequently in Adriana's home, became lovers. Adriana was perfectly content to collude in cuckolding her son, packing the wretched Monoculus off to the family estates near Bassanello. Lucrezia was thus raised in a harem-like atmosphere, where the will and desires of the Borgia sultan were the only laws. She was close to both Adriana and Giulia, describing them in a later letter as her 'mother' and 'sister' and generously praising Giluia's superior beauty, but there are indications that at times she found the brilliance of the girl who had outshone her at her own wedding rather difficult to endure.

A description written the winter following Lucrezia's marriage to Giovanni Sforza by her brother-in-law depicts the women at home. Giulia is 'a most beautiful creature. She let her hair down before me and had it dressed; it reached to her feet, never have I seen anything like it, she has the most beautiful hair. She wore a headdress of fine linen, and over it a sort of net, light as air, with golden threads woven in it. In truth it shone like the sun!' Lucrezia was obviously put out by the comparison, as she left the apartment and returned having changed her dress, a Neapolitan robe similar to Giulia's, to a violet velvet one. The writer here is Lorenzo Pucci, brother to Puccio Pucci, a Florentine who had married Giulia's sister Girolama Farnese. Girolama reported on the one-stop shop for papal favours that the three women managed from their home in the Palazzo Santa Maria. Adriana, a shrewd, intelligent woman who recognized the wealth and advantages that would accrue to her if she continued as Giulia's protector, organized the visitors and their requests, while Giulia and Lucrezia saw to it between them that they reached the pontifical ear. Lucrezia, commented the Mantuan envoy, 'had great access and could not be better, and certainly for her age she has great intelligence ... the majority of those who want favours pass through this door'. Every day, gifts from suitors arrived for the women, including not only the delicious and fashionable carp from Lake Garda but also more durable bribes in the form of valuable jewellery.

The young Countess of Pesaro, then, did not find her condition greatly altered by her marriage, except insomuch as she was now considered an adult woman and could put her share of the family passion for politics to good use. Her husband, however, had little reason to be pleased with his brilliant alliance. Giovanni Sforza had hung around the Holy City kicking his heels for several months after the ceremony, but since neither his wife nor his father-in-law seemed inclined to take much notice of him he had used the pretext of a plague epidemic in the city to receive permission to return home to Pesaro. In September, Alexander discussed his son-in-law with Ascanio Sforza, deciding, according to a letter sent to the Florentine archives from Urbino, that Giovanni should be invited to return to Rome where he would receive Lucrezia's dowry payment in full and be permitted to 'accompany his wife in everything' (i.e. consummate the marriage). In this age of deception little could be held as conclusive, but this certainly indicates that until this point, Lucrezia had not slept with her husband, and while Giovanni eventually appeared in Rome in November, he was back in Pesaro by January. It was known that he had come to 'pay his duties to His Holiness and to establish his full position with his illustrious wife'; it remains debatable whether he ever did so.

Giovanni began to realize the perilous diplomatic situation in which his ambiguous marriage had placed him. Thus far, he had passively acceded to the wishes of both Sforza and Borgia, but a situation of deepening political crisis on the peninsula began dividing his obligations in an alarming manner. By early 1494 it became clear that King Charles VIII of France was about to invade Italy with the intention of pursuing his claim to the crown of Naples, which had been disputed since the death of King Ferrante in March 1494 and was a matter of legal, rather than dynastic, succession.

The second French claim in Italy threatened Milan. Not only were the Sforza relative parvenus who had successfully promoted themselves through the marriage of Francesco and Bianca Maria Visconti; Ludovico il Moro feared that even this claim to the duchy could be proven to be legally dubious.* If the French had ambitions across the Alps, Ludovico needed to protect Milan by diverting Charles VIII's attention. Supporting his claim to Naples offered him a realistic protective tactic.

The situation of the Borgia Pope was quite different. Despite his cultivation of the Sforza connection through Lucrezia's marriage, he had begun to recognize that his own position was vulnerable

---

* The first Visconti Duke of Milan, Giangaleazzo, who had died in 1402, left a daughter, Valentina Visconti, by his first wife Isabelle de Valois of the French royal house, and two sons by his second. Giangaleazzo Visconti had supposedly left a will stating that Milan could pass to the heirs of Valentina should the male line fail. This had indeed occurred when the third Duke of Milan, Giangaleazzo's second son Filippo Maria, was obliged to nominate Francesco Sforza as his successor in right of his marriage to his illegitimate daughter Bianca Maria Visconti. Valentina Visconti had married Louis de Valois, by whom she had a son, Charles, whose own son succeeded to the French crown as Louis XII. The French kings, according to the purported will, had a better claim to Milan than the Sforza. Chroniclers talk of the existence of this will, but Ludovico supposedly had all copies destroyed.

without the support of Naples, and to incline to an anti-French policy. With the death of King Ferrante in 1494, it became necessary for all the players on the peninsula to choose their sides.

Giovanni Sforza's letter to Ludovico that month describes his divided loyalties:

> Yesterday His Holiness said to me in the presence of Monsignor [Ascanio Sforza], 'Well, Giovanni Sforza! What have you to say to me?' I answered, 'Holy Father, everyone in Rome believes that Your Holiness has entered into an agreement with the king of Naples, who is an enemy of the State of Milan. If this is so, I am in an awkward position, as I am in the pay of Your Holiness and also in that of the State of Milan ... I do not know how I can serve one party without falling out with the other.'

If Giovanni had possessed the intelligence to see it, he would have known that he was rather well placed, as Pesaro was of potential strategic importance; but rather than parlay his country for a stake in the proceedings, he succeeded only in irritating both Alexander and Il Moro, who agreed at least that he was better off out of the way.

Plague struck Rome again, and it suited the pope to have Lucrezia and his beloved Giulia removed to more sanitary surroundings. A visit to Pesaro, supposedly at the request of its people, who clamoured to see their new countess, put the best face on the whole awkward situation. Accordingly, Lucrezia, Giulia and Adriana, along with their ladies, set off on 31 May for Urbino, where they rested before travelling on to Pesaro, arriving on 8 June.

Lucrezia was delighted with her reception, as well as with the new clothes which the journey had given her the opportunity of ordering. Giulia Farnese wrote exultantly that the girls looked so magnificent that it seemed as though they had ransacked Florence for brocade. But Giovanni Sforza was being cornered into committing treachery by the Pope's demands. Alexander proposed to his daughter that her husband should leave the service of the Milanese Sforza, who were barely paying his *condottiere*'s salary, and agree to serve under the Neapolitans. Sforza dithered, then attempted rather pathetically to accept the command while communicating the movements of his troops to his Sforza cousins via the Milanese envoy Raimondo di Raimondi, thus making a gesture of continued allegiance. Giovanni Sforza's personal dilemma of conflicting loyalties reflected in microcosm the shreds of ruptured alliances which, in 1494, would soon plunge the peninsula into a devastating war.

CHAPTER 10

Sibling Rivalry

1493–1495

'So there is no risk of us being alike'

ISABELLA D'ESTE

In October 1493, any residual loyalties between the ruling dynasties of Ferrara and Naples were weakened with the death of Duchess Eleonora. She had been unwell since the previous year, though she kept the gravity of her condition from her daughter Isabella, who was expecting her first child. When the news of her death did leak out, Isabella, though greivously struck by her mother's death, typically met it as a fashion challenge. Spies were sent to investigate what sort of mourning her sister Beatrice had ordered, and Isabella wrote that 'since we are obliged to wear black crepe during this very sad time', it had better be of the finest quality. She was informed that Beatrice had opted for a *panno bruno*, a dark woollen dress, though the informant was frustrated by not being able to get a good look at the Duchess of Bari as 'she was always locked up in deep discussion with the Duke'.

The sisters grieved over their mother's death, though they remained competitive. The approaching wedding of Bianca Maria Sforza* was a source of rivalry, though as they were in mourning they ought not to have attended. Beatrice succeeded in having the strict mourning code waived for a day and described gleefully to Isabella the dark velvet dress with gold panels she was having specially made. She added that since the dress was so sombre, 'I have decided to have a belt designed to look like that of a friar's, only

* The eldest legitimate daughter of Duke Galeazzo Sforza, by Bona of Savoy.

this belt shall be made of giant pearls, clasped at the waist by a very large ruby.' Another letter added condescendingly that 'I don't really want new inventions because of the pain of our mother's death, but I must dress appropriately for the occasion, painful though it is. I have therefore sent a drawing by Niccolò da Correggio so that you know what I shall be wearing in case you don't want to wear the same clothes.' For once outdone, Isabella replied curtly that she would not be using Correggio, 'so there is no risk of us being alike'.

Beatrice's secretive discussions with her husband were doubtless on more serious subjects than dresses. Bianca Maria's wedding to the Holy Roman Emperor elect, the thirty-four-year-old Archduke Maximilian, was the final step in Ludovico's long-plotted scheme to claim Milan as his own. In return for a huge dowry of 400,000 ducats and a trousseau worth 100,000 more Maximilian had agreed to marry Bianca Maria and ensure Ludovico's investiture with the Duchy of Milan – since the duchy was an Imperial fief, Maximilian could confer it on whom he pleased. There was one more clause attached, more for the sake of propriety than of law. Giangaleazzo, Bianca Maria's brother and Lord of Milan, had to die.

Bona of Savoy was once more trundled out of exile for the proxy wedding ceremony, so too Giangaleazzo and his Duchess Isabella d'Aragona. News of Ludovico's investiture had begun to leak, so Isabella knew her days as Milan's First Lady were numbered. Heavily pregnant, she dragged herself through the wearying ceremonies, shortly afterwards giving birth to a daughter, Ippolita, named for her own mother Ippolita Maria.

The imperial marriage turned out to be Giangaleazzo's last appearance in public. Isabella had been nursing him through an illness, and the duke travelled straight from the wedding ceremonies to his sickroom at Pavia. His condition worsened daily, with some chroniclers noting that the ducal couple were kept so chronically short of money that they lived on gruel (though household accounts demonstrate that some expenditure was admitted for a display of public parity in the matter of the quality of Isabella's dresses). Isabella and Giangaleazzo suffered the cruellest deprivation of all, that of hope – the hope that the duke, his Neapolitan princess and their children would ever have a future in Milan.

The gloomy atmosphere of the Lombardy was lightened in December, when Beatrice received news of the birth of a niece, Isabella d'Este's daughter Eleonora Violante Maria. Isabella's own cold reception in the world had clearly left lasting scars, as she proceeded to welcome her own daughter in a similarly frigid fashion. She wrote resignedly, 'you will have heard that I have a daughter and that both she and I are doing well, though I am sorry not to have a son. But since it is the will of God, she will be dear to me.' Francesco Gonzaga was less equivocal, delighting in his daughter and showing her off in her cradle to Giovanni de' Medici, who had come to Mantua as proxy godparent for Lorenzo di Pierfrancesco de' Medici. (The child might be a girl, but when it came to godparents Isabella was as ever determined to have only the best.) Eleonora's birth introduced a note of sweetness into the correspondence of the d'Este sisters which had been absent for some time. Relations between their husbands became increasingly suspicious, and Beatrice wrote as though she wished to restore confidence within the family, lovingly congratulating her sister and concluding 'Quello che desidera la Signoria Vostra'.

Domestic relations elsewhere also boded ill. Archduke Maximilian was an amiable character, athletic, somewhat eccentric, always short of money and full of madcap schemes which never quite came to realization. Initially he seemed satisfied with his wife, as he endeavoured to expand his power base in the peninsula and, moreover, she had come complete with a ceremonial sword consecrated by Pope Alexander VI. Yet the Visconti strain of peculiarity soon began to manifest itself, and Bianca's habit of suddenly rolling around on the floor at dinner in what she obviously considered to be a playful and winning fashion soon began to grate. Bianca occupied more and more of her time in rolling about the palace, despite which Maximilian failed to get an heir. Thoroughly disgusted, the unfortunate archduke began to absent himself from his wife, whose mental health grew more unstable with every year she spent away from Milan.

Despite its unsatisfactory results, Bianca's marriage had nevertheless served its purpose, as Ludovico Sforza felt closer to achieving the long-awaited investiture. Isabella d'Aragona, despairing at Pavia, grasped at the possibilities opened up by the death of her grandfather King Ferrante of Naples soon after the birth of Isabella d'Este's daughter. Ferrante had been trying desperately to preserve relations with Milan and had decided on an embassy to the duchy, but fell ill with fever as he was planning the voyage to Genoa. The Kingdom now passed to Alfonso, Duke of Calabria, the widower of Ippolita Maria Sforza, and in her father Isabella found a sterner champion than the old king. Alfonso had been enraged with Ludovico ever since Isabella had written to him complaining of her treatment at the birth of Beatrice's son, and had pressed for action at the time, but he was overruled by his father's long-term political plans. Now secure in his inheritance of the Kingdom, he was determined to challenge the power of a man whose ambitions appeared increasingly crazed and despotic. Alfonso's inheritance was confirmed by a letter from the Milanese envoy to Rome which informed Ludovico that Alexander VI intended to address his condolences to King Alfonso II; but Charles of France also pressed the Pontiff to acknowledge his own claim to the Kingdom. Italy, France and Isabella d'Aragona held their collective breaths.

The Duchess of Milan and her father were not the only ones weary of Ludovico's increasing grandiosity. After Bianca Maria's wedding he and Beatrice had retired to their country residence at Vigevano, where in a superbly illuminated document Ludovico endowed Beatrice generously with lands near Pavia, Cussago and Novara. Isabella, Marchioness of Mantua began to feel irritatingly like a poor relation in comparison with her sister's ever more brilliant status. She wrote to her husband that she was tiring of the peremptory 'requests' she received from her brother-in-law Ludovico. Francesco Gonzaga had been approached for alliance over the Naples question by both the French and the Aragonese, but Isabella confronted him with her own conflict of political loyalty in the matter of fresh fish for the Milanese court. 'I am quite willing that fresh fish be sent to Milan regularly,' she grizzled, 'but not every week as he requests in his imperious fashion, lest we should appear as his feudatories and the fish a tribute due to him.' Isabella had a well-earned reputation as a dreadful skinflint when it came to any expenditure other than her own. The jealousy of the Gonzaga couple for the Sforza was rooted in good old-fashioned snobbery, though its manifestations were distinctly suburban. The Gonzaga and the d'Este were of the ancient nobility, yet seemed to be nobodies in comparison with the upstart but monied Sforza. While Isabella had to pawn her jewels, Beatrice could order ten times their value every week. Worse still to Isabella's mind, Francesco was shown up as very much the country squire to Ludovico's metropolitan sophisticate. While Ludovico took pleasure in the reconstruction of the Duomo and patronage of Milan's university, chats with Leonardo da Vinci and studies in his library, the stubby, hairy Marquis of Mantua could think of no greater joy in life than a night under canvas in anticipation of a good battle.

While Isabella d'Este scribbled away on stately matters such as Lake Garda's fish, her cousin Isabella d'Aragona made a pilgrimage to Loreto to pray for Giangaleazzo's health and Charles VIII announced his intention of receiving the crown of Naples and continuing onwards for a crusade in Jerusalem. Ludovico had carefully embroidered a brilliant chivalric tapestry to smother the rather feeble brains of his young ally. The distant claim to Naples, dating back to the thirteenth century, and the promise of the everlasting glory of Holy War, such as no French king had achieved since the days of St Louis, conjured up for Charles the most alluring notions of romance and adventure. Charles was desperate for death or glory, but Ludovico urged him to stay his hand until it could be discerned where the crucial papal allegiance would lie.

The French king had little to recommend him personally as an ally. The envoy Guicciardini claimed he was bodily weak, 'foul and deformed ... more of a monster than a man' and a cretin to boot. Charles was given to rages and was more than usually susceptible to flattery, dismissing any adviser who dared disagree with him. He was extravagantly generous, but even this was dismissed as incontinence, deriving from 'coldnesse and slacknesse of the spirit'. Charles had an outsized head and a mouth so wide it resembled a gash from a knife. Stuttering and spluttering, his speech sounded as ungainly as his misshapen body looked, and even Philippe de Commines, who discerned a certain sweetness in his character, felt obliged to concede that he was 'little' in sense as well as stature. Charles may have been possessed of a childish kindness, but what graces he had were immature in comparison with the sinuous reasoning of a hardened politician such as Ludovico. Il Moro distracted Charles by sending Galeazzo Sanseverino on an embassy to France.

Galeazzo, who was descended from a disaffected Neapolitan family and would soon marry Il Moro's natural daughter Bianca and become his son-in-law, was a beautiful, exceptionally arrogant man, charming when he wished, murderous on the battlefield and in the bedroom. He proved a great favourite with Ludovico, who was delighted when the French king offered his favourite 'son' an intimate visit with certain royal ladies. Charles invited Sanseverino to choose from among the royal mistresses a lady with whom he 'could spend a few hours in private discussion', reporting that Sanseverino had a very good discussion, without much talking. He also flattered Charles's reputation as a sensualist with gifts of scent, jennets from Spain and armour for the royal steed, while the French queen received a Spanish gown of the utmost sumptuousness. Ludovico occupied himself in the meantime with an exciting new plan for the castello's privies.

Under pressure from the powerful Orsini clan in Rome, the Pope finally declared for the Aragona in April. Alexander extracted a high price from King Alfonso, whose natural daughter Sancia became betrothed to his youngest son by Vannozza, the barely pubescent Joffre Borgia. Joffre would receive the principality of Squillace, Juan Gandia those of Tricario, Carinola and Calrimointe, while Cesare Borgia saw his benefices hugely augmented. It was the moment for Ludovico's alliance to march into action, but Charles dallied on at Lyon, caught in a snare prepared by Alfonso. Charles was so accustomed to women leaping eagerly into the royal bed that any who resisted him became all the more fascinating. Alfonso sent a particularly beautiful girl who was to be rewarded if she did *not* submit to the king, and she managed Charles so effectively that Alfonso had time to get himself crowned and send an emissary warning Ludovico that if the rumours of the French pact were true, 'Signor Ludovico will be the first to rue the day when the French set foot in Italy'. In June Alfonso sent a force to attack Ludovico's duchy of Bari and declared war on Milan.

Pandora's box had been opened, but Ludovico Sforza had not as yet realized it. In July 1494, Louis Duke d'Orléans crossed the Alps at the head of the French army and stationed himself at Asti in Piedmont, a fief he had inherited from his grandmother Valentina Visconti. Louis was Charles's senior by a decade and a far more capable man than his cousin. Ludovico agreed to meet the man who would become his nemesis at Alessandria on the 13th. Their encounter featured the usual elaborate theatricals of Renaissance courtesy, but Ludovico had finally become alive to the fact that this time the stakes were higher than ever before. The parvenu duke's pact with the superpower prince would appear in the end as a bargain with the devil, with Charles as a deceptively bumbling Mephistopheles.

Naturally, the Gonzaga were agog to keep abreast of developments. Isabella received minutely detailed reports from her envoy Benedetto Capilupi as to Beatrice's part in events. Such a great prince as Louis had Beatrice's ladies giggling with anticipation, and the duchess arrived at the head of a squadron of her most glamorous women, all desperate to discuss the burning question of whether Louis would kiss them, French-style, or adopt an Italian greeting. Would they all receive a kiss from His Highness, would he kiss some and not others, ought they to kiss him back? Beatrice rose to the occasion by announcing that once more she would be obliged, regretfully, to leave off her mourning 'and dance, and be kissed by the duke who will kiss all the maids of honour and all the ladies of the court according to French fashion'. In the event, Beatrice was deprived of her *bisous*, as the duke appeared more concerned with the imminent conflict. The Neapolitans took the war northwards with a naval raid on Genoa, a Milanese possession. Keen to display Ludovico in the best light, commentators on the war council sneered at the brutal habits and appearance of the French, and their unsophisticated goggling at all things Italian. Isabella d'Este agreed with them. She had avidly taken up Ludovico's invitation to inspect the troops as they marched through the city of Parma, but admitted that the martial parade was more like a ragtail provincial circus, with the horsemen unable to discipline the pace of their mounts, and Louis himself decidedly foolish-looking, with a head so tiny it appeared it could barely contain any brains at all.

Appearances aside, it seemed that the French would meet with no resistance in their progress down the peninsula. Gianandrea di Boccaccio, the Ferrarese envoy to the Holy See, felt confident that the Italians would recognize what was happening and react in time, but they appeared 'mesmerised by the French advance'. Guicciardini damned the King of France, saying 'he brought all these calamities to Italy' and that he was 'void of almost all the gifts of nature and the mind', but in fact the misery descending on the peninsula was a consequence of the Italians' own blindness. The French chronicler Philippe de Commines took a gentler view of Charles, describing him as enjoying the expedition with the gaiety of a child arranging his toy soldiers. Neither he nor Ludovico Sforza understood the power of the demon they had unleashed.

After hearing, to the astonishment of this largely illiterate nobility, a Latin oration of welcome by a young child at Asti, Charles and his company rode on to meet Duke Ercole of Ferrara in early September. Ercole remained suspicious of Pope Alexander and planned to give the French free passage through his duchy, riding out with Ludovico to greet them. Beatrice finally had her chance to meet His Most Christian Majesty at the castle of Annona nearby, accompanied by Ludovico's daughter Bianca and her new bridegroom Galeazzo Sanseverino. Beatrice held a banquet for Charles, determined to impress upon him the superiority of the Italian lifestyle in all its sophistication, riches and refinement. Beatrice accompanied her choir, musicians, and, to cater to Charles's well-known tastes, eighty of her most attractive ladies, gorgeously dressed, their hair styled in the latest modern fashion and glittering with gems. She wrote exultantly to her sister: 'At about noonday the King came here to pay me a friendly visit with the chief lords of his court and remained for about three hours with me and my ladies, conversing with the greatest familiarity and affection. I assure you that no prince in the world could have made himself more agreeable.' Dancing with her ladies, she added, seemed to give the king 'much pleasure', and she herself was reported to have performed the unfamiliar French dances 'wonderfully well' (though the other pleasures the party took among the ladies of Milan were disastrous for the country, as they introduced syphilis as well as French kissing). Charles's sister, the Duchesse de Bourbon, had sent her envoy with his party with the express mission of describing the attire and conduct of the glamorous Italian ladies. A portrait of Beatrice was painted for the Duchesse, and the envoy was able to describe her:

> First of all, when she arrived, she was on a horse with trappings of gold and crimson velvet. She herself wore a robe of gold and green brocade and a fine linen *gorgette* turned back over it. Her head was richly adorned with pearls and her hair hung down behind in one long coil with a ribbon twisted round it. She wore a crimson silk hat, made very much like our own, with five or six red and grey feathers and with all that on her head sat up as straight on horseback as if she had been a man.

Twenty-two ladies rode out with the duchess, with more following in six chariots hung with green velvet and cloth of gold. The next day, that of Charles's visit, the king found the duchess: 'magnificently arrayed after the fashion of the country in a green satin robe. The bodice of her gown was loaded with diamonds, pearls and rubies, both in front and behind and the sleeves were made very tight and slashed so as to show the white chemise underneath, and tied up with grey silk ribbon which hung down almost to the ground. Her throat was bare and adorned with very large pearls ...'.

Charles's progress was interrupted by a brief attack of smallpox, but by October the French were at Piacenza, and then moved on to Pavia. Two boar hunts and a magnificent banquet thrilled Charles and his entourage, who were also struck by the rich fertility of the countryside and expressed themselves impressed by Ludovico's hobby-horse, his model farm, and the racing stud supervised by Sanseverino. Thus far, the supposed war had more the air of a gallant progress, but at Pavia reality suddenly became more sinister.

Accounts vary as to the details of Charles's meeting with his cousin Giangaleazzo Sforza, but most chroniclers concur that it took place. The young duke's condition was still precarious – seeing him at Bianca Maria's wedding, his mother Bona of Savoy is reported to have cried out in tears that her son was 'ridotto a un larva' (reduced to a larval state, a shadow of himself). Charles arrived at Pavia to the customary fanfare of triumphal arches, singing maidens and magistrates' speeches, and toured the famous university, but he was anxious about the possibility of assassination and requested to be lodged in the castello, where Giangaleazzo and Isabella d'Aragona were living in semi-confinement. Ludovico proudly showed off the castello's treasure, its library, pictures and sculptures, but this failed to disguise the real motive for Charles's presence. According to the Venetian diarist Marin Sanudo, Isabella d'Aragona refused to see the king, then grabbed a dagger and held it to her breast, crying that she would kill herself rather than meet her father's most dangerous enemy. Prevailed upon to speak with Charles, she then threw herself at his feet and implored him to save Alfonso and his throne. Another version has Isabella welcoming Charles at the great entrance to the castello, holding her son Francesco, the supposed heir apparent to Milan. Giangaleazzo himself appeared finally cognisant of his position and begged the French king to take care of his wife and children, adding that Charles must protect his little son by ensuring his inheritance.

Charles was vague about the fate of Naples, but took Francesco in his arms and comforted Isabella, reassuring her rather obliquely that he would protect the child 'as if [he] were my own son'. Charles later told Philippe de Commines that he had been shocked by the condition of the ducal family, and had it not been for the hovering presence of Ludovico, whose support Charles needed at the time, he would have done more. Commines reported that 'The King spoke with him [Giangaleazzo] and told me their words, which only related to general subjects, for he feared to displease Ludovico; all the same he told me afterwards that he would have willingly given him a warning. And the duchess [Isabella] threw herself on her knees before Ludovico, begging him to have pity on her father [King Alfonso] and brother. To which he replied that he could do nothing and told her to pray for her husband, or rather for herself who was still so young and fair a lady.'

Giangaleazzo fatally weakened and the physicians declared him mortally ill, and sinking. Those obliged to enter his sickroom felt overcome by the sickly stench emanating from his diseased body. Unable to rise from his bed, the Duke of Milan lay with the shutters drawn and the curtains closed; through his shirt his skeletal frame could easily be discerned. Giangaleazzo's condition, as well as Isabella d'Aragona's shrieking hysteria, painfully embarrassed Ludovico. He rushed his royal guest off to Piacenza in the middle of October. Giangaleazzo, his stomach now protruding with malnutrition, had given up hope. As though wishing to die, he called for spiced wine, apples and pears, and forced them down, despite the agonizing pain this caused him. He was able to swallow a sleeping-draught, and his four physicians (whose attentions were quite as deadly as the acidic, bloating fruits), sent messengers after Ludovico to reassure him that although not out of danger, Giangaleazzo seemed more cheerful and composed. On the evening of 20 October, Giangaleazzo asked for his two favourite horses to be brought to his chamber, and appeared gratified by the sight of them. He asked his servant whether Ludovico had been saddened by his condition, and the man replied soothingly that he believed so. Giangaleazzo then made his confession and asked for his greyhounds, stroking them and chatting with his wife before falling asleep. He died that night.

CHAPTER II

Pandora's Box

1494–1495

'Put not your trust in princes'

PSALM 146

The French advance moved down the peninsula with the speed of a contagion. The Italians' astonishing complacency in the face of the invasion may perhaps be attributed to the fact that, for generations, they had nearly always bested foreign invaders. In the 1440s the celebrated *condottiere* Bartolomeo Colleoni had trounced the French in the battles of Bosco Marengo and Romagnano Sesia. Besides, despite the fact the Milanese had been defeated by the Swiss at Giornico in 1478, they had received their revenge nine years later at the Battle of Ponte di Crevola. Yet diplomacy and cunning had served the Italians more effectively than martial planning, in that conflict was resolved, or avoided altogether, by minor skirmishes, the assassination of individuals or back-room plotting.

Unlike the French, who retained the memory of the Hundred Years' War in the third generation, the Italians had believed themselves secure, immune to the reality of conflict which remained at the centre of European dynastic politics. The French were seasoned, and they were savage. Even so, the 30,000 soldiers who had crossed the Alps with Charles VIII were not an entirely different breed from the mercenaries who fought for the city states. But the French had a large and highly mobile artillery train, with cannon firing metal shot. It is possible that Charles had negotiated separate strategies with the rulers of each of the states he passed through; when faced with the prospect of the French army encamped beyond the city

walls, those states remained largely passive. Having ineluctably enabled the French advance, it was now too late for them to resist. What
would a refusal to allow French passage achieve except for burned
countryside, razed towns and massacred citizens?

Piero de' Medici declared that Florence would stand firm against
all invaders and continue her support of Naples. His strong line,
however, could not be described as entirely representative. The
Medici no longer held Florence in their thrall; the powerful grasp
held by Cosimo *Pater Patriae*, Piero 'the Gouty' and most of all by
Il Magnifico had weakened steadily since the death of the last. The
precarious position of the Medici bank and the increased wealth of
the junior branch of the family as opposed to the senior, were causing dissent between the two sides of the family, while Piero's neglect
of the Medici client network had diminished their influence in the
republic. Nevertheless, they maintained an appearance of harmony
and, even as the French prepared to swarm down the peninsula, the
Florentine elite were planning their traditional spring social season.
But the suppressed tension within the Medici ranks flared up when,
at one such event, Piero and Giovanni quarrelled over an attractive
and certainly not invisible woman. Piero publicly slapped Giovanni's
face and left Giovanni unable to issue the challenge which convention demanded of such treatment. With the dispute made public,
Piero felt he had to contain his unruly relatives and accused Giovanni
and Lorenzo of corresponding with Charles VIII, a charge which
subsequent events made likely to have been accurate. The two men
were placed under house arrest at Cafaggiolo, the family villa in the
Mugello, where they sat out a fearsome Tuscan summer.

In early September 1494 the Neapolitan troops of Alfonso II,
moving north to confront the French, succeeded in taking the
Ligurian coastal town of Rapallo, which came under the jurisdiction of Genoa in the Sforza domains. On the 8th, 2,500 Swiss Guards
retook Rapallo, massacring its citizens in the process and claiming
it for Charles VIII. Alfonso was forced to march for Naples with
his tattered army. There remained 250 miles of country between
the French and the borders of the Kingdom. Venice declared herself neutral, while the Pope sanctioned the free passage of Charles's
troops across the Territories of St Peter. With only Florence standing

between the French and the Neapolitans, Charles halted the march at the border of the republic's territories and demanded that his men be permitted passage. Piero returned no answer for five days. To encourage him a little, the exasperated Charles attacked the Florentine fortress of Fivizzano and made examples of every last member of the garrison. He sent another envoy to Piero, insisting that Florence surrender.

Many members of the Signoria refused to support Piero's initial policy of resistance, and he was further undermined when Giovanni and Lorenzo escaped from Cafaggiolo and rode to join the French, where they informed Charles of the dissent behind the city walls. Piero tried to rally the Florentines, ordering that the fortresses be placed on alert and attempting to summon the city mercenaries, but received little or no support. Desperate, he set out to seek a personal audience with Charles at Sarzana. Though it was a chivalric gesture, especially for a Florentine, Charles received it with less than *parfait courtoisie*. He rudely insisted on the immediate cessation of the port cities of Pisa and Livorno plus a number of strategic fortresses, and Piero did not have the stomach to call the king's bluff. Charles could hardly have continued his advance with a hostile fortress such as Sarzanello – all but impregnable at the time – at his rear. When Piero returned to Florence on 8 November and went to announce his decision at the Palazzo della Signoria, he found the great doors had been closed on him.

From the relative safety of the Palazzo Medici, Piero could hear his name being cried through the streets as a traitor. Those who had advised the city's immediate surrender now conveniently forgot that it was only Piero who had attempted some sort of resistance and denounced him for betraying the republic. Piero's acquiescence had in the end saved the city and its treasures, a gesture for which he has never been recognized and for which the cultural world has reason to be grateful. He also realized that he had been outmanoeuvred and that, with Lorenzo Il Magnifico gone, the Florentines were no longer prepared to give the Medici their unequivocal support. In the dawn of 9 November, Piero, his wife and two small children quietly slipped out of the palazzo and left Florence through the Gate of San Gallo. Next day, the Signoria formally pronounced a sentence of exile in perpetuity. Lorenzo Il Magnifico's son had become an outcast with a price of 4,000 florins on his head.

On 17 November Charles VIII rode into Florence in the van of an army of 20,000 troops. The much vaunted but long-suppressed republicanism of the Florentines had finally been reawakened, and already they had done all they could to eradicate the reminders of their city's greatest dynasty. Medici emblems were stripped from their palazzi, the Palazzo Medici itself was looted and the homes of two principal Medici administrators were put to the torch. The Signoria sent troops to occupy the Palazzo Medici and began removing the family's collections in the name of the republic. They carried off anything that could be moved, including the remains of Lorenzo Il Magnifico's hoard of jewellery and Donatello's statue of David. It may have pleased the Florentines to compare their city with the biblical underdog, but for now Goliath was in the ascendant. Charles remained for eleven days in Florence, lodging in the few rooms of the Palazzo Medici that the mob had left unsacked. The king proceeded to ask the Florentines for a colossal sum, threatening otherwise to sack the city. But by quartering his troops within the walls he had placed himself in a trap, something both he and his hosts knew all too well. Eventually a settlement was reached, and the king departed with his troops, headed for Rome.

Pope Alexander awaited the French arrival in the Holy City from within the fortress of the Castel Sant'Angelo. As New Year's Eve approached, word arrived that Charles's armies had been sighted, and by 31 December the French guns stood trained on the castle walls. In a masterstroke of theatre, Alexander announced that if a single salvo were fired, he would appear in person on the battlements with the Host raised above his head. This placed Charles in an impossible dilemma. He could hardly fire on God's anointed, let alone the Holy Sacrament. Given that the French were welcomed as a liberating army as they marched through the Porta del Popolo, Alexander may well have sat quaking on his throne, believing that his papacy was doomed if Charles called his bluff. His enemy Cardinal della Rovere, himself covetous of the tiara, had demanded a general council to be summoned to call for the Pope to be removed, and Alexander knew that if he lost the support of the Romans della Rovere would be able to oust him.

Charles might have waited until the old Borgia fox showed himself before his lair, but the fleshpots of Rome proved too seductive. Making no attempt to control his troops, he gave himself up to the beauties of the city, whether or not they welcomed his attentions. His soldiers followed their leader's example. Women and young girls were repeatedly raped and then killed, either from the internal wounds or the expedient of a slit throat. The victims' bodies were abused so cruelly that even the most primitive of the 'barbarian' invaders had no taste for them. Assassination became endemic, with Romans paying Frenchmen for the discreet settling of scores, and the streets became a horrific carnival of rapacious, carousing soldiers. Convention decreed, *noblesse oblige*, that the property of grandee belligerents be left mutually unmolested, but now the noble families of Rome found their property sacked and desecrated in the most vulgar and savage fashion. Even Alexander's former mistress had her palazzo sacked and looted.

Thus the French managed to alienate their sympathizers while their King was too busy rutting to notice. The news of their activities spread across the peninsula, causing particular concern among Jewish communities. Alexander, for all his myriad faults, held an enlightened policy towards Jews and left them unmolested, but the French now seized the Roman 'Christ-killers' and put them to death with the garotte. Any anti-French protests were similarly silenced and the bodies of the victims strung up as a warning to others in the Campo de' Fiori. Since Rome depended on imports for survival (an atavistic reminder of the Empire), its only industries being pilgrims and tourists, supplies now ran low and hunger began to spread among the populace.

Yet still Charles felt himself unable to take the Castel Sant'Angelo. Fate conveniently intervened on 10 January 1495, when a large section of the fortress walls collapsed, killing three of the papal bodyguard. Charles made use of the breach in the fortifications not to impeach or imprison Alexander, but to fling himself at the holy feet. The story of Alexander's magnificent facing-down of the French cannon had now spread, and psychology and Charles's stupidity carried the day. Those who had treacherously welcomed the French recognized their probable fates. If Rome fell, the French were keen to press on to Naples and the Romans equally anxious to be rid of their ghastly guests. Alexander quickly perceived that he had a sapling to play with, and one that could be used to sweep his house clean. A few cosy strolls in the gardens of the Vatican, with the Pope calling the king 'my first-born son', soon evaporated any of Charles's rhetoric about papal abuses. They spent hours each day together, Alexander playing the sagacious adviser to the young man who was obliged to carry such heavy burdens. The temporal and spiritual monarchs soon came to a cheerful agreement and signed a pact of non-aggression, permitting French passage through papal territories. Finally, on 17 January, a Mass was held for the departing troops.

Alexander had managed what few men could have achieved by holding their nerve. The boy king, who had had all Italy at his mercy just two weeks previously, had been completely bamboozled by the supremely able Spanish pope. Even on the question of Naples he received no satisfaction, the Pope only answering that he would give 'careful investigation' and 'close examination' to the French claim there. Charles would have done well to heed the maxim 'Put not your trust in princes', for in truth this prince of the Church had utterly outwitted him.

On 28 January the French left for Naples. Cesare Borgia rode in the vast procession, promised to Charles as a hostage for his father's continuing favour. Naturally, the Borgias had already worked out a plan of escape, so when the French halted at Velletri Cesare simply exchanged his clothes for those of a groom and galloped back to Rome. Charles was incandescent, remarking that 'all Italians are dirty dogs – the Pope is the worst of them all'. But he continued south, and Cesare's flight was soon put out of his mind by the arrival of the Spanish ambassador, Fonseca, representing Their Majesties Queen Isabella and King Ferdinand of Spain. Fonseca implored Charles to heed a message of protest from the Spanish monarchs, but Charles grandly declared that the Pope was to judge his actions once Naples was secured and this was the only decision that he would heed. When Fonseca refused to accept this, Charles took the extraordinary diplomatic step of telling the truth, saying that since he had come so far he was not about to turn back. Fonseca then tore the Franco-Spanish treaty to shreds before arrogant Charles's eyes. The pile of parchment at the king's feet now meant that his only friend was his beloved Alexander VI, who had already deceived him.

Meanwhile Ludovico Sforza had anticipated the direction of events for some time. Even as his French allies reached Rome, he had written an appraisal of Charles VIII which disingenuously considered that: 'the King of France is young and of poor judgement; he is not advised as he ought to be ... the King is haughty and ambitious beyond all imagining and he has esteem for no one'.

Isabella d'Este had also altered her attitude towards the French, whose commander, Gilbert de Montpensier, was after all her brother-in-law, the husband of Francesco Gonzaga's sister, Chiara. She now invited Chiara to stay with her while the French were campaigning, though her growing revulsion at the news of French barbarities in Rome might have put a strain on the family visit. As opinion of the French soured, Ludovico realized it would soon be time for him to turn his coat. Anxious to secure the support of Isabella and Francesco, suspecting the latter of a secret correspondence with Alfonso II, the now exiled King of Naples, he issued an urgent invitation to Isabella to visit Milan, with the aim of assisting at the birth of her sister Beatrice's second son.

Isabella was indeed present at the birth of Francesco Sforza in January 1495, bringing fulsome congratulations from her husband, though politically he and Ludovico were becoming increasingly estranged. The day after her arrival from Mantua she took the opportunity to visit her childhood friend, the Dowager Duchess of Milan. With the news of her father's exile from his kingdom, Isabella d'Aragona lost what remained of her wits. Draped as ever in black and heavily veiled, she spent her days in hysterics or sunk in a depressive stupor. Much to Ludovico Sforza's irritation, she insisted on referring to him as 'Il Maestro'. The Marchioness of Mantua reported to her husband:

> I found her in a large room with the walls hung with black and the windows covered so barely any light could enter and only just enough air to prevent me suffocating; she was wearing a black

cloth cloak and a black veil over her head. Her profound mourning
moved me and filled my heart with compassion and sorrow to such
a point that I could not prevent shedding tears myself. I condoled
with her on your behalf and my own, she was extremely grateful
for my sympathy. Then she sent for her children and seeing them I
could not restrain my emotions.

Shocked at the Dowager Duchess's condition, Isabella was anxious to return to Mantua; but she remained not only until baby
Francesco was christened, holding him at the font, but until the
end of the Carnival season. This gave her an opportunity to see her
brother Alfonso d'Este, also in Milan with his Sforza bride, Anna.
Their marriage had been unhappy from the start, as Alfonso had a
taste for low-class prostitutes of both sexes and took no trouble to
conceal this from his wife; but Isabella and Anna took comfort in the
magnificent Carnival entertainments organized in a city that was
being transformed by Leonardo da Vinci. Isabella wrote, describing the parties, feasts and drives through the parks, conceding that
Ludovico was indeed a 'maestro' of lavish entertaining, and that his
skill would incite 'envy' in Mantua. Although the new Duke and
Duchess of Milan seemed almost at the zenith of their power and
popularity, Isabella admitted that she felt uneasy and that Ludovico
seemed nervous. Isabella was torn. Her political sympathies now
lay with her husband against the French, but to wish them failure
would be to undermine, so far as she understood it, the position of
Beatrice and her husband. She returned to Mantua towards the end
of February loaded with good wishes and a present of two fat oxen
as a gift from Ludovico to Francesco Gonzaga. Ludovico provided
her with gold brocade cloths embroidered with doves as tokens of
his esteem and wish for concord, and the two d'Este sisters parted
emotionally. Later Beatrice was to write, 'whether I am outside or
in I seem to see your face everywhere. I miss you and feel a terrible
grief.' Isabella d'Aragona was now incapable of reason and flitted
ghostlike about the castello, muttering like a shrouded Cassandra as
the marchioness took her leave.

Isabella d'Este was not present to hear the bells of Milan pealing
in celebration of the crowning of Charles VIII in the Cathedral at

Naples. For Ludovico, those bells rang a different tune, his own mastery of the political quickstep. On 27 February he wrote two letters: one to Charles congratulating him on adding the crown of Naples to those which he already wore, the other to the Doge of Venice, ratifying Milanese support of a Holy League against the French.

Charles's trust in the Borgia Pope had been ludicrously misguided. Barely had the dust settled behind the French on their road to Naples than Alexander VI put in train a diplomatic novelty – a pan-European alliance against the French. The Holy League, or League of Venice, was proclaimed on 31 March 1495, just a month after Charles's coronation. The papacy, Milan, Venice, the Aragonese and the Holy Roman Empire agreed to combine to drive Charles from the peninsula. Twenty-five thousand troops were to be mustered under the command of Isabella d'Este's husband Francesco Gonzaga. Six weeks later, on Palm Sunday, the League's ambassadors processed slowly around St Mark's Square in Venice to receive a formal blessing. Ludovico wrote that 'today brings the dawn of peace and prosperity for Italy'. His cynical manipulation of the vain and foolish French king might have brought him his coveted dukedom, but Ludovico still believed he could save Milan and the peninsula from destruction.

CHAPTER 12

The Immaculate Duchess Lucrezia

1494–1498

'Thankless and treacherous Giulia ... you signify and declare
your intention of not coming here ... Though we judged the
evil of your soul and that of the man who guides you, we could
not believe that you could act with such perfidy and ingratitude.'

POPE ALEXANDER VI

The spiritual leader of Christendom remained sexually possessed by
the twenty-year-old woman Giulia Farnese. Alexander VI's obsession with her had not diminished; indeed, writing to her now in 1494,
with Charles VIII's troops poised to advance on Rome, it seemed
that he cared for nothing but the recovery of his mistress.

Giulia had not returned from Pesaro at the end of the summer as
the Pope had expected. Anxious for the safety of his beloved in the
light of the imminent French invasion, Alexander wanted Giulia in
Rome where he could protect her. Giulia, though, had been summoned to her family home at Capodimonte, where her brother
Angelo lay desperately ill. She and Adriana left Pesaro immediately
without seeking the Pontiff's permission, which inspired an angry
letter from Alexander to Lucrezia, who had remained behind: 'Truly,
Lord Giovanni and yourself have displayed very little thought for me
in this departure of Madonna Adriana and Giulia: for you should have
remembered ... that such a sudden departure without our knowledge would cause us the greatest displeasure.' When Giulia and her
brother Cardinal Alessandro Farnese arrived at Capodimonte, it was
to find their brother dead, the shock of which made them both ill
with grief. Alexander thought to send them one of the papal doctors,
but was determined to see Giulia as soon as possible. From Pesaro,
Giulia had reported to her lover that despite the entertainments laid
on daily by Giovanni Sforza to welcome his wife Lucrezia, the new

Countess of Pesaro, she could take no pleasure in the visit as 'your Holiness is not here and my every happiness and wellbeing depends on Your Holiness'. 'All is mockery,' she wrote, except being at her lover's feet. She had disingenuously described the appearance of a visitor to Lucrezia's little court, Caterina Gonzaga di Montevecchio, and Alexander had replied like a besotted teenager: 'Giulia, darling daughter . . . although you extend yourself in your description of the beauties of that person who could not be worthy to fit your shoes . . . everyone who writes to you says that next to you she appeared as a mere lantern next to the sun . . . we thus understand your perfection, of which truly we have never been in doubt.' Of everyone in the world, he assured her, it was he who loved her most. Yet despite these exchanges, Giulia now appeared oddly reluctant to return to Rome. Her husband Orsino Orsini had been summoned to join the Neapolitans in Umbria, along with the rest of the Orsini men, but he lingered at Città di Castello, claiming illness, before slinking off home to Bassanello, the Orsini property between Orte and Viterbo.

Perhaps the precarious position of the Pope in regard to the French advance bolstered his courage, but Orsino Orsini now decided to make a stand against the man who had been cuckolding him for years. Even were he to lose his life and his possessions ten times over, he declared, he would not permit his wife to return to Rome, demanding instead that she join him at Bassanello. Alexander could not afford a scandal, given Charles's insinuations that he intended to call a General Council of the Church and have him deposed, and this was precisely what Orsino threatened if Giulia did not comply. Orsini's confessor wrote to Giulia describing the 'torture' and 'displeasure', as well as the rage and 'abnormal behaviours' her husband was experiencing at her apparent obstinacy.

Giulia's brother the Cardinal, notwithstanding the immense favours he had received from the Borgia, felt that the affair had gone too far now that Orsini was no longer complicit; 'it would be a blot on your honour to subscribe to this grave fault,' he wrote courageously, 'which would end in a break with Orsino for a thing of this kind, and so public.' He sent Adriana to Rome to persuade Alexander to desist. She returned with a demand that Giulia must leave immediately. While the whole peninsula awaited the arrival of the invaders, Alexander was initiating a private war of his own with a minor client in his provincial castello.

Giulia, perhaps irritated by the Pope's assumption that he owned her, perhaps touched by Orsino's reckless devotion, perhaps capricious and taking pleasure in reducing the Pope himself to a pleading suitor, proceeded to play the moral card and said she could not contemplate returning to Rome without her husband's permission. Envoys and Borgia fixers were despatched back and forth, while Alexander worked himself into paroxysms of frustrated lust. To Giulia he wrote furiously that she was risking her life by going to Bassanello 'with the purpose, no doubt, of surrendering yourself to that stallion. We hope that you and the ungrateful Adriana will recognize your error and make suitable penance.' To Adriana, he insisted that she had 'laid bare the evil and malignity of your soul,' and both women were threatened with excommunication if they dared to countermand his wishes and continue their journey to Bassanello.

To Giulia, Alexander may have described Orsini as a stallion, but elsewhere he jealously described her husband as a 'monkey', and it was the latter epithet rather than the former which perhaps best described Monoculus. For, having made his stand, he lost his nerve and the next month Giulia and Adriana were on the road to Rome. Gilulia's resistance to Alexander's threats proved dangerous, as by September the French were in Italy, and when she set out to rejoin him in late November the countryside crawled with Charles's troops. They had barely begun their travels when a group of soldiers commanded by the dashing Yves d'Allègre stopped them. The French took the women prisoner in the politest fashion and courteously insisted they accompany them to Montefiascone. Impressed by the gallantry of her captors, Giulia acknowledged that d'Allègre arranged everything for their comfort, but this could not disguise the fact that they were prisoners of war.

Alexander was frantic at the news and appealed to Galeazzo di Sanseverino, Ludovico Sforza's man, to intercede with the French king. He sent his chamberlain Giovanni Marraves with the 3,000 scudi that the French had demanded as a ransom. With Charles's permission, the prisoners were freed and Alexander rather pathetically got himself up in a military-style outfit complete with sword to welcome his lover home. However, Giulia's marital family, the Orsini, now defected to the French, leaving Alexander little choice but to give Charles free passage into Rome. It would be excessive to suggest that poor Monoculus's marital difficulties had any bearing on the Orsini decision, but Giulia's honour was perhaps not irrelevant in a culture which paid at least lip service to chivalric codes. There is no record of Giulia's whereabouts during the French occupation, though her brother the cardinal continued to grieve somewhat disingenuously over her relationship with the Pope and attempted at least to dissociate himself from further Borgia patronage. 'I understand they are making rings worth 1,000 ducats for Madonna Giulia,' noted a Florentine correspondent, 'and the poor Cardinal has nothing to live on.'

With the departure of the French, Lucrezia Borgia now joined her father in Perugia, before returning with him to her old home at the Palazzo Santa Maria. Here she was joined for a time by her husband Giovanni Sforza, but by March 1496 he had left, remaining away for some months. In May the Mantuan envoy reported that Sforza had left 'in despair, leaving his wife beneath the apostolic mantle'. He remained in Pesaro, deaf to Alexander's apparently encouraging offers that he should return. It was not until January 1497 that he responded to a papal 'invitation' requesting him to appear in Rome within fifteen days. Sforza wrote to the Duke of Urbino expressing his misgivings about the trip, but acknowledging that he could no longer run the risk of papal displeasure.

Initially he received a welcome as one of the Borgia family, participating throughout February and March in the public festivals of the Church calendar. Lucrezia, moreover, seemed delighted that her husband had finally returned. However, Sforza influence in Rome had been vastly diminished since the conflict with the French, despite the best efforts of Cardinal Ascanio, and Giovanni Sforza began to sense that he was dispensable. On Good Friday he visited Lucrezia in her apartments early in the morning and told her he planned to spend the day as a pilgrim in the churches of Rome. Instead, with a small group of companions, he rode for his life to Pesaro.

The chronicler Monaldi reports that Lucrezia concealed a servant of Giovanni's, Giacomino, in her chamber, where he could overhear a conversation between herself and her brother Cesare which made it clear that Giovanni's name featured on the Borgia hitlist. She instructed Giacomino to report the conversation to his master. An objection to this story has been made in that it would have been perfectly possible, and much simpler, for Lucrezia to inform her husband herself, but this method allowed her to claim with perfect truthfulness to Cesare that she had not betrayed the plan. Another chronicler confirms that Lucrezia found a means of warning Giovanni, which suggests that she did feel some concern, if not affection, for him. For his part, the fleeing Giovanni left a letter for his wife urging her to join him at Pesaro as soon as she could. Alexander informed Giovanni that he would only see Lucrezia again if he returned to Rome, and that he need not seek help from his powerful Sforza kinsmen as they had already come to an accommodation with him. Clearly, what little use Ascanio and Ludovico Sforza had had for their poor relation was now exhausted.

By May, the situation was becoming embarrassing as Giovanni Sforza still refused to budge. Alexander sent an envoy to Pesaro to suggest that the marriage be annulled, either on the grounds of non-consummation or on the basis that Lucrezia remained technically the property of her second betrothed, Procida. Lucrezia had evidently consented to this arrangement, since her father signed the papers on the 26th, yet she was anything but passive, as on 6 June she left abruptly for the convent of San Sisto where she had spent time as a child. Her father claimed that she had done so at his instigation, the convent being a fitting place for a woman whose marriage was being annulled to spend time. But on 12 June he sent a band of armed men up the Appian Way to retrieve her. Lucrezia held out, and the Pope's attention was shortly distracted by a far graver family tragedy.

On 14 June Vannozza Cattanei gave a supper party in a pleasant vineyard she owned near Santa Lucia in Selce. Among the guests were her sons Cesare and Juan, Duke of Gandia. As the evening proceeded, an unknown masked man appeared at Juan's side; and when the party broke up they left together, Juan instructing his groom to wait an hour in Piazza degli Ebrai and then return home. Though some of the group had misgivings about the young duke disappearing with a stranger, they were familiar enough with Juan's womanizing habits to assume he had an assignation with a courtesan and took leave. Two days later, the battered body of the Pope's best-beloved son was hauled from the Tiber with a slit throat. His murderer was never caught, and historians are divided as to whether or not the assassination had been ordered by Cesare Borgia, who certainly stood to profit from his brother's death.

Pope Alexander saw no one for two days, writhing in uncontrollable grief, and then declared a total reform of the Vatican. God had punished him for his sins, he claimed, and from now on there was to be no more worldliness and nepotism. He even went so far as to declare to the King of Spain that he wished to renounce his tiara and spend the rest of his days doing penance as a monk. Naturally, these good resolutions did not last; but suspicion for the murder had also fallen on the Sforza, and though Alexander had formally acquitted both Cardinal Ascanio and Giovanni of any involvement in the crime, he now insisted that the cardinal bring his kinsman to order, a demand which Ascanio was hardly in a position to refuse.

Giovanni now made an incognito visit to Milan to seek Il Moro's help; but the latter, aware of the extent of the papal spy network, insisted that he show himself publicly in his proper rank. He then proceeded to humiliate his cousin by a series of important if somewhat salacious councils which aimed at proving that Giovanni had consummated his marriage to Lucrezia. Would the two care for a second honeymoon on a Sforza property? Perhaps Giovanni could acquit himself of the charge of impotence by making a 'trial' with a Milanese prostitute before witnesses? Had not Giovanni's first wife, Maddalena Gonzaga, died in childbirth – surely this was proof enough of Giovanni's virility? Giovanni resisted all attempts to prove his manhood, being obliged to declare miserably that according to rumour he had provided a stud to father Maddalena's child. Il Moro affirmed to the Ferrarese ambassador poor Giovanni's undoubted impotence – a claim which Lucrezia herself had justified in her assent to the annulment, stating that 'She had been transferred to [Giovanni's] family for over three years and was still without any sexual relation and without nuptial intercourse and carnal knowledge, and that she was prepared to swear and submit herself to midwives.' In Ludovico's view, had Giovanni been capable of sexual congress he would have proved it, and it would take only 'two twists of the rope' to make him confess.

At this juncture Giovanni made an extraordinary accusation, one which has haunted Lucrezia Borgia's reputation for centuries. In his correspondence with Ludovico, he had hinted at a secret he dared not commit to print, and now confessed that he feared Alexander's motivation in separating him from Lucrezia was that he wished to become his own daughter's lover. The Ferrarese ambassador reported that Giovanni claimed 'that he had known his wife an infinity of times, but that the Pope had taken her from him for no other purpose than to sleep with her himself'. Whether he believed this himself is open to question – certainly, had he thought that Lucrezia had committed incest he could hardly have been so anxious to have her back. The rumour, made by one who had been an intimate member of the Borgia family circle, has obstinately stuck ever since.

The Pope himself declared explicitly that he wished Lucrezia to be publicly pronounced a virgin, as he intended to make another marriage for her, which would have been a risk had he had personal knowledge to the contrary. Lucrezia, still immured in the convent and grieving for her brother, began to hope that she might be transferred to Spain. Despite her gesture of defiance in entering San Sisto, she remained at this point true to her upbringing, acquiescing in her father's wishes and deriving her sense of self from the use he made of her. Perhaps her submissiveness hints at something darker in their relationship; but far more likely that she accepted her role as a diplomatic tool in accordance with the mores of her culture and education. Finally, under threat of the withdrawal of papal protection from Pesaro, Giovanni capitulated. Having held out for an annulment on the less shaming grounds of pre-contract, his resistance finally collapsed and in November 1497 a conclave met in Pesaro to pronounce the annulment, with a memorandum sent to Ascanio Sforza permitting him to pass it on the basis of non-consummation.

The declaration that Lucrezia Borgia was still a virgin was met with derision. A correspondent from Perugia wrote that all Italy was laughing: 'it was common knowledge that she had been and then was the greatest whore there ever was in Rome'. On 22 December

Lucrezia had been present at the Vatican for the pronunciation of her divorce, where she made a speech in Latin that one observer compared to Tully 'for grace and sweetness'. During the proceedings, she was solemnly announced to be *virgo intacta*. Three months later, according to Cristoforo Poggio of Bologna in a memorandum dated 18 March 1498, Lucrezia gave birth to a child. Hardly surprising, then, that the Borgia campaign to assert Lucrezia's sexual innocence was met with howls of laughter.

Lucrezia's decision to move from central Rome to the convent is now cast in a different light. If she knew in June 1497 that she was pregnant, then discretion was obviously necessary if she were to comply with her father's wishes regarding the annulment. Several writers have suggested that Lucrezia began an affair after she entered San Sisto with Pedro Caldes, known as Perotto, a Spanish attendant in her father's household. Perotto's presence 'awakened feelings of trust and friendship in Lucrezia which developed into affection and *finally* into passion.' That it was given out that he was the father is supposedly confirmed by the fact that, on 8 March, Perotto 'fell not of his own will into the Tiber of which there is much talk in the city'. The diary of the papal master of ceremonies adds that Pantasilea, Lucrezia's waiting-woman, had also been found dead in the river. This would suggest that Pantasilea had known of or perhaps assisted Lucrezia in her relationship with Perotto, whom Cesare Borgia appeared to believe was the father of her child, at least given that he pursued her supposed lover through the Vatican with a drawn sword. However, a consideration of the dates suggests that Perotto was merely the straw man, a disposable cover for a situation which looked set to thwart the Borgias' plans. If Lucrezia began her alleged affair with Perotto after she had entered San Sisto, any resulting pregnancy would give a delivery date later than March. The likely father of Lucrezia's child, if the absurd theory that it was her father is discounted, was her husband, Giovanni Sforza.

Throughout the divorce proceedings, Giovanni had been in and out of Rome, and not all of his visits were documented. According to Lucrezia's biographer, Lucrezia 'saw her husband at all times of day' – that is, they lived on familiar terms, terms which Giovanni had always insisted included full sexual intimacy. If Lucrezia was pregnant with a Sforza baby, this would have altered the entire complexion not only of Alexander's plans that she separate from Giovanni, but also potentially the loyalties of Ascanio and Ludovico Sforza. No confirmation of the degree of Lucrezia's relationship with Perotto exists, and it is possible they may have had a sexual affair during her pregnancy, or that she herself may have been unsure of the paternity of the child; but it was more convenient for the Borgias to put out that Perotto had disappeared for 'having made His Holiness's daughter, Madonna Lucrezia, pregnant' than for the truth to be known. The allegations are complicated by the fact that a child, Giovanni Borgia, known as the 'Infans Romanus', was certainly born at this time. At first it was believed that the child was Cesare's, but a later papal bull of 1502 claims the boy was Alexander's, probably by Giulia Farnese. It was not implausible, given that Giulia's relationship with the Pope was well known, as was her 'sisterly' relationship with Lucrezia, that she agreed to pass the latter's child by Giovanni Sforza off as her own. No definite solution has as yet come to light, but given the circumstances of Lucrezia's divorce, this is the theory which at present seems most convincing.

With the evidence of the scandal at least less obviously visible, the Pope and Cesare Borgia had more freedom to select a politically useful husband for Lucrezia. Curiously, one candidate proposed by Cesare was Ottaviano Riario, Caterina Sforza's son, presumably with an eye to retaining papal influence in the ever-vital counties of Forlì and Imola. But Cesare also had marital ambitions of his own. He wanted to cast off his cardinal's robes and found a dynasty, and for his bride he wanted Carlotta d'Aragona, a daughter of the King of Naples, whose breeding suited the swelling ambitions of the Borgias to become a quasi-royal European house. As a means of establishing an initial relationship with the Aragonese, it was proposed that Lucrezia should marry Alfonso d'Aragona, an illegitimate son of Alfonso II of Naples and brother to Lucrezia's sister-in-law Sancia. Alfonso was to be granted the dukedom of Bisceglie and Lucrezia would bring a dowry of 40,000 ducats, even greater than that which the unfortunate Giovanni Sforza had been obliged to return. In July 1498, Lucrezia's newly betrothed appeared in Rome. Alfonso appeared to be a good-looking man with fine manners, and the prospect of such a husband pleased Lucrezia.

Unfortunately, this wedding too left something to be desired. As ever, Lucrezia was wonderfully dressed, in a French-style robe of gold brocade with a silk underskirt studded with jewels, a magnificent pearl necklace and a pearl cap on her unbound hair, a style which traditionally symbolized virginity. Once again, on 5 August, Lucrezia knelt beneath an unsheathed sword to pronounce her vows in the Vatican, but hardly had the solemnities concluded when a fight broke out between the attendants of Cesare and Sancia d'Aragona, in which two bishops were badly beaten up, and the Pope himself took a few punches. The servants ran away in fright and even an elegant supper at which Cesare Borgia appeared in the masquerade dressed as a unicorn, symbol of purity and loyalty, did little to restore decorum to the proceedings.

On 7 August, Cesare gave an entertainment in the Villa Belvedere. Beneath Mantegna's frescoes, Lucrezia and Sancia danced with their host, dressed as the lay magnate he was determined to become in crimson satin and white brocade. Supper was served at one in the morning, then the dancing continued until the announcement that breakfast had been laid out in the loggia in the summer dawn. At the same time each member of the family was presented with a flattering sugar sculpture. Alfonso received a Cupid carrying love poetry, Lucrezia the virtuous Roman matron Lucretia. For the rest, the principal part of the amusements consisted in laughing at the 'many tricks' of 'some buffoons'.

CHAPTER 13

Fortune's Child

1495–1497

'To satisfy her appetites'

The spring of 1495 brought Ludovico Il Moro's long-cherished ambitions to fruition as he prepared for his official investiture as Duke of Milan, despite the fact that, thanks to the Holy League, the alliance which had brought him the coronet was now in tatters. With Charles VIII still precariously ensconced in Naples, the great families of the peninsula prepared themselves for a party. For Isabella d'Este, her brother-in-law's investiture presented as ever the problem of how to present the best possible *bella figura*. On a visit to her father at Ferrara, Isabella received anxious letters from her husband Francesco, who took time away from his military preparations to request that she lend him her jewels for the forthcoming *festa* in Milan.

Isabella replied that she had recently pawned the best of her collection in trying to obtain a cardinal's hat for Francesco's brother Sigismondo Gonzaga. The tone of Isabella's letter is warm, even beneath the conventional hyperbole of submissive, wifely courtesy, and it seemed that at this juncture the Gonzaga marriage was cordial, with Isabella proud of her husband's achievements with the League, not to mention his splendid salary. While the Sforza celebrated, Charles VIII wrote to his brother with a quite exceptional want of perception declaring Naples 'the fairest city I have ever seen. You would never believe what beautiful gardens there are here. So full of rare and lovely flowers and of delicious fruits that nothing, by my faith, is wanting except Adam and Eve to make this place another Eden.' The Neapolitans thought differently, as their southern paradise was in the process of being despoiled by the debauched and brutal French troops.

Charles remained in Naples until 21 May, despite finally having been informed of the treachery of Il Moro and the formation of the League. Fortunately for the French king, Louis d'Orléans realized early on that Charles would need a safe corridor to pass through Italy and over the Alps, and mustered 2,000 troops at Asti. Ludovico threatened an attack, but what nerve he had was lost when Louis occupied Novara in early June. Panicked that d'Orléans would turn on Milan, Ludovico rushed with his family to Pavia. It was Beatrice who acted like a true Sforza, assembling the nobility of Milan and rousing them to defend their city. Beatrice was still so young, so obsessed with her gay entertainments and divine clothes that it took everyone by surprise to see her coolly take command, inspecting the city's ramparts with her hair bound in pearled ribbon and her pretty mouth red with specially commissioned Florentine rouge. If Novara could be retaken, it would be possible to attack Charles without the threat of a rearguard action from Louis, and Beatrice's decisiveness bought the League enough time to call its Venetian divisions north and besiege the city.

It was hardly the Sforzas' finest hour, but Charles's failure to negotiate a peaceful retreat in July gave Francesco Gonzaga his place in history. Charles, though a poor commander, at least had the foresight to send an advance party to occupy Pontremoli, at the head of the pass which would give the French access to the Alps and freedom. But beyond the summit the 12,000-strong army of the League awaited, under the command of the Marquis of Mantua. On 6 July, the French – fewer than 10,000 of them – advanced. The victory of Fornovo, as it became known, was claimed by the Italians as a great triumph, though Philippe de Commines commented wryly, 'I have never seen such great armies so close to each other go their ways without fighting'. Gonzaga himself undoubtedly fought bravely: having had three horses shot from under him he continued on foot with his sword until even that was broken in his hands. But confusion in the ranks of the Albanian mercenaries, known as the *stradioti*, who were unaccustomed to artillery fire, allowed the French to retreat in a body after suffering about 3,000 casualties. Francesco wrote to his wife that 'if others had fought as we did, the victory would have been complete, and not a single Frenchman would have been left alive'. In fact, the French abandoned their baggage train, and among the few notable prisoners seized figured Charles's illegitimate brother the Bâtard de Bourbon, who spent the eight weeks of his captivity with Isabella at Mantua. For the present, the French threat had vanished.

Aside from the Bâtard, Francesco had amassed other valuable spoils of war, including Charles VIII's own sword and helmet and the sacred bone of St Denis which formed part of the royal regalia. Ludovico Il Moro wrote teasingly to Isabella that since she was such an excellent rider she ought to have been with the League to pursue the French and their treasures. Isabella was enraged when her husband graciously returned the regalia to Charles, arguing that he ought not to have kept the trreasure, instead she had to content herself with some precious hangings and a book which the lecherous king had commissioned containing the portraits of the most beautiful women in Italy. Perhaps she was peeved not to find herself among his planned paramours. Isabella's cupidity was soothed by the praises heaped on her husband, comparing him with every military hero from Hannibal, as well as a payment of 1,000 ducats to her as the wife of the newly appointed Captain-General of the Armies of the Republic. Predictably, she went shopping, ordering the finest 'tabby' silk from Damascus and retrieving the jewels she had pawned.

To the fury of his allies in the League, Ludovico Il Moro concluded a separate, independent peace with the French at Vercelli; but the taking of Novara appeared to have had a damaging effect on his nerves. Despite the apparent success of all his plans, Ludovico was depressed and withdrawn, and began an affair with a former lady-in-waiting to his wife, Monna Lucrezia Crivelli. Beatrice d'Este remained ignorant for a while, but when her husband began to promote members of La Crivelli's family she became suspicious, and her family were obliged to inform her that they had known of the relationship for some time. A Ferrarese chronicler wrote that 'The latest news from Milan is that the Duke spends his whole time and finds all his pleasure in the company of a girl who is one of his wife's maidens. And his conduct is ill-regarded here.' No one expected fidelity from princes, but Beatrice's popularity meant that her husband's careless indiscretion was viewed unfavourably. Ludovico adored Beatrice, but felt squeamish about making love to his wife while she was pregnant, a condition which Beatrice broken-heartedly accepted, though by November 1496 Crivelli too was expecting a child.

Nor was Ludovico's uncharacteristic callousness towards Beatrice the only sign that all was not well in Milan. The duke had sent word to his painters, including da Vinci, that they must have their present works at the Rocchetta completed in time for the duchess to give birth, but his request was met with resentment. Milan was rapidly heading for bankruptcy and minor riots were erupting as artisans found their bills unpaid. Servants, artists, even the scholars at the renowned University of Pavia found their stipends unforthcoming. At least Leonardo remained cheerful. When Ludovico asked him why he had not yet completed the face of Judas in 'The Last Supper', the artist replied that he had trawled the lowest quarters of Milan in search of a suitably vile candidate, but since he had discovered nothing perhaps the face of the Prior of Santa Maria delle Grazie would serve. They laughed a great deal at this idea, probably the last time that patron and protégé laughed together. That month, the estranged ducal couple were united in their grief at the sudden death of Ludovico's beloved natural daughter Bianca, who had been the wife of Galeazzo di Sanseverino for just five months. They travelled gently by water to Pavia to await Beatrice's lying-in, though Ludovico was distant and preoccupied by his financial worries. Between his pressing debts and his daughter's death, it seemed that the security he had struggled for all his life had been exposed as alarmingly fragile.

In the winter of 1496, the small, rather sleepy court of Caterina, Countess of Forlì received a glamorous visitor. Giovanni 'il Popolano' de' Medici, aged twenty-nine, was considered one of the handsomest and most brilliant of the young Florentine aristocracy. He was also a Medici of the junior branch that had remained in Florence as the senior line had been exiled for all eternity. His grandfather Lorenzo had been the younger brother of Cosimo de' Medici, and the cadet branch of the great dynasty had been spared the opprobrium which fell on other Medici males after the overthrow of Piero in 1494. He and his brother Lorenzo had been exiled from Florence due to their hostility to Piero, but had joined with Charles VIII in exile. After Piero was driven out of Florence they returned to the city, taking the name of Popolani as an indication of their severance from their Medici roots. By 1496, the Medici di Popolo brothers had become successful merchants, and Giovanni acted as an unofficial ambassador for Florence in the matter of purchasing grain from the Romagna. Ever since Pisa had rebelled against Florentine rule during the French invasion, grain prices had been rising in the city republic, as the supplies bought in from France and shipped through the Florentine port of Livorno were constantly under attack from the Pisans, with whom the Florentines remained in a state of war. It was natural, then, that the city should seek a supply closer to home territory, and natural that Giovanni de' Medici il Popolano should enter into correspondence with Caterina Sforza about the possible sale of grain from her lands.

When Giovanni visited Forlì, Caterina found herself extremely attracted to him. She had loved her second husband, Giacomo Feo, but it had been a sensual love, while Giovanni treated her not only as a beautiful woman but as an intellectual equal. Through the winter evenings they discussed political and economic issues and Caterina became increasingly bound to the younger man as their conversations revealed his intelligence and judgement. Ludovico il Moro was informed that Giovanni's stay had long outlasted his purported reason for visiting Forlì and that Caterina might well remarry 'to satisfy her appetites'. Caterina dismissed the rumours in a letter to her anxious uncle in a bantering tone: 'I am not, however, of an age to which others might ascribe such juvenile appetites,' but gossiping correspondents reported that the relationship was progressing. Giovanni now lodged in the late Giacomo Feo's apartments, with his own household, and paid daily solicitous visits to Caterina, who had fallen ill.

Ludovico sent his orator, Tranchedini, on a visit to Forlì to

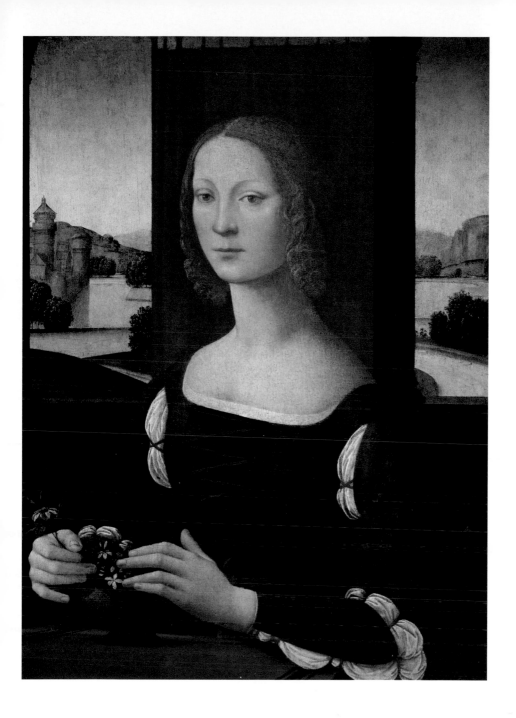

Caterina Sforza, the Lady of Forlì, combined mettle with
sensuality to a high degree – and she always got her man.

Bona of Savoy, the de facto duchess of Milan, whose abundant girth sadly did not correspond to an equipollent amount of political acumen.

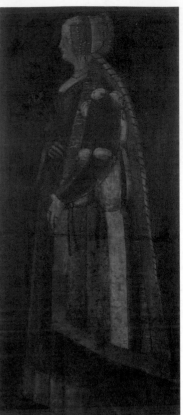

Galeazzo Maria Sforza undoubtedly preferred the bed of Lucrezia Landriani to that of his wife. And who could blame him?

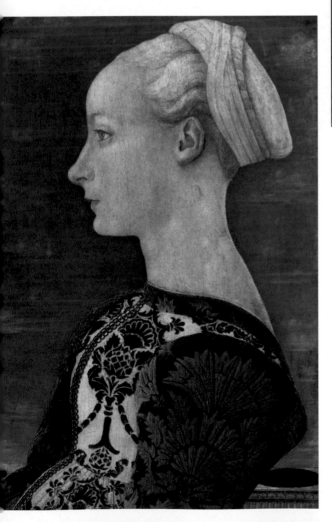

Galeazzo Maria Sforza, the lecherous, cunning, violent and cruel de facto Duke of Milan, was a far cry from the virtues of his Arthurian namesake, Galahad.

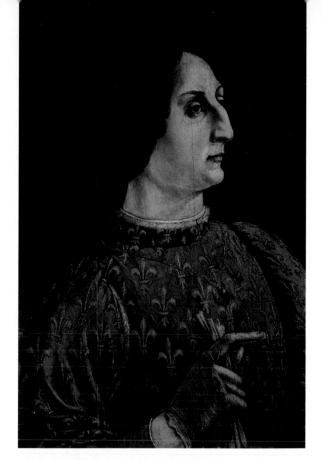

'Keep your friends close and your enemies closer.' Unfortunately, Galeazzo Maria Sforza sometimes could not keep enough distance from people for his own good, as this 1476 woodcut of his murder shows.

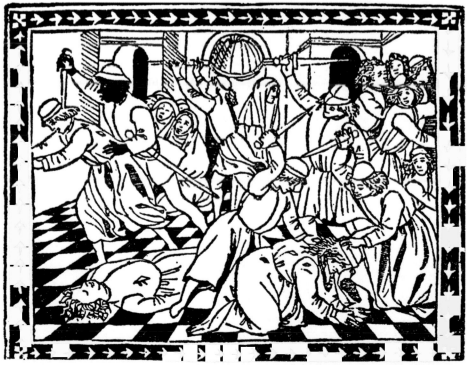

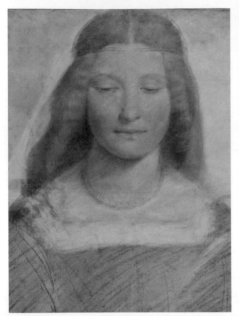

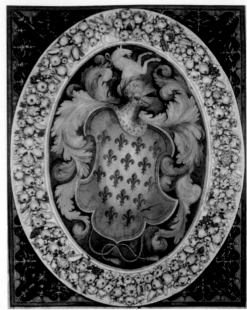

ABOVE The coat of arms of
the Farnese: once petty nobles
from the Latium countryside,
the family owed their fortune –
including a cardinal's hat and the
papacy – to Giulia's sway over
Alexander VI.

ABOVE LEFT As the
unfortunate wife of the equally
unfortunate Gian Galeazzo
Sforza, Isabella d'Aragona at
least had the satisfaction of
seeing her nemesis Ludovico
Sforza die a prisoner in France.

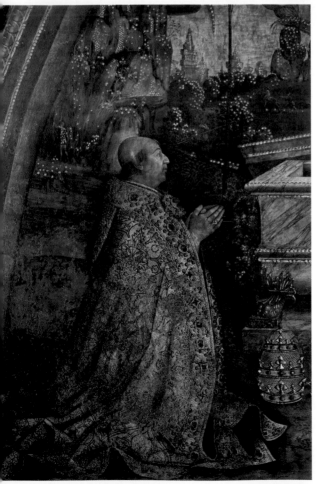

LEFT Alexander VI was a
wonderful family man, who
never allowed his frequent
crises of conscience to
overcome his ruthless desire
to favour his offspring.

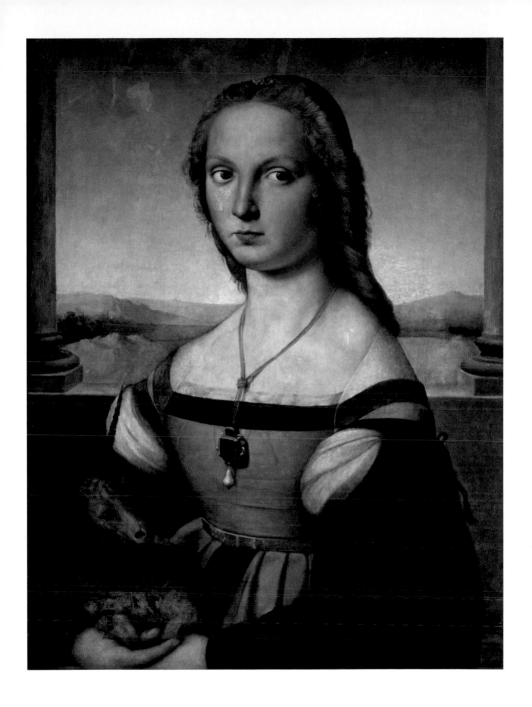

In Raphael's portrait Giulia Farnese appears rather more matronly than when she made Alexander VI's head spin, but 'Giulia la bella' retains the beauty that justly made her famous.

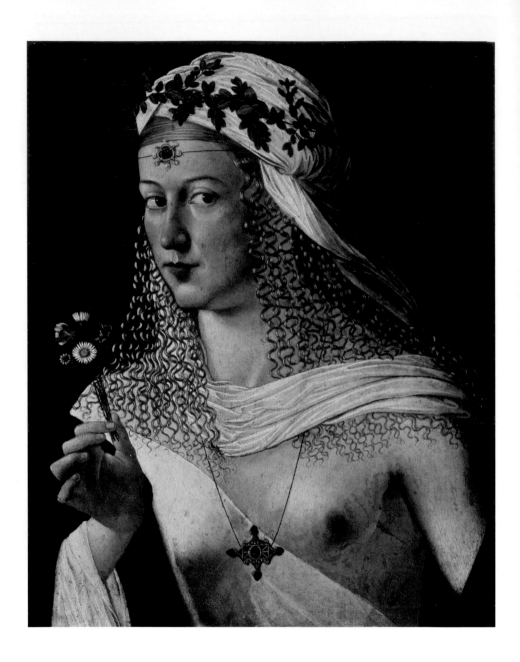

Lucrezia Borgia has received more than her share of calumny,
even before being savaged by television producers – her husband
Alfonso d'Este would have had them fired… from one of his guns.

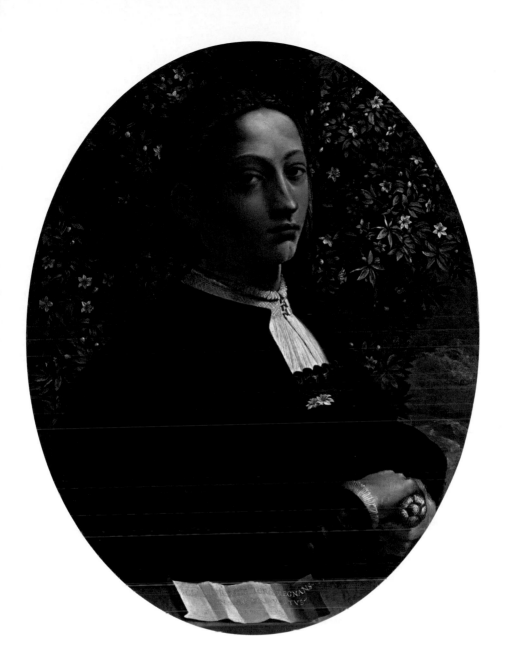

A more mature, meditative Lucrezia, in this portrait by
Dosso Dossi – devout in her Christian beliefs, an excellent
administrator, yet still with a twinkle in her eye.

One had to be cautious when accepting an invitation to dinner from Cesare Borgia, Duke of Romagna – the Tiber was already polluted enough.

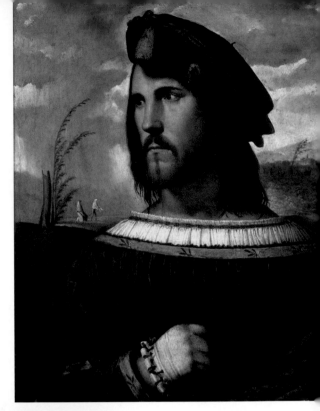

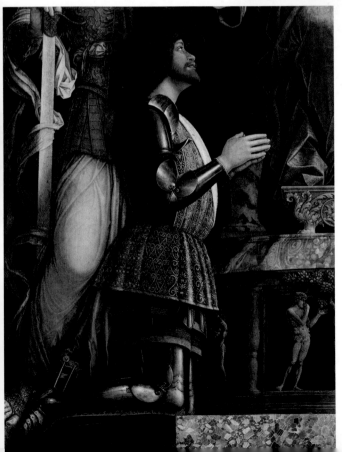

Even an accomplished court painter like Mantegna could not conceal entirely Francesco II Gonzaga's notorious ugliness. The Marquess of Mantua nevertheless enjoyed success with the ladies, notably his acquired sister-in-law Lucrezia Borgia.

obtain more reliable information. Caterina continued to insist that Giovanni was merely a dear friend with whom she enjoyed satisfactory business dealings, a story which Giovanni himself confirmed on a visit to Tranchedini the next day. Both Ludovico and the Doge of Venice accepted the orator's reassurances that he saw nothing in the relationship, but poor Tranchedini felt mortified shortly thereafter when he was obliged to explain in a letter of 23 January 1497 that Giovanni and Caterina had indeed been through a secret marriage ceremony. Officially, Caterina continued to deny her marriage until August that year, when she found herself pregnant, though she and Ludovico continued their correspondence on a variety of other matters. Caterina was canny enough to know that she could not admit to her relationship with Giovanni as Florence was still pro-French and she needed the support of Ludovico, who was allied with the League; but given the demands she was to make on him in the coming year, she was not quite playing her uncle fair.

For the first time in years, Caterina found herself at peace. After the violent struggles and losses of her twenties, she had evolved into a mature woman, respected by her people, with a husband whom she admired and loved at her side. Finally she was able to attend to both the spiritual and frivolous demands of her nature, ordering exotic animals to adorn her parklands and simultaneously establishing her patronage of the Florentine convent of the Murate, which would continue for the rest of her life. On 6 April 1498 her happiness was crowned with the birth of a son, christened Ludovico but afterwards known as Giovanni in honour of his father. The little boy, exceptionally pretty and lively, became Caterina's favourite child, but she did not neglect the future prospects of her other children. In January 1498, for example, she had refused Isabella d'Este's proposal of a marriage between her son Ottaviano and Isabella's daughter. To Il Moro she explained that 'the prevailing turbulence and bad state of Italian affairs obliged her to set aside every consideration but the preservation and weal of her state'. In March she did the same with Pope Alexander himself. Caterina's Sforza blood recoiled at the prospect of her eldest son's marriage to the notorious Lucrezia Borgia, even if her uncles Ludovico and Ascanio were keen to retain a family connection. 'When I want a wife for my son,' she wrote

haughtily, 'I will think to give him such a person who is not repug-
nant to me, and so contrary to my peace and my needs.' To the Pope
she delivered her message with rather more respectful words. She
made it clear that she understood his intentions perfectly. Instead
of marriage, Ottaviano was to go soldiering, receiving a *condottiere*'s
commission from Florence for 17,000 florins in June 1498. Caterina
ensured that he was equipped with the best, and he left Forlì that
month at the head of a troop of 100 men-at-arms and another 100
cavalry. Proudly, Caterina had commemorative medals struck showing Ottaviano astride his horse.

Ottaviano's departure signalled that once again the Romagna was
in turmoil. Caterina's precious period of happiness had been briefer
than the latest peninsular war. The Florence–Pisa conflict had
dragged on for two inconclusive years when the Venetians decided
to send a consignment of troops to the Mugello in support of the
Pisans. To dissuade Caterina from acting against them, the Venetians
employed two pretenders to her territories who had been displaced
by the Riario – Antonio Maria Ordelaffi, once her proposed bridegroom, and Taddeo Manfredi, whose family still claimed a right
to Imola. To counter the Venetian threat, Florence had appointed
Giovanni de Medici as commissioner for the Romagna. Caterina
wrote to Ludovico il Moro to solicit his influence in persuading the
Manfredi to refuse the Venetian alliance, while to the Signoria in
Florence she sent letters of advice on garrisoning the passes of the
Apennines. Aware that if the Venetians succeeded with the Pisans
against Florence her own lands could be threatened, she also had
the walls of Forlì reinforced. On 23 July, in recognition of her mar-
riage and her support for the republic, the Signoria granted Caterina
Florentine citizenship.

In August, the Venetians under Ordelaffi entered Forlivese lands
and Caterina wrote urgently to Ludovico asking for reinforcements,
as so far she had only received a modest consignment of Milanese
troops. She was reassured by the return of her husband on the 18th
and they were able to spend a week together at Ravaldino, though
Giovanni felt unwell, possibly suffering from gout typical of the
Medici. On the 28th he left to take the waters at Bagno in hopes of a
cure. Alone once more, Caterina renewed her ever more impatient

requests to her uncle, who, despite his promised intentions to appear in the Romagna himself, sent her only a measly company of fifty men-at-arms and the same number of light cavalry. 'States cannot be defended with words,' she wrote angrily.

Already desperately worried about the political situation Caterina did her best to prepare Forlì for war when she received the terrible news of Giovanni's sudden death at Bagno on 12 September. A courier was sent urgently with the news that he had fallen desperately ill, but Caterina arrived only to find that her husband had died in the night. His body was taken to Florence for burial by his brother Lorenzo, and Caterina had no choice but to return to Forlì, where despite her grief she continued her preparations. Undaunted by Ludovico's diffidence, she deployed what troops she had to inhibit the Venetian advance. Yet her bitterness increased when the Venetian attack finally came. Thanks to her efficient network of spies, Caterina had been able to warn the Florentines of an attack on the town of Marradi, a crucial mountain outpost at the border of Tuscany and the Romagna. Despite the early warning she had given the Florentines, the garrison was ill-prepared and the castle was taken. Caterina exploded with fury that her advice had been ignored and that she had been dismissed as timorous and 'womanly'.

In October, though, fearful of the oncoming winter, the Venetians chose to retreat. 'Florence,' writes the scholar Ernst Breisach, 'who had contributed to this victory two captains, few soldiers, many good intentions and not a single coin, could now be considered secure on its north-western borders. The lady of Forlì, fighting like a lioness, saved the situation.'

Caterina's impatience at the apparent lassitude with which Ludovico had greeted her demands for support shows that she expected him to behave as she did, as a Sforza. She had succeeded in putting aside her own grief for Giovanni to concentrate on war, but Ludovico seemed incapable of doing the same. In early January 1497, the Duke of Milan had lost his duchess. Beatrice had been delivered of a stillborn son at Pavia, having gone into labour while at prayer on a cold winter's afternoon. Her funeral is described in a letter by Antonio Costabili, the ambassador to Duke Ercole of Ferrara:

The obsequies ... were celebrated with all possible magnificence and pomp. All the ambassadors at present in Milan, among whom was one from the King of the Romans, two from the King of Spain and others from all the powers of Italy, lifted the corpse and bore it to the first gate of the Castello. Here the privy councillors took the body in their turn, and at the corners of the streets groups of magistrates stood waiting to receive it. All the relatives of the ducal family wore long mourning cloaks which trailed on the ground and hoods over their heads.

The cortège proceeded to Santa Maria delle Grazie with a large company of monks and priests carrying silver and wooden crosses. Beatrice, dressed in one of her most sumptuous gowns, was laid out on a bier before the altar draped in cloth of gold with the Sforza arms. Some of the greatest *condottieri* of the peninsula were among the mourners and were seen to weep at the lifeless eyes of this beautiful, vital girl, now closed for ever. Under Bramante's cupola, Beatrice d'Este, Duchess of Bari and Milan, had found her final resting place, where she had so recently prayed for the safety of her little sons, beside the daughter whom she had loved and lost.

CHAPTER 14

'You are Only a Woman. I Forgive You.'

1498–1500

'The ruin of Italy is confirmed ... given the plans which father and son have made; but many believe the Holy Spirit has no part in them.'

CATTANEO

Madama Margherita,

... You will understand how I came to Avignon to speak with Lorenzo of the matter which we discussed together, so that our interest may be well served in this matter and Lorenzo has received me with the best possible countenance, and has told me that he is all mine, and in the matters in which he may serve me, he will be at my disposition. Thus I believe that he will do all that he will ... it seems to me that he has the malady of San Lazzaro* in his face. Also Pietro is none too well of his malady. Lorenzo and Pietro will soon depart from here to do business with M. Cristoforo.

Ludovico Sforza did not have a high opinion of feminine intellect, but he was not averse to disguising himself as 'Madama Margherita' in his secret correspondence. In this letter of 1498, 'Margherita' is receiving news from her spy as to the activities of Giuliano della Rovere ('Lorenzo'), Cesare Borgia ('Pietro') and Louis XII, newly King of France ('Cristoforo'). Within a mere two years of Beatrice d'Este's death, Ludovico would be forced to witness the collapse of his life's ambitions in the face of the relentless advance of the Borgia. Ascanio Sforza had dared to suggest that the Pope was inviting the ruin of Italy by seeking another return of the French, to

* Secondary syphilis.

which Alexander VI calmly and accurately replied, 'Monsignore, I may have let them in, but was it not your brother who opened the door?'

One of Ludovico Sforza's first acts on the death of his wife was to evict Isabella d'Aragona from her home. Every step of her feet, he claimed, reminded him of Beatrice, but was he really haunted by the ghosts of those whom he had wronged? In his ceaseless struggle to legitimize his appropriation of the ducal title, Ludovico had shown himself guilty not only of treachery, but of hubris. His father Francesco Sforza, the first of his line to rule Milan, and his elder brother Galeazzo had been acknowledged as Lords of Milan by their people, who by popular acclaim called them Duke, and they had felt justified if not invested. Perhaps, Ludovico now realized, this ought to have been sufficient for him. In his pursuit of the dukedom he had summoned his own destruction and Milan's, losing his father's hard-won prestige and popularity as well as the claim to Sforza dignity derived from the nobility of their Visconti forebears. Yet he seemed addicted to tyranny, unable to resign himself either to his grief or his rightful place in the succession.

He ordered Isabella to live in a palazzo in the city, but her child, little Francesco, was to remain behind, a futile hostage to his uncle's misery and need for vengeance against God for his wife's death. As the grave, mourning court assembled to take their leave of her, Isabella screamed out at Ludovico that he had robbed her son of his state – did he now intend to deprive him of his mother? After a while, Ludovico answered in a cold monotone, 'You are only a woman. I forgive you.'

Over the subsequent months, Ludovico did not cease to grieve, but sat in a darkened room, refusing to see his sons, only conducting business when absolutely vital, and on condition that the councillor in question did not mention Beatrice's name. The Venetian ambassador reported that 'the Duke has ceased to care for his children or his state, or anything on earth, and can hardly bear to live'. Isabella d'Este had loved her sister despite their petty rivalries, and wrote to their father, 'I do not know how I can ever find comfort.' Her husband attempted to soothe her, as did her sister-in-law Elisabetta, who made a visit of condolence from Urbino; but Francesco Gonzaga admitted that he had never seen his wife brought so low, and that her grief was more horrible to see in one 'who has always shown herself so strong and of manly courage in adversity'.

Beatrice's loss was not the only one which the Sforza and d'Este sustained, for in November 1497 Alfonso d'Este's wife Anna Sforza died in childbirth. Despite his infidelities, Alfonso mourned Anna, whose wedding had been celebrated simultaneously with that of Ludovico and Beatrice. Isabella resorted to the family custom of bringing on the dwarves, and sent her best fool, Mattello, to distract her brother. Alfonso was so cheered that he wrote back to Isabella saying that he could not have been happier had she given him a palace, as Mattello's antics had succeeded not just in making him smile, but had induced roars of laughter. The unfortunate Mattello had been unwell for some time; it transpired that he had been struck by cancer, and his constitution could hardly have been improved by an excess of somersaults and Alfonso grew bored when the poor man could barely stand up, his pain increasing with time. He received permission to lie on his bed when he eventually returned to Mantua. Isabella graciously visited him but rather callously reported that, entertainer to the last, Mattello had made one of his best ever jokes from his bed, and then he died. Her shrieks of laughter and hilarity can almost be heard as she told and retold the wonderfully amusing story. Not everyone felt as Isabella did and the court went into mourning for the loyal and devoted 'primo matto nel mondo'. This baffled Isabella somewhat as she did not quite consider her dwarves to be fully human, but Mattello had earned his place among the coffins of the Gonzaga princes. Perhaps they hoped to hasten the opportunity of humour in the next world.

United in mourning, the two families also shared political unease. Since 1496, when Ludovico had met Maximilian, Holy Roman Emperor-elect, at Mals, the peninsula had been preparing for a second French invasion. The sudden death of Charles VIII at Amboise on 7 April 1498 meant that Italy was threatened by a far more serious adversary – his successor Louis Duke d'Orléans, now Louis XII, who had signalled his intentions unequivocally on his accession by taking the titles of Duke of Milan and King of Sicily. Isabella d'Este worked to bring about an understanding between

Ludovico Il Moro, Emperor Maximilian and the French King; but, as ever, incessant bickering and power-jockeying undermined efforts at diplomacy. Maximilian offered Francesco Gonzaga the leadership of the Leagued armies of Milan and the Empire, but Gonzaga insisted on the title of Captain-General in addition to the 30,000 ducats a year promised by the Emperor (a post then held by Ludovico Sforza's son-in-law Galeazzo Sanseverino). Ludovico refused to disparage his protégé and a disgruntled Gonzaga made suit via his brother to the Venetians, claiming he would prefer to fight for them. Tensions were such that Ludovico declared he must visit Mantua 'to show the world what confidence he placed in his brother-in-law'.

With the visit planned for June, Isabella was thrown into a competitive panic at how best to impress Ludovico. She borrowed plate, hangings and other valuables to decorate the castello at Mantua and wrote to Capilupi, her agent in Milan, to ask what hangings he thought the Duke would prefer in his chamber. She wrote:

> ...we intend to lodge the Duke here, in our rooms at the Castello, giving him the Camera di Pinta, with the ante-chamber, the Camerino del Sole [the sun being Ludovico's personal device], the Camera del Cassone and our own camerino and dining room. And we mean His Excellency to occupy the Camera del Cassone himself, which we will drape with black and violet hangings as although we hear that he still wears mourning, we think this will look rather less melancholy and show that here at least there is reason to celebrate on this occasion.

What did the duke like to eat and drink, did he plan to bring his own hangings? And ought she to wear black, since Ludovico had not put off his own mourning? Isabella felt quite prepared to set herself at odds with her husband over this visit, Francesco's leanings inclining more towards Venice, but the Venetians had also withheld the title he craved, so perhaps he might still prove biddable. Ludovico arrived with a suite of 1,000 attendants and remained in Mantua for three days, seeing the principal churches, the greatest of Mantegna's works and Isabella d'Este's hoard of treasures. Francesco condescended to give tournaments and stage plays for the duke, but despite this show of family unity, the other ruling houses of Italy saw clearly that the Sforza sun was setting.

In December of the previous year, Ascanio Sforza had reported from Rome that Cesare Borgia was 'working harder every day to put off the purple'. With the insatiable ambition of the Borgias now resting in him, it was imperative that Cesare be released from his clerical status in order to take a wife and found a dynasty. Increasingly, it seemed that the genesis of such a dynasty would depend on a papal alliance with the French. Not only was Carlotta d'Aragona, his intended Neapolitan bride, living at the French court under the new King's protection, but following the Peace of Vercelli it seemed all but inevitable that Italy would have to accept the presence of two contending foreign powers, France and Spain. Venice was now anti-Milanese and increasingly pro-French; Florence, politically ruined, tended to lean the same way, while the embattled Kingdom of Naples depended entirely on the Spaniards. For his part, Louis of France urgently required a papal dispensation in order to divorce his childless wife Jeanne de France and marry the widow of Charles VIII, Anne of Brittany, to prevent her duchy from passing out of French control.

While Ludovico Il Moro was being entertained at Mantua, Alexander VI and Louis XII exchanged embassies, as a consequence of which Louis promised tremendous concessions to Cesare Borgia in return for the crucial dissolution. Cesare was promised the county of Valence, which was to become a duchy, as well as that of Diois, the revenues of both being supplemented to bring him a total of 20,000 gold francs; the command of a brigade of lancers to be maintained at Louis's expense; a grant of a further 20,000 gold francs per year from the royal treasury; the Order of St Michel, and, conditional upon the successful conquest of Milan, the lordship of Asti. Cesare had made his final appearance in ecclesiastical garb on 21 April 1498 and formally renounced his cardinal's hat on 2 August. From now on he was a soldier, the most magnificent that Italy could boast.

With Cesare concentrating on preparations for his departure, he ordered a new wardrobe, featuring prominently the black velvet with which he was to become associated and which flattered his elegant, athletic physique, which he hardened by taking vigorous exercise, including gymnastics and mounted bullfighting. From the famed Gonzaga stud he ordered warhorses which were to be shod in silver, while a privy fit for a prince was commissioned, draped in gold and scarlet brocade with silver appointments for his use on the voyage to Marseilles. He sailed on 1 October.

En route for his appointment with 'Cristoforo', 'Pietro', his face indeed blotched with the spread of secondary syphilis, paused at Avignon as the guest of Giuliano della Rovere. Knowing his guest's tastes, whatever their risks, Cardinal Giuliano prepared a suitably worldly entertainment for his quondam colleague, ordering that 'He must be honoured at the City Palace by ladies and beautiful girls who should know how to entertain him with dances, because the aforesaid Don Cesare finds pleasure in this.' Though della Rovere was keeping his options open by maintaining contact with Ludovico Sforza's spies, he was personally certain that with the arrival of Cesare in France the Sforza were doomed. When the marriage of Louis XII with Anne of Brittany was successfully celebrated the following January, both della Rovere and Cardinal Sforza were proved correct.

Cesare's arrival at the French court at Chinon was extraordinary, even by the standards of a prince of the Church.

[He was] preceded by twenty-four handsome mules carrying trunks, coffers and chests, covered with cloths bearing the Duke's arms, then again came another twenty-four mules with their trappings halved in red and yellow, the colours of the King, then twelve mules with coverings of yellow striped satin. Then came six mules with trappings of cloth of gold ... and after came sixteen beautiful great chargers, led by grooms, covered in cloth of gold, crimson and yellow ... after these came eighteen pages, each one on a fine charger, of whom sixteen were dressed in crimson velvet, the other two in cloth of gold ... Then came six fine mules richly equipped with saddles, bridles and trappings in crimson velvet, accompanied by grooms dressed in the same. The two mules carrying coffers and all covered in cloth of gold ... Then after came thirty gentlemen clad in cloth of gold and silver, followed by three musicians ... dressed in cloth of gold according to the style of their country, and their rebecs had strings of gold. They marched between the gentlemen and the Duke of Valentinois, playing all the while. Then came four with trumpets and clarions of silver, richly dressed, playing their instruments without ceasing. There were also twenty-four lackeys all clad in crimson velvet halved with yellow silk, and they were all around the Duke.

Cesare may have been doing all he could to display that vital component of Italian pride, *la bella figura*, but despite the awed gasps the Duke of Valentinois drew from the crowds, the French courtiers were inclined to find all this splendour rather ridiculous, while Carlotta d'Aragona maintained that she wanted nothing to do with the projected marriage. Despite pressure from King Louis, Carlotta insisted that she would never marry Cesare, a position which carried the full backing of her father, whose envoys baldly declared that 'to a bastard son of the Pope the King [of Naples] not only would not give his legitimate daughter, but not even a bastard child'. Back in Rome, Alexander VI was increasingly concerned as to the consequences should Cesare fail to secure his bride. Anti-French factions were beginning to unite against him, with Naples and Milan the most powerful among them. The Roman Colonna dynasty backed the anti-French cabal. Both the Spanish and Portuguese envoys to the papal court were overt in displaying their royal masters' disgust at the Pope's manoeuvrings, while the Holy Roman Emperor Maximilian also let it be known that he could not sanction a Borgia-French axis. Only the marital family of Giulia Farnese, the Orsini, professed themselves to be pro-French, and Alexander had had dealings with their sinuous treacheries during the first French war.

Just as it appeared that the Pope was beginning to waver, Cesare pulled off a coup. On 12 May 1499 the Duke of Valentinois married Charlotte d'Albret, the daughter of the Duke of Guyenne. Presumably the magisterial travelling privy was put to good use, as some courtiers had played a *charivari* trick on the groom, replacing the tablets of Spanish Fly Cesare had requested to boost his performance with laxatives. Nevertheless, between dashes to the lavatory, Cesare managed to consummate his marriage no less than eight times after the ceremony, a fact which Louis XII reported in a ribald

letter to the Pope and which Alexander had proudly read aloud for
the edification of the Roman populace. As ever with Borgia weddings, an element of indignity was introduced when the students of
Paris, less impressed than their Roman counterparts by the virility
of the Spanish papal bull, staged a seditious satire which concluded
in a riot.

While Cesare was at work in the bedroom, Louis XII was concluding a series of diplomatic bargains which would ease his way
across the Alps. He made agreements with the Swiss and Philip, the
Habsburg ruler of the Low Countries. In February 1499 he settled
with Venice that Milan would be divided and the Venetians rewarded
with Cremona and Adda in exchange for a payment of 10,000 ducats
into the French war chest. Ludovico Sforza sent frantic diplomatic
missions all over the peninsula in an attempt to muster allies, but
though the city states were generous with consolatory words, their
leaders provided neither troops nor money. By mid-July, when plans
for the French invasion were nearing completion, Sforza supporters began to slink out of Rome. Ascanio Sforza left on the 14th for
the Colonna fortress at Nettuno, joining Ludovico in Milan three
weeks later. Lucrezia Borgia's husband, the Duke of Bisceglie, rec-
ognizing that his homeland was doomed, also sought refuge with
the Colonna at Genazzano, abandoning his wife in the sixth month
of her pregnancy with her full support.

Even now, the *condottiere* blood of the Sforza could not be quelled.
With the Sanseverino brothers as lieutenants, Ludovico prepared
Milan for a last stand against the coming onslaught. Troops were
raised in the Sforza territories and garrisoned on the duchy's borders. If the city held for a time, Ludovico reasoned, perhaps the
power of the Holy Roman Empire could be brought to bear.

By 10 August the French army had mustered at Asti, with 17,000
infantry, 1,500 *lances fournies*, 15,000 heavy cavalry and 6,000 Swiss
Guards. At the end of the month they besieged Alessandria, which
held for four days under the command of Galeazzo Sanseverino,
until the latter, realizing the hopelessness of the odds, fled. *Sauve
qui peut* was now the order of the day. On 2 September, Ludovico
Il Moro emptied the treasure chests designed for him by Leonardo
da Vinci of 240,000 gold ducats and the major part of his legendary

jewel collection and took to the hills, heading towards Como and the Tyrol. He had left the castello in the charge of his most trusted companion, Bernardino da Corte, who, in a gesture entirely Milanese, promptly sold it to the French for 150,000 ducats. The city had neither defenders nor defences.

When Louis and Cesare Borgia made their triumphal entrance into the city on 6 October, their men used da Vinci's vast clay model of a statue of Francesco, the first Sforza duke, for target practice.

CHAPTER 15

Caterina's Loss, Lucrezia's Gain

1499–1500

'If the French despise the baseness of its men at least they must
applaud the ardour and valour of Italy's women.'

ISABELLA D'ESTE ON CATERINA SFORZA

During the freezing days of November 1499, those who worked
within the massive walls of the papal fortress of Castel Sant'Angelo
hurried about their business and most likely shuddered as they
heard the faint sound of agonized screams emerging from prisoners held for interrogation in the special chambers below. Two voices
among the chorus of those fainting with pain came from servants of
Caterina Sforza. Torture, the common method of extracting information, held an inherent and fatal flaw. Should a name be blurted
out by the wretch writhing in unimaginable pain, or nodding his
head in bloody assent, how did his tormentors know whether or
not their captive had given them valid information in the misguided
hope that, by appeasing his persecutors, he would be set free if he co-
operated? The supremely persuasive tactics used by the brutes who
worked in the bowels of the fortress made the system anything but
ideal. The Pope claimed the two men had been involved in a bizarre
plot and had acted upon their mistress's orders to assassinate him.

An outbreak of plague had ravaged Forlì and Alexander accused
Caterina of taking the shroud from the corpse of one who had suc-
cumbed to the virulent disease and rolling a piece of the winding
sheet into a cane tube. The contaminated wrapper contained letters that had been falsified by the countess, though they appeared
to be from the citizens of Forlì begging to surrender their city to
the Pope. The Borgias made it be known that the countess's deadly

missives had been intended to carry the pestilence into his hands. One Tommasino, to whom Caterina had entrusted the tube, had foolishly told another attendant of his mission, though he had been assured the fellow would take the secret to his grave – usually a guarantee that it would become the talk of the tavern within twenty-four hours. Both men had been quickly apprehended and soon made satisfactory confessions during their torments at the Castel Sant'Angelo. In Rome, crowds of the faithful flocked to Santa Maria della Pace to hear a thanksgiving Te Deum for the Pope's life, though in Forlì the incident was barely noticed. The Venetian diarist Sanudo wrote 'credo fusse vania' (believed to be false), and few considered it more than a stunt orchestrated by the Borgias to justify their imminent plans for an attack on Forlì.

Caterina Sforza had many talents, and enjoyed a reputation as an accomplished amateur chemist. Alongside dabbling in the fashionable science of alchemy, she created her own beauty remedies and sunburn creams and her commonplace book contained recipes for aborting unwanted babies and notes on the efficacy of slow-working poisons. Given these interests, it seems unlikely that she would have lent herself to a method as clumsy and uncertain as sending Alexander documents within a swatch of deadly winding cloth. It proves telling of Caterina's terrifying isolation and desperate situation that the Borgias could make such a claim sound plausible.

After the conquest of Milan, the next step in the Borgias' dynastic ambitions focused on the provinces of the Romagna. If Cesare had the ability to unite these ever-unruly city states, it would not only provide him with an appanage to rival the greatest prince on the peninsula, but would also substantially strengthen the position of the Church; and once his father died, Cesare would rule a huge buffer zone between the French to the north and the Spaniards to the south. A set of tactics which became a Borgia convention were now put into play. First the spiritual threat: Rimini, held by the Malatesta, Pesaro, by the lordship of Giovanni Sforza, Imola and Forlì, under Caterina Sforza, as well as Faenza, under the Manfredi, all held the official status of vicariates within the Territories of St Peter. The Pope declared these states forfeit under penalty of interdict, supposedly as a punishment for non-payment of the census. A bloody and determined temporal attack followed. On 9 November 1499, Cesare Borgia left Milan at the head of a combined French and pontifical force of 14,000 men destined for Forlì.

Since the arrival of the French in Milan, the countess had been making vigorous preparations for war. At first, she sent her own agents to join the desperate crowd of magnates who were forcing themselves through the rituals of courtly entertainment in the sinister atmosphere of the Castello Sforzesco. Louis XII had made his intentions transparent. 'In response to the request of Our Holy Father the Pope, and ... wishing to aid him in the recovery of his lands and lordships of Imola and Forlì ... we have constituted our dear and well-beloved cousin Cesare the Duke of Valentinois as our lieutenant.' In response to a direct appeal from Caterina, Louis returned blandly that he could not interfere in matters which fell under papal jurisdiction. Caterina's spies initially assured her that there was hope, but by 31 October they were writing, 'Your Ladyship is betrayed ... by Rome, whence all evil comes.' Until the previous day, they reported, the matter had been suspended in dispute, but as of the morning, it was concluded. Caterina sought support from Florence, but the Florentines risked losing the chance of retaking Pisa if they offended the Pope, and, as in the case of her uncle Ludovico, were able to offer no more than good wishes. Nor did the Manfredi, the marital family of Caterina's daughter Bianca, lend their allegiance, as their state of Faenza came under the protection of the Venetians and they felt powerless to act without their sanction. Publicly, Caterina demonstrated her typical courage. She ordered new coursers from Spain, refusing to allow even Cesare Borgia to interfere with her pleasure in hunting, and wrote of her intention to stand alone, claiming that Borgia would not find her people so easy a target as he was persuaded. Yet Caterina knew in truth that, with her fellow Romagnol rulers abandoning her, she was isolated, with only the loyalty of her people to depend on.

The Countess of Forlì personally oversaw every detail of the preparations for the attack she now knew was coming. In a gesture worthy of Castiglione, she appointed the poet Tarchianota of Constantinople as the chief of the civic defence and set about razing trees and farm buildings within a quarter-mile of Forlì's walls, furnishing each substantial dwelling with four months' supply of food, calling in all monies to a central bank with a promise of restitution after the siege and setting a watch to warn the citizens of an enemy advance by the ringing of the bells. The fortress of Ravaldino had been much improved, but needed strengthening if it was to counter bombardment by sophisticated French artillery, so Caterina installed a new parapet and a series of cannon niches along the perimeter wall for the more modern light artillery she had ordered.

Even Caterina's feckless son Ottaviano rose to the call of his mother's bugle. The countess had engaged two bands of German and Gascon mercenaries who were taunting one another in the piazza, calling out 'Francia' and 'Spagna'. Confused, many Forlivesi interspersed themselves, calling 'Riario! Riario!'. Just then, the bells of the city rang a practice warning and panic broke out, the citizens believing they had been infiltrated by the enemy. Several people were killed in the ensuing affray, but Ottaviano managed to calm the riot. Between 4 and 13 November, Ottaviano stayed at Imola, supervising similar preparations to those instigated by his mother at Forlì. On his return he worked alongside volunteers of all ranks from gentleman to peasant to reinforce the city gates of Porta Schiavonia and Porta San Pietro, the labourers pausing at midday to take their lunch together. When the work was finally completed, there remained nothing to do but wait.

When Borgia's troops drew up before Imola on 24 November, Caterina once again found herself betrayed. The diarist Sanudo reported that her people, who had only recently sworn their fealty to her, lay down before Cesare 'like whores', but this is not quite true. The city gates had been barred, with the exception of one, the Porta Spuviglia, that had probably been left vulnerable by an agent acting inside.

The enemy entered without any engagement. Yet Caterina, mistress of Renaissance realpolitik, had not relied on the sycophantic words of her counsellors. Instead she had taken the precaution of bringing the wife and children of Dionigi Naldi, castellan of Imola, to Forlì as hostages. Naldi refused to give up the citadel and trained its cannon upon the town. Naldi held out for a fortnight, swearing that he would prefer to die than break his word to his Countess. Yet when the French finally occupied the citadel on 7 December, Naldo was obliged to concede, though Cesare gave him free passage from the city with five mules carrying his personal effects as acknowledgement of his honourable stance.

When Caterina heard the news from Imola she sent away her jewels, her valuables and her documents, as well as her younger children, to safety at one of the Medici villas in Florence. Briefly, she debated retaining Ottaviano. Fighting for his birthright would be honourable for him and a source of pride for her, but she prudently rejected her wishful thinking, and on 12 December, Ottaviano left for the city republic. Poignantly, it was in the Romagna, not Milan, that the warrior dynasty of Muzio Attendolo made its last stand. Caterina was joined by her sister Chiara and brother Alessandro, children of Lucrezia Landriani, and her half-brother Galeazzo, the elder son of Duke Galeazzo Maria's favourite mistress the Countess of Melzo. When the citizens of Forlì desperately invoked the example of their uncle Ludovico Il Moro, urging Caterina to go into voluntary exile, she stood firm. This generation of the Sforza would remain true to their ancestors and would go to their deaths rather than surrender.

The citizens of Forlì took a more practical view. The high-flown language of chivalry was a meagre return for a sacked city. Led by one of the city councillors, Luffo Numai, they determined to make a private agreement with Cesare rather than suffer the fate of Imola. Accordingly, when Cesare's troops arrived before the city on 17 December they surrendered, even as Caterina let fly her artillery from the fortress of the Rocca. On the 19th, Cesare took formal possession of Forlì, riding into the piazza with his lance contemptuously lowered, a conqueror rather than a combatant. The garrison of the Rocca watched cautiously from the ramparts. However impressed Caterina may have been by the sight of this undeniably beautiful young man in his black velvet cap with its white plume and gleaming French armour under a quartered silk jacket, it was a small satisfaction to her that he was unable to complete the traditional gesture of possession – three circuits of the piazza on horseback – due to torrential, freezing rain.

The Forlivesi hoped that Cesare would deal with them benevolently in return for their ceding the city, and indeed it was a characteristic of Borgia's methods that he treated the people of conquered cities well, as a means of retaining their loyalty. The same, however, could not be said of the French. Pathetically, the Forlivesi had wheeled out the statue of the city's saint, as a reminder to the French troops that their countrymen had been defeated there in 1282. History was obviously not a strong point among the enemy, though, as they gaily ransacked the city, looting, raping and turning the council chamber, the hallowed Sala degli Anziani, into a tavern. Forlì, wrote the chronicler Bernardino, was subject to 'the pains of hell', while the Venetian diarist Sanudo wrote that the Forlivesi deserved their 'damage and shame' as they had so swiftly betrayed their Countess. Whether Caterina was saddened or grimly satisfied to see the treatment of those who had deceitfully sworn loyalty to her, she did not allow it to affect her sense of humour. When the French artillery drew up on 23 December, she decided that under no circumstances would Cesare Borgia enjoy a merry Christmas. On the day of the feast, when hostilities were suspended, the French were horrified to see the standard of Venice raised over the Rocca. Did this mean that Forlì was now under Venetian protection, as was the case with Faenza and Rimini? Of course it was not, but it took some frantic couriering to ascertain that this was so, and Caterina was assured that her enemies spent as gloomy and anxious a Christmas as she did.

On the 26th, Cesare presented himself before the walls of the Rocca, splendid 'as a paladin' according to Bernardino, in the first of two consecutive attempts to parlay directly with Caterina. She refused to receive him, but did permit her brother Alessandro to speak with him, concealing herself behind him so she could whisper suggestions. Perhaps Cesare too should have brushed up on his history, as he attempted to get at Caterina through her children, offering them a papal remittance of 4,000 ducats a year and free passage from the city with her belongings. This, he argued, would prevent the ruin of her family. Via Alessandro, Caterina responded that she was no slave to her children and that she would rather die. So it was war. Cesare put a price on Caterina's head: 5,000 ducats for her corpse, 10,000 for the living Countess. She responded by putting her own ransom out on Cesare: 10,000 ducats, dead or alive. This 'incandescent atmosphere of rivalry' proved infectious both to historians and the contemporary imagination. Rumours abounded that Caterina had called Cesare out, to settle the matter in single combat, and that she had attempted to trap him behind the drawbridge when he came to speak with her. The combat began in earnest on 28 December, when the French guns began to bombard the fortifications of the Rocca. Caterina, wearing a breastplate over her gown, was visible everywhere, rallying her men along the ramparts and directing the fire, which early on succeeded in killing the French artillery commander. Yves d'Allègre admitted admiringly that his master the King of France would have given ten crowns to bring him back to life. Awestruck, Isabella d'Este wrote that she had heard that, during night sorties, Caterina had personally killed a number of French troops, running them through with her own sword, dressed 'à la turcha'; 'Madonna defended herself gallantly'. Indeed, many writers concurred that Caterina was an inspiration to the dawning century. In the *Chroniques de Louis XII*, Jean d'Auton observed that 'under a woman's body she showed a virtuous and virile heart, for no danger, even the closest, caused her to retreat', while Machiavelli reported that she had undertaken an exercise which neither the King of Naples nor the Duke of Milan had dared to attempt.

For a short time it appeared that Caterina might actually succeed. On 4 January 1500, the Marquis of Mantua wrote to Lucrezia Borgia's ex-husband Giovanni Sforza that Ludovico Il Moro was about to arrive in Italy with an army. If the Countess of Forlì could hold out a little longer it would hearten Giovanni, as Pesaro had been chosen as Cesare's next destination. Yves d'Allègre would now be required in Milan. Meanwhile Cesare's funds were running dangerously low, and his unruly mercenaries remained unpaid. Moreover, the frightful weather was beginning to take its toll on his men. Yet her countrymen's praises could have been of no consolation to Caterina when the French guns finally breached the walls of the Rocca on Sunday, 12 January. Dining with his French gentlemen, Cesare Borgia accepted a bet that by Tuesday 'the Madonna will be in our hands'. The final assault on the Rocca cost the lives of 400 of

Caterina's troops and took 4,250 shots from the huge French guns. While the walls of the Rocca were being 'split to their foundations', two barges brought from Ravenna and wooden ladders were laid across the moat in order to create a makeshift crossing.

Until the last moments, Caterina still ran among her men, urging them to show courage; but now Cesare drew up before the ramparts, had the trumpets sounded and offered Caterina a choice. She could come quietly or watch the remainder of her garrison put to the sword. Softly, she replied 'My Lord Duke, I am with you.' Before either had time to move, a constable representing Cesare's French captain, the Bailly de Dijon, rushed up to Caterina and claimed her as his prisoner in the name of the King of France. In the twilight, Caterina was led out into the city, through streets strewn with bleeding corpses, to Cesare's lodgings.

Caterina was apparently preoccupied with the well-being of a man many assumed to be her current lover, the military commander Giovanni di Casale, while a dispute broke out as to who should now have possession of her. The ever-gallant Yves d'Allègre considered it was not form to hold a woman while the Bailly de Dijon was determined not to surrender his prize. Eventually, it was concluded that Caterina had officially surrendered to the French but would be held by Cesare Borgia on the authority of the King of France, and the Bailly was pacified with a ransom of 4,000 ducats. Thus, in Machiavelli's words, 'Madonna was sold to Valentino'.

Caterina's relationship with Cesare during her time as his captive has proved a rich source of salacious discussion. Some chroniclers claim that Borgia completed the Countess's humiliation by raping her, committing 'injuries on the body of our poor and unfortunate lady, Caterina Sforza, who was possessed of great physical beauty'. Others argued that the thirty-six-year-old Caterina, who had become notorious for her taste for young, athletic men, was a more than willing victim: 'There is news that the lady of Forlì has been sent to Cesena, and it seems that Duke Valentino has gone there, and, as I hear, was keeping the said lady, who is a most beautiful woman ... day and night in his room, with whom, in the opinion of all, he is taking his pleasure.' Perhaps in the adrenaline-charged atmosphere of the ravaged city, it was inevitable that two such powerfully sensual figures as Caterina and Cesare should discover an erotic attraction. 'Both ambitious and volatile, both *lussoriosi*, both above law and morality', drawn together like two characters in a troubadour romance, they escaped into one another for a few nights' caprice before respectively returning to the brutal everyday struggle for the Romagna.

Cesare's intention had been to continue the conquest of his putative duchy, but the arrival of Ludovico Il Moro at Como with 8,000 Swiss and 500 Burgundian troops now required the immediate presence of the French. D'Allègre and his troops left for Milan on 27 January, leaving Cesare with a much diminished force of 500 horse and 1,000 infantry. Wisely deciding against pushing on through the Romagna, he returned to Rome for a Caesar's triumph, complete with a captive princess. Caterina Sforza entered Rome along the Via Latina on 26 February in the Duke's train, in some accounts dressed as the Queen of Palmyra, wearing black velvet and led by a restraining gold chain around her neck. It was Carnival, and the already frenetic atmosphere of the city was intensified by the thrill of Cesare's return. Over two days, the former Cardinal of Valencia vaunted his success in a series of appearances which drove the doting Pope wild with joy. A hundred grooms with 'Cesar' picked out in silver on their chests, wagons bearing tableaux of the triumph of Caesar, endless mules in silken trappings and, presumably, the silver privy, made up the spectacle.

Alexander VI received his declared enemy the Countess of Forlì with a show of courtesy and at first she was lodged in the elegant Palazzo Belvedere in the Vatican grounds. But when she refused to sign a document formally relinquishing Forlì and Imola, he set a guard of twenty soldiers to watch her, day and night. Caterina remained defiant and with the help of a Milanese friar, Lauro Bossi, she attempted to escape from the Belvedere in late March. Betrayed by one of Bossi's messengers, she was easily apprehended by the guards. Alexander commanded she be taken to less salubrious quarters, and Caterina found herself unceremoniously dragged into the Castel Sant'Angelo and locked into a small, dark dungeon. It was not long before the damp and airless chamber took its toll upon the prisoner; often ill and prone to fevers, Caterina remained incarcerated in the degrading squalor of her surroundings and, according to the Mantuan ambassador, 'heartsick' at the behaviour of her sons.

As a child, Ottaviano had been exposed to the terror of the rebellion in Forlì, and according to some accounts had been very directly involved. He had been horrified by Caterina's marriage with Feo and had been imprisoned by his mother on suspicion of complicity in his murder. Perhaps he had noticed the attention she lavished upon her baby son by Giovanni de' Medici, who had been baptized Ludovico but changed his name to Giovanni after the death of his Medici father. Perhaps he resented being moved to safety before the attack on Forlì, claiming that she had denied him the chance to fight honourably for his birthright.

It is likelier that his mother's ability to rule her son's territories with no sign of handing them to their legal heir angered the epicene youth, who probably had little stomach for a role that had killed his father. The flabby boy grew to resemble his father both in looks and personality, even inheriting Girolamo's feelings for Caterina, his hatred of her courage and the innate sensibilities she displayed to survive for as long as she had in her prominent and perilous role.

Caterina had always been a devoted mother to her small children, but the rigour and fearlessness of her Sforza heritage may also have made her an unsympathetic one to the older children. Certainly, she appeared to inspire little filial feeling in Ottaviano and Cesare. They did write to Alexander, offering to make over Forlì and Imola in return for their mother's freedom and the benefice of a diocese for Cesare, who was already Archbishop of Pisa; but when this was rejected they wrote to Caterina, telling her to expect no more help in this matter from them. Their callousness outraged the courtier Fortunati, who protested: 'I truly believe that the devil has taken your feelings and your memory from you – recover yourselves, in the name of God, and remember what your mother is, and that she loves you all.' This had little effect, though her sons' negligence did not extend to preventing them from asking Caterina for money, which she provided, signing letters of credit to the Medici for them before her incarceration.

Whatever hopes Caterina had of her uncle's return to Milan came to an end in April 1500. In February Il Moro had been briefly restored and was in the city with Ascanio Sforza, events which may have encouraged Caterina in her attempted escape. But the Milanese had turned against the Sforza, and without popular support he was unable to hold the duchy. Ascanio Sforza barely had time to write a gloating letter to the Pope before Il Moro once again capitulated to the French on 10 April. Caterina had lost everything – her state, her standing, her family, her riches. For a woman of her irrepressible vitality, the confines of prison proved a torture, and the comments of the Mantuan ambassador might nowadays be read as implying she was deeply depressed. There seemed no prospect before her but a lonely, lightless life followed by a forgotten death beneath the city in which she had once been considered a queen.

The Borgias' alliance with the French also held implications for Lucrezia. Like Caterina Sforza, she had now to play the role of a man. During the preparations for the second French invasion of Italy, in the summer of 1499, Lucrezia had become a close confidante of Ascanio Sforza. Her Neapolitan husband, Alfonso Duke of Bisceglie, a natural Sforza ally, as both Milan and Naples suffered the ominous threat of the French taking their lands, so Lucrezia was thus drawn into the factions forming around the Spanish envoys who were determined to prevent the Borgia alliance with Louis XII taking effect. Ascanio visited Lucrezia frequently, calling on her first for news before attending meetings at the Vatican, in the clear hope that Lucrezia's well-known influence with her father would turn him once more towards the Sforza cause.

However, it soon became clear that Cesare and Louis were moving on Milan and Ascanio took flight, as did Alfonso. For Lucrezia, her husband's abandonment was a terrifying shock. They were a genuinely affectionate couple, even if their romance was not so intense as Lucrezia's more romantically minded biographers suggest, and Lucrezia was six months pregnant. The child was particularly precious to her as she had suffered a miscarriage during some energetic games at a garden party eight months previously. Not only did she miss Alfonso at such a vulnerable moment, she had also to bear the shame and humiliation of being so publicly deserted. Roman gossips were quick to report that Giovanni Sforza of Pesaro was enjoying his former wife's discomfiture, considering himself well rid of his Borgia connection; and Alexander only made things worse by crassly evicting Alfonso's sister, Joffre's wife and Cesare's former lover, Sancia d'Aragona, in retaliation. The rumour-mongers reported that the Duchess of Bisceglie 'did nothing but weep'.

To console Lucrezia and save face, the Pope appointed her to a serious civic position usually reserved for high Church officials. She was invested as Governor of Spoleto and Forligni, a serious respon-sibility in a time of approaching war; an extremely unusual post for a young, inexperienced and heavily pregnant woman. Alexander knew that Lucrezia's Borgia pride would seize upon the responsibil-ity and hold her to her new residence in Spoleto, which was moreo-ver several days' ride north of Rome and thus even further away from Alfonso, who begged his wife to join him. Lucrezia arrived in Spoleto with her brother Joffre, only recently released from incar-ceration for his appalling antics, on 14 August 1499 at the head of forty-three carriages and a large company of attendants. Alexander had wished her to travel with the magnificence due to a Borgia duch-ess, and had commissioned a golden palanquin with a gold damask shade which allowed her to ride upright rather than reclining in her scarlet satin litter. This sumptuous contraption bore Lucrezia into the courtyard of the hill fortress of Spoleto, where she dismounted and presided over her first chancery court, acquitting herself with grace and a courteous display of interest. Her new duties included supervising the garrison, attending the meetings of the city authori-ties, provisioning the castle and its armaments and adjudicating the requests and complaints of petitioners. A real job, in short, and one which provided Lucrezia with welcome occupation until the Aragonese, in a conciliatory gesture to the Pope, permitted Alfonso to return to her on 19 September.

The young couple enjoyed their time together in the beautiful surroundings of the Umbrian autumn before returning to Rome in mid-October to await the birth of Lucrezia's baby. The child, a boy, was born on 1 November. As ever, an event in the Borgia household provided an occasion for splendid display, and tiny Rodrigo, named for his grandfather, was christened in the chapel of Santa Maria in Portico with sixteen cardinals, the Governor of Rome and the

Imperial Governor in attendance. Lucrezia presided from a state bed draped in red satin with gold borders, her chamber hung with blue velvet. The noise of the crowds of visitors was muted by Spanish carpets and tapestries, though according to the papal maître d'hôtel Burckard there were so many ladies thronging forward to view the baby that the cardinals were shoved from their seats and had to make do at the back on the chilly marble floor.

Presumably Lucrezia witnessed the triumph of Cesare Borgia when he returned to Rome in Carnival season, though there is no evidence that she visited his unhappy prisoner Caterina Sforza. Having provided an heir, Lucrezia was more than ever in favour with her father, just as the Countess of Forlì had once been, constantly receiving presents and letters from the Vatican, and acting as the principal woman at grand entertainments. Yet Cesare's return proved ominous for the young woman who, perhaps for the first time in years, was enjoying a period of satisfaction and contentment. On 29 June 1500, Alexander VI was awaiting a visit from his family in the papal apartments when the sky outside turned black and a flurry of hailstones dashed against the shutters. As the Pope's two companions, the Bishop of Capua and a chamberlain, Gaspare, rushed across the room to close them, they were arrested by a horrifying noise, a tremendous crack followed swiftly by the sound of the building heaving and collapsing. The Pope had disappeared under a heap of fallen stone, barely visible through a thick black cloud of dust. The upper apartment, usually occupied by Cesare, had been struck by lightning. For some time it was believed the Pope must be dead, and a wave of hysteria spread through the crowds of pilgrims gathered in the city for the Carnival. After hours of panicked digging, however, Alexander was recovered, still seated on his throne and almost unharmed. The coincidence could not have been more ominous – if God were striking against the Borgia, then the devil himself must be protecting them.

Two weeks later, Alexander was recovered and gave a banquet in honour of Lucrezia, her husband the Duke of Bisceglie and his sister Sancia, who had married Joffre, the putative youngest son of Borgia's children with Vannozza Cattanei. The Duke of Bisceglie left the Vatican at around ten accompanied by his man Tommaso

Albanese and a groom. Crowded as the city was with pilgrims, many were sleeping in the piazza before St Peter's, and the three men had to pick their way between the huddled shapes on the ground. Suddenly, a group of these sleeping forms sprang to life, drawing swords from beneath their cloaks. Alfonso was an impressive swordsman and, drawing his own weapon, he fenced them off until he had too many wounds to stand. The groom hauled his body in the direction of Santa Maria in Portico, but saw another group of waiting assassins, so made for the Vatican, with Albanese fighting in the rear to cover their retreat. When Lucrezia saw her husband, wounded in the head, shoulder and thigh, she fainted, but recovered herself and acted quickly, ordering a room in the papal apartments for Alfonso and sending for the Neapolitan ambassador. The next day, as the hunt for his attackers began, Lucrezia summoned the royal surgeons of Naples to treat her husband.

There was little doubt in Rome as to who was behind the attempted murder of the Duke of Bisceglie. Cesare Borgia's methods were already well known. The assassins of his brother Juan Gandia had never been caught, and though his involvement can never be proved, many contemporary accounts attribute the crime to him, as only with Gandia gone could Cesare realize his dreams of a worldly principality. A series of mysterious killings in 1499 had also been linked to Cesare, beginning with the death of a former favourite, the Spanish-born constable of his guard, who had been found in the Tiber bound in a sack like a Turkish concubine. Juan Cervillon, another Spaniard close to both the Aragonese and Borgia factions, was a close enough family friend to have been entrusted with presenting Lucrezia's baby son at the font. Shortly afterwards, Cervillon, who was known for his forthright, outspoken criticisms of his superiors, asked permission to join his family in Naples. As he was leaving a supper party on 2 December he was stabbed to death. According to the diarist Sanudo, he was quickly buried and no one was permitted to view his corpse. In Romagna, the Portuguese Bishop of Ceuta who, despite having travelled in France with Cesare, was attached to a hostile crown, was killed, supposedly having died from wounds incurred on campaign. What these three victims had in common was connections with the Spanish/

Portuguese/Aragona group who were so determined to prevent Cesare's ongoing French-backed success.

Cesare recognized that, despite the setback cause by the momentary return of the Sforza, his hope for the Romagna depended on Louis XII, which would in turn require him to support the latter's projected attempt to reclaim Naples. All ties with the Aragona, despite the customary leaning of the Borgia towards Spain, had to be ruthlessly cut. Cesare had personal reasons for disliking the Aragonese royal family since Carlotta d'Aragona's contemptuous refusal of his suit. Alfonso d'Aragona also irritated him, being handsome, young, a fine soldier, genuinely royal and, it seemed, beloved of Lucrezia. Despite Alfonso's attempts to disassociate himself from the Aragonese party in Rome (he had declared at the time of his flight that he wished to live 'privately' with Lucrezia on his estates at Bisceglie), he was a potentially threatening link with the doomed Neapolitan Kingdom, and he had to be disposed of.

The poet Vincenzo Calmeta, in whose home Tommaso Albanese had taken refuge, reported in a letter that 'every man considers that the Duke of Valentinois brought this about', while Sanudo hints that 'it is not known who committed the assassination but it is said to have been perpetrated by the same hand that murdered the Duke of Gandia', while the Neapolitan Notar Giacomo added 'Valentinois brought it about through envy'.

Numerous other writers saw Alfonso's brother-in-law as responsible; but, maddeningly for Cesare, Alfonso was now recovering in a chamber decorated with Pinturicchio frescoes, Lucrezia and Sancia attending on him personally. The two women never left his side, even sleeping on cots at the foot of his bed. Only the Neapolitan royal doctors were allowed to see him and Lucrezia prepared his food with her own hands for fear of poison. The accounts of the Florentine and Venetian ambassadors differ as to what precisely occurred on the evening of 18 August, but agree insofar as Cesare's second attempt was successful:

... then burst into the chamber Michelotto [Miguel da Corella], most sinister minister of Cesare Valentino; he seized by force

Alfonso's uncle and the royal envoy and having bound their hands behind their backs, consigned them to armed men who stood behind the door, to lead them to prison. Lucrezia, Alfonso's wife, and Sancia, his sister, stupefied by the suddenness and violence of the act, shrieked at Michelotto, demanding to know how he dared to commit such an offence before their very eyes and in the presence of Alfonso. He excused himself as persuasively as he could, declaring that he was obeying the will of others, that he had to live by the orders of another, but that they, if they wished, might go to the Pope, and it would be easy to obtain the release of the arrested men. Carried away with anger and pity ... the two women went to the Pope and insisted that he give them the prisoners. Meanwhile, Michelotto, most wretched of criminals and most criminal of wretches, suffocated Alfonso ... The women, returning from the Pope, found armed men at the door of the chamber, who prevented them from entering and announced that Alfonso was dead.

Lucrezia and Sancia went wild with grief and fury that they had been tricked, not believing for a moment Michelotto's hasty story that Alfonso had been struck by a sudden haemorrhage. Their sobbing provided the accompaniment for Alfonso's funeral cortège, a rabble of priests who scuttled alongside the corpse as Michelotto's men bore it hastily to the tiny church of Santa Maria della Febbre, where presumably a grave was waiting. Cesare soon brought his father round, claiming that Alfonso had been plotting against the Borgia family for the Aragonese, and that he had even tried to murder Cesare himself with a crossbow. Whether or not Alexander actually believed the story, he appeared to do so publicly. Lucrezia, though, made her grief embarrassingly public. The day after the murder, Cesare insouciantly paid a call on his sister, surrounded with a huge number of bodyguards to back up his story that the Aragon had tried to kill him. Lucrezia did see him, though what passed between them is unknown. However, the court at Mantua received a report that 'the Pope has sent away his daughter and his daughter-in-law because in the end they were wearisome to him'. On 4 September, Lucrezia departed for her estate at Nepi, either in disgust or disgrace, but Cesare and Alexander knew that she was too valuable a political tool to be permitted long to mourn. Within a month of Alfonso's murder, they were receiving fresh, and it must be admitted, brave, suitors for Lucrezia's hand.

CHAPTER 16

Lucrezia and Isabella do Battle

1500

'The shame, my Lord, is that you have all done this to me ... but I have found a remedy'

OTTAVIANO COLONNA

Aged just twenty, Lucrezia Borgia had received the blame for the violence and threats to her first husband, and the successful murder of her second; ferocious death stalked her and those whom she loved. She agonized that she brought tragedy in her wake, perhaps personified by her brother and her father.

Her adult life had proved a litany of scandal and bloodshed. Divorced from her first husband, Giovanni Sforza, on the grounds of non-consummation, she had buried her second bridegroom, the Duke of Bisceglie, bastard son of Alfonso d'Aragona and his mistress Truzia. Lucrezia had not only genuinely loved her beautiful young husband and borne him a posthumous son, but she had been an unwilling witness to the youth's murder by her brother Cesare's men. The known birth of a dubious child in 1498, not to mention the darker rumours so successfully put about by Sforza, hardly made her a desirable catch. Initially, Lucrezia herself was apparently opposed to marrying again.

In September 1500, Louis de Ligny, a cousin of Louis XII, offered for her hand in return for a large dowry and the lordship of Siena – 'These Frenchmen will do anything for money,' sniffed Cattanei, but Lucrezia claimed she did not wish to leave Italy. Francesco Orsini, Duke of Gravina, was the next to throw in his hat, making a great display of consigning his mistress to a convent before presenting himself at the Vatican. A Roman grandee, Ottaviano Colonna, received some consideration as a possible candidate. Betting in the Holy City showed Gravina as a clear favourite. Lucrezia confounded the gamblers when she declined the latter's formal offer of marriage. According to the diarist Sanudo, the Pope demanded her reasons and his widowed daughter delivered the tart response, 'Because my husbands have been very unlucky,' and stormed out of the room. As early as November, however, the Dowager Duchess Lucrezia, still a young woman, had changed her mind and hoped that the fatality and misfortunes of her bridegrooms might yet cease; and the family looked at another union for Lucrezia. It appears that Cesare had already proposed the alliance to his grieving sister when he visited her at Nepi en route for the Romagna that autumn. This time the Borgias had set their sights high, and their gaze had fallen upon one of the most ancient and greatest dynasties on the peninsula. The groom was the widowed Alfonso d'Este, brother of Isabella and son of Duke Ercole of Ferrara.

For Lucrezia, the marriage meant an escape from Rome, home of unhappy memories, and an opportunity to take the place for which she had been educated, as the Lady of a truly influential and cultivated court. Pesaro and Bisceglie appeared pathetic provincial backwaters when compared to Ferrara. Furthermore, with a significant, rather than a weak and dependent husband, she might finally be free of the control of her father and brother. As a mature woman, Lucrezia now saw how she might exploit Alexander VI and Cesare's need of her, as they both felt particularly desirous that the Ferrarese union take place. Cesare's insistence that the Borgias abandon the Neapolitan Aragonese had proved correct, as in November 1500 Louis of France and the Spanish King Ferdinand of Aragon and Spain came to a ruthless agreement partitioning Naples between them. Louis would have the kingdom of Naples and various other territories, while the Spanish would take Puglia and Calabria. To boost their legitimacy, the territories carried the added cachet of the title 'papal fiefdom'. This put Alexander VI in a powerful position, much more significant than that of the Duke of Ferrara, also allied with the French. For Cesare, Ferrara could act as a loyal buffer zone between his intended Duchy of Romagna and the hostile territories of the Venetians. Both Cesare and the Pope felt certain that any objections from the Estense Duke of Ferrara could be smoothed over. Accordingly, in February 1501, the Cardinal of Modena wrote to the Duke of Ferrara to propose the alliance.

Duke Ercole's immediate reaction to the Cardinal's news had been abhorrence at such a connection, sentiments heartily shared by his daughter Isabella d'Este. Had Lucrezia's reputation been spotless and uncompromised, the idea could barely be considered a joke. The idea that the bastard daughter of the Borgia from Valencia, otherwise known as *marranos*, made the marriage a preposterous fancy. The d'Este had been rulers for 250 years and had been present in Ferrara since the eleventh century. The late Duchess Eleonora had been a royal princess, Beatrice had taken Ludovico Sforza of Milan as her husband, her brother Alfonso d'Este had married Ludovico's niece and daughter of the former Duke Galeazzo Sforza. Isabella's connections had been no less exalted, for she had been joined in marriage with the Marquis of Mantua.

Ercole came up with what seemed a sound argument for not being able to deliver his elder son. He wrote to the Vatican stating the marriage would be impossible because of Alfonso's recent betrothal to Louise d'Angoulême. Word arrived from the Pope. Silken words, serpentine in their soothing tone, appeased the Duke of Ferrara. Alexander quite agreed, but his words hit their mark when he affably stated that a compromise would solve their problem. Lucrezia could marry the third d'Este brother, Ferrante, instead of the unavailable Alfonso. He added that nothing could be simpler than the small matter of separating Modena from the other d'Este holdings and providing the young couple with a fief, suitably maintained, of course, at the Duke's expense.

One thing the Duke feared more than the Borgias was the division of his estates, and Louise was heard no more of. There was also the small matter of the papal bulls which so conveniently dispossessed any magnates who displeased the Pope. The duke had not wish for Ferrara to suffer the fate of Imola and Forlì. In desperation, Ercole turned to the French as his last hope. Louis needed the papal investiture of Naples far more than he needed the duke. The d'Este had to proceed cautiously, and Isabella's consummate skills at spread-betting continued to appease by requesting Cesare to be godfather to her first son, Federico, born amid great jubilation in May that year.

Cesare wrote graciously to Mantua, 'I heard of the fortunate and much-desired birth of Your Excellency's little son with exultation as great as if it had been my own, and gladly accept the honour you propose to do to me.' Isabella loathed the Borgias though she had a good sense of realpolitik and that compromise solved most problems. She prepared to swallow her pride and hitch her baby to the coat tails of the man who looked likely to become Italy's most powerful prince. Isabella's delight in finally taking out the fabulous d'Este cradle, a gift from her father which had been so long gathering the dust of despair, was marred further a few months later when Cesare proposed a betrothal between baby Federico and his own newborn daughter with Charlotte d'Albret, Luisa. Isabella conceded in a letter that, despite Cesare's courtesy, she doubted the wisdom of sending an envoy to Valentinois to discuss his daughter's possible dowry, 'because [Cesare] has little respect for me ... It has been agreed to use the means of the Illustrious Lady Lucrezia,' a line which acknowledges Lucrezia's influence within her powerful family despite Isabella's unabashed horror at the connection with her.

Cesare demonstrated the contempt which Isabella's political and diplomatic instincts had intuited after a visit to Urbino at Carnival in 1501. The court had been captivated by a beautiful Mantuan girl, Dorotea Malatesta, the intended bride of the Venetian *condottiere* Gianbattista Caracciolo. Cesare declared himself smitten, but the Duchess of Urbino, Elisabetta Gonzaga, ran a strict and modest household and any attempts at flirtation were stamped out quickly.

As Dorotea set off after Carnival for her Venetian wedding, her party was set upon by a group of masked horsemen, among them Cesare, particularly easy to recognize thanks to the silly and rudimentary disguise of a bandaged eye. Dorotea reacted in a manner that seems similar to Caterina Sforza's own resistance when taken by Cesare. She submitted quite willingly to his attentions in private, but the abduction naturally caused a scandal. Cesare, careless of both public opinion and his *inamorata*'s reputation, suggested that she had been having an affair with one of his Spanish captains, to whom she had given a gift of some embroidered shirts. Beyond this, he claimed the affair had nothing to do with him. This must surely have provoked a fit of polite coughing throughout the peninsula, certainly among those who knew Cesare. The only unwanted result for the latter had been that, because of Dorotea's Mantovese origins, the kidnapping had been a grave slight both to the Gonzaga and d'Este families. The abduction provided yet another reason for the family at Ferrara to fear the marriage with Lucrezia.

The events of the following spring destroyed what hope Duke Ercole had that the King of France might step in to save his family from disgrace. A force of over 20,000 was assembled in Lombardy, commanded jointly by Cesare Borgia, the Duke d'Aubigny and Francesco de Sanseverino. A month later, the Pope co-operated by promulgating a bull depriving the King of Naples of his crown and confirming the division of territories decided by Louis and Ferdinand of Aragon. By July the French had sacked Capua with their customary thoroughness and King Federigo recognized the hopelessness of his position. Before the dread French guns had even been hauled into position he came to an accommodation with Louis, and spent the rest of his life in comfortable exile in France.

The historian Guicciardini commented on the Ferrarese marriage: 'Although [it] was most unworthy of the house of Este, wont to make the most noble alliances, and all the more unworthy because Lucrezia was illegitimate and stained with great infamy, Ercole and Alfonso consented because the French King, desiring to satisfy the Pope in all things, made strong importunities for this union.' In other words, they knew when they were beaten. Duke Ercole, resigned, sent a sarcastic letter to Rome in which he expressed his joy at the marriage of Lucrezia and Alfonso; 'God had touched His Holiness's heart, and inspired him to unite the blood of his house with ours ... pray God that we may be worthy of it.' His last hope was that Alexander would refuse his exorbitant dowry demands, but the Pope was reported to be so delighted at the prospect of such a thoroughly respectable marriage that the Roman gossips sniggered he would have pawned the papal tiara to see his daughter a d'Este duchess.

Lucrezia was to bring 100,000 ducats, another 75,000 ducats' worth of valuable goods in her trousseau, and the castles of Cento and Pieve. Alexander reduced the toll of Ferrara as a papal vicariate from 4,000 ducats to 100 for the next three generations, guaranteed the investiture of the duchy to any male heirs of Lucrezia and Alfonso, and provided Cardinal Ippolito d'Este with even greater ecclesiastical benefices. Lucrezia rode out to Santa Maria del Popolo for a thanksgiving Mass accompanied by the French and Spanish ambassadors and an escort of 500, all dressed in cloth of gold. Her Spanish dwarves tumbled about her, proclaiming their lady's goodness, while fireworks lit up the dusk, and the next day Lucrezia gave the dress she had worn to church to her jester, who donned it and rollicked through the streets, demanding homage for the Duchess of Ferrara.

And what of the bridegroom? Alfonso had been vain or curious enough to have his portrait painted and sent to Rome for Lucrezia to examine. He was not bad-looking, and had succeeded in turning his pet hobby of casting iron into a lucrative artillery manufacture – 'he was destined to become perhaps the first great gunner of history'. His other pastimes were less appealing. His taste for coarse companions and squalid nightlife had proved a constant humiliation to his first wife, Anna Sforza, who had taken to cross-dressing and making love with women as a consolation; and of late Alfonso's behaviour had become not so much base as bizarre. He was occasionally to be spotted marching naked through the streets of Ferrara, his drawn sword in one hand and his penis proudly gripped in the other. At least that worked, as his first wife had perished in childbirth. Lucrezia seemed sure that she could tolerate her new husband's eccentricities, perhaps even welcoming them if it meant he would not be a demanding lover, and at least they shared a taste for dwarves.

While the settlements were being finalized, Alexander made another gesture which demonstrated his love for and trust in Lucrezia, and, like the governorship of Spoleto, allowed her publicly to demonstrate her talent for exercising authority in a conventionally masculine sphere. Extraordinarily, when he departed for Rome to tour the papal dominions he made Lucrezia his regent in the Vatican. Burchard reports that 'Before His Holiness, our Master, left the city, he turned over the palace and all business affairs to his daughter.' Although she did not perch her fashionably dressed form on the papal throne, as later chroniclers reported, she was invested with full authority to open all papal correspondence not dealing directly with ecclesiastical matters and presided over the assemblies of cardinals with calm and efficiency, much assisted by her old confidant Cardinal Giorgio Costa, the Bishop of Lisbon. If the other members of the conclave were shocked, they dared not show it, and Lucrezia's time as governess of the Vatican proceeded with a great show of co-operation and cordiality.

In December, the news arrived in Rome that Lucrezia's escort had left Ferrara to fetch her. The Pope was extremely nervous, moody and erratic. He was sure his daughter was beautiful enough to triumph over the ladies of her new court, but, to be certain, he ordered 20,000 ducats' worth of pearls to be stitched onto one of her new dresses and provided her with a hat which cost half as much again. As ever, vast lengths of gold brocade and striped velvets and silks were made up to ensure that Lucrezia would dazzle her new subjects. The d'Este party arrived on the 23rd, having journeyed in torrential rain throughout, and were not pleased to be kept waiting for two hours outside the Vatican while Cesare organized his 4,000-strong escort. At last they were greeted by the cardinals, then Cesare, flanked by his bumblebee-striped halberdiers. As they proceeded towards their audience with the Pope, the guns boomed out from Sant'Angelo, where Caterina Sforza would surely have heard them.

Lucrezia met her escort the next day, casually arranged on the steps of Santa Maria in Portico in a mulberry gown banded with gold under a gold jacket lined with sable. She wore a necklace of huge rubies and pearls and her hair was bound in a snood that seemed to be made entirely of gemstones. The bride was breathtaking, a fact which even the most hostile chroniclers were obliged to admit. Much to Isabella d'Este's disgust, her spy Il Prete reported: 'She is singularly graceful in everything she does and her manners are modest, gentle and decorous. She is also a good Christian ... as regards good looks she has quite sufficient but her pleasing expression and gracious ways make her seem even more beautiful than she is. In short, she seems to me to be such that there is nothing to fear, rather the very best to be hoped in every way.'

The furiously competitive Isabella was even more incensed when she received breathless reports of the skill and captivating sensuality with which Lucrezia danced. On St Stefano, Lucrezia gave a party where her Moorish blood was displayed as she performed an exotic Eastern dance in a black satin dress slashed with gold. Isabella demanded that Cardinal Ippolito, who had become a great crony of Cesare Borgia, should discover what this new dance was and send a dancing master to teach it – though given that Isabella was on her way to becoming the fattest woman in Italy, the effects might not have been so pleasing. Other novelties provided by the Borgia for their guests included a bullfight in which Cesare took the part of the matador, and a succession of masques and entertainments proceeded until Epiphany.

The proxy marriage took place on 30 December. For all the d'Estes' much vaunted aristocracy, they could be as penny-pinching as Florentine housewives, so when the fabulous collection of Este jewels was opened before her, Lucrezia was disappointed to find that, rather than plunging her hands into the casket, she was permitted to retrieve only the wedding ring, lest she die on the journey and the gifts pass out of the family to her son Rodrigo. The Ferrarese treasurer also insisted on biting the ducats of the dowry to ascertain that they were not wood overlaid with gilt. More painful to Lucrezia was the parting with her son, who was only three. She had arranged for him to be given the dukedom of Sermoneta and the great income which came with it (some lesser properties had been made over to the mysterious Infans Romanus), and had consigned him to the care of her cousin Cardinal Francesco Borgia. As she knelt to kiss him goodbye, the little boy tried to hug her, but was prevented from wrapping his tiny arms around his mother by the stiff brocade about her neck. It was a fitting image for the sacrifices demanded of the new Duchess of Ferrara. His mother never again saw Rodrigo after their last, awkward embrace as he died ten years later, aged thirteen.

On 6 January 1502 Lucrezia rode out through a snowstorm for her new home. Her route took her through Cesare's newly conquered territories of Imola, Forlì, Pesaro and Rimini. Thoughtfully, Cesare had had the roads repaved for his sister's comfort. Just before Bologna, Lucrezia paused with the immortal excuse that she needed to wash her hair. She had reason to be nervous about greeting the Bentivoglio family, the ruling house of Bologna, as her former aunt-in-law, Giovanni Sforza's relative Ginevra, presided there. As she had progressed through the Romagna, Lucrezia could not but be embarrassingly aware of the hostility provoked by Cesare's conquests in the region; and there were also fears for her safety from the revenge of Gianbattista Caracciolo, whose bride Cesare had kidnapped (albeit with her seeming consent) the previous year. Perhaps for this reason, Alfonso d'Este arranged that the customary 'surprise' meeting between the betrothed couple should happen near Bologna. Lucrezia's gold curtain of hair took so long to dry that it was still damp when Alfonso appeared, and they had an unusually unchoreographed first encounter, Lucrezia *déshabillée* in a muslin gown. Alfonso had resigned himself to his duty, but it had never occurred to him that it might be a pleasure to do it. He had hardly bothered to consummate his marriage to Anna Sforza, beyond the pregnancy which killed her; but when he saw Lucrezia, who had just had time hastily to comb her shining hair, he felt the beginnings of what became a genuine, protective love.

Isabella d'Este had travelled to her home city to act as First Lady of Ferrara, though she had left her husband behind, on her father's advice, since Alexander VI had made it clear that he disapproved of the marquis, who, he claimed, was harbouring Borgia enemies and speaking his mind too freely in criticizing the Pope. Isabella threw herself into the preparations, even going so far as to diet in her attempts to compete with Lucrezia. When she was not having fittings for new clothes of the latest and most luxurious fashion, she was taking lessons with her dancing and singing masters, convinced that she would show the Spanish bastard who was the greater lady. When Lucrezia, accompanied on the last stages of her journey by Elisabetta, Duchess of Urbino, arrived on the steps of the ducal palazzo, she was greeted by a glacially correct and condescending Isabella, who comported herself more like the Queen of Italy than the Marchioness of Mantua. Isabella's women wrote to Mantua with loyal spite that their mistress had far outshone La Borgia, but no one really thought so. Isabella had neglected to consider the sophisticated education Lucrezia had received during her time in Rome and she found herself thoroughly and infuriatingly routed. 'Her face is very pretty with adorable eyes, full of life and gaiety,' described the chronicler Zanotto, while Cagnolo di Parma enthused about the 'good humour and gaiety' which seemed to suffuse 'her whole being'. Isabella d'Este reportedly wept 'hot tears' at the sight of a stupendous ruby, formerly the property of her mother Duchess Eleonora, clasped about Lucrezia's neck.

Isabella attempted to embarrass Lucrezia after the wedding when, at the request of the exhausted bride, who had been receiving the Ferrarese nobility for hours without having sat or eaten since the morning, the entertainment was cut short and she and Alfonso retired. Isabella's love of the coarse humour of her dwarves was also reflected in the pleasure she took at wedding-night bawdy – when her daughter Eleonora was married, she burst into the bridal chamber early next morning and asked her son-in-law the most embarrassingly explicit questions; but Lucrezia was hardly a blushing virgin bride. The bedroom door was firmly closed on the Marchioness of Mantua and the Duchess of Urbino, and Isabella's attempts the next morning to jolly the couple along with the buffoonery known as the 'joyous awakening' were met with the same chilly refusal. Isabella huffily concluded that the marriage night had been 'a cold one', but she was ashamed by Lucrezia's sophistication and self-possession. Herself an inveterate early riser, Isabella was also enraged by Lucrezia's calm unwillingness to leave her chambers in the Torre Marchesana before noon: 'Yesterday we all had to remain in our rooms ... because Donna Lucrezia takes so long to rise and dress herself ... Your Lordship should not envy me for your not being here at this marriage because it is of such a coldness that I envy anyone who remained in Mantua,' she bitched to Francesco Gonzaga.

Isabella did all she could to emphasize her own importance in the proceedings at Lucrezia's expense. She complained that the balls and comedies provided were dull, but of course she had no time to write because her attention was in such demand from her brothers and

the women of the Ferrara court, whom she was obliged to entertain while Lucrezia lolled in bed. The Gonzaga secretary Capilupi
unfavourably compared Lucrezia's oratory with that of Isabella and
Elisabetta of Urbino when they responded to the formal farewells of
the Venetian ambassadors: Isabella had spoken with the 'eloquence
and prudence' of a consummate orator, but Lucrezia, notwithstanding her experience, 'got nowhere near their prudent replies'. Isabella
was especially enraged because from the evidence of all accounts,
Lucrezia was dazzlingly well dressed and Isabella, despite enormous effort and expenditure, appeared at her side as a portly provincial. Jealousy and malice drips from every word of Isabella's pen,
heightened by the fact that both Duke Ercole and Alfonso seemed
delighted by the Borgia merger: 'His affection and honour for her
... is a great thing,' commented Isabella's spy Bernardino di Prosperi
of Alfonso. Yet there was a sincerely emotional component to her
anger at Lucrezia's glamour and precedence, as she saw the remaining memories of her beloved mother Eleonora being supplanted.

Nowhere was this more evident than in the rooms which were
redecorated for Lucrezia's arrival. Eleonora's apartments and
garden were made over to Lucrezia, including a bathroom suite
with marble warming rooms and a *necessarium* with marble benches
and marble steps leading down to a deep bath lined with linen. The
garden had as its centrepoint a marble pavilion with sixteen columns, surrounded by a pool fed from lion's head fountains. Roses,
jasmine and rosemary scented the air among ornamental fruit trees,
sheltered by walls espaliered with vines. A flower garden and herb
garden, a fishpond and an outdoor dining room beneath a loggia
made the duchess's garden an enchanting retreat. Isabella returned
bitterly to Mantua leaving Lucrezia in possession not only of her
mother's jewels and rooms, but also the affection of her father, who
wrote approvingly to the Pope: 'before the most illustrious Duchess,
our common daughter, arrived here, my firm intention was to caress
and honour her, as is fitting ... Now that Her Ladyship has come
here, she has so satisfied me, by the virtues and worthy qualities that
I find in her that I am not only confirmed in this good disposition,
but the desirer and intention to do so have greatly increased in me.'

★

The French conquest of Naples had effected Lucrezia's marriage, but it also had consequences for Caterina Sforza, who had spent the preceding year in surroundings far less charming and salubrious than Duchess Eleonora's garden. In June 1501 Yves d'Allègre presented himself in Rome, where he demanded Caterina's release in the name of Louis XII. Alexander conceded, but only in exchange for her formal renunciation of Imola and Forlì. Caterina signed the document on 30 June and quit the castello, where her adventures as a politician and a warrior had both begun and ended. She remained in Rome for a few days as a guest of Raffaele Riario, seeing old friends and a number of prelates and cardinals. Two thousand ducats from Florence were authorized for her return journey there, but she still chose to travel by night for fear of further Borgia plots, embarking incognito at the port of Ostia for Livorno. Alexander was hypocrite enough to write to the *Dieci di Balia* (the Florentine magistracy in charge of military and foreign affairs, also known as The Ten), recommending Caterina to them, for whom he felt a paternal affection and whom he claimed to have treated with clemency. Caterina kept a strained silence, though she wrote to her confessor that, if she chose to do so, what she had to tell of the Borgias would 'stupefy the world'.

Caterina was elated to recover her boy, Giovanni, of whom she had eagerly sought news as soon as she was released from prison. 'He has grown and is a beautiful, gallant boy,' reported a relative. Yet Caterina was almost immediately plunged into the kind of controversy which seemed to have ended for ever with her incarceration. Lorenzo il Popolano de' Medici, her brother-in-law, had assumed the guardianship of her son when she was imprisoned and now wished to administer his patrimony. When he left Florence with the child Caterina launched a legal battle for justice. She wrote to Mantua and to the imperial court in Germany, and tried to sway her sister Bianca Maria, her friends and their extended kinship network to her cause. As long as the legal proceedings were drawn out, Caterina could not see her son, and was fearful for his life. Caterina had removed to the Medici villa at Castello, wearied by the harrying of Lorenzo and the incessant financial demands of her other children; but in July 1502 Lorenzo attempted to chase her out, a move which scandalized the republic. Caterina responded with some of her old vim that she was determined never to leave other than in pieces. Caterina returned to the city for a short time before setting out once more for the villa, writing sadly to her son Ottaviano, 'the shame, my Lord, is that you have all done this to me ... but I have found a remedy'. Caterina tried to maintain a decent household, consisting of twenty-four 'mouths', five horses and three mules, but such was her desperate lack of funds that she had to beg for tablecloths and linens; the prior Fortunati remonstrated with Ottaviano for his ingratitude and asked that he request the necessary linens as well as six forks and spoons for his mother. While Caterina was reduced to these pathetic requests, the man who had been her nemesis and her lover was reaching the apogee of his power. As the Countess of Forlì struggled to retain a modicum of her stolen dignity, Cesare Borgia received his official confirmation as Duke of the Romagna.

CHAPTER 17

Lucrezia's Embarrassment

1502

'And truly the Heavens cannot give a man a greater opportunity
for glory'

NICCOLÒ MACHIAVELLI, DISCOURSES ON LIVY

At the same time as Caterina Sforza emerged from her confinement at the Castel Sant'Angelo to face her struggles in Florence, the
people of her former state of Forlì had been witnessing the arrival
and departure of large trains of goods. During the end of June 1502
caravans of over 180 mules arrived almost daily to deposit their cargo,
before returning to fetch more. The carts carried treasures and other
spoils of the Romagnol rulers dispossessed by Cesare Borgia, now
Duke of Romagna. The latter had decided to deposit the treasures
and other loot at the scene of Caterina Sforza's greatest triumph and
later undoing: the Rocca di Ravaldino.

Six months earlier, a few miles outside Rome, Lucrezia Borgia
had endured the departure of her brother Cesare; her huge bridal
caravan halted to allow her to say goodbye. The siblings' farewell
to each other seemed to kill rumours put about by the enemies of
the Borgia that a satanic bond united them. Witnesses saw only the
deepest mutual love and affection, an extraordinary connection that
had largely been created by Lucrezia's willingness to defend her
brother's actions even when detrimental to her own happiness. The
relationship might have been difficult for outsiders to comprehend,
but those accompanying the pair, each upon a momentous journey,
could see that nothing sinister lay in their love for each other.

Pragmatic as ever, Lucrezia realized that much depended upon
Cesare's presence with their father now. She watched him prepare

to leave for Rome with an expression of impassivity. Only those who knew Lucrezia well understood that her complete stillness betrayed her deep concern over what lay ahead. She would be passing through territories either already taken by Cesare, or states which he imminently threatened to make part of his new dominions. The ultimate destination also risked unnerving her usual adamant determination, and without her brother or her father for protection, the future Duchess of Ferrara would need to put her full arsenal of guile and dissemblance to use, if only to disguise her fears. She watched Cesare and Cardinal Ippolito d'Este, her future brother-in-law, turn their horses and ride back towards the Holy City.

Cesare had much to occupy his thoughts. The past two years had seen a distinct shift in power; he appeared to have become the dominant partner in the relationship with his father, the Pope, but at times the Pontiff did not seem to realize what his eldest surviving son had planned. When word arrived of a new conquest in the Romagna, the Pope was as surprised by the news as those closest to him. Of late, Alexander had been clearly dismayed by some of Cesare's latest victories, as these had another name to those not in the Borgia camp. They saw the young duke's actions as outrages. Cesare's love of action, quick thinking and sly deceptions, as well as the other resources he had at his disposal, had brought him within sight of his final goal. Believing his oft-repeated prediction that he would die young, Borgia was spurred on in his hurry to take the states he had yet to capture, to complete his duchy and, he hoped, prevent his own fall at his father's death.

In October 1488, aged seventeen, Guidobaldo da Montefeltro, Duke of Urbino had taken Elisabetta Gonzaga as his wife. Considered one of the finest-looking noblemen of his day, the tall, blond-haired Duke had an unusually long, thin body disproportionate to his short legs, and poor health quickened his wish for the marriage to his betrothed, the sweet-natured Elisabetta. The eighteen-year-old bride and younger sister of Francesco, Marquis of Mantua also suffered from a delicate constitution, not helped by a most hazardous bridal journey to her new mountain state.

The d'Este sisters complained bitterly over the journey to Milan two years later, but the nearest they came to real harm was the cold weather and a lack of the usual vast amount of food they expected to be served. Elisabetta, by contrast, arrived in Urbino having survived rock falls and flash floods of cascading water gushing from mountain ravines that also brought down large trees. Graciously she thanked her entourage, and wrote: 'If it had not been for devotion I should not have reached Urbino alive.' Benedetto Capilupi, Francesco's secretary, described the journey to his master as 'The most detestable weather for weddings ever known.'

Despite her constitution, Elisabetta enjoyed much acclaim as one of the best-looking young women on the peninsula. Those who saw the handsome pair considered them well matched for their arresting looks. To a contemporary eye, however, the portraits of the ducal couple – their long, pale faces startled, as they stare fixedly from their frames – are quite expressionless.

Elisabetta had been befriended by Isabella d'Este in Ferrara while breaking the journey to her new home and husband in Urbino, and the pair remained close friends for the rest of their lives, though Isabella's forceful character had a baleful influence on Elisabetta's innate goodness, particularly when they spent long periods together. Isabella had latched onto her rich and pliable sister-in-law. She had visited Urbino, her eyes bulging with greed, for rarely had a father and son created such a diverse and discerning collection of books, pictures, statues and other precious items. When the Montefelto were newly wedded, Francesco Gonzaga, Marquis of Mantua, visited his sister whenever homesickness overpowered her. Francesco, already despised by Isabella, proved a touchingly solicitous brother to all his sisters.

The Christmas before Elisabetta's marriage, the eldest of the three sisters had organized a special *festà* for their brother. They had special reason to celebrate for Chiara Gonzaga, married to the Comte de Montpensier, had not been home since her marriage five years earlier. When the marquis had to travel over Christmas the three sisters wrote urging him to come home in time to celebrate the New Year: 'We pray you earnestly, by that brotherly love you bear us, to come and console us in the New Year and taste the pleasures we have prepared for you in our *festà* ... which will certainly gratify you and give us the greatest possible delight.' Francesco Gonzaga must have wondered why he and his wife did not enjoy the same harmonious relationship that he could claim with any one of his sisters.

The new duchess's homesickness might certainly have been remedied by the love of her husband. When apart they wrote to each other daily, and seemed almost as young lovers throughout the vicissitudes they would suffer during their life together. The marchioness considered the soppy exchange of letters silly; she treated Elisabetta as being touched in the head when it came to marriage, particularly when Elisabetta panted with impatience to receive the courier bringing her Guidobaldo's daily letter. Isabella had managed the perfect marriage, and it had been easy enough to arrange. She saw her husband as little as possible, eased by Francesco's frequent and long absences on military or diplomatic missions. During these periods, she took over as regent and enjoyed running Mantua, a job at which she became highly competent. Her somewhat simian husband became exasperated by his wife, avoiding her when not campaigning, increasingly choosing to lose himself in sporting activities, not always in the field. It did not occur to Isabella that her own marriage might not be considered the most successful within the family. The thought of the deviant uxorious devotion that Guidobaldo held for his wife and the couple's evident desire for physical proximity frankly disgusted the marchioness.

In her own marriage she managed her husband's lust as best she could. Isabella turned two blind eyes to the ever-growing number of familiar-looking children playing in the streets of Mantua. Unfortunately their origins could hardly be doubted, for they had been stamped with Francesco's hirsute genetic imprint. Upon hearing from her sister-in-law that the young duke's hyperactive libido continued to plague him, she sympathized for Guidobaldo. Elisabetta told the Marchioness that she felt particularly worried about the duke's health due to his exertions. She confided to Isabella that he leapt upon her at every opportunity, spending hours trying to consummate their union fully, until finally the couple both lay exhausted by yet another failure. The news left Isabella both bewildered and revolted in equal measure. Shortly after his marriage, physicians had confirmed the ducal couple's worst fears. Guidobaldo suffered from incurable impotence, rumoured to be the result of a wicked spell once cast upon him, though no further explanation was provided for this malevolent act. Elisabetta's love for him redoubled and he gratefully returned her feelings, though she feared her highly sexed husband's alarming episodes.

In 1498, the vexing question as to who should eventually succeed Guidobaldo was put by Cardinal Giuliano della Rovere. The Cardinal proposed that their shared nephew, Francesco Maria della Rovere, son of Guidobaldo's sister Giovanna and della Rovere's brother Giovanni, be named heir to the dukedom of Urbino. This required Alexander's official approval and, given the hatred between the Pontiff and Giuliano della Rovere, the two families expected a long-drawn-out struggle. Yet papal ratification arrived promptly, permitting the desired succession. In 1501 Giovanni della Rovere had died, leaving his wife Giovanna da Montefeltro as regent of Sinigaglia for her son. Francesca Maria would eventually combine the domain with Urbino.

Throughout her marriage, Elisabetta spent a great deal of time with Isabella d'Este. The Marchioness of Mantua needed her friend more than ever since the death of her sister Beatrice, and the sickening of her father. Isabella did not lack for occupation, and had plenty of projects between the embellishment of her art collection and, during Francesco's absences, the running of Mantua. The worsening situation as Cesare Borgia greedily took the weaker Romagnol states, as well as there being two French invasions, had left Isabella as regent of her husband's small but important state for much of her married life. During that critical period, which required supreme diplomacy, she feared that her husband, a creature not gifted with the necessary slippery talents, could cause real harm to the couple and their state with one of his ill-tempered and overly frank outbursts.

The marquis had a reputation for nurturing grudges and remembering perceived insults. At this precarious moment, with foreign powers on the peninsula, as well as the Borgia duke capturing one central Italian state after another, a bravura sally from Francesco could prove fatal. The ambitious marchioness, with her labyrinthine mind, her supple ability to send honeyed words to yesterday's enemy, filled his place more than amply.

Isabella had shown a particular capacity to maintain good relations with Cesare. At the beginning of 1502 the Gonzaga couple had agreed to Borgia's suggestion of a betrothal between his daughter Luisa and two-year-old Federico, their adored only son and heir to Mantua. However, Francesco had to make use of the proposed betrothal to gain his brother, Sigismondo, a long-sought cardinal's hat. Isabella had to keep on good terms with Cesare, despite her inner disgust at such a bride for the heir to Mantua. Upon Lucrezia Borgia becoming Isabella's sister-in-law as well as the future Duchess of Ferrara, the rotund and snobbish marchioness, obsessed with her own lineage, had described the Borgia beauty as a common bastard, accusing her of being ugly, lazy, witless and without grace or talent of any sort. It pained her to think of yet another marital link with that *marrano* clan, and in particular for her darling Federico. Three days after Cesare's letter to Isabella about the betrothal of their children, he rode out of Rome and towards the Appenine mountain range. He had unfinished business there.

In April 1502 the Pope sent his vassal Guidobaldo an urgent request for the use of his cannon. At the time the Urbino guns had a reputation for being among the best on the peninsula. Cesare Borgia needed the artillery for his campaign against Camerino and its tyrannical da Varano Lord. Dutifully, Guidobaldo, who felt nothing but horror at the methods da Varano used to subjugate his citizens, had sent the cannon, draught oxen and a generous supply of grain. Thus when a further request arrived at the beginning of June, this time from Cesare, asking for 1,000 men to aid the citizens of Arezzo who had revolted against their Florentine masters, Guidobaldo had been unable to help. He wrote a letter to his dear friend Cesare in which he explained that he dared not anger the powerful Florentines. He sent the Duke of Romagna a beautiful horse bred for battle as a gift to keep their relationship intact.

In the late afternoon of 20 June 1502, Guidobaldo left Urbino on horseback. The sun shone as he departed by the easterly gate to dine with his great friend the prior of the Zoccolanti convent, a few miles outside the city.* After dinner the duke bade the prior to come outside into the night-scented garden to continue their theological discussion. The young Montefeltro had been born of the peninsula's greatest *condottierre,* Federico Duke of Urbino, and raised to become a great commander. Guidobaldo had suffered poor health since childhood and would never equal his father's achievements in the field. He might, though, exceed Federico's famed artistic and cerebral accomplishments, for he enjoyed intellectual pursuits far more than the martial obligations which he dutifully fulfilled, having been pressed upon him as the son of the legendary soldier.

Sitting in the long summer night, the Zoccolanti's prior and the duke had fallen into earnest discussion, laughing and countering each other's words with fresh argument. At about eight o'clock the two noticed a messenger coming towards them at full speed. He brought terrible tidings. Cesare Borgia had penetrated the state of Urbino from several directions and a contingent was heading their way. Guidobaldo da Montefeltro had not a moment to lose. The breathless young courier stood before his astonished master, who finally cried 'I am betrayed!'; realizing that he had no hope of stopping Cesare's men, the Duke hurried back to the palace to collect what he could to sustain him and his wife for their inevitable exile. He worried too about the safety of his nephew Francesco Maria, whose uncle Cardinal Giuliano della Rovere, a mortal enemy of the Borgia, had written about the boy's well-being as early as April that year. Scenting trouble from the Pope and his son, the cardinal had suggested that their mutual della Rovere nephew come to live with him in safety at his home town of Savona, on the Ligurian coast – a safe distance from Rome and the Romagna.

Shortly before midnight the duke and his nephew left the city of Urbino, making their way past the advancing invaders. He took only a small party of household servants, three chamberlains and a handful of archers. Cesare had planned his attack well for at almost every pass, mountain track or forest path the party had to turn back, warned by shepherds and locals that men had been seen in

---

* Historians do not agree on where the duke dined on 20 June, though most concur that he was outside the city at a religious house for dinner, enjoying a lively discussion with the prior, though possibly at the Franciscan house of San Bernardino.

the area. At last the desperate Guidobaldo dismissed the rest of his party. The exhausted young Francesco Maria would have to make a perilous journey to reach his uncle Cardinal Giuliano, travelling many hundreds of miles across Italy, with only a small company to protect him. Guidobaldo retained only the three chamberlains, said a speedy though affectionate farewell to his by now frightened and tired nephew, and wished the lad's protectors well. The parties then set out in their different directions. About a mile further along the forest path the company found themselves set on by a band of brigands with clubs and axes. Guidobaldo signalled for his men to gallop away, for they had far superior horses. Unfortunately the Duke's favourite chamberlain had been restrained and surrounded by the robbers, and, unable to follow his master by spurring on his horse, he had been seized by the men and pulled to the ground. Seeing a large and bulging leather pouch clutched by the loyal servant, they pulled it from the wretched fellow, whom they had to club to death before they could hack it from his tenacious grasp. Inside they found all the gold coins that Guidobaldo had grabbed in his dash to the palace before escaping, which he had hoped would pay for his exile.

On 20 June Isabella and Elisabetta left Mantua for the pleasant countryside outside the stifling city. The two women had decided to stay at Porto, one of the country estates that 'My Lord has given me ... for my pleasure,' though Isabella often complained that the many properties Francesco had bestowed upon her made barely enough money for their own upkeep. She, Elisabetta and little Federico took a few ladies with them and settled down to enjoy the cooler air and fresh breezes, which they found a great relief after the sultry heat of the city. Less than a week after their arrival Isabella and Elisabetta witnessed a shocking sight. Before them stood Guidobaldo, who had crossed 200 miles to reach his beloved wife. The skeletal and ailing duke told his wife and her family of the calamitous situation wrought by the deplorable betrayal he had suffered at the hands of Cesare Borgia. Guidobaldo had used his wits, as well as luck, to escape Cesare's murderous search parties circling the countryside inside and around the Urbino. Cesare had placed a heavy price on the Duke of Urbino's head. Guidobaldo's wife and in-laws fed him, tending his aching body and agonizing gout. On 28 June, the day after his arrival in Mantua, the duke wrote to his friend and kinsman, Cardinal Giuliano della Rovere, confessing, 'I have saved nothing but my life, my doublet and my shirt,' continuing to describe Borgia's duplicitous action against him and his state. He added: 'Such ingratitude and treachery were never before known.'

At dawn on the morning following Guidobaldo's escape and the capture of Urbino, Cesare rode through the city gates just as the sun rose. He and a company of his troops glimmered as the early shafts of light reflected off their armour. The Borgia duke passed through the city, his company of immaculately turned-out bodyguard riding briskly in crisp formation. The victor of Urbino installed himself in the vast ducal residence, where he proceeded to have his special team fillet the beautiful palace of its treasures; this they did with well-practised precision, ensuring that all items removed should be logged and accounted for.

Lucrezia Borgia, now well into her pregnancy, cried out when she heard of the unprovoked attack on her kinsmen by marriage, one of the most popular couples within the ruling elite of Italy. Lucrezia knew well that Elisabetta had fallen under Isabella's malignant thumb, and the usually kind duchess found a mean streak that Lucrezia's sensitive antennae picked up, but did not show. Sorry as she was for the couple, the consummate actress trained at the Vatican school of drama and diplomacy may have felt more than a scintilla of satisfaction at her brother's latest success. La Duchessa's* presence in Ferrara, until now so odious to Isabella, served to preserve the state for the d'Este. It was perennially galling to the chubby marchioness that her father and his state enjoyed their protected status to the bastard Borgia's marriage to its heir Alfonso.

Isabella clucked in concern around the Montefeltro couple and, busy as she was, she managed to find time to write indirectly to the man who had stripped Elisabetta and Guidobaldo of all their

---

* Since Duke Ercole had long since been a widower, the people of Ferrara, who had taken to Alfonso's new bride, had started calling her La Duchessa, since there was no other, and she would become the duchess upon Ercole's death.

belongings, their state and the status it gave them in princely circles. Just three days after da Montefeltro had arrived, she sat down to send an urgent message to her brother:

> Most Reverend Father in God, my dear and honoured Brother ... The Lord Duke of Urbino ... Had in his house a small Venus of antique marble and also a Cupid, which were given him some time ago by His Excellency the Duke of Romagna. I feel certain that these things must have fallen into the said Duke's hands, together with all the contents of the palace of Urbino in the present revolution. Since I am very anxious to collect antiques for the decoration of my studio, I desire exceedingly to possess these statues, since I hear that His Excellency has little taste for antiquities, and would accordingly be the more ready to oblige.

She added that she did not feel sufficiently intimate with the young Borgia and asked her brother to intervene for her.

Worried that one of their letters or couriers might go astray, she asked her brother to use both messenger and letter 'in so effectual a manner that both you and I might obtain satisfaction'. Isabella, for whom quantity could quite easily be as satisfying as quality, had stumbled upon a rare and wonderful Cupid. Far from being the antique she believed she had, at last, got her hands on, it proved to be the work of the young Michelangelo Buonarroti, already making a great name for himself in Rome.

Cesare proved more than ready to part with the two statues, and on 22 July they duly arrived in Mantua, where Isabella quickly placed the items in her famed *Grotta*.* Later, when Guidobaldo found himself in a more favourable position, he asked his sister-in-law for the

---

* Isabella's *Grotta* in the old castello at Mantua housed her principal art treasures. Her collection began from the beginning of her marriage, and her methods for building the collection demonstrate her character. She could sit among her beloved objects attained through 'perseverance and tenacity ... no chance of enriching her collection ever went uninvestiged'. Having been given rooms on the ground floor by her husband, the original *Grotta* needed enlarging as she required more space for the pieces. By the end of Isabella's life her extraordinary collection spread over a suite of rooms and included bronzes, paintings, statues and other items of great beauty and value. Notable are the paintings by Titian, Mantegna, Perugino and Costa. Michelangelo's Cupid was later bought by Charles I of England.

return of the Cupid. Instead of a shamefaced denial, Isabella wrote that she felt exuberant at the Duke regaining his possessions but compelled to point out that the item he desired now belonged to her. Isabella, efficient as ever, proved her point by producing a letter Guidobaldo had sent to Cesare Borgia at the time of his ousting in June. In the document he gave his permission to the Duke of Romagna for the Marchioness of Mantua to receive the Cupid. He had never intended this as a gift, but a means of procuring the Cupid to Isabella's safekeeping and hoped to have it once again in his own hands. The statue remained in the *Grotta* and, closing the matter, the Marchioness received a letter from her brother-in-law, in which he assured her 'that his person and property were altogether at her disposal'. Any irony intended proved words wasted, for they drowned in Isabella's rapacity.

Isabella and Francesco did not waste time playing hosts to their family members Duchess Elisabetta and Duke Guidobaldo. Their presence, however, exasperated Cesare Borgia, who now occasionally signed himself Duke of Urbino among the many other fabulous and noble-sounding styles he could avail himself of. Cesare made it clear via an envoy that Francesco must not harbour the former Duke of Urbino, or he would regard this as an unfriendly act.

As soon as Guidobaldo could stand unaided and move about without help, it became clear that the couple must press on. Venice had always been Guidobaldo's preferred destination. He needed a place from which he could operate with the support of a state large enough not to feel terror every time Il Valentino rode out in the morning. The couple proceeded to Venice in September, where they received a warm welcome, a dignified palace in Cannaregio and a pension to live on. On 5 October, Isabella wrote to say how glad she felt upon receiving the news that they had been welcomed in Venice and then droned on about how boring life was without Elisabetta there to console and amuse her. Elisabetta was torn, for as the couple lived meagrely on their Venetian allowance, she felt it her duty to consider most seriously a proposal from the Queen of France, Anne of Brittany, to take a position and generous allowance at her court. The Duke of Romagna also made what many have perceived as a cruel insult to the Montefelto. His offer of financial aid to the impotent former Duke of Urbino carried a condition: that he agreed to renounce Urbino, have his marriage annulled and take the red hat of a cardinal (some sources say that he even suggested that Guidobaldo should join the priesthood with no cardinalcy offered). Upon fulfilling all these conditions Elisabetta would be given a worthy annuity, and if she wished, Cesare would find another husband for the beautiful duchess. This offer is often wrongly misrepresented as a public slap to the highly sexed Duke, though it offered Cesare an easy and bloodless way legitimately to become the Lord of Urbino. Guidobaldo and Elisabetta, however, vowed not to be parted. The news of his impotence had little effect, since many had guessed it and Borgia's public offer did not humiliate Guidobaldo; rather it strengthened his resolve to triumph and recover his state with his wife beside him.

Upon taking Urbino, Cesare next needed to deal with Florence. There had been an uneasiness between Louis and Cesare about the city republic. At first the French King had warned Cesare off Florence, but when distracted by bad news from his campaigning, Louis was in no position to stop Borgia in his tracks. As fortune favoured Cesare's plans, he took the opportunity to call two emissaries who could speak on behalf of the republic. The Signoria decided upon Niccolò Machiavelli and Bishop Francesco Soderini as their representatives. The two exhausted men arrived after nightfall and, having barely dismounted, they found themselves being ushered before Cesare. The scene had been orchestrated for a display that would overpower the envoys; it did not help the visitors' nerves when Cesare's stern-faced bodyguards proceeded to lock the doors behind them. The pair had difficulty seeing Cesare, seated behind a table at the end of the carefully lit room, which not only added to the suspense but avoided exposing how much loot had already disappeared. Niccolò Machiavelli, who would later express great admiration for Cesare though at the time loathed him, listened with alarm to the ultimatum issued against Florence. The conditions seemed simple enough: either they ally themselves to him, or he would take the republic and force her to bend to his will. As the pair departed, Cesare increased the pressure by stating forcefully that the Florentine Signoria had only four days to reply.

To Machiavelli, Cesare seemed to have the qualities of Pluto's Abatos and Æton.* In his despatch to Florence he wrote: 'He arrives at a place before anyone is aware that he has left the place he was at before, he is beloved by his soldiers and he has in his service the best men in Italy. All this makes him victorious and formidable, particularly in the light of his constant good fortune.' Little known to Machiavelli, Cesare's luck had already begun to turn.

---

* Abatos and Æton were mythological horses; Abatos was inaccessible, and Æton moved with the swiftness of an eagle.

CHAPTER 18

Cesare's Troubles

1502–1504

> 'The duke [Cesare Borgia] allows himself to be guided by a spirited self-assurance, and believes other people's words to be less hollow than his own.'
>
> NICCOLÒ MACHIARELLI

As he sat in the huge, and now almost empty palace of Urbino, Cesare had more than the stubbornness of Florence on his mind. His principal mercenary leaders had surpassed his orders; having found that to expect the worst had served him well in the past, he pondered upon his situation and how to pull his commanders back in line before they went rogue. Having seen the successes of their leader, what would stop them – some of the best soldiers on the peninsula – from pursuing their own aims, and turning against him? Alone but for a few servants, Cesare paced the echoing halls of the palace; the first chill of foreboding came as he surveyed the mountain range from the windows.

Alexander VI added to his son's worries. The Pope had become the junior partner in Cesare's enterprise to make a state so powerful that it would rank among the greatest on the peninsula. Cesare's own independence had seemed to aggravate his father, who now became a dangerous, albeit unwitting, liability. Having arrived a month earlier, the Venetian envoy to Rome found himself placed in the midst of a tense drama. On 1 July he wrote that the Pope 'cannot refrain from saying some word which indicates his mind'. The state of Alexander's mind reminded Cesare of what a formidable ally his father had been, but the Pope had suffered a series of small strokes and showed signs of ageing. Once secretive, he had started to babble, speaking of matters that echoed past discussions made with his son and the plans they had made. He announced that he would be 'clipping the Orsini's wings, so that he alone remains master of the synagogue'. Alexander's verbal incontinence betrayed his intention of punishing those disloyal to him and his son, and that 'he would help King Louis to punish [Vitellozzo Vitelli]* ... until his death and total destruction'.

His other preoccupation, the ousting of the Montefeltro of Urbino, actively displeased most rulers on the peninsula, for the attack had been entirely unprovoked and no one liked to see Cesare flout the opinion of former supporters and future subjects alike. His capture of the mountain state had acted as 'banging gong and crashing cymble' and finally roused those rulers still in possession of their dominions to action. It worked just as well for those who had been disposed to join with his other enemies. They formed an anti-Borgia alliance and travelled to Milan, where it had been said Louis planned to arrive at the end of July. They sought the French king's help in regaining their states and restraining Cesare. As the newly created league of allies headed for Milan, the object of their disgust remained quietly in Urbino.

Cesare had more to worry about than growing anti-Borgia sentiment, for his newly wed sister had been suffering a difficult pregnancy, her first with Alfonso d'Este. As Cesare's would-be destroyers gathered, he wrote with an apparent lack of concern about himself, referring to the taking of Camerino: 'There could be no more salubrious nor more efficacious medicine for your present indisposition than the reception of good and happy tidings ... [yet] with your illness we can find no pleasure in this, nor in anything else ... from your brother who loves you as himself.' He received nothing to indicate any improvement in Lucrezia's condition and heard sufficient intelligence to warrant sending both Gaspare Torella, his own physician, as well as Niccolò Masini of Cesena, to examine her. The Pope's personal doctor also arrived. This army of well-meaning but bewildered physicians would have been enough to alarm the pregnant Lucrezia, but the thought of their hair-raising remedies of the day proved the young woman's true courage. Lucrezia lay bled and

* Vitellozzo Vitelli was one of Cesare's most important commanders.

unfed, but for repulsive cordials and the essential cardamom seed placed beneath her mattress that, in most cases, the medical men concurred, ensured a successful pregnancy and an easy birth. Yet she did not seem to respond to their treatments. The experts cast about for an answer, looking in their dreaded medical books.

On 27 July a mysterious Knight of St John, accompanied by only three horsemen, galloped at full speed from Forlì towards Ferrara. As Lucrezia languished with a fever at the Palazzo Belfiore, a beautiful island palace on the Barco near the northern edge of Ferrara, an epidemic struck many in the city. Lucrezia, already suffering from her pregnancy, fell ill from the flux, and Duke Ercole had been told that his daughter-in-law and her unborn baby would almost certainly die. Yet Lucrezia rallied, and now she received news that the knight turned out to be Cesare in disguise.

She did not attempt to dissemble her joy at her brother's visit, and they sat together talking for many hours. Cesare left her much cheered, but now had little time to lose. He headed north to meet Louis XII, riding part of the way with his brother-in-law Alfonso.

When Isabella had received the Urbino statues from Cesare's chamberlain, he remained behind with the marchioness, who played hostess to him – albeit a nervous one. Feeling his appraising eye casting about on behalf of his master, she was prompted to write urgently to her husband. She asked that he send a letter praising Cesare, in order that she could demonstrate the high esteem in which he was held. Gonzaga did as his wife said but penned a letter of such lukewarm feeling that Isabella felt compelled to rewrite it. Secretly she had the letter delivered to her husband in order that he might copy the strident and admiring tones she had written, even including high praise of Lucrezia. She begged him to hurry and send back her version of the letter in his hand. Isabella did not like Cesare's snooping chamberlain, whose presence augured ill. She also worried that Francesco failed to take sufficient precautions over his own security by allowing only the lowliest of his servants to attend him. Events would shortly conspire to make her instinctive diplomacy seem as redundant as her security precautions. By the summer of 1502, the world had become a place for more brutal exchanges.

Louis had already entered Milan on 28 July, where the anti-Borgia alliance all but fell upon the French monarch. They came en masse, pouring their woes out before the king. Louis entertained and discussed, sympathized and listened. He now seemed ready to pronounce upon the matter of Cesare Borgia. On 5 August, as King Louis received those who wished to see Cesare brought to justice, he called the Governor of Milan to him and, using theatrical gestures, contrived a whisper that almost everyone in the large chamber could hear. He announced to the Governor that Cesare would shortly be arriving. Louis then rose to meet him. Some of the former plaintiffs followed the king, but most of those standing in the audience chamber stood petrified by the news, quite unable to comprehend what they had just heard.

Niccolò da Correggio wrote to his friend and relative Isabella, describing the welcome Louis gave to Cesare, which could not have been warmer: 'Embracing him with great joy [he] led him to the castle, where he had him lodge in the chamber nearest his own.' Other witnesses' accounts concur with the reception Cesare received. Louis noticed that as Cesare had no baggage he ordered before everyone present that he 'dress in his own shirts, tunic and robes. In short he could not have done more for a son or a brother.'

The only person who had been more nonplussed by Cesare's arrival than the lords present in Milan had been his own father in Rome. The Pope had been kept in the dark because of his loose tongue, and soon realized that his son had pulled off a brilliant coup. Francesco Gonzaga's boast that he wished to fight a duel with the 'bastard son of a priest' had been firmly squashed by the king; Louis asked Gonzaga and Cesare to leave aside their quarrel and publicly embrace as brothers. This did little to quieten Isabella's anxiety in general and, in particular, her terror at Cesare's well-known desire for revenge, which threw her into a state of almost unparalleled anguish. Rarely had she felt so little appetite for life as she did when receiving the news from her husband, whom she now considered with scant regard to be an idiotic simpleton.

Cesare had pulled off his bold manoeuvre by promising aid to Louis in his campaign to Naples, offering to bring men and fight beside the French king himself. However, not everything went

Borgia's way, for on 3 September Lucrezia, already ill with the fever that still plagued Ferrara, had started suffering small fits. Two days later those doctors who had not already died of the epidemic themselves, helpless about what to do, declared that the only chance of saving Lucrezia's life would be if she gave birth to her child. The same day La Duchessa suffered a convulsion so terrible that in one spasm her back arched with a severity so extreme that it brought about her labour.

Screaming in the agony of the birthing pains, Lucrezia delivered the stillborn baby, a daughter she had carried for seven months. Cesare had travelled to Genoa with Louis when he heard of her condition. He took a company of men and, with his Navarese brother-in-law Cardinal d'Albret, took his temporary leave of the French King. Cesare rode his horses hard, desperate to reach Lucrezia and lend her some of his own strength, for he feared she would die without him beside her. He arrived two days after the stillbirth to find his beloved sister on the point of death.

Puerperal fever had struck Lucrezia as well as the fever she had been fighting since early July. Cesare begged the physicians to save his sister. One of those attending her wrote to Duke Ercole: 'Today at the twentieth hour, we bled Madama on the right foot. It was exceedingly difficult to accomplish, and we should not have done it but for the Duke of Romagna, who held her foot. Her majesty spent two hours with the duke, who made her laugh and cheered her greatly.' This time Cesare remained with his sister for two days. He departed for Imola once she had been declared out of danger, leaving her greatly improved. Alfonso, clearly relieved at Lucrezia's recovery, made a pilgrimage of thanks to Loreto, while Duke Ercole and Alexander, papal grandfather-in-waiting, agreed that they should congratulate themselves upon the fact that Lucrezia had only been carrying a girl.

Suddenly, on 13 September, Lucrezia suffered a dramatic relapse and, weak as she was, managed to check her own pulse. Upon finding nothing to indicate that her heart was still beating, she cried out 'Oh God, I am dead.' She fell back upon her pillows as though she had just expired, but a feeble voice issued from where she lay. Lucrezia ordered that her will be brought from Rome and changed in favour of her son Rodrigo, the young Duke of Bisceglie, whom it had torn her heart to leave for the glorious marriage she had made.

Ercole and his advisers became most alarmed; if Lucrezia died now it might be said that she had been poisoned, particularly for not providing an heir to follow Alfonso. The rumours flew about the Italian courts, yet both Ercole and Alfonso's love for the future duchess had been demonstrated by providing in every way for her recovery and survival. By October Lucrezia had recovered sufficiently to enter the convent of Corpus Domini, where she fulfilled her pledge to wear only grey and spent almost a week away from the prying eyes of those who reported back to their masters, most especially the verminous lickspittle Bernardino di Prosperi, who wrote almost daily to his mistress Isabella.

Urbino provided the next thorn in Cesare's side when, on 2 October, a successful uprising took the garrison there by complete surprise, allowing Guidobaldo's return. Hurrying from Venice, on 18 October he arrived to find his home and state pillaged but his people cheering his return. Guidobaldo had become weak from the long journey. After giving thanks to God for his restoration at the Cathedral, he spent most of his time receiving visitors while lying on his bed. Machaivelli happened to be with Cesare when news arrived of the revolt at Urbino. He seemed unworried and said only: 'Let them go. I have taken the duchy once, and I have not forgotten how I did it.' It became clear to Machiavelli that Cesare had expected something of the kind, and that it was part of a plot by his chief commanders to turn on their leader.

Guidobaldo had little time to enjoy his return to Urbino, for the league formed against Cesare in July, when the city had first been taken, collapsed. He made a farewell speech to his people before leaving again on 8 December for Venice. He begged them not to put up any resistance, despite women offering their jewels to finance a fight and men offering to go into battle with him. Sitting in the deep snow of Imola, Cesare now decided it was time to deal with the rogue *condottieri*. On 26 December he bolstered the number of troops at his disposal, yet separated them in order to keep the treacherous commanders who served as his chosen few from guessing he had more than a small force, and ordered that Sinigaglia be taken in his name. Guidobaldo's sister, the regent Giovanna della Rovere, mother to Francesco Maria, had fled before Oliverotto da Fermo's troops took the small town on 26 December. Other messages passed back and forth between Cesare and his formerly loyal commanders to meet him at Sinigaglia on 31 December. Stating that he required room for his own men, he ordered that all but da Fermo's garrison leave the town and camp a few miles away. He then arranged to meet with his senior *condottieri*, having previously agreed that they too should garrison their troops a few miles outside Sinigaglia.

Expecting a bedraggled group of men led by a beleaguered Cesare, his once trusted favourites approached the agreed meeting point and saw him riding in his shining armour with standard flying and surrounded by a formation of Swiss pikes and his men-at-arms, looking equally spruce. This came as an unpleasant shock to his captains, whom he proceeded to greet in the friendliest manner, embracing each of them. As they cantered towards the small town, where the gates with one exception had been locked, Cesare's men-at-arms split into two and stopped either side of the bridge.

Cesare had managed to cut off the traitors from their men; they could do nothing but follow him to the house that had been specially selected by Borgia for his horrid plan. Each man tried to excuse himself, but Cesare insisted they dismount for a council meeting in his room. Following Cesare up a small staircase, they sat down, the nervous *condottieri* beginning to relax as they spoke for a while about their tactics for the following days. Cesare rose saying he must relieve himself, but would return in a moment. As he closed the door behind him, the executioners entered and tied the captains' hands behind their backs. Each blamed the other until finally Michelotto, Cesare's henchman and the murderer of Lucrezia's second husband Alfonso of Bisceglie, fulfilled his master's orders to garrotte the treacherous scum. Cesare then left the scene and spotted Machiavelli with three Orsini prisoners* who had been part of the rebel group and would shortly be strangled in the

---

* The Orsini whom Cesare took prisoner and had executed were Paolo, Geronimo Borgia's father-in-law, Francesco, Duke of Gravina and Roberto Orsini.

castle of Sarteano. Borgia leaned towards Machiavelli, saying: 'This is what I wanted to tell the Bishop of Volterra [Francesco Soderini], when he came to Urbino, but I never trusted the secret to anyone, thus, the occasion having come to me, I have known very well how to use it ...'.

It transpired that the *condottieri* who had once enjoyed much fame and success with Cesare had, with the connivance of the castellan, planned precisely the same fate for their former master in Sinigaglia as he succeeded in carrying out on them. Machiavelli called it 'an admirable deed' and Louis sent a message to the duke describing his actions as 'worthy of a Roman hero'. Even Paolo Giovio, an historian known for his hatred of the Borgia, called Cesare's coup 'a most beautiful deception'. Using Machiavelli's own words, most Italian states agreed that the captains had 'behaved in a manner unworthy of their past life'. For this they had received just punishments. Most of the Italian states concurred and Cesare made capital out of his revenge.

Isabella d'Este, ever the first to be on the winning side, wrote to Cesare: 'The happy progress of which your Excellency has [informed] us in your amiable letter has caused us all the liveliest joy, owing to the friendship and interest which you and my illustrious husband feel for each other. We therefore congratulate you [and hope] we may be able to rejoice ... at the success and advancement of your Excellency.' The duplicitous marchioness added that, in order to celebrate his 'glorious victories', she had sent one hundred Carnival masks with her letter. She fawned further: 'We, of course, know how slight is this present in proportion to the greatness of your Excellency.'

Cesare wrote back to thank her; one observer remarked that he examined each mask and made the ambiguous observation that they reminded him of people he knew or had known.

At the same time the Marchioness of Mantua wrote to her husband at Loches in France, where he was staying with King Louis and Queen Anne. Isabella asked him to speak to the king about how to proceed with Cesare. As Francesco Gonzaga sat, in high favour, feasting yuletide with the King and Queen of France, did he remember that beneath him, in a dungeon deep in the bowls of the grim fortress, languished a prisoner, his brother-in-law, the former Duke of Milan, Ludovico Sforza?

Lucrezia could feel relief in her position at Ferrara thanks to her brother's success. All outstanding matters about her marriage settlement no longer appeared to present a problem to Duke Ercole, who dealt with the annoying details between himself and the Pope. It is not surprising that the querulous exchanges over relatively minor amounts of money now seemed of little consequence to Ercole, who agreed to do as the Pope wished on all counts. Glad to be alive, La Duchessa set out to enjoy herself and to feel more at home in and around Ferrara. In the course of her happy expeditions, Lucrezia managed to become familiar with a Venetian named Pietro Bembo, one of the greatest *literati* of the Renaissance, whom she met late in 1502.

In January 1503 Lucrezia attended a dance in her honour given by the poet Ercole Strozzi. During the early summer of the previous year Lucrezia had taken her ladies and travelled in her fabulously painted bucentaur out to Strozzi's villa, Ostellato. The splendid villa looked out upon the water and Bembo confessed himself surprised and delighted by the ladies he saw before him, led by La Duchessa, the best of them all. Verbal parrying of a self-consciously witty nature, as encouraged by their Humanist education, had the pair hooked upon their own cleverness and the other's appreciation of it. They had started writing flirtatious letters to each other and exchanged poetry. By June Lucrezia had taken the codename f.f. as she drifted into a situation fraught with risk. On 18 July Bembo had to leave Ferrara for a few weeks and wrote with drama and desire: 'I am leaving, oh my dearest life, and yet I do not leave and never shall ... All this night long, whether in dreams or lying awake, I was with you ... My heart kisses your ladyship's hand which so soon I shall come to kiss with these lips that are forever forming your name ... I entreat you to cherish yourself most dearly...'. By the summer of 1503, Lucrezia and Pietro had passed from friends to lovers. Bembo found himself egged on by Strozzi, who loved intrigue and, though lame and dependent upon crutches, found this no impediment when it came to horizontal activities, enjoying numerous affairs himself. The sudden arrival of Cardinal Ippolito in February made

Lucrezia's situation hazardous. She knew that he, with whom she laughed and flirted safely and who had keen powers of observation, would spot the slightest hint of any amorous activities. Nor should she seem too excited. Any change in her usual behaviour would be tantamount to an admission.

Isabella paid a visit to Ferrara in April, for rumours had reached her of Lucrezia's increasing love of taking the country air, and making other excursions. The marchioness had decided she must come and appraise Bembo and see what she could make of her sister-in-law's behaviour. Lucrezia seemed well in command of the situation as she graciously welcomed Isabella, whom she knew despised her. For her part, Isabella behaved with a sweetness that was not part of her nature. Lucrezia had laid on a number of particularly extravagant and sophisticated entertainments for the marchioness, who returned to Mantua without having been able to catch the slightest glimpse of Bembo. The marchioness and La Duchessa exchanged letters in which Lucrezia wrote of her relief to hear of Isabella's safe return home. Isabella reprimanded Lucrezia for her formality: 'There is no need to use such terms of reverence to me being your cordial sister.' The pair continued the charade, though the short stay with her father had shown Isabella that La Duchessa had become far more popular than she had been led to believe.

In Rome, Cesare and the Pope could often be found closeted together discussing the future. The Orsini posed a problem, for not only had they conspired against Cesare but, upon hearing the news of Cesare's coup at Sinigaglia, Alexander had arrested Cardinal Orsini and Rinaldo, Archbishop of Florence, the late Lorenzo de Medici's brother-in-law, now an old man in his eighties.

Cesare's and his father's main concern, however, were the two international powers that threatened to crush them in their fight for their possessions on the peninsula. In the north a large force of French troops prepared to move against the Spanish in Naples. Yves d'Allègre, once Cesare's brother-in-arms, had held out against the Spanish army in the southern Kingdom with only a small remnant of the French troops. The Orsini had finally come to their senses and rallied those barons around Rome to face the Borgia in a showdown. All eyes focused upon Cesare, expecting him to disappear; he re-emerged having managed yet another fabulous success that would only serve to increase his power. Yet the Borgia duke remained with his father and the pair seemed intent on raising money by resorting to every legitimate and illegitimate trick. When citizens or aged cardinals with great riches died, the Pope seized their property in the name of the Church. Some of them had certainly been poisoned. *Cantarella* or *aqua tofana*, as these most fashionable venoms were known, usually contained arsenic acid that caused either cerebral-spinal fever or, more commonly, gastric fever. The victim would fall ill and appear to rally as the fever came and went, until the doomed patient died, mercifully freed from the poison's agonizing effects. The Borgia had become more Italian than Spanish, especially when killing certain victims. The peninsula had been called 'the apothecary shoppe of poison' not without reason. A later admission of one of the Borgia henchmen told of being paid 1,000 ducats to empty a phial of a deadly toxin into a cup from which Cardinal Michiel drank. The cardinal, a fabulously rich Venetian, died shortly afterwards. Alexander promptly helped himself to his properties and fortune.

The weather became hotter than usual as the French arrived in the papal territories. The Orsini, having mustered all their forces, caused the Pope and his son to turn towards Spain. The Pope had always been remarkable for his jovial character, but as July turned to August he seemed filled with apprehension. He made the morose remark 'This month is fatal to fat men,' Alexander's uncle, Pope Calixtus III, having died in the pestilential heat of Rome in August, as had his predecessors Pius II, Sixtus IV and Innocent VIII. The fighting outside Rome trapped the pair in the city, and Cesare waited with anguish to see what the outcome would be and how he could turn matters to his own profit. The bleak mood in the Vatican seemed to infect all those stuck there. Alexander, vigorous as ever until now, appeared visibly aged and barely inclined to indulge in his former favourite diversions. Among them Giulia Farnese waited; she had reappeared in the Pope's life following the death of her husband Monoculus. Though several other women had done their best to fill her place during her several years' absence, none had proved her equal. Giulia La Bella held her place in the highest firmament of beauties. The Pontiff and Giulia picked up their relationship but she no longer enjoyed the stellar adoration she had once sparked in her lover. Her brother, Cardinal Alessandro, had prospered, and ignored those who mocked him for allowing the Pope to have his sister on her back, calling him Cardinal *Fregnese*.*

On 7 July a Florentine working in Rome wrote: 'Here many are sick with fever and people are dying in great numbers.' The fever turned into an epidemic and by August anyone who could leave the Eternal City had already done so. The Pope and his son did not have the luxury of this option. Cesare had his army move from Perugia to Rome and, with the French approaching, did not wish to commit his men to their cause but to keeping the Romagna stable. He planned to leave for his duchy, but on 5 August, before his departure, the Pope and Cesare dined with Cardinal Castellesi at his vineyard at Monte Mario. On Saturday, 12 August Cesare and the Pope fell ill with a fever. They both had high temperatures and were seized with fits of vomiting. The Vatican became a closed house; no information about the illness of the Pope or Cesare could be permitted to leak out. Amazing everyone, Alexander seemed to recover, though the physicians despaired of Cesare, who be appeared to be dying. On Tuesday, 14 August the seventy-two-year-old Pope required bleeding. The physicians took ten ounces of blood, which appeared to animate the elderly man, but his fever-addled mind focused more upon his son. Cesare lay on the brink of death, and only the most drastic treatment might save him. Lying in the rooms above him, Alexander's son was lifted out of bed and lowered into a vast olive jar filled with ice and freezing water. The cure brought down the duke's fever, but the skin all over his body blistered and peeled off in large sections. Cesare's attacks of high fever came and he suffered 'strange fits'. He managed, however, despite his utterly deplorable state, to send essential messages, one summoning his troops. On Thursday the 17th his condition stabilized, though he heard the awful news that his father was sinking. In the early evening of Friday, 18 August 1503 the announcement came that Pope Alexander VI had died at the hour of vespers.

* The word *Fregna*, still a slang term in some parts of Italy, refers to the female genitals.

Cesare got up from his bed when his father died. With what little strength he had, he ordered Michelotto to close and lock the doors to the late Pope's apartments, and explained where to find the hidden store of treasures. Most belonged to Alexander, though some could only be considered as the papacy's inalienable property. In a small ante-chamber that lay behind the Pontiff's bedroom they found 300,000 ducats' worth of treasure, including silver coins in chests, jewels and other valuables. In their desperate haste, Cesare's core of loyal men overlooked a further niche filled with gems, silver and gold that included the papal tiara. They removed all they could find of any value, including the late Pope's entire wardrobe, before hurrying to the Castel Sant'Angelo where Joffre and a large number of soldiers held the fort. Thanks to Cesare's forethought in sending his message to recall his men a few days earlier, many of them had already arrived and made their camp outside the city.

Barely able to stand unaided, Cesare found the will to write hurried letters to all those vital to him now. He assured his Romagnol fiefs that he had recovered and, knowing that the Orsini would certainly kill him, sent a message to the Colonna and made a contract with the Roman clan to act in concert with him. This inclined him towards the Spanish side, yet neither the French, from whom he had also received lavish commitments in return for his allegiance, nor the Spanish, delivered more than ominously ambiguous answers. For a short time Cesare held the power to bargain in his hands. He negotiated hard, and refused to leave – nor would his men – until he felt assured of the papal election. This conclave of cardinals would prove crucial to his survival. Much in the same way that Caterina Sforza acted following the death of Sixtus IV, Cesare would not leave Rome until he had extracted every possible guarantee. While he held the balance of power and Rome to ransom, Cesare Borgia, the Duke of Romagna, finally left the city on 2 September, still awaiting the outcome of the election. Unlike Caterina Sforza, Cesare had been in a position to create enough vassal cardinals to place some insurance upon achieving the outcome he desired. Those who understood the loyalties and politics of the Vatican counted that one third of the cardinals could be described as belonging to him.

During Cesare's exertions, Alexander's corpulent remains had been lying in the Sala del Pappagallo on the table where, as Pope, he had given many merry feasts. The heat called for prompt action, for, as with his recent predecessors who had died during the swelter- ing summer, his body had already started to swell, and the stench of putrefaction reeked throughout the chamber. No one stood vigil for him, and he would have been the first to understand that Cesare had more pressing matters to occupy him, now that their splendid and successful partnership was over. Coffin makers arrived to find the late Pope's corpse as wide as it was long. The box they had made for him had allowed for some swelling, but not the gruesome lump of blackened flesh that lay stinking on the table. They decided to roll up the corpse in a carpet that had been overlooked during the looting by Cesare's lieutenants. The workmen endeavoured to push the Pontiff's remains into the box, but the coffin's lid would not fit properly. The porters joined in with the carpenters, pounding and thrashing the rolled-up carpet until the top of the lid finally closed over the coffin.

Alexander's mortal remains suffered the fate shared by many popes of the turbulent Renaissance period. The undignified end demonstrated to observers the nature of power; for, having expired, the man who had proved himself able to outwit some of the ablest diplomats and rulers in southern Christendom now rotted alone. Though a man of the flesh, little is now said about Alexander's devout Marianism and his simple faith that was the least com- plex part of him. Able to combine piety and indulge in his healthy sexual appetites and his love of entertainment, he did not have the air of tortured suffering of so many for whom redemption seemed impossible. His behaviour while enjoying himself could hardly be described as fitting for a man wearing the papal tiara. His successes, however, while working in that elevated office, far outweigh his human weaknesses.

Most of Alexander's critics at the time and since have been guilty of hypocrisy on a grand scale. Pope Alexander VI did not care for humbug, and while he proved a great administrator and a bril- liant diplomat and politician, his faith was as real as his belief in human nature was cynical. Once Alexander paired with Cesare, he allowed violent acts to be committed in his name, and that of the

Holy Mother Church. A kind and benevolent man who loved his family, and enjoyed his rank, he has been judged by his principal sin: the death of many innocents in the name of his plans. He strengthened the papacy and the long and bloody process of uniting the Romagna started by Nicholas V, Sixtus IV and Innocent VIII. Each had espoused more fantastic nepotism than his predecessor, yet few recall their behaviour. The Borgia Pope was an unapologetic Catalan all his life, which only fuelled the outraged accusations of his xenophobic critics, whose words often remain the last ones when summing up the life of a great man. Sixtus is remembered for the Sistine Chapel, Innocent is remembered for doing nothing too egregious, but Alexander's name is recognized the world over for the wrong reasons. The chauvinists' tales, circulated shortly after Alexander's death, are loaded with exotic themes including Faustian pacts, incestuous children, bloodlust and cruelty that hardly fit the picture of the Borgia Pope's jovial and yet often beleaguered life. The stories told immediately after his death still held an extraordinary medieval flavour and they quickly hardened into fact, cruelly misrepresenting the Pope. In truth he was a man of his time, charged with the office and duties of a papacy at a time when Italy became overrun by foreign invaders from both north and south.

Machiavelli wrote that everything can be learned from history, for it repeats itself. While nothing is inevitable, the political and military estrangement the invaders brought with them adumbrated the end of the small Italian states, their glory days, patronage and their *condottieri*. The duchy of the Romagna, had Cesare been given time to complete it, would have provided a buffer state tough enough to stop most invaders. Ultimately he dreamt of a united Italian peninsula. In his *Discourses* and other writings, Machiavelli's enthusiasm for a strong, united country is evident, as is his hope that the leader would be a man of Cesare Borgia's stature. Fixed on criticism rather than forward-looking, the Borgia legend became a heap of fantastical stories and lies.

PART THREE

1500–1527

CHAPTER 19

The Duke of Romagna and the Borgia Die Out

1500–1510

'The more I try to submit myself to God the more he sends to try me'

LUCREZIA BORGIA

In 1500, Isabella d'Aragona, Dowager Duchess of Milan, returned south. She had nothing left to hope for in Lombardy, and the fall of Ludovico Il Moro had released her from the effective house arrest which she had endured in the years of her widowhood. When Louis XII arrived in Pavia, Isabella had petitioned him to give the duchy to her own son, Francesco, but yet again she was deceived and disappointed. Claiming he wished the boy to marry his own daughter, Louis had him sent to France, where he was promptly locked up in a monastery. Isabella uselessly petitioned the Holy Roman Emperor for Francesco's return. Fearful of the consequences should Il Moro be restored to power, she surrendered the last of her hopes and went back to the Kingdom she had left as a royal bride eleven years previously.

Just as Beatrice d'Este had usurped Isabella's title, so Isabella now found herself Duchess of Bari, her cousin's fief when she had first come to Milan as a bride. The duchy was conferred on Isabella by King Federico of Naples in 1501, but predated to April 1500. Even as Duchess of Bari, Modugno and Palo del Colle, Isabella's position remained precarious, as in another neat irony the title to the dukedom was properly the right of Beatrice's son Francesco Sforza. Isabella would never see her own son again, as he was killed in a hunting accident in Angoulême in 1512.

Now in her early thirties, Isabella established herself with her daughters Bona and Ippolita at the Castello Normanno-Svevo in Bari, where, bearing in mind her previous experience, she made it her priority to reorder the castle's defences, modernizing the fortress to take the latest artillery. Her time in Milan had also influenced her understanding of government. Finally free to act with the autonomy she craved during her marriage to the idiotic Giangaleazzo, she introduced various reforms, including more rigorous surveillance of public officials, who were notoriously corrupt. These reforms had much of the spirit of her mother, Ippolita Maria Sforza, who had been noted for her efforts to relieve the poor as well as for her love of the new learning, and here again Isabella followed her example. She summoned the writer Amedeo Cornale to her court, which also witnessed the printing of Bari's first book. Her public works in her territories included the embellishment of the castle, the rebuilding of the mole which protected the harbour and the construction of a canal around the citadel to act as a defensive moat.

Tragedy followed Isabella. Her youngest daughter Ippolita Maria died aged four in 1501, leaving only Bona as the focus of her mother's aspirations. She hoped to marry the girl to Beatrice d'Este's son Massimiliano, and thus restore the rightful Sforza bloodline to Milan, but the Sforza hold on the duchy proved too weak in the fourth generation for this to be viable. Instead, Bona was betrothed to Sigismund I, the King of Poland, and extra taxes were raised in Bari to pay for the wedding, which was to be in Naples in 1517. Isabella hoped until the end of her life that she would be able to make the journey to Poland to visit Bona, but as ever her plans were thwarted. However, her life was brightened by the addition to her household in 1506 of young Don Rodrigo of Bisceglie, Lucrezia Borgia's son by her second husband Alfonso, who came to live with her after a time in the care of Sancia, Joffre Borgia's wife.

Fever-stricken, only moments before his death, Alexander VI had repeated the same whispered anxiety: 'I do not know if he will be able to keep what he acquired.' Cesare Borgia, who had been working ceaselessly to ensure that his father's worries would prove groundless, now awaited the outcome of the papal election. On 16

September 1503 thirty-seven cardinals, the largest conclave ever at that time, began their deliberations.

Cesare had left Rome and withdrawn with his men as agreed, though his sickness had returned due to his exertions and he was too weak to ride. Eight of his halberdiers carried their duke, who lay inside a palanquin decked in crimson damask, but with the curtains drawn as he did not wish to be seen in his weak condition. Thanks to the fever, the sculpted muscularity of his beautiful physique had wasted away. The severe high temperatures also caused circulatory problems, leaving the soles of his feet agonizingly swollen. Following the closed litter came his magnificent battle horse, decked in black velvet trappings and bearing the distinguishing marks of Borgia's ducal coronet.

The wily duke left Rome by the Porte Viridaria, nearest to the Vatican, although he had arranged to meet Prospero Colonna at the Porta del Popolo, where he stood waiting for Cesare as agreed. From here they had planned to proceed together to the Spanish camp. Cesare had sent a small number of his men acting in concert with the Colonna plan, hoping to put the pro-Spanish grandee off his guard. Shortly before taking the road away from Rome, Cesare met the French envoy; the pair had a brief meeting until the soldiers with whom he had fooled Colonna arrived. Cesare had not a moment to lose. The Borgia caravan, including 'women of all kinds' and a large baggage train, headed for the small duchy of Nepi, while an enraged Prospero Colonna, who had told the Spanish ambassador that he feared Borgia might 'play us a bad turn', realized too late that he had been right.

Cesare, the new leader of the Borgia clan, took them to Nepi. Joffre, who had rarely had to concentrate for longer than it took him to choose the silk with which to slash his tunic, became his brother's determined aide. The pair had brought their mother Vannozza with them; Cesare had also taken his sister's sons, Don Rodrigo, Duke of Bisceglie, Giovanni Borgia, Duke of Nepi (Infans Romanus), and his own two bastards, Girolamo and Camilla Lucrezia. The fate, during that perilous period, of his nine additional illegitimate offspring, fathered with various women, is not known.

On 22 September 1503, the jubilant pealing of church bells all over Rome passed the happy tidings throughout the city that the Catholic Church had a new pope. The ringing bells almost drowned out the announcement that the aged Cardinal Francesco Todeschini Piccolomini had been elected unanimously, and had taken the name Pius III, in honour of his revered uncle the late Pius II. The ailing Pope could neither walk nor kneel, and had barely the wherewithal to find a place to sleep, Cesare and his men having thoroughly scoured the Vatican of its movable valuables.

Pius had been elected as a compromise candidate, and for Cesare he held the same value. Initially the new Pope protected Cesare, who risked being caught in the crossfire between the opposing armies of the French moving south to meet the Spanish troops coming up from Naples. Cesare used his illness in his appeal to the Pontiff that he be permitted to return to Rome from Nepi, though in truth once the French troops pulled out of the area the duke felt increasingly exposed to attack from a number of his local enemies.

Pius agreed. On the evening of 3 October Cesare returned, bringing with him 750 men-at-arms and installing himself in his main residence at the Palazzo del Cardinale di San Clemente, which Alexander had bought for his son on his election to the papacy in 1492. Perhaps the Pontiff's rheumy eyes had hopes of seeing the glint of Borgia's treasure.

Both Cardinal Giuliano della Rovere and Raffaele Riario hurried to Pius and told him that he had made a grave error allowing the Borgia incubus into the Eternal City, adding there would be no peace while he and his troops remained. The Pope, who might have been crowned lying down, but for his ulcerous leg being cut twice before the ceremony, found himself under such increasing pressure from all who had suffered injury under the Borgia that he could find no rest. Nor could Cesare, who heard his enemies ride past his palazzo during the night shouting 'Let us kill the Jew dog!' and 'We shall loot your house before any others.'

Unsurprisingly, as each day passed so the number of Cesare's men decreased. Receiving the news that the Borgia's enemies had united against him had been a particularly unhelpful development, and an exodus left Borgia with only seventy men.

The superannuated Pontiff had become too ill, meanwhile, to

participate fully in any decisions, except when Cesare's situation had deteriorated from perilous to desperate. Making plans to flee from Rome, Borgia found himself swiftly surrounded and ended up in the Vatican. There Pius saw him briefly and ordered his move into the Castel Sant'Angelo to stand trial for his crimes. But Pius's death on 18 October, after only a twenty-six-day papacy, left many pressing matters unresolved and Cesare enjoyed yet one further miraculous change in his circumstances.

In the coming conclave, the war between France and Spain provided the central rift. The Spaniards and pro-Spanish cardinals played off the French and their Cardinal d'Amboise. Cesare, who had lived through far less salubrious dealings in the Vatican than these, and knew many of the protagonists, seemed the reconciling influence among the pro-Spanish cardinals, making them the dominant party.

The Orsini, who had been patrolling the streets around the Castel Sant'Angelo, received orders to quit Rome before the cardinals entered the conclave, as well as a further command to honour Borgia's safe conduct issued by the papacy when he first returned to Rome. Cesare began to receive numerous visits, even from his deadliest foe, Giuliano della Rovere. After what must have been a great number of discussions, a secret meeting took place between Cardinal della Rovere and Cesare, witnessed by the Spanish cardinals. Articles were drawn up for della Rovere to sign, allowing Cesare his former position, provided that he support della Rovere as his Captain-General and *Gonfaloniere* of the Church. As Cesare and della Rovere had wished, the pro-Spanish cardinals agreed to vote for della Rovere. Many historians criticize Cesare's support for della Rovere, yet he had no other options worth entertaining. Since the death of Alexander, della Rovere, a vigorous man of sixty, had become strong. Cesare held a crucial number of cardinals, but once they went into conclave which one of these would not be tempted by della Rovere, the determined and most successful nephew of Pope Sixtus IV? Better to support the winner, Cesare had reasoned. He lacked not courage and would rather attempt to work with his enemy of yesterday, and see what opportunities presented themselves; but he would face della Rovere, not run from him.

The election of Giuliano della Rovere to the throne of St Peter was over in less than twenty-four hours, the shortest conclave ever recorded. On 1 November 1503, Giuliano took the name Julius II. Known to history as the Warrior Pope, Giuliano had waited for his moment. Helpless, he had watched as Cesare moulded a success-ful and well-run state wrested from generally tyrannical rulers. The early conditions of a viable, well-organized duchy were evident to those returning to take back their states. With a strong judiciary and order where there had once been tyrannical caprice and cruelty, Cesare's subjects had almost invariably found themselves far better off than before his arrival and many lamented his loss silently. Now the new Pontiff felt a burning desire to bring the Romagna back under his control, the Venetians having already mobilized with the same view in mind. Depressed by how few places within his duchy remained to him, Cesare had nothing but the Romagna in his heart either.

On 18 August, when the news of Alexander's death arrived in Ferrara, Duke Ercole asked his son, Cardinal Ippolito, to send word to Lucrezia Borgia. He also informed Lucrezia that her brother lay in an appalling condition, father and son having suffered the same tertian fever. Collapsing on her knees, she cried and admitted later that she thought she would die from the tears and convulsive sob-bing. Ercole found Alfonso and he arrived soon afterwards, but it is doubtful she noticed. Pietro Bembo recalled the tragic sight of her on 21 August, 'lying in a darkened room and in that black gown, so tearful and disconsolate ... for a long time I knew not what to say ... [and] I withdrew as you saw, or might have seen'.

Bembo counselled that Lucrezia give away her feelings as little as possible, an ability which had been bred into her at the Vatican, though this would prove the most difficult test yet. She tried to get money and help to Cesare, as she watched his duchy fall back into the hands of those he had ejected. Lucrezia's detested first hus-band Giovanni Sforza re-entered Pesaro on 3 September, only two weeks after her father had died. Wondering about the fate of the small Borgia children, in particular Don Rodrigo Bisceglie, added further to her anxiety. Cardinal Ippolito and Cardinal Cosenza had been charged by Cesare to be his guardians. Cosenza wrote to the

anguished mother in Ferrara saying that, while Giovanni and probably his infant sibling would be tolerated near Ferrara, there could
be no question of her adored son by Bisceglie coming to live in
the Estense state. Long discussions with Ercole ensued and finally
Lucrezia, who had for a time favoured sending the boy to Spain,
decided that his father's home state of Naples might prove a fitting
home for him before the longed-for reunion could take place. Thus
Rodrigo was entrusted to Isabella d'Aragona.

As Julius II moved into the Vatican, he invited Cesare to leave his
depressing accommodation in Castel Sant'Angelo. He was offered
the Vatican's finest apartments, the Camera Palace guest suites, built
by Innocent VIII. Cesare had a household of over forty, and as he
looked from his windows he could see Julius in the palace where his
father and his family had lived. Meanwhile he was hearing daily news
of the Romagna, where anarchy had erupted and chaos reigned.

Probably the most benign of the lords dispossessed by Cesare
had been Guidobaldo da Montefeltro. On 28 August 1503 the duke
returned to Urbino alone, for he did not want to inflict the journey upon the easily tired Elisabetta without feeling assured of her
safety. On seeing the shocking transformation of their home and
their state, he feared she might become seriously ill. Guidobaldo
meanwhile received an emotional and joyous welcome from his subjects. Hailing his safe homecoming, Count Baldassare Castiglione
wrote, 'The very stones seemed to rejoice and to sing for gladness.'
In Urbino at least, chaos did not rule the day. Julius kept Borgia
close, and as a number of strongholds in the Romagna refused to
submit, Cesare found himself in ever less exalted surroundings.
Daily calls for restitution and applications to investigate murders
during the Borgia papacy thrilled Julius who, as one commentator
wrote, 'occupied himself more with the Duke, almost to the exclusion of his other business'. On 2 December Guidobaldo met Cesare,
having arrived in Rome a few days earlier.

Of all the men Cesare had dispossessed and wronged, Guidobaldo
had been the most innocent and trusting victim. It is said the pair
met in an anteroom before one of Montefeltro's aides, who stood
close enough to hear and witness the extraordinary scene played
out between them. Upon seeing the crippled duke sitting with his

painful feet upon a stool, Cesare knelt and begged forgiveness for the wrongs he had done him. Guidobaldo carefully stood up and took Cesare's shoulders to raise him from his knees. Cesare spoke of his youth and the evil counsel he had received from his father and swore to return the treasures of Urbino, all of which he had stored in the Rocca di Ravaldino. He also confessed that he had given the extraordinary Trojan tapestries to Cardinal d'Amboise and felt it highly unlikely that these would be rendered to their rightful owner. However neither man mentioned the two statues that Isabella d'Este had taken into her care. Both held the dubious honour of being the marchioness's brother-in-law and it is likely that a mutual understanding of their illustrious relative kept them from speaking of the treasures she had hidden away in her already famed *Grotta*. Whether Cesare knelt before the Duke in abject misery and contrition is not known for certain, but reports reached Urbino of their meeting and the pathetic drama. It is quite possible, as Cesare would employ any such means to achieve his aim, as well as to please the increasingly hostile Pope, who loved Guidobaldo.

By December 1503, Cesare had lost his army, most of his treasure sat inside various strongholds of the Romagna, and both the French and the Spanish had turned their backs on him. Julius had effectively separated Cesare from what little power he had. Two huge cartloads of treasure that had been on their way to Lucrezia in Ferrara were stopped. Julius also coveted the valuables Cesare had hidden in the various forts throughout Romagna. But Cesare, who commanded extraordinary loyalty from his men, now faced the difficulty of trying to convince certain captains to surrender their strongholds. They would not yield to the papal bulls of Julius, nor the encroaching Venetians, who had taken the opportunity to bite a sizeable chunk out of the Romagna. Yet, during those tumultuous days, the loyal men held out for their beloved leader. The Ramirez brothers, two of the most reliable, though perhaps least sophisticated, of his castellans received a visit from de Oviedo and an emissary from the Pope. According to proper procedure Cesare sent a letter attaching the agreed signs, official stamps and signatures. The two castellans looked at the documents, and in one voice accused the piteous de Oviedo of treachery and slung him from a wall of the fortress with a rope around his neck. To the papal envoy, despairing of his own fate, they sent a message: they would not surrender their fastness until their master was a free man. Nor would they carry out orders contrary to his will.

Cesare and Julius continued to circle each other. Finally, after endless struggles and near-escapes, the Pope reached a secret agreement with the Spanish commander Gonzalo de Córdoba to take the charismatic prisoner and deliver him to Spain. Cesare, believing that he had safe conduct from Córdoba, travelled to Ostia; the galleys awaiting him had been held in Naples harbour due to the stormy winter weather. On 19 February 1504 Cesare found a horse, which he rode as far as Nettuno where he stole a small boat. Staying close to the shore, he rowed to within thirty miles of Naples. He landed the tiny craft, found a mount and rode to the palazzo of his cousin, Cardinal Ludovico Borgia. There he was met by his family as the children, Joffre and the cardinals had been sent on when matters had looked their bleakest.

Preparing men and materiel for his journey to Pisa, and the planned recapture of the Romagna, Cesare had everything ready on 26 May. He mounted the steps of the Castel Nuovo to thank Gonzalo and tell him that he had finished his preparations and would leave the following morning. As Cesare turned to leave, his business finished, a Spanish gentleman inclined towards him saying in soft tones that he was under arrest. The arch-deceiver had been deceived and on his deathbed Gonzalo said this act of treachery was one of three actions of his life that he truly regretted.

The remainder of Cesare's desperate and unceasing struggle included several years' suffering in La Chinchilla, the Valencian fortress standing nearly 1,000 feet up in the mountains.

It is fitting that the last act of Cesare's that held any significance would be the final handover of the Rocca di Ravaldino at Forlì. On 11 August 1504, Guidobaldo and the papal troops sat outside the Rocca. They watched the castellan ride out of the scene of Cesare's triumph and now his final act of significance on the peninsula. As a man serving under the erstwhile Duke of Romagna, the castellan rode out with solemn dignity, his lance rested low upon his thigh in a traditional gesture of submission. The smart turnout of his troop and his own shining breastplate did not speak of defeat, merely of following the orders of his commander; a herald led the way who loudly proclaimed Cesare as the Duke of Romagna. At that moment a clap of thunder could be heard in the sultry summer weather and heavy rainfall followed immediately. Bernardi reported an eclipse of the sun, though the moment, already laden with drama, did not require any gilding.

Lucrezia heard the news of her brother's death at Ferrara, a month and a half later. Ippolito d'Este, who had bravely broken the news of Alexander VI's passing, could not face the task of bringing worse horror to his sister-in-law, so Fra Raphaele, a priest preaching at court during Lent that year, told the Duchessa of her brother's fate. It came as the darkest blow she had suffered during her young life. Since their father's death she had followed Cesare's movements closely and tried to help in every way possible without endangering her position. She had written letters interceding for him, and sent what money she could. Ironically, Lucrezia had been enjoying a moment's rest from her cares, for, knowing her brother had stayed in the friendly territory of Navarre, she believed him to be in relative safety.

She screamed with horror when she heard the news, but quickly gathered her feelings to herself and regained her composure. Before excusing herself for the demonstration, for many of the court were present, she said only: 'The more I try to submit myself to God the more he sends to try me.' She added the words, 'God's will be done.' She disappointed her enemies, who had hoped for tears, maintaining an inscrutable mask. Her ladies reported that only at night while sleeping did Lucrezia cry out the name of her adored Cesare. As one correspondent wrote to Isabella in Mantua: 'She loved her brother as much as if she were his mother,' and a large part of Lucrezia died with him.

Cesare had never stopped hoping and planning to get back to Italy and fight for the Romagna and died in a spectacular charge, an ambush awaiting him, while fighting for his brother-in-law, the King of Navarre. Speaking to Machiavelli during one of their long discussions while he remained as Julius's captive, Cesare said, 'I had planned for everything that could happen at my father's death, except that when he died, I too should be struggling with death myself.' Of all the women he had known during his life he admitted he had admired and respected only three: his mother, his sister Lucrezia and Caterina Sforza, whose attitude and courage resembled his own in so many ways. Although his wife, Charlotte d'Albret, did not manage to find her way onto her husband's list, yet upon Cesare's death she wore black until the end of her life, and redecorated the Château à La Motte Feuilly by draping whatever she could in mourning. Even the couple's daughter had to wear black. Charlotte spent her days doing good works and living quietly until her death on 11 March 1514. Upon her tombstone she had engraved the words: 'Here Lies the heart of the most high and powerful lady, Charlotte d'Albret. In her life the widow of the most high powerful prince Don Cesar, Duke of Valentinois, Count of Diois, Seigneur of Issoudun and of La Motte Feuilly . . .'.

Lucrezia eventually succeeded in bringing Cesare's son and daughter to live with her in Ferrara. Her namesake Camilla Lucrezia, who was legitimized on 8 August 1509, is described as the daughter of Cesare Borgia and an unnamed woman, possibly Dorotea Caracciolo. Having received her education in a Ferrarese convent, she became a nun in 1516, eventually rising to abbess, and lived until 1573, having achieved a saintly reputation. Lucrezia appointed Alberto Pio as tutor to Cesare's son Girolamo, who in 1537 took to wife a daughter of the Lord of Capri with whom he had two daughters. The girls received names to honour the d'Este – Lucrezia and Ippolita. Unfortunately Girolamo did not earn the same glowing reputation as his sister Camilla Lucrezia. There is good evidence that in 1542 he attempted to assassinate a rival named Chastron. The first effort, botched by assassins, was followed four years later by a second and successful effort.

Freed by the death of Sancia in 1506, Joffre remarried, taking one Maria de Mila as his wife. Joffre, who must go down as one of history's lightweights, showed spirit and courage immediately after his father's death, helping his brother take their family to safety in Nepi; but once at Naples he reverted to the superficial ways of a nincompoop. While Cesare had been betrayed by Córdoba, Joffre could be seen taking daily rides, galloping along the beaches of Naples, choosing as his companions the young men of the Spaniard's family, and sometimes even riding out with the great man himself. Joffre died in 1517. Lucrezia made the proper noises and wrote the usual decorative Renaissance letters properly expressing herself, though it is doubtful she felt anything but disgust at the passing of her empty-headed, vain brother.

Vannozza, who had loved Cesare best of all her children, was now left without the protection of Pope Alexander VI, her former lover. Uneasy about the vulnerability of her possessions, which Julius might snatch in his search for Borgia spoils, she proved more than able to hold her own. As the angry Pontiff's hunt reached Vannozza she had been canny and quick, and already placed her assets, largely property, in the name of the Church. She had made the gift with the proviso that she might have full use of her assets until her death.

Lucrezia had not seen her mother for seventeen years, and always felt closer to Adriana de Mila, who had played the maternal role in her life. The d'Este archive contains nine letters from Vannozza to Ferrara, of which only two she addressed to her daughter; and these consist almost entirely of Vannozza's covetous wheedlings. Seven of her letters to Ferrara are addressed to Cardinal Ippolito, who had obviously made the mistake of replying favourably to an early missive. Vannozza latched onto the Cardinal as a more sympathetic audience to her constant demands. She dictated her letters, implying that she wrote poorly or that she wished as a status symbol to show that she had a scribe. She signed herself 'The fortunate and unfortunate Vannozza de Cattaneis', or when writing to Lucrezia, 'Your fortunate and unfortunate mother, Vannozza Borgia'. She used the Borgia name only in private.

As with so many rich, mean people, Vannozza claimed to be perpetually staring into the abyss of financial ruin. In reality she had, over the years, established herself as an excellent businesswoman of Lucrezia Tornabuoni's ilk. The pious Medici matriarch might have baulked at renting out rooms to prostitutes, but Vannozza had no such scruples and spent much of her immoral earnings in later life on the church of Santa Maria del Popolo and other virtuous causes. She chose the chapel as her place of burial and endowed it for this purpose, featuring splendid marble ornaments by Andrea Bregno. Vannozza enjoyed many visitors, who she believed had come to pay her their respects, though in reality she remained a living witness to the recent past whom many felt they had to meet out of curiosity.

After her death aged seventy-seven in November 1518, the diarist Sanudo reported: 'News of her death was cried through Rome as befitted a celebrity of her stature.' Her well-attended funeral was that of a virtuous Roman matron; among the mourners were papal chamberlains and the obsequies were served 'with pomp almost the equal of a Cardinal'. For once Sanudo understated the situation. Vannozza ensured that she would make the transition of curious relic of the past to the place she believed her endowments had bought her in Heaven. In an act of almost unparalleled egotism, Cattanei provided for a sumptuous funeral. To the foremost burghers and nobles of Rome, it did indeed seem as if almost the entire city attended her funeral. For a landlady with a highly colourful past, Vannozza could congratulate herself upon a more than respectable send-off.

Giulia Farnese, the other woman who had enjoyed the favour of the late Alexander VI, had inherited Bassanello upon the death of her husband, the sulky cuckold Monoculus. She had also become mistress of the small domain of Carbognano, awarded to him by Alexander for keeping his mind on matters other than his own matrimonial affairs. Carbognano stands in the midst of Farnese territory, in the countryside north of Rome. Giulia La Bella had taken to living respectably and quietly; she kept her head down during Julius's raving searches for papal treasure, or offspring. She had become a respectable mistress of her properties when tragedy struck her sister Girolama Farnese.

Lucrezia would doubtless have been pleased when, in 1509, Giulia remarried. It seems that Giulia could afford to buy a new husband, for she had plenty of money. Her husband was a petty nobleman name Giovanni Maria Capece Bozzato who, according to Canossa, in a letter to Isabella d'Este, was 'very well endowed though not in property'. The couple led a happy life, mainly in Carbognano, until his death in 1517. Giovanni was kind to his wife Giulia who, like Lucrezia, had married and been a mistress to enhance her family's standing and did not question her duty. In the end she had married for love. On 14 March 1524 Giulia, who had been unwell for some time, drew up a short will in which she left all her properties to her two nieces, should her beloved Laura die without issue. There remains no portrait of the great beauty, except the statue of Justice in St Peter's. Originally the sculpture had bare breasts, though upon her brother Alessandro's later elevation to the papacy it is said that the image was changed to make her appearance more seemly.

In Italy today there is a remarkable flexibility of attitude. The Borgia legend still lives on but is no longer held as fact. History has proved that Alexander VI, Lucrezia and Cesare were paradigmatic people of their time and position – indeed some of their actions have made them exemplars of their day.

CHAPTER 20

The Medici Restored

1503–1519

'The Medici wandered over Europe like members of an outcast tribe.'

CHRISTOPHER HIBBERT

Of the male descendants of Cosimo de' Medici, four remained alive by 1503: Giovanni and Giuliano, the youngest sons of Lorenzo Il Magnifico; Giulio, the illegitimate offspring of Lorenzo's brother Giuliano, murdered in the Pazzi conspiracy of 1478; and Lorenzo, the son of Piero the Unfortunate and his widow Alfonsina Orsini, now the matriarch of the dynasty. As Piero's wife, Alfonsina had been most immediately affected when her husband was exiled from Florence in 1494. Unlike Lucrezia Tornabuoni and Clarice Orsini, Alfonsina was obliged to take a public, as well as an active political role. Since women were technically exempted from the sentences of exile passed on their menfolk, she was in a position to negotiate where her husband could not. Piero Parenti records that 'the wife of Piero de' Medici ... a woman of authority and managerial ability, together with several male accomplices of Piero, attempted to persuade the French king that her husband had been unjustly expelled and should be allowed to return'. But her activities made her extremely unpopular in a city which was determined to eradicate all traces of its Medici past.

Alfonsina was accused of trying to bribe Charles VIII with money and jewels to get Piero reinstated, and when she attempted to return to the Palazzo Medici she and her mother Caterina di Sanseverino were surprised by a group of citizens who burst in on them and tore the jewels from the women's hands and gowns before unceremoniously evicting them. The diarist Bartolommeo Cerretani records with a degree of gleeful *Schadenfreude* that 'they sent them crying to the convent of Santa Lucia'. Codes of behaviour which had pertained in the previous generation no longer served, as was further evinced by the reaction to Alfonsina's attempts to recover her dowry. This was her legal right, as dowry settlements were not normally subject to seizure by the Signoria even if all other assets had been made forfeit. Nevertheless, her insistence on her due was seen as 'damaging and completely hateful to our city'. Alfonsina's struggle for her dowry money took many years, and in the meantime she was concerned with bolstering the family's unstable finances. Like Lucrezia Tornabuoni in her need for funds after the Pazzi conspiracy, she pawned jewellery, paintings and books and borrowed money where she could, principally from Francesco d'Agostino Cegia.

Piero the Unfortunate had not shown much character, but never lost hope of returning to Florence, egged on by his wife, who joined him in Siena in 1495 before moving to Venice with her children. In 1497 Piero attempted a *coup de main* against the city; two years later he joined a Venetian invasion of Tuscany, and when the Florentine town of Arezzo rebelled in 1502 (thanks to Cesare Borgia's machinations) he made it his headquarters for a planned attack on Florence. His career concluded in characteristic bad luck at the Battle of Garigliano in 1503, when the ongoing conflict between the French and Spanish over domination of Naples was resolved in favour of the latter. Piero was drowned when a raft capsized as he attempted to ferry artillery to Gaeta. His death left Giovanni de' Medici as the head of the senior branch of the family.

The year 1503 marks the advent of a new political strategy for the Medici, which some historians attribute to the legacy of Lorenzo: 'instead of serving the Church as bankers, the Medici should now attempt to infiltrate it, and thus attain an even greater source of wealth and power. No record of such thinking survives, but the evidence suggests that deathbed conversations [between Lorenzo de' Medici and his heirs] ... must have included such a strategy.' Certainly before he died Lorenzo had been able to achieve from Innocent VIII the cardinal's hat for Giovanni, when the boy was just thirteen. After the expulsion of the Medici in 1494, he had judged it imprudent to go back to Rome and spent five years travelling in Europe before returning to the city on Piero's death. At this point, the family began to cultivate their connections with Giuliano della Rovere, who after the demise of the Borgia Pope and the brief reign of Pius III, succeeded to the tiara in October 1503.

Piero's death also enabled Lorenzo Il Magnifico's daughters Lucrezia and Contessina to attempt the rehabilitation of the Medici in Florence. Whereas the interventions of Alfonsina Orsini had been compromised by her 'foreign' status, the sisters did not have to contend with such prejudice. In 1505 they set up a wax statue of Giuliano de' Medici in the church of Santissima Annunziata, connecting the present generation of Medici with figures such as Lucrezia Tornabuoni, Lorenzo and the murdered Giuliano, all of whom had had images placed there after the Pazzi conspiracy. In 1502, Piero Soderini, *Gonfaloniere di Giustizia* for life and brother of Cardinal Francesco, had attempted to associate the shrine with his own family; hence the placing of the image at this particular juncture symbolized a spiritual return of the Medici to one of the city's most holy places.

In 1507 Alfonsina Orsini also returned to Florence to arrange the betrothal of her daughter Clarice, as Cardinal Giovanni determined she should marry a Florentine. In her attempt to woo the republic's elite, 'she was visited and entertained by many citizens who had belonged to the Medici party ... She went about entertaining those that seemed to her of possible benefit to the Medici.' Alfonsina also conducted secret audiences on Clarice's behalf. Yet apparently no Florentine was willing to commit himself to the marriage, for fear of government reprisal, despite Clarice's hefty dowry of 7,000 scudi. The person with the guts to come forward was Filippo di Filippo Strozzi, whose family had traditionally been enemies rather than allies of the Medici. Indeed, so extraordinary was this alliance that for some time the Florentines refused to believe it, and it caused 'great agitation' according to Cerretani. Indeed, Filippo had to face not just his relatives' opposition, but also the accusation of not being a true republican for marrying the daughter of a public enemy – one secret memorandum, believed to have been drafted by Machiavelli, maintained that Clarice, being the offspring of a rebel, was herself a rebel. Eventually, the Strozzi relented, the government did not manage to get Fillippo convicted, and the couple married in Rome.

Clarice, Lucrezia and Alfonsina now worked closely with their male relatives in gauging and cultivating the political contacts who would ease the family back to power. It is notable that when this was achieved, the women of the family were able to participate in strategic discussions in the Medici palace itself: 'This complete displacement of the locus of government effectively meant that the rigid distinction between a "private" female domestic arena and a male "public" political one – which had slowly been disintegrating from the 1460s onwards – now completely collapsed.' Perhaps it is not going too far to say that the examples of politically active women such as Caterina Sforza and Beatrice and Isabella d'Este had infiltrated even into the sequestered environment of elite Florentine women. At last, with the ascendancy of figures such as Alfonsina, the Medici girls were moving with the times.

Caterina Sforza's position in relation to the principal branch of the Medici family was ambiguous. As mother to a Medici heir, Giovanni, their restoration would naturally be advantageous, but until 1503 she was occupied both with her precarious finances and the struggle against her brother-in-law Lorenzo for the return of her son. Lorenzo's death in 1503 put the guardianship dispute to an end while in mid-1505 Caterina was finally able to recover her dower settlement from her marriage to Giovanni il Popolano. No longer reduced to selling off her remaining scraps of jewellery, Caterina could entertain a wide circle of friends from Lombardy and the Romagna in her home, including her mother Lucrezia Landriani. The restitution of her son proved the greatest joy of this last, relatively peaceful phase of her life. Established in Florence with six-year-old Giovanni and Carlo, her son by Giacomo Feo, Caterina now divided her time between spirituality and domesticity, though neither pursuit entirely assuaged her hunger for the political tumults of the Romagna.

In educating Giovanni, who was to become the last great Italian *condottiere,* Caterina was determined that the martial brilliance of the Sforza should flourish once again. Almost as soon as the boy was returned to her, she wrote to one of her former *condottieri,* Baccario di Cremona, to request that he pick out a horse for him, small, but spirited and gallant. Although Caterina insisted on the best masters to give the boy the thorough Humanist education she herself so admired, there was no doubt even in childhood where his talents lay: 'ogni giorno di piu si rivelava geneticamente uno Sforza' ('every day he revealed himself more as genetically a Sforza'). Though Giovanni was her joy and comfort, Caterina continued to interest herself actively in the lives of her other children. In 1503 her daughter Bianca married Troilo di Rossi, a Romagnese noble whose family estates lay near Parma, and the two women corresponded frequently and affectionately. During Bianca's second pregnancy, Caterina had her first grandchild, Pietro Maria, to live with her. Of her sons, Cesare and Ottaviano were respectively at Rome and Viterbo, from where they continued to harass their mother with demands for money – and, in the case of the now obese and embittered Ottaviano, for her influence in securing a cardinal's hat. Francesco Sforza, 'Sforzino', lived in Florence until appointed to the see of Lucca in 1517, while Galeazzo, the most intelligent and devoted of her elder boys, married the sister of the Duke of Urbino, Maria della Rovere, and spent much of his life in Bologna. Cesare and Ottaviano were undoubtedly disappointments to Caterina, but she continued to assist and promote them as far as she was able.

Now in her forties, Caterina was keen to spend what time she could spare from Giovanni's education in continuing her 'experiments', a passion since her time in Forlì. Increasingly, these were concerned with beauty treatments, and she wrote to her *farmacista* there, Albertini, for ingredients and hints, though her enthusiasm rather exceeded her budget, as a debt of 587 florins outstanding after her death shows. Caterina was delighted to receive from Luigi Ciocca in Mantua the secret recipe for the hand and face creams used by Isabella d'Este. Other experiments were medical: cures for headache and stomach ache, aching joints, troublesome liver and even the plague. Given her romantic career, it is unsurprising that Caterina also took an interest in love potions. A test for virginity involved giving a girl *pietra armoniacci* dissolved in water to drink, while an encouragement to masculine virility – 'to make your member thick' – involved the juice of red ants blended with castor oil and marinated in hot horse dung for six days, after which it should be massaged into the recalcitrant organ. It is not recorded on whom Caterina tried this particular formula, but another recipe of newts and Greek nettles to keep a man 'standing' all night hints that the Countess of Forlì had not entirely abandoned her penchant for lovers, though they too were no longer as young as they might have been.

Other satisfactions came in the form of correspondence with those Romagnol subjects who still nurtured passionate loyalty for the Madonna of Forlì. Giambattista Tonelli, a long-standing Riario partisan, wrote from Imola to tell her of a group of faithful subjects who met in one another's houses in the evenings to talk over the old days and dream of her return, while Gabriele da Casola Valsenio wrote that he would 'still die for her a hundred times over', lamenting that without her advice he and his commanders were 'abandoned like a ship at sea without a sail'. In 1507 she received two rather sentimental sonnets in her praise from Piccoli, though Caterina might well have wished that the Forlivese had been as forthcoming in deeds in 1499 as they were in words after the Borgia attack.

Caterina died in 1509, three years short of the return of the Medici to Florence.

On his ascension to the papal throne, Julius II's principal objective was the ousting of Cesare Borgia from the Romagna, allying with the French to rid papal territories of usurpers. In the grand tradition of the Church militant, he took to the field in person, insisting that he be accompanied by twenty-four cardinals, whose girth and cowardice made them a 'most lamentable sight'. Only Cardinal Giovanni de' Medici, a superlative horseman despite being fat and short-sighted, could keep up with him. Hoping to evict the Venetians from the Romagna, Julius managed to put together a broad alliance, the League of Cambrai, which included the French, Spanish and

Imperials. Despite some initial defeats, the Venetians held their ground, in the process capturing Francesco Gorizaga. Julius then summoned the Holy League once more to rid himself of his former allies, though Florence remained neutral, a decision motivated by widespread sympathy for the French in the city and fear of reprisals against Florentine merchants in France. Louis XII was suitably disgusted and retaliated by summoning a college of French cardinals at Pisa, recently restored as a territory of the republic, with the aim of deposing the Pope.

Florentine indecisiveness here served the Medici well. Julius was angered by the city's refusal to participate in his war, but his first strike was against the French at Ravenna at Easter 1512, where the papal-Spanish force of 16,000 under Ramon de Cardona met 23,000 French commanded by Gaston de Foix. Cardinal Medici, acting as papal legate, rode with the troops in his red ecclesiastical robes, while doing his best to look noble – a posture, as Guicciardini spitefully observed, which was somewhat compromised by 'the imperfection of his sight'. Although outnumbered, the league's forces did bravely, but the slaughter on both sides was appalling: 12,000 killed, two-thirds of them belonging to the league; since the French sustained marginally fewer casualties they declared themselves the victors. Giovanni himself was captured as he tried to administer the sacraments to the dying, which must have been a novel experience for him. Taken to Milan, he was ordered to be brought to France by Louis XII but he managed a daring escape and arrived back at camp via a sojourn in a pigeon coop. That summer he participated in the congress of Mantua, which decided to reinstate the Medici in Florence. As soon as the news of Ravenna arrived, the Florentines had thrown their lot in with the French. But while the remaining Spanish troops had retreated in a body, the death of Gaston de Foix had left the French leaderless and by June the remains of the victorious army scurried across the Alps to France. Already enraged with the Florentines because of the Council of Pisa, Julius II had decided to put an end to Florence's ruling regime.

In mid-August an army 6,000-strong under Cardona crossed the Appenines, bypassing Florentine defensive positions and descending on the town of Prato, Giovanni de' Medici riding with the invaders.

Prato was defended by about 2,000 militiamen – the Roman-style citizen army being Machiavelli's brainchild – ill-trained, with few provisions and behind old fortifications. On 26 August the Spanish, 'like rabid dogs', assaulted a breach created in the town's walls, over-powering the militiamen who took to their heels after sustaining two losses. The uncontrollable Spaniards, whose bloodthirsty repu-tation had rendered them the terror of Europe, sacked the city for two days. Giovanni did his best to corral as many women as he could in the safety of a church, but the Spaniards were eager for flesh as well as blood and raped their way through the small city, assaulting nuns and laywomen alike, until in their desperation mothers were reduced to pushing their daughters into wells and leaping in after-wards. This was the first time a Medici prelate had dealings with the Spanish furies; but, unfortunately, Prato does not seem to have left a significant impression in the family lore. When news of the sack reached Florence, a pro-Medici uprising forced the *Gonfaloniere* of the Signoria, Piero Soderini, to resign and make for Siena, leaving the city clear for a chastened Medici triumph.

For the first four years of the Medici interregnum, the Florentine government had been controlled by the compelling Ferrarese friar, Girolamo Savonarola. His passionate sermons and his exposure of the luxurious lifestyles of the Florentine elite during the increasing wretchedness provoked by economic stagnation even before the French wars made him as loathed as he was worshipped. His spiritu-ality influenced many in the city, including a young Michelangelo. When the Medici fell, only Savonarola had the charisma get the necessary reforms pushed through, inaugurating a Grand Council to consist of an assembly of 3,000 citizens over the age of twenty-nine whose families had held magistrates' office back to the third generation. An incongruously puritanical spirit now prevailed in the city. One of Savonarola's followers' first acts had been to reconfirm the laws against homosexuality and in 1497 the Piazza della Signoria hosted the extraordinary 'Bonfire of the Vanities', a conflagration of the accoutrements of worldly delight, collected by the friar's zeal-ous followers, often, but not invariably, through force. 'At its base were to be seen false hair, false beards, masquerading dresses, rouge pots, cards and dice, mirrors and perfumery, beads and trinkets of

Leo X, with cardinals Giulio de' Medici (left) and Luigi de' Rossi. His remark, 'Let us enjoy the papacy, since God has given it to us,' sums up in full the attitude of many Renaissance popes.

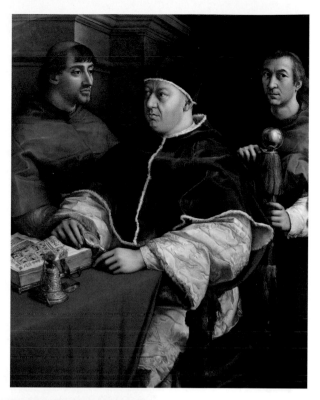

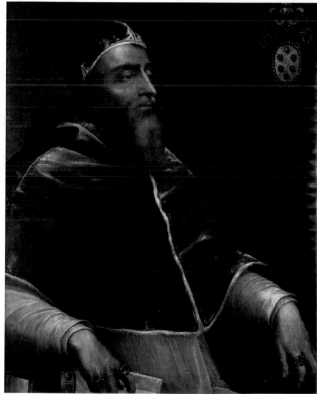

Clement VII, or 'il papa Che-mente' ('the lying pope') as he was known to his enemies, whose dithering and indecision brought catastrophe upon Rome and his own family.

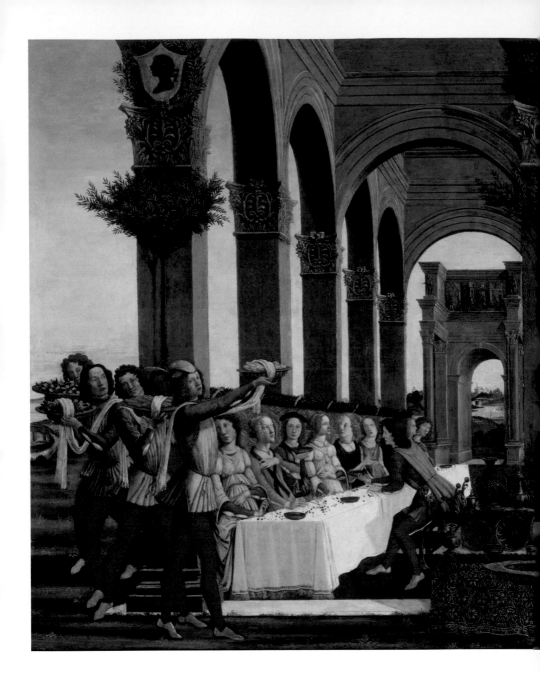

The setting of this wedding reception by Botticelli, with its
Roman-style arcade and the plasticity of its figures, synthesizes
the idyllic vision of a world dancing on the edge of the abyss.

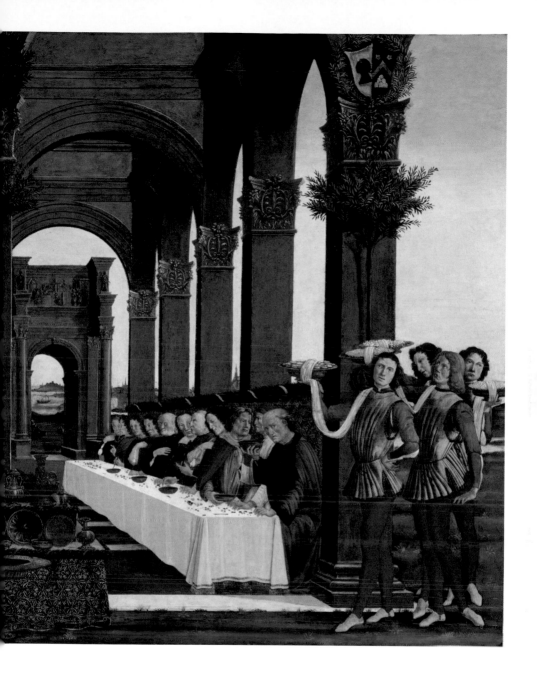

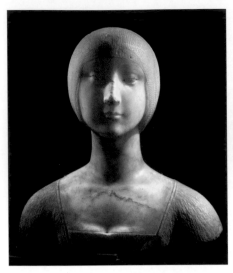

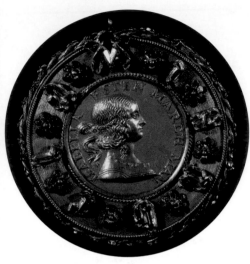

Eleonora d'Aragona's gentle features belie her political ability, steely determination and a taste for culture – in these respects, her daughter Isabella was a chip of the old block.

Widespread as the love for the classical world was, Isabella d'Este always managed to take it a step further, as this medal struck with her image demonstrates.

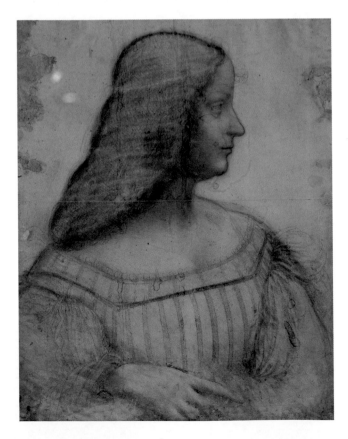

In order to escape Isabella d'Este's clutches, Leonardo da Vinci could only resort to a polite lack of flattery, as seen in this portrait – and it certainly worked.

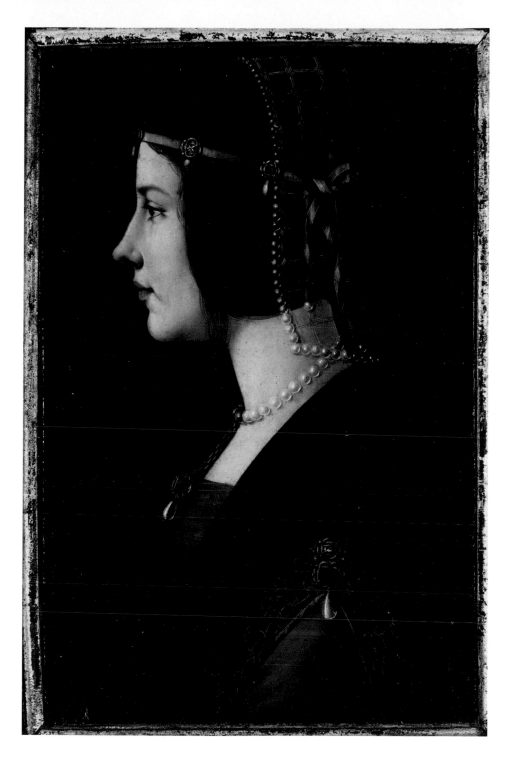

The rich jewellery displayed here by Beatrice d'Este, future duchess of Milan, reflects not only the attentions of a doting husband but the manifestation of wealth and power – of the sort that made her sister Isabella green with envy.

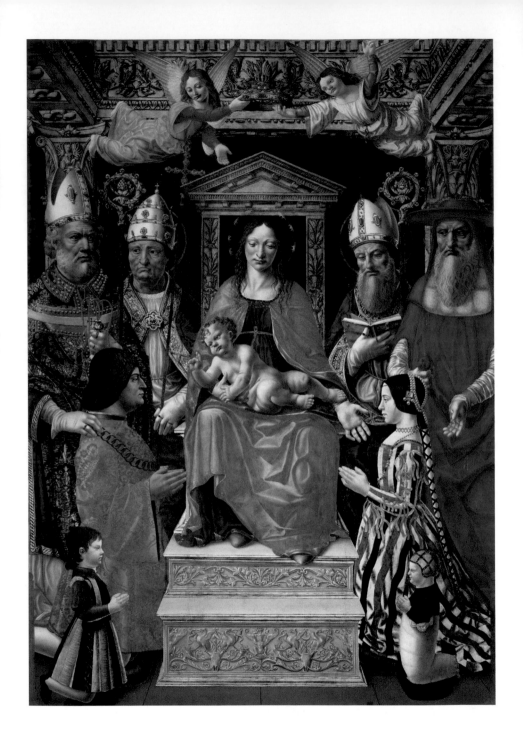

Ludovico Sforza with his wife Beatrice d'Este and their children. The formal composure of the ducal couple kneeling at the feet of the Virgin Mary, belies the domestic tensions created by il Moro's questionable activities, private as well as public.

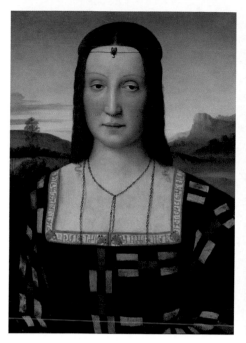

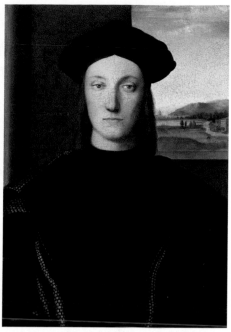

Elisabetta Gonzaga, duchess of Urbino – the victim both of Cesare Borgia's ambition and of her 'friend' Isabella d'Este's avarice.

Her husband, Guidobaldo da Montefeltro, was a good-natured, ineffectual man, who somehow managed to survive, of sorts, amid the turmoil of Italian politics.

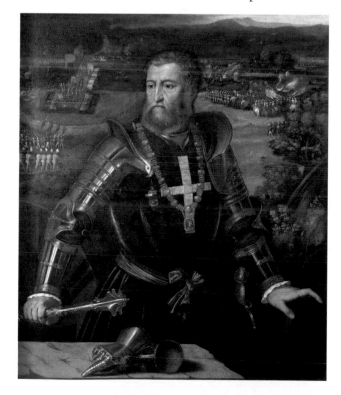

Alfonso d'Este, duke of Ferrara, whose passion for gun-casting was more than matched by that for the fair (and sometimes the unfair) sex.

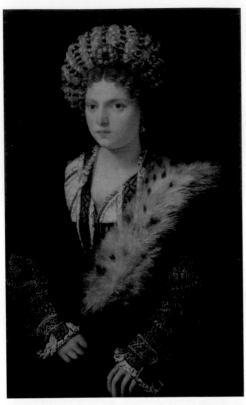

Titian's portrait of Isabella d'Este catches all too well her grasping determination to be *abitra elegatiarum* of Italy – and woe to those who dared to outshine her.

Ludovico il Moro's claim to fame proved to be as empty as the tomb he had made for himself and his wife Beatrice.

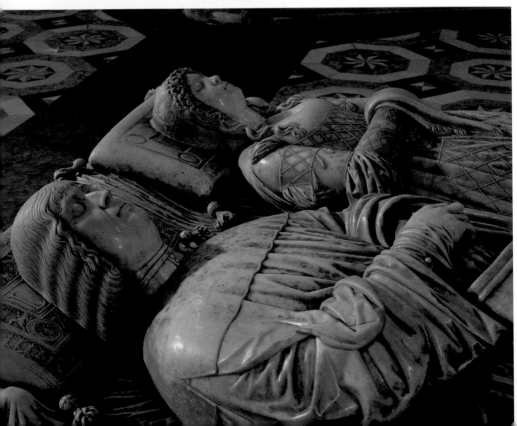

various sorts. Higher up were arranged books and drawings, busts and portraits of the most celebrated Florentine beauties.'

Not content with depriving the citizens of their false beards, Savonarola now set about attacking the corruption of the Pope in Rome. Irritatingly, he was too safe in Florence for Alexander VI to consider murdering him, but he sent agents to infiltrate the Signoria and boost the anti-Savonarola faction which succeeded the following year in bringing the friar down. He was hanged and burned on 23 May 1498. The frenzied atmosphere in Florence – that beacon of humanism (Savonarola being himself a Humanist) – anticipated the excesses of the religious wars in the following century. Guicciardini confirmed that 'It is difficult to imagine a city so thoroughly shattered and ill-regulated as ours was at this time.' The continuous wars, rebellions and divisions of the following years produced virtual political anarchy, until in 1502 Piero Soderini was appointed *Gonfaloniere* for life following a constitutional reform.

Giovanni did not remain long in Florence. His ambition, as well as his inclination, was for Rome, and he deputed Giuliano, who had spent much of the interregnum at the court of Urbino, to govern the city. In 1513, the Medici scheme for ecclesiastical domination came to fruition in Giovanni's election as Pope Leo X on the death of Julius II. Giuliano, who in accordance with the model established by his grandfather Cosimo had ruled moderately, lived unassumingly and had taken care to adhere to Florentine customs, saw his chance and promptly departed for Rome where he was appointed *Gonfaloniere* of the papal armies. Leo was at pains to find a replacement: his cousin Giulio had been a cardinal and had no intention of leaving the Eternal City. Despite the pope's misgivings, Alfonsina Orsini's son Lorenzo was directed to handle Medici interests in Florence.

The Medici restoration elevated the family to a status of which their predecessors had hardly dared to dream. Lorenzo may have been *magnifico*, but he had remained in essence a tradesman, an outsider in the world of the European aristocratic elite. The marriage of Caterina Sforza's son Giovanni to Maria di Jacopo Salviati brought together a stream of the great Italian dynasties in an exemplar of the Medicis' arrival as players on the Continental stage. The bride and groom were cousins of the senior and junior branches of the family: Maria was the daughter of Lucrezia Medici's marriage with Jacopo Salviati, Giovanni the son of Il Popolano, hence both were descended directly from Giovanni di Bicci, the founder of the Medici bank. Through Giovanni's mother, Caterina, the Medici were now linked with the dynasties of Sforza, Este, Gonzaga, Montefeltro, Malatesta and Orsini. Jacopo Salviati had been a friend to Caterina Sforza on her first arrival in Florence, lending her money, and was subsequently appointed executor of her will and guardian of her son Giovanni. The union of the two estranged branches of the Medici, as well as Caterina Sforza's connections, saw the marriage universally approved as being of 'great quality'.

Yet Giovanni's was not the greatest marriage among the new Medici generation. In 1515 Giuliano was sent to France as the papal representative to congratulate François I on his accession. The dynamic young French King was eager to reconquer Milan and Naples, for which, as ever, he required papal backing. To encourage Leo X, François offered Giuliano the dukedom of Nemours and the hand of his aunt, Filiberta of Savoy, in exchange for the lordships of Parma and Piacenza, which Giovanni had bestowed upon his brother. But 'the marital alliance between the ruling house of France and the merchant Medici was as thrilling to the latter as it was to prove short-lived', as Giuliano died within a year of the wedding, leaving no heir save for a bastard son, Ippolito. In a sense, Giuliano's death was timely. Leo had planned to install him as Duke of Urbino, but Giuliano had objected to dispossessing the current duke, Francesco della Rovere, nephew to Guidobaldo da Montefeltro, on the grounds that it was unjust to Urbino's rightful heir. Even as he was dying, Giuliano was begging his brother not to prosecute his plans for the duchy, but Lorenzo II de' Medici, the Pope's nephew, had no such scruples, egged on by his ambitious mother who had been pestering Leo for years to give her son a state.

In March 1516 the papal armies were sent against Urbino with Lorenzo in command. The della Rovere were put to flight and the duchy taken without difficulty within a month. On 30 May the Pope created Lorenzo Duke of Urbino. The acquisition did nothing to benefit Florence, since Lorenzo was a vain if not unintelligent individual, and the only material effect was to involve the city republic in a five-year struggle against the della Rovere. Further stupendous expenses were incurred when Lorenzo travelled to France with his brother-in-law Filippo Strozzi and a retinue of Florentines in new crimson velvet outfits for the baptism of François I's heir and his own betrothal. At least the sixteen-year-old bride, Madeleine de la Tour d'Auvergne, had plenty of cash with which to replenish the Medici coffers. Descended from the royal line of Vendôme-Bourbon on her mother's side and the great magnate Jean de la Tour on her father's, her inheritance encompassed lands in Auvergne, Castres, Clermont, Berry and Lauraguais. The marriage established the Medici for the first time as an influential dynasty beyond the confines of the peninsula, and though the Duke and Duchess of Urbino both died within months of their return to Italy, their daughter Caterina, 'La Duchessina', would one day become the first and the greatest Medici queen of France.

It was with the Medici, ultimately, that Caterina Sforza chose to associate herself in death. In her last years she had continued her donations to the convent of the Murate in Florence, which would eventually become the home of the orphaned Caterina de' Medici, as well as religious houses in Forlì. In the months before her death she also planned a pilgrimage to Loreto. In her will, drawn up in May 1509, she made bequests to the Murate, the church of Santa Caterina and that of San Girolamo in Fiesole. Among all the bequests to her children, the most poignant is perhaps that of her black slave, Moro Bona, whom she dedicated to the service of her son Giovanni. She died on 28 May and was buried, according to her request, at the high altar of the Murate, in a plain, unostentatious tomb. The engraving, which her grandson Cosimo, Grand Duke of Tuscany, had reset in white marble, read simply *Catharina Sfortia Medices*. In death, the Countess of Forlì chose to neglect all mention of the state for which she had battled for so many years, for which she had been imprisoned and ruined, and which had contributed most to her legend as the Madonna of Forlì. Yet there was still something of the warrior. Her will also made provision for the rebuilding of Florence's walls, defence against the unexpected having ever been dearest to her Sforza heart.

CHAPTER 21

Lucrezia the Duchess

1508–1515

'She is a highly intelligent and clever woman: you need to have
your head on straight [when dealing with her].'

'IL PRETE' ON LUCREZIA BORGITA

Much in the manner of Caterina Sforza, who had found true fulfil-
ment with her third husband, so too did Lucrezia Borgia, once freed
of her family's demands, find satisfaction in her own third marriage,
though for quite different reasons.

By 1503 Lucrezia had grown used to her husband's strong physical attraction for her and his nightly conjugal visits. The coupling
between them would be brief and basic, though the rough and rustic
manner of Alfonso's love-making corresponded perfectly with the
rest of his personality. To the despair of Duke Ercole, the Ferrarese
heir would spend his days wearing an apron, working in his forge,
creating innovative cannon and artillery pieces made from an alloy
he had invented himself. Alfonso also used the ovens to fire attractive majolica; he made delicate vases which he painted and found
this pastime a contrasting, as well as an enjoyable, distraction from
producing weapons of death and destruction.

The duke failed to appreciate the increasing acclaim his son
received as one of the foremost artillery experts in Christendom.
Personally designing and casting his 'engines of war' gave Alfonso
a unique understanding of their deployment, and he evolved into a
superb general tactician and commander. Alfonso is credited with
changing the art of warfare, and enjoyed the soubriquet 'Earthquake
d'Este', or 'Terremoto'. Tight-fisted Duke Ercole could not imagine that the trade in artillery Alfonso had started to build up would

provide a wonderful fillip to feed the coffers of the Ferrarese treasury. An old-fashioned man, Ercole considered his son's alternative daytime activities far more appropriate, if somewhat inelegant and lacking in style. These merely revolved around whoring and taking up almost permanent residence in various foul taverns with his equally revolting companions who shared Don Alfonso's low tastes of long habit.

Having survived several miscarriages and stillbirths, Lucrezia had yet to provide a living child for Alfonso. The situation filled the duke with disquiet. His clan had been notable for the number of bastards among its rulers and the consequent question of rights of succession. Alfonso's brother Ippolito enjoyed considerable popularity, though for all his elder brother's rough edges, the smooth cardinal had no edges at all, and might prove unstable and slippery. The courtiers approved of the raffish young Ippolito, so much their own image of what a prince should be; yet the people found his temper foul and his interest in them nonexistent. Their younger brother Ferrante had loved women, and held positions that brought little responsibility, large remuneration and no work.

Ercole's illegitimate son Don Giulio had resisted all Ercole's persuasive attempts to arrange a lucrative ecclesiastical career for him; his foremost two loves could be counted as himself, and looking at reflections of himself. There is no doubt that the young man had been blessed with male beauty, and that his soft brown eyes beckoned lovers to the bedchamber. Sigismondo had not even begun to worry his father Ercole, who felt that Alfonso and Ippolito needed to remain genuinely harmonious, even though they were polar opposites. Alfonso found himself popular with the people for his whoring, his drinking, his majolica vases and for forging cannon with his own hands. To the uncomprehending nobles at court he remained anathema. They understood Lucrezia better than they did her husband. Or she allowed them to believe so.

Lucrezia's romance with Pietro Bembo had essentially petered out by 1504. The pair saw each other when Pietro came through Ferrara on a visit to Rome, though the warmth between them seems to have flared again briefly in 1505. Bembo's father had heard of the attraction and possible affair between the two, and hauled Pietro out of Ferrara, fearing for his son's life. The d'Este had an essentially strict policy when it came to their women taking lovers – the rule being that, if caught, it could be fatal for both parties.

Lucrezia enjoyed the risks and peril their romance engendered, as well as Bembo's poetry to and about her. Three centuries later Lord Byron, fascinated by Lucrezia's reputation, and relating to Bembo's feeling, created an imaginary bond with both the lovers. He wrote, 'so pretty and so loving, it makes one wretched not to have been born sooner'. In a typical gesture of pseudo-daring, Byron, who wanted to increase both his romantic and dashing reputation, visited the archive in Milan to steal a strand of her golden locks, and memorized the letters with them.

Ercole I, Duke of Ferrara, wily and tight-fisted over money when the matter did not concern any of his own favourite pastimes or interests, proved a kind father-in-law to Lucrezia. After Alexander VI's death, Ercole had been politically cautious but showed much affection toward Alfonso's young bride. In May 1504, when the ageing duke heard of Cesare's final capture in Naples, he demonstrated his real attachment to the stricken Lucrezia again, writing to her: 'Be of good heart, for even as we love you truly and with all tenderness of heart as our daughter, so to shall we not fail him, and pray we are to him a good father and a good brother in all things ... [Then] hope in our Lord God who does not abandon those who put their faith in him.'

In April 1504, Lucrezia found herself abandoned in a potentially dangerous situation that imperilled their future. Alfonso had left Ferrara on the 13th of that month on a long voyage that he planned would incorporate many of the important courts in Christendom, although he wished to play a minimal diplomatic role. His purpose was to inspect the different countries' uses and types of artillery as well as their fortifications; his passion for martial expertise would lead to regular absences of this sort in the future.

Lucrezia feared that her father-in-law's health could collapse at any time, but she had already enlisted the support of a man who she knew would help her, despite his loathing for Alfonso, who returned the sentiment heartily. Francesco Gonzaga and Lucrezia had first met in the late 1490s. La Duchessa had been corresponding with Isabella's husband since her arrival and wrote to him herself, as evidenced by the sharp-pointed letters she formed when writing. Lucrezia, far less easy with her sister-in-law, used her secretary when communicating with Isabella.

From the first her letters to Francesco are inflected with a gay and playful tone, artfully conveying the scintilla of flirtation she hoped to impart. Delighted, Francesco responded in the same vein – he had long since given up hoping for anything but dreary lists of instructions and thinly veiled complaints from his wife. He admired Isabella's abilities but had been pained by the way she ignored their daughters, and his sisters. By 1500, when she gave birth to the couple's heir Federico, her letters deteriorated from the ornamented lists of demands and complaints, but contained every possible reference to Federico. Almost every stage in the infant's development is recorded, from his first steps, his first words and his obvious genius – for, as she wrote in one glaringly tactless moment of forgetfulness, she believed the boy had inherited more from his mother than from Francesco. Absenting himself from his state more frequently than ever, usually at a military encampment, the sight of a courier carrying a letter from his nagging wife made him droop, while reading the contents generally bored him to sobs.

Lucrezia had found life even lonelier of late. A short while before Alfonso's departure, his younger brother, the inscrutable though amusing Cardinal Ippolito, had been forced out of Ferrara. The cardinal had also enjoyed the amusements and intrigues of the larger, international Vatican court, and had found his sister-in-law a definite adornment to life in Ferrara, a backwater compared to the papal court. Lucrezia felt a kindred spirit in Ippolito, a man both entertaining and witty, whom she had known as a friend to Cesare, which made him especially dear to her. Yet her instincts and informers told her to pay careful attention as she whiled enjoyable hours away with him. Her jaundiced eye had long since spotted the elegant Ippolito's insinuating ways, and how his apparently laughing manner teased information from unwitting people, particularly the Ferrarese bumpkins. Although it had been said that the cardinal 'owns the Madonna by day, and Don Alfonso claims his ownership at night', Lucrezia, an old hand at these games, proved more than able to keep her own counsel in all matters that might affect her interests, or those of the duchy.

Not helping matters, Pope Julius II, who loathed the d'Este, found provocation when he sent an envoy to Ippolito with the unwelcome news that the Estense cardinal must surrender a number of his lucrative benefices. The irascible Pontiff intended to bestow them upon one of his own favourites. Ippolito, every bit as hot-headed and impetuous as Julius himself, received the news and punched the papal envoy. He followed this up with a thorough beating. Raving furiously, he went to his father to tell him of the Pope's latest insult to their family.

Ercole listened, appalled at his son's behaviour, and insisted that he write to the Pontiff immediately and apologize for his loss of control and the wretched emissary's subsequent beating. When Ippolito refused to do so, Ercole banished his son to Mantua: 'you need not wonder that we have dismissed your from our State, because behaving yourself as you do, we do not think you are worthy to be near to us'.

Julius wished to incorporate Ferrara into the papal sphere, and Venice always cast a hungry expansionist eye on the duchy, geographically sandwiched between her predators. The Duke of Ferrara feared that his death would leave the duchy vulnerable to its natural enemies, while weakened by his own ambitious sons or nephews nurturing secret desires to supplant his legitimate first-born son Alfonso. The people of Ferrara discussed little but what would happen when 'that poor old man' died.

Lucrezia had made a secret arrangement with Francesco Gonzaga that, should the need arise, he would come to the ducal couple's aid. The Mantuan marquis, who earned his living as a *condottierre* and had become as renowned for his equine expertise as for his sexual appetites, had agreed that the cry of the people 'Turco' would be the cry of Alfonso and Lucrezia's supporters; but as his correspondent, confirming this, wrote: 'You alone, my Lord, can do more in this city than the house of Este together.' Ippolito had been brought back during the late spring by Francesco, who effected both the reconciliation between father and son and Ippolito's immediate return to his home country.

As Alfonso hurried back from England, Lucrezia took a second important step by telling the Venetian ambassador that her husband considered himself a friend of Venice and recommended 'the most Reverend Signory ... that she serves you willingly'. The letter continued in the same vein, adding that, despite malicious gossip stating otherwise, the new Duke would not be changing his allegiance from Venice.

Alfonso returned in August, and on his arrival the situation quietened somewhat. The heir to the dukedom visited Venice in September to reiterate the message sent by his wife during his absence. He preferred Venice to the papacy, for the latter, led by the Warrior Pope, had become a real threat – particularly since Julius showed Ferrante great favour (implying papal support), and he returned from Rome puffed up with the notion that he would be the next duke if his brother did not get back to Ferrara before their father died.

Duke Ercole's condition deteriorated and he lay listening to the gentle music played on his favourite clavichord. Sinking slowly, with the family gathered about his bed, Ercole beat time to the music with his hand. On the evening of Friday, 24 January 1505, the physicians insisted upon administering a good dose of *auro portabile* (a mixture of gold and water), upon which the patient suffered a stroke. The following morning Ercole I d'Este, Duke of Ferrara, died. One historian compared him to his fellow rulers on the peninsula, calling him 'the one sympathetic [and] almost only not ignoble figure'. A notable absentee at her father's bedside had been Isabella; she could no longer attempt to guide the rule of both Mantua and Ferrara as she had been wont over the past years.

Snow had been falling heavily during the night and had filled the piazza and streets, as a gelid wind blew through the city. The fast-falling snowflakes muffled the tolling palace bell. It announced Ercole's passing, and called the council of magistrates. The former republic had elected its ruler; the tradition, though a formality, characterized the succession process. Following the anachronistic ceremony, the company entered the new duke's Camera della Stufa Grand. Alfonso appeared regal and magnificent, wearing a white-plumed velvet cap; a mantle of heavy white damask lined with squirrel revealed the brilliant gems studded into his collar as well as the gold and chains of precious stones that hung from his neck, falling onto an immaculate white silk tunic. Invested with the ducal insignia, the sword of state (representing him as its defender) and sceptre, Alfonso listened to the official speech proclaiming him Alfonso I, Duke of Ferrara.

After making his reply, filled with the recipe's usual ingredients, he swore to be a good, just Lord and to love his people. Volleys of cannon fire could not drown out the cheering of 'Alfonso!' and 'Duca!' as he emerged from the palace, walking between Ippolito, dressed in his cardinal's crimson taby, on his right, and on his other side the Venetian Visdomino. Ferrante and Giulio followed directly behind. Alfonso mounted his magnificent grey horse and with his fraternal and Venetian escort rode through the icy blizzard to the Cathedral, where the bent and aged figure of Tito Vespasiano Strozzi greeted the new ruler of Ferrara and, in the coronation service that followed, crowned the new duke.

Lucrezia was dressed in a white taby gown fringed with gold and a white cloak lined with ermine, through which brilliant white sleeves showed off the slashing of gold and crimson. The Duchess of Ferrara wore her hair loose and among the blonde curls glinted superb gems as she stood watching her husband return through the piazza. By the time the proclaimed and ordained Duke Alfonso arrived at the palazzo steps his wife had descended and watched her husband dismount. As he turned towards Lucrezia, she dropped in a beautiful deep reverence before her newly elevated husband. As she took his hand to kiss it, Alfonso held his wife's shoulders and lifted her from the curtsey, and 'with happy faces' the couple smiled as the duke kissed Lucrezia on the mouth, and then led her to the balcony where the pair received ecstatic cheers from the large crowds whose feet had cleared the snow. After bowing and nodding to their joyful subjects for some minutes, Lucrezia returned inside and left her husband to be acclaimed by his people.

Their first public appearance as Duke and Duchess had driven the crowds wild, with shouts of joy and felicitation. Both husband and wife looked regal and perfect for the part life had chosen them to play. Alfonso finally returned inside the palace and out of the cold, and led Lucrezia to the celebrations and banquets ahead, which would last for a full twenty-four hours. Lucrezia had to be careful not to exhaust herself, for she had discovered that she was pregnant again, and the couple sat with their favourite fool, 'Il Barone'. The court would go into mourning the following day, and the accession banquet and celebrations were enjoyed by all, one contemporary noting that the duke and duchess sat 'in great joy'.

Lucrezia's Borgia instincts and experience had taught her that these moments do not last long, and she lent herself to the festivities wholeheartedly. She could also congratulate herself upon sitting on the throne of one of the most important duchies on the peninsula, as the legitimate wife of the duke; and she prayed that the baby growing in her belly was a son.

When any new monarch ascends his throne some changes are made due to the exigences of the time, others merely because of different interests, beliefs, friends and favourites. As Ercole had been confounded by Alfonso's love for getting himself hot and dirty working in his forge, he found the other interest that made his son hot and dirty far less disconcerting. Alfonso had been equally baffled by his father's veneration for nuns. Music did not interest him, and the musical soirées held and performed by the ducal family in his mother's day did not interest him.

Alfonso knew that Ferrara had been greatly impoverished by the war but he found his father had left the state in a parlous financial condition. Ercole had been selling offices and pardons for some time before his death. The new duke found a serious challenge before him – restoring his duchy to its former economic stability.

Alfonso needed to head off any potential trouble from his brothers. He often spent the mornings hawking or hunting with them, returning to the city to take care of the varied and immediate issues that required addressing. His father had given each of his sons a palazzo, but – having almost bankrupted Ferrara in his modernizing and rebuilding of the city, doubling it in size during his reign – the treasury had been left perilously empty. One of Alfonso's first acts upon becoming duke provided for a generous sum to be paid to each of his brothers in order that they could live in the style required of them and that they had enjoyed all their lives.

Fortunately for Lucrezia and all concerned but the green-eyed Isabella, the young Borgia bride had shared Duke Ercole's passionate fascination with ancient nuns and they petitioned, pleaded and cajoled the Church to permit these semi-mystics to come and live within convents in Ferrara. The new duchess did not confine her attention to these holy relics, who, in one or two cases had proved less than genuine and courted favour with the duke and his daughter-in-law, who in turn lavished gifts on these ravaged old Brides of Christ. Lucrezia favoured poetry and poets; she also enjoyed music. The late duke had built up the largest choir of the princely courts in Christendom, once the boast of Galeazzo Maria Sforza. Women were not permitted their own choirs, but Lucrezia circumnavigated this problem by having musicians in her own apartments playing for her while she and her ladies sat confined there due to poor weather or while she indulged in her fragrant southern habits, which involved long hair-washing sessions and other hygienic rituals that, according to Isabella's spies (who exaggerated greatly), kept the court waiting for her to appear.

Isabella might have done well to take note of Lucrezia's habits, making herself somewhat more feminine and attractive at the same time. Comparisons are odious, particularly between the Marchioness of Mantua and the Duchess of Ferrara, yet Isabella continued to ask her spies and correspondents to make them, and the fawning or evasive replies did not cause her to question her supremacy. Which of them could be called the greater beauty? Since Isabella had only ever enjoyed the good looks of youth, and she had never been beautiful, so this question defied parallel. Which of the two women danced more gracefully? The tubby marchioness enjoyed dancing, though even as a child the sycophantic dance master dared not expose himself to ridicule by describing Isabella as a ballerina. The acquisitive Marchioness of Mantua enjoyed fine clothes and jewels, and as her body expanded so did her vast wardrobe, bursting with furs, hats, capes, mantles, gloves (a huge luxury, often chased in gold or silver, with fur and a number of exotic linings) as well as other adornments. Her collection of jewels, almost invariably at one of the pawnbrokers, comprised a host of fine pieces.

The marchioness would have done better to consider her immense strengths: her commanding personality, her majestic attitudes, and, above all, her keen political sense would have allowed a far more even result between herself and her sister-in-law.

Lucrezia came to Ferrara as a foreigner – not just a Roman woman but a woman imbued with the ways of her father's country, its Moorish invaders, even oriental treatments whose habits had been adopted by his people. The duchess approached her health, her style and her entire presentation with all that she had learned at the far more exotic Vatican court, and the practices of her father's homeland.

A paradigm of feminine perfection, Lucrezia was in her early thirties; and, while she had always been a beauty, she reached the high point of radiant womanhood at this age. Her long blonde hair still reached her knees and to keep the thick curls clean and fragrant it required washing every three days. This process amounted to an almost religious ritual. The method favoured by rich women of her day, and used by Lucrezia herself, included a mixture of vine stock ashes, liquorice root (with the outer bark removed) and shavings of cedar thrown into boiling barley water, creating a wet paste to which scrapings of horses' hoof, myrrh, saffron, cumin and rock alum were added. The compound had to be applied to her scalp using a broad, flat knife and left to harden before rinsing. Women dried their hair by a fire or brazier while brushing it with combs. In Lucrezia's case these would have been made of the finest ivory or tortoiseshell, or painted wooden combs, inlaid with precious stones, which could also be of decorative use when putting her hair up.

One of her favourite ways of whiling away the little time she had in privacy was to design her own dresses, while listening to the musicians play and her ladies chatter. Often she would take one or two of her favourite ladies and lie in the huge bath originally made for Eleonora d'Este, which Alfonso had restored as a gift to his wife.

Braziers lit with scented wood filled the air with a pungent oriental aroma, as Lucrezia and her attendants enjoyed the scented water wearing only shroud-like long shifts, their hair tied up in gold nets to keep it dry. Lucia, her maid, kept the bath filled with fresh supplies of hot water.

A firm believer in what would be called a natural look, Lucrezia officially banned Pomatum, the cosmetic paste in common use by upper-class women to whiten their faces, necks, hands and other visible parts. One variant of the cosmetic killer is described by Marinello, a Venetian beauty expert of his day. Marinello advocated a high forehead by plucking and a coating of mastic over the depilated skin overnight to keep it smooth. To achieve 'skin whiter than alabaster', the recipe required two young white doves, their heads removed, plucked and drawn. The undeterred beauty-seeker ground the birds with four ounces of peach stones, four ounces of washed melon seeds, two ounces of sublimate of mercury and a spoon of bean flour. Ground pebbles infused for a day and a night in milk required blending with two young cabbages, a fresh cheese, preferably made at that hour, fourteen whites of fresh eggs, half an ounce of camphor, an equal amount of borax, and four bulbs of the white lily. Once given a final grinding and mixing, the ghastly swill was placed in vials. The instructions advised the wearer to add water to suit and 'use at your pleasure'.

Variations upon this theme could be found in most beauty recipes, but the deadly ingredients blended with the rest of the exotic list that sounded as though it belonged in the alchemist's almanac made Lucrezia rebel. Since childhood she had seen the grim effects the lethal unguents left upon those who used them. Tiresome and difficult to paint on, once the pomatum had dried upon the face, it became a white mask requiring rouge and other paints. Disinclined to repeat the procedure, most women at court left their make-up on, refreshing it occasionally; finally the skin beneath became destroyed by over-use. Lucrezia, whose small white teeth had been greatly admired as a very young woman, believed in clean, clear skin. She freshened her breath by chewing herbs, ate sparingly and brushed her teeth using elementary toothbrushes with ivory handles and badger's hair to apply the paste of soot and salt, or the preferred and more usual white wine mixed with fresh urine. If it was not possible to use one's own urine, then a young girl's urine would do the job admirably.

On the Sunday following the ban on their way into Mass, Lucrezia and her ladies walked through a staring crowd who had 'come to see the duchess's naked face'. No extremist, Lucrezia allowed the use of rouge to continue. Watched and reported by Isabella's spies, Lucrezia began to set her own style and assert herself. Isabella thought only of her sainted late mother and bemoaned every change.

Lucrezia had never sought the rivalry with her sister-in-law and the two women could only be described as laughably different when compared physically. The marchioness's instinct told her that, when in doubt, add yet more gold brocade, more fur or more gems to a gown before feeling certain that she would trump her sister-in-law. Yet Lucrezia invariably won the day by wearing an unadorned robe with a clever cut, device, or an original twist of some sort. Lucrezia understood elegance and had an eye for style. Isabella might have outshone her Borgia sister-in-law, but only on the technical grounds that she had almost entirely covered herself in gems. The Duchess of Ferrara followed a 'less is more' aesthetic, but for Isabella, more was always better. To her the question answered itself.

Yet the two women had much in common, though they used their talents differently. Both the Duchess and the Marchioness had repeatedly proved adept and clever; forced during times of crisis to act alone, they had shown speed and initiative. Both bold and courageous, they had each been forced into the male world of politics, successfully manoeuvring around obstacles that most would find impassable.

Listening to petitions and taking up the administrative duties as duchess, Lucrezia felt uneasy as spring 1505 turned to summer. She dreaded the scrutiny of the court should she suffer another failed pregnancy. As she went about her duties and received senior women of Ferrara, Lucrezia managed to make her mourning elegant. Her gowns of soft stuff were cut in order to pronounce her slim body and movements, and she invented a confection that she perched upon her head with a veil covering her face, calling it a 'Bologna veil'; this allowed her to escape the heavy black drapery normally worn, and yet fell within the bounds of respectability. She had moved from wearing black into brown, and ordered her ladies to follow, their light new veils adding a dash of white or yellow that suggested laughter lay ahead.

In May plague struck Ferrara. Lucrezia, with only a few months left before her longed-for child's birth, dared take no risks and left the city with her household.

Alfonso had moved to his 300-room palace at Belriguardo; Ippolito had left town and stayed near Alfonso. The two seemed to have agreed some sort of accommodation, if not understanding, with each other. The two brothers had lived in noticeably greater harmony since the death of their father.

Lucrezia headed for Modena and, meaning to travel on to Reggio, she found that Giulio, Duke Ercole's illegitimate son, had decided to join the ladies on their journey. The duchess had a great affection for the beautiful youth, though she feared trouble. The d'Este bastard had decided that he had found someone as beautiful as he; he had become enamoured of Angela Borgia, Lucrezia's illegitimate cousin and part of the duchess's household.

It is rare that contemporary accounts agree, yet in the case of the Borgia girl's beauty, there is complete accord. Unfortunately, Angela's intelligence did not match her looks. The teenager knew well she had the power to attract tremendous admiration, though she proved heedless when wielding that power. Her flirtatious glance, jealousies thoughtlessly provoked, and playful spirit gave her more circumspect cousin the duchess plenty to worry over. Lucrezia had more than sufficient concerns to burden and distract her attention, though she feared Angela would fall into some mischief or problem if she left her alone.

While the duchess turned to Francesco Gonzaga for personal comfort as well as help of a more official nature, he enjoyed the fragile beauty's need for a strong protector as well as practical support. He sent grain supplies to keep the city fed while the plague raged, and comforted her with promises that he would do all within his power to free her brother.

Leaving Modena for Reggio, the duchess suffered light fevers but nothing that caused undue alarm. The baby kicked, reminding her of the new life inside her – a son, she prayed, if only God would give her a son. On 19 September, to her rapture, Lucrezia gave birth to a son whom she named Alexander, and she sent out separate couriers, one to Francesco and the other to her husband, with the news of her son's arrival. But the infant would not feed and Alfonso hurried to his wife. Lucrezia had suffered a serious fever but it had not lasted for more than a few hours. She had complained of a lack of feeling down her legs, and the midwives wrapped hot cloths around them. Lucrezia's letters following Alexander's birth are little more than health bulletins to those she trusted, while she and Alfonso replied formally to the congratulations that arrived from officials and those sent from outside Ferrara.

By mid-October Isabella, pregnant and complaining of feeling unwell, waited in Mantua for her great favourite Beatrice de' Contrari to join her for the birth of her child. Lucrezia had made Beatrice a member of her household and, despite the alarm she felt for her son, sent Contrari to Isabella. The wet-nurse whom Isabella had also requested received last-minute orders to remain with the duchess. She hurried to ask Francesco's pardon for keeping the *comatre*, explaining: 'Our son has been gravely ill in these past few days, and although, thank God, he has begun to take the breast he is in such a condition that he will not be able to do without the Comatre.' Her first-born Estense son, the male heir she desperately wanted for Alfonso, died three days later on 16 October. Lucrezia did not write of her pain to her husband; instead she poured her grief and tears into a letter she sent to Francesco and made plans to meet him on her way back to the Duke at Belriguardo.

Pietro Bembo heard of the child's birth and sent prompt and formal congratulation; in December he wrote again, having only just heard of Alexander's death. With an astonishing lack of tact, Lucrezia's former lover enclosed a chart that he had ordered to be drawn up 'by a man skilled in astrology' as soon as heard of Lucrezia's infant's birth. He seemed to have been thinking of their own moribund relationship rather than their predictions for Alexander, judging by his somewhat martyred tone, writing: 'we are truly in great part ruled by the stars'. Regrettably the chart itself is no longer available, for rarely do seers tell bad news to great people, though it must be assumed their predictions for Alexander were brief. Bembo, so recently ensnared by Lucrezia's beauty and golden hair, found himself miraculously freed. He did not write to his former lover again for seven years.

Upon receiving word that Lucrezia would meet him at Borgoforte, Francesco fell into raptures at the thought of their assignation with neither the entire court nor their sibling spouses ogling at them. 'We would not wish to have acquired a great[er] treasure,' he trilled, and hurried to transform the forbidding fortress into a lovers' bower. He sent tapestries, furniture, plate, paintings and other touches to lighten the tenebrous atmosphere of the bleak fastness and transform their crenulated arbour. Under different circumstances, the ideal person to cheer up, if not clutter up, the stronghold, would have been Isabella, who believed she had been born to design the interiors of a palazzo or castle. It is fortunate that, heavily pregnant and feverish, she had been unable to attend. Had the graceless touch of the marchioness's decorative style been imprinted upon the Borgoforte, it would probably have squeezed the life out of the romance before it could flourish.

It is at Borgoforte, to lyrical tunes played by the musicians Gonzaga had summoned, that the relationship between the marquis and Lucrezia is most likely to have become physical. Famed for his sexual appetites, the marquis was set aflame by the duchess's unique blend of strength and fragility, while remaining superbly feminine. He wanted to have Lucrezia and to make her his own. She could identify with Gonzaga far more readily than with her Estense husband or his tribe, and saw his concentrated potency and powerful masculinity as just the antidote to Alfonso who, while no weakling, gave her little sense of security. Almost invariably, when trouble threatened she turned to Francesco before she approached her husband.

Lucrezia had lost Cesare, her exemplar and protector, to a Spanish gaol, making Gonzaga sexually appealing on the most basic level. With him she felt safe. Two people of such prominence as the Marquis of Mantua and the Duchess of Ferrara engaging in a physical love affair, fraught with risks, excited them both. Lucrezia wrote to her husband that the marquis had insisted upon hosting her party at Borgoforte, and he, Alfonso, had no idea 'how much resistance I put up'; she added that Gonzaga had insisted she pay a visit to Isabella and he would then send the party back on his bucentaur wherever she wished.

Isabella seems to have rushed Lucrezia on a treasure tour. The duchess did not interest herself in fine collections; she admired great work, though she had become inured to Isabella's bobbish excitement over ownership. Since her first teenage years, during her life at the Vatican and Rome, the duchess had watched the great masters at work, and had received exotic gifts offered by potentates from all over the known world. As well as owning gems of staggering value and rarity, she had lived in palaces filled with her own collection of pictures, sculptures and tapestries, all of the highest quality, and of such rarity that the provincial marchioness would have been mute with awe.

Yet Isabella wanted to show the jumped-up Borgia duchess, who had no sensational collections of her own at Ferrara, that she had stolen a few marches on her in her quest to become the foremost collector of valuables. Indeed, Isabella had purloined a fair amount of what she displayed in a vain attempt to impress her detested sister-in-law. She had barely left a drawer unopened in her desperation to amaze the duchess, who uttered little more than polite appreciative remarks, or commented with genuine interest when she saw a piece she truly admired. Mantegna being the official court artist of Mantua, Lucrezia's cultural programme could hardly have avoided a number of the Master's finest works. Before the duchess's departure, the marchioness proudly told Lucrezia how she admired his pictures and murals. In truth Isabella had been furious with Mantegna for over fifteen years, for he had displeased her with a portrait that she found unflattering, and had managed gradually to freeze him out.

Despite Francesco's continued loyalty to Mantegna, the marquis found he could hardly stand being in the same state as his wife for long, and had lost touch with the paintings being commissioned unless specifically by him. As wars had raged along the length of the peninsula since 1494, his duties (and earnings) as a soldier had had to come first. Without Francesco's presence, Mantegna found himself in an increasingly penurious situation as the Gonzaga family commissions dried up. By 1504, old and ill, Mantegna knew that the marchioness craved his antique sculpture of the Empress Faustina. He felt heartsore to lose his favourite piece, but the old man decided he must ignore wretchedness, and wrote offering to sell the bust to Isabella for the sum of 100 ducats.

The marchioness wished to punish Mantegna and did not bother to reply to his letter. From a distance she kept a beady eye on the bust, and used her spies to ensure it was not sold. Then she waited. A few months passed and Mantegna fell into further debt; his commissions were rare and he had aged a great deal due to increasing financial concerns. Isabella picked her moment and swooped quite suddenly upon the painter, taking the treasured bust of the Roman empress against the promise that she would pay the asking price of 100 ducats direct to his creditors.

Tradesmen rarely pursued their rulers for payment, particularly one who could be as vicious in acquisition as Isabella d'Este. The concept of a timorous tailor importuning the illustrious marchioness for a small payment on account for 'Ser Mantegna's mantel' leads to the conclusion that Francesco's miserly consort had found a devious method of getting her hands on yet more treasure for her hoard without it costing her a single ducat. Isabella placed the bust in her *Grotta*, where it stood in a special niche of honour. A month after her swindle, Andrea Mantegna, the court painter and long-time friend of the Gonzaga family, died.

Having met Alfonso at Belriguardo, Lucrezia prepared to set out for Ferrara and wrote several letters to Francesco. In one she commented, 'things have been going well there [Ferrara]'. Unfortunately the duchess had allowed her attention to focus on matters far from Ferrara and had not kept up-to-date with the latest events in the city, where sibling rivalry had caused deadly mischief. Ippolito and Giulio both loved music as much as their father had; a squabble had arisen over one Don Rainaldo, a chaplain and master of music who had worked in Giulio's household but had apparently died shortly after Duke Ercole.

When Giulio discovered that Don Rainaldo was not only alive, but had secretly agreed to join his half-brother's household, he boiled with anger. Furthermore, the deceit had required that Don Rainaldo disappear for a while and to that end he had agreed to be tucked away, as far as possible from the main family traffic. La Rocca del Gesso, a stronghold belonging to the Count of Scandiano, fulfilled all the criteria.

Giulio, being a spoiled hothead, did not wait to think about how to resolve matters intelligently but gathered a force of men, some armed with crossbows, whom he met at a place near Carpi where Ferrante happened to be staying. Giulio disappeared with his men to the fortress of Gesso and, without having to fire an arrow in anger, he scooped up Don Rainaldo, leaving him with Ferrante.

It did not take long for the news of his chaplain's abduction to reach Ippolito. Being on the closest terms with Alfonso, he demanded reparation. The duke commanded Giulio and Ferrante to attend him at Modena, where he exiled his young half-brother and used the offence upon the Count of Scandiano as his excuse. Alfonso sent Ferrante to Brescello, where he placed him under restraint to move no further than a two-mile radius from the town.

A hideous fuss ensued among the rest of the family. Isabella wrote and begged Alfonso to pardon Giulio, 'who not from malice but from lack of thought has fallen into error ... this is no time to remember affronts and hatred and if [Ippolito] is of this way of thinking, I would remind him of the same'. Fond of both her younger brothers-in-law, Lucrezia wrote to Alfonso, who sent his wife a peremptory message ordering her not to interfere in the affair except to have his secretary tell Don Giulio 'to obey us because if he fails to do so, your ladyship may know that we will proceed to other means'. Alfonso would brook no feminine pleading. Finally Ippolito rode over to Belriguardo to discuss the matter with Alfonso, the result of the meeting being an appeal to Marquis Francesco that the Gonzaga inner circle resolve the dispute. The brothers returned but the reconciliation affected merely masked hidden hatreds within the fraternal circle. On 12 October Isabella's spy di Prosperi wrote sycophantically: 'I judge this case to be settled, thanks to the good offices of Your Ladyship.'

The 'graceful and elegant' maiden, Angela Borgia, who worried Lucrezia over her reckless flirtations and the mischievous use of her powers to ensorcell her admirers, had captured the attention of the two most prominent men in Ferrara: she had cast her eye upon Cardinal Ippolito and the breathtakingly handsome Don Giulio. The former had changed since the episode over the chaplain; once gay and full of ideas with which to entertain the Duchess and her ladies, he now sat in her apartments noticeably brooding.

Anxious to find a husband for the eighteen-year-old Angela, whom she loved best of all her household, Lucrezia no longer had the vast means at her disposal to offer a huge dowry to Angela's prospective husband, and the price of her dowry had just gone up for she had almost certainly started a serious physical love affair with Giulio. Unthinking and childlike – consequences and responsibility never seemed letters addressed to her – she could enjoy the best of everything with Lucrezia's protection, and two of the late Duke Ercole's sons chasing her simply added to the dizzying fun.

Angela flirted outrageously with Ippolito though Giulio had captured her heart (and body, as later events would bear out). According to Guicciardini, soon after the theatrical reconciliation between the cardinal and his bastard brother, Angela lolled about her two panting princely admirers, and with the attitude of a spoiled child she looked at Ippolito and laughed, saying: 'Monsignore, your brother's eyes are worth more than the whole of your person.'

Cardinal Ippolito, the epitome of elegance with his carefully curled hair, sublimely cut clothes and soft-skinned white hands, perfectly manicured, found himself at a loss. To his late father's frustration the cardinal rarely wore the red robes that announced his status as a prince of the Church, but equally rarely did he find himself playing cat and mouse games with a girl who thought of nothing but her own beauty, her next pleasure, or an expensive gift from the duchess. The playful rejection did not appeal to his ear and a burning, irrational desire for Angela grew for her to submit to him.

Ippolito did not give his heart, but his libido and ego required constant nourishment. He enjoyed taking risks and he had even bedded Lucrezia's sister-in-law Sancia d'Aragona while under her holy father-in-law's roof; to add to the danger, Cesare used her as his sometime mistress.

As he sat with the duchess and her ladies, his wit hovered above the others' reach; but the wretched Angela eluded him. He tried his well-oiled seduction routine. Usually this charmed the female prey into the sophisticate's toils, but not Angela.

Ippolito became dark in his pursuit of Angela. As she ran giggling from his embrace his determination aggravated his need for the foolish teenager. Foolish indeed, for she had entered the last trimester of pregnancy and the clues pointed to Giulio as being responsible for the girl's swollen belly. Lucrezia's travels during the late summer had partly been an attempt by the duchess to keep her cousin out of sight and harm's way. Even as they returned it is probable she strove to keep the pregnancy secret. The pregnancy might explain Ippolito's furious efforts at seduction with almost anyone biddable within Lucrezia's household. One of the bolder maidens commented, 'My Lord Cardinal touches all the young girls and caresses them, saying: "I am your shepherd and you are my little lambs."' The calculated liaisons that he had been wont to conduct did not appeal to Angela. She preferred a male beauty who mirrored her own glorious looks.

On 1 November 1505 Giulio left Alfonso at Belriguardo and rode towards Ferrara in high spirits. On the road he came across his half-brother with four of his men, riding towards Lucrezia's palazzo. Whether an ambush had been set is not known, but upon stopping Giulio in an amiable fashion, Ippolito spoke the words: 'Kill that man. Take out his eyes!' He watched as his men, apparently accustomed to such work, moved efficiently and quickly unhorsed Giulio and stabbed him in the eyes, the eyes that Angela loved more than Ippolito himself. The cardinal's men having taken their knives to Don Giulio's eyes, then lifted him up and threw him on the grass near the side of the road. Perhaps the sight of his brother's blood startled Ippolito from his madness. He turned his horse and galloped for the border to leave Ferrara.

How long Giulio lay on the blood-soaked grass is not known, though when found he was immediately carried to Alfonso's palace of Belriguardo. The wailing from Angela's and Lucrezia's despair is not recorded, though the sinister attack would certainly have reminded Lucrezia of that upon her beloved late husband, the Duke of Bisceglie. Had she travelled so far only to find she had returned to a strange facsimile of her old home at the Vatican, and the bloody deeds she had witnessed and endured within her own family?

Alfonso felt stunned disbelief at the news that Ippolito, his brother, wisest counsellor and right arm, could have committed such a horror. Having urgently called the best physicians and surgeons to attend to Don Giulio, four days passed. Finally Alfonso felt recovered sufficiently to write to Isabella. Unwittingly, he betrayed his position, as well as the truth. The four men had been captured, and upon questioning they had denied any knowledge or complicity by the cardinal of their attack upon his brother. He then wrote a postscript telling his sister that Don Giulio had met his brother. 'The Most Reverend Cardinal our brother ... commanded "Kill that man: cut out his eyes."'

The following day Alfonso wrote to Francesco and included both versions, though he asked his brother-in-law to burn the letters. This exhortation is usually a guarantee that the document is filed carefully away by the recipient. The Gonzaga despatched the finest surgeon and physician from Mantua to aid the work of the Ferrarese doctor. Incredibly, the wretched Giulio's sight returned in the left eye, though he could only see dark and light with his right. The muscle having been cut, he had to open the right eye with his fingers. The pain 'is almost unsupportable', he wrote in a letter to Francesco and Isabella. He thanked them for the solicitude, no longer the gay fellow in love with life and himself, and perhaps he thought of Angela.

Alfonso, understandably panicked by the monstrous nature of the fratricidal attack, turned to the other sovereign prince within his own family, Francesco Gonzaga, as well as his sister Isabella. He knew well that Ippolito's foul deed merited punishment of the most extreme severity, yet he became befuddled by the thought of punishing a prince of the Church, his most capable adviser and his brother. Alfonso could not admit it to anybody, but he feared Ippolito, the most able of them all, and he did not fear Giulio. He had laid the guilt at Ippolito's feet in the letters to Francesco and Isabella, who were calling for Alfonso to exact the proper retribution from the Cardinal. The Duke knew that he would only weaken his house if it was seen tearing itself apart by brothers at war over a loose young woman, who had not only disgraced herself but caused the Duchess opprobrium with her behaviour.

The news filtered quickly through to Rome, where Julius summoned the Ferrarese envoy and quizzed him about the attack, calling the crime 'most audacious'. As ever, his keen nose tried to pick up the scent for a reason to attack Ferrara. Without too much difficulty he pulled the facile official version of the crime apart, informing Beltrando Costabili: 'the events occurred in another manner than Your Excellency's account'. He ordered that the delinquents be captured should they be found within the papal territories; unsurprisingly, the assailants evaded capture and fled as far as Hungary. Alfonso worried that if he did not effect peace within his family, Julius might make his next move against Ferrara itself.

The duchess's part in this is not recorded, having been told to mind her own business. Di Prosperi wrote telling Isabella tame tales of her rival's activities. These had been restricted to decorating her new apartments. He complimented Her Ladyship's judicious touch and the delightful result of her efforts, which included creating new rooms at the castello in the Torre Marchesana. She also worked on the passage 'from the rooms of his Lordship her Consort without being seen from the piazza unless they wished it, connecting their private rooms'.*

As Ercole had always wished for his illegitimate son to have an ecclesiastical career, Lucrezia had also been busy writing to the Prior of the Gerosolimitani in Venice requesting a position for Giulio among the Knights of Malta, which she hoped would appeal to him under his changed circumstances. Angela, the brainless beauty, had to have a husband as quickly as possible. She was about to give birth, yet with her connections Lucrezia found a husband for her cousin

---

* Alfonso's apartments were in the Palazzo del Corte and Lucrezia's in the castello.

with ease. She would become the wife of a minor local lord named Alessandro Pio, Lord of Sassuolo. The d'Este must have breathed a sigh of relief as they could now wash their hands of the problematic, wilful child. Angela gave birth to the baby in early January 1506.

The Duchess arranged for the marriage to Pio, taking care of the details, dowry and other matters. The Borgia had become fewer and poorer, but Lucrezia generously supplemented the girl's dowry and wardrobe. The wedding took place in Lucrezia's apartments in early February; because the mother of the groom was a forbidding woman born of the Bentivoglio family, the affair had to be kept secret. In high good humour the couple followed Lucrezia into a chamber to consummate the marriage. The newlyweds emerged after two hours with shrieks of laughter, and a small celebration followed. The formal ceremony took place at the end of the year, when the matronly Bentivoglio could do nothing but fume impotently at her son's mésalliance.

Giulio had been brought back from Belriguardo to stay at the Corte, and Lucrezia moved into her husband's rooms. Alfonso, while affecting a normal routine, felt stricken by the attack on Giulio, and desperately needed Ippolito by his side to guide him. He sought reconciliation between the two brothers and the sooner it could be brought to pass the better it would be for all.

On 24 December 1505, Ippolito and Giulio met before the young duke. Niccolò da Correggio had been asked, as a wise elder statesman and member of the family, to be present as a witness. Ippolito did not speak when Giulio was brought into the duke's presence, Alfonso spoke for him. For once, Ippolito must have felt lost for words, whether facile or sincere, at the sight of Giulio's disfigured face. It seemed as though the beautiful youth had been supplanted by a pathetic and monstrous-looking creature.

Alfonso swore that Ippolito regretted and repented what he had done. Ippolito said graciously that henceforth he would be a good and loving brother to Giulio. Alfonso added that his young half-brother would benefit greatly from the Duke if he could forgive Ippolito. Giulio spoke first to Alfonso: 'My Lord you see how I am,' and then, to Ippolito, he said he felt humble gratitude to God and the Holy Virgin for the return of his sight, and that despite the 'cruel and inhuman' acts against him though he had committed no fault, he forgave the cardinal and promised to continue to be the good brother he had always been.

Alfonso tried to speak but could not say more than 'love each other' and urged them to 'enjoy the state with him'. The flow of his tears choked his voice and, at the duke's signal, da Correggio had to end the proceedings with the kiss of forgiveness. As Giulio, the Adonis turned Caliban, embraced his half-brother, Ippolito is likely to have remembered the old wisdom 'keep your friends close, and your enemies closer'.

Not long afterwards Bernardino di Prosperi wrote ominously: 'Something sinister is afoot, I do not believe things will ever be right again between Don Giulio and the Cardinal.'

Carnival of 1506 passed with frenetic gaiety. Lucrezia and Alfonso led the revels with a determination. They both wanted to dance away the memories of the first year of his reign, a year fraught with strife and sorrow. As the festivities proceeded with frantic enjoyment, Giulio, once the leader of the revels, lay in his bed. His sight might have been poor, but his hearing had not been affected. He felt tortured by every joyful shriek, the beat of dancing feet, lovers' laughter and the strains of music, for each sound reminded him of his happy past.

Alfonso had neglected to make any 'more provision for Giulio considering his condition'. It had been his promise that he would reward Giulio for the fraternal reconciliation, yet so far nothing had been forthcoming. Cardinal Ippolito took an eager part in the traditional celebrations, and found he had not a moment to visit his half-brother, though Ippolito's secretary arrived with a cursory greeting from the dancing cardinal.

Not wishing his disfigured face to be seen, Giulio remained in his room. Angela had forsaken him, and lay in the arms of another. He no longer cared, for Giulio had found a new love and spent the days and nights tenderly embracing his new mistress and companion: bitterness.

Lucrezia enjoyed the celebrations with apparent delight, eager to forget her dead baby, her adored son Rodrigo far away in Bari and the tragic injuries suffered by Giulio. She initiated new fashions in Ferrara, wearing gowns of gold 'bordered with fringes of silk' and white gowns striped with black velvet, the vast detachable sleeves lined with fur. Ferrara had not seen the like since her arrival as a bride. Lucrezia appeared glowing with happiness. She took part in the Battle of the Eggs, rode masked through the streets until dawn, and at one ball danced with Alfonso, who had dressed 'à la turcha', 'showing himself very gallantly and with more joy in his heart than usual'. Comedies, masques or other entertainments took place each night and di Prosperi wrote of the duke and duchess 'as if they were in the greatest state of happiness in the world'.

It is unaccountable that the sensitive duchess did not visit Giulio, but abandoned herself to the pleasures of Carnival. When an entertainment had ended and the duke had retired, Lucrezia took up the habit of bringing guests to her apartments. They spent an hour or two listening to restful music, talking and winding down from the frenetic mood of the evening. The late duke had been ultra con servative in his last years and banned any real amusement. Alfonso wanted to shake the horror of the last year off too and, anxious to avoid the imprimatur of his first year as duke being the savage and wanton violence between his brothers, he allowed Carnival to be celebrated in full. He ended the prohibition that his father had imposed upon the Ferrarese during the last years of his reign, permitting theatrical performances, dressing-up and jousts, games and races, one novel entertainment being a man fighting a maddened pig. It seems that Ferrara did not wish to look as though it did not know how to have fun, and could teach the other courts to follow. Whether or not men fighting mad pigs ever became the *sine qua non* of Carnival games during the early sixteenth century is not recorded, which perhaps speaks for itself.

Lucrezia had other duties that fell to her at that time of year. As her household served as a finishing school (at least in theory) for local well-born maidens, she found husbands for these girls who had to arrive in her care before they reached the age of twelve. Here they were 'to be brought up otherwise than usual in work [embroidery] and in learning virtue'. It could hardly have been a good advertisement for Lucrezia or the curriculum when her illegitimate cousin had become pregnant, borne a child out of wedlock, caused a murderous quarrel between the Estense brothers and become the pampered, empty-headed bride of a young nobleman, stamping her well-shod feet until the duchess requited her latest demands. Angela Borgia could easily have served as a prototype for Thackeray's anti-heroine Becky Sharpe with her outrageous behaviour, social climbing, her seduction of upper-class dandies, heedless manner and reckless spending. The one important difference between the fictional Becky and the all-too-real Angela that needs to be taken into consideration is that Becky had brains, as opposed to Angela's narcissism, and – had she but realized it – blinding stupidity.

Angela had become the spoiled monster created by a loving Lucrezia. Disregarding the cost, Angela took a huge palazzo for the winter, though she lacked the means, demanded that her trousseau be of a ruinous splendour, and did not cease greedily nagging her aunt until she received both a dress of cloth of gold and a carriage that was an exact copy of the duchess's, which duly arrived upholstered in satin and velvet. Even Lucrezia's patience and purse had been stretched to accommodate the grandiose flibbertigibbet and her absolute necessities.

Those girls who joined the duchess's household to receive their education and training also received a husband whom their mistress would seek out for the *donzelle*, though many of these young men would head for the border when it became time for their marriage. Lucrezia is recorded as being most severe with those youths who had changed their minds. On one occasion the groom of La Dalara could not be found on the day of their marriage. Lucrezia refused to be denied and sent word round to the home of the runaway's parents, stating that they would be fined 1,000 ducats if he did not reappear to marry the embarrassed Dalara. She had greater marriages to organize for her more senior ladies and these took considerably more time and effort.

While the whole of Ferrara seemed bent upon enjoying Carnival as never before, Giulio had started to receive visitors. Ferrante came daily, and his presence pleased his half-brother most. Ferrante had always idolized his gay and amusing brother and, having seen Giulio's butchered face, he fell into talking with him about Ippolito.

The bastard brother spat his name, and he repeated the account of Alfonso's dastardly night of reconciliation, repentance and restitution. Giulio used foul language, which had not been his habit before. The pliable and empty-headed Ferrante soon picked up the habit as the two scornfully discussed the duke's pathetic efforts to make his own life easier. Giulio saw all too clearly that there had been no attempt at repentance or restitution, and any real word of reconciliation had come from the miserable wretch who had suffered the crime. Alfonso's weakness with Ippolito had led to mitigation and qualification; he remembered the silken cardinal's seemly and suitable words, smoothing over his own beggarly contrition. The duke must bear the guilt too, for he had permitted the offence to go unpunished.

The two brothers thought of dark plans, and the Old Testament was frequently quoted with the 'eye for an eye' ethos that Giulio and Ferrante adopted. Ferrante had had his empty head filled while visiting Julius II, and the foolish young prince believed the Warrior Pope's glorious words about the young Estense's suitability as Duke of Ferrara; they had sounded like promises, but he could not be sure. After a while Ferrante convinced himself of Julius's support should he supplant his brother; the Pontiff's empty waffling and clever delivery had become as solid as the troops of men he saw in his mind's eye.

Finally the resentful brothers' resolve hardened – or rather, as the pair talked about their hatred for their elder brothers, retribution became both regicide and fratricide. Giulio and Ferrante decided to kill Ippolito and Alfonso. It is difficult to imagine a more colourful or eclectic mix of would-be killers than that collected around the brooding brothers. These included an elderly Lord, Albertino Boschetti of San Cesario. Alfonso had challenged Boschetti's rights to the ownership of his small dominion. He was supported by his sons, Gherardo and Roberto; the former held the promising post for a would-be assassin of Captain of the duke's guard. Joining the conspirators came the inspiring figure (if only for his size) of Gian Cantore di Guascogna, a blond, white and corpulent priest whose voice Duke Alfonso particularly favoured. The fat priest had no discernible motive and none has yet been discovered. These five members of the conspiracy had no experience in such perilous matters nor, did it seem, could they form a plan upon which they all agreed. Some wished only to kill Ippolito, others the duke, until finally they realized that they could not dispose of one without the other.

The method of murder was no easier to decide upon. Stabbing with poison-tipped daggers seemed favoured until the choice of poison became a heated source of argument. Without ruling out poison, the gang agreed that as an alternative, they set an ambush for the duke and Ippolito. The motion was approved and passed among the muddlers.

Giulio sat at home experimenting with different types of toxins upon dogs, cats and doves, trying to decide which would be best to use upon his brothers. The ambushing had not been going according to plan. On two occasions the plotters had missed the brothers altogether and on another they had quailed at the thought of their hazardous mission and run back to their horses, consoling themselves with the thought that there would always be another night when the brothers could be caught.

Alfonso's boon companion when on his saturnalian outings happened to be the fat Gascon priest and singer Gian Cantore. Cantore tipped his dagger in poison on one of the several evenings the duke went visiting prostitutes with the Gascon. An ideal moment presented itself at one whorehouse, when Alfonso insisted upon being bound hand and foot to each corner of the girl's bed. The tall and muscular duke normally wore mail beneath his clothes. His body had become powerful thanks to the hours spent forging cannon. Lying naked, spread-eagled and tied down, the duke seemed satisfied and amused. Laughing incontinently about the sexual episode that had just taken place, the plotters' victim had nothing to cover his skin, far less protect him, from one of the assassins. Cantore pulled out the dagger, which engendered further laughter from the duke; instead of killing Alfonso the fleshy Gascon used the poison-tipped dagger to cut his victim free, and the pair left the whorehouse.

Alfonso journeyed to Venice. He wished to tell the Most Reverend Signory that he planned a pilgrimage – at least so it had been said.

Alfonso made Lucrezia Governor of the city. He gave the duchess strict orders: he asked not to be disturbed by her about any matters unless it involved a grave crisis threatening the state or his family. As Easter approached, the duke moved his wife into his own rooms in the Palazzo del Corte. *Landsknechts** hired by the duke moved into the palazzo with the usual men-at-arms to ensure the safety of his wife. These precautions seemed excessive for a short visit, especially since the duchess had taken herself to the convent of Corpus Domini, as was her habit during Holy Week.

Alfonso departed at dawn on a date far later than he had announced. He returned again before setting out for the south-eastern coastline, where he planned to visit his cousin Isabella d'Aragona, who had become Duchess of Bari. It is not known whether or not he saw the young Duke of Bisceglie, but Lucrezia believed she would soon visit her son, perhaps during the summer of 1507.

Lucrezia spent a good deal of time with Cardinal Ippolito and sensed that something was afoot. She worried about Giulio, and urged him to leave Ferrara during Alfonso's absences. It seems that even Alfonso suggested Giulio leave Ferrara, but pleas disguised as suggestions fell upon deaf ears.

On 24 May Ippolito's men arrested a servant of Don Giulio's. Nearly three weeks later the same fate befell Andrea della Matta, who happened to be in the Romagna when he was taken and ordered back to Ferrara. News arrived that one Girolamo Tuttobono, another of the lesser conspirators, had also been taken. Upon hearing this Ferrante wrote to his sister and begged her to get Giulio to Mantua and out of Ippolito's way. With the duke absent it would be child's play to do away with Giulio. Isabella eventually persuaded her brother to travel to Mantua, though Tuttobono and Andrea della Matta had been released.

The fat priest had been travelling with the duke when orders for his arrest went out. Cantore escaped before the Ferrarese had time to capture him. He had been about to board a ship with Alfonso, when he excused himself saying he felt sick. His plan had been to poison the duke once on board, but, as with the other opportunities

---

* German mercenaries.

presented to him, it is doubtful that Cantore would have had the nerve to follow his dread plan through. He ran not from the cross-bowmen that came to arrest him; but, having lost his taste for murdering the duke, who had shown him great friendship, he knew that the other conspirators would try to kill him for fear that under questioning he would gabble their plans out to the last hazy detail.

Alfonso returned in early July but arrived earlier than expected, and with his fleet habits of travel missed his brothers the cardinal and Ferrante, who had ridden out to meet him. Giulio seemed relaxed, especially after della Matta and Tuttobono had been released and Boschetti had been given no warning of imminent danger either – rather they had received small signs of favour most unusual to them after their recent territorial disagreements with Alfonso. The duke became angry at the news of Giulio's visit to Mantua, taken without permission. He promised safe conduct provided that Giulio's hurried trip to Mantua had been taken with no ill intent against his own person. Giulio did not return but remained safely with Francesco and Isabella until the duke's anger quietened.

On 22 July an inquiry had been instituted, and Albertino Boschetti was arrested three days later. This caused Ferrante to forsake any courage he had, for he proceeded to denounce his half-brother and wrote to Francesco begging him to take him into his care and release 'Don Julio [sic] ... for having facilitated Julio's escape ... Despite the punishment I might merit ... I pray your Lordship to have more respect for my safety than that of Don Julio and to grant me this grace'.

As the details poured from the captured conspirators, Ferrante had been taken into custody and the de Roberti were seized from the estate, as Ippolito and Alfonso ensured that, one by one, members of the conspiracy were taken. Even the fat Gascon, who had managed to find a rich patroness in Rome, the mistress of a cardinal, had to submit to the extradition orders that came through. The final member of the plot, Giulio, arrived from Mantua in shackles accompanied by two gigantic henchmen who worked for the Gonzaga. Forced to concede that Alfonso had the right to demand his brother's return, Francesco complied, but the bad blood they had felt for each other grew as a result.

Francesco passed through Ferrara on his way to meet the Pope, and Alfonso escorted him to the duchess, his lover, to whom he paid a visit with the formalities attendant upon their position. He had to hurry on his journey to meet the Pope, on the brink of his campaign against the Bentivoglio of Bologna. His visit coincided with the wretched Giulio's arrival in chains.

Lucrezia attended a service of solemn Mass at the Cathedral with the noblewomen of Ferrara, followed by a procession through the town which Alfonso and Ippolito joined as well as the noblemen and people. They proceeded through the town in thanksgiving; bonfires had been lit and the church bells rang out for three days in gratitude that the conspiracy had been discovered in time.

The two brothers watched as their co-conspirators suffered the typically cruel public executions that traditionally took place in the piazza. Giulio must certainly have wished that his vision had not been returned to him for the horrid sights he saw that day. The crime having been read out to the public, the executioner took his first prisoner, who had been blindfolded, and cut his head off with an axe; he then quartered the body. On 8 October both Ferrante and Giulio received the death sentence. At last the flabby Gascon arrived, the priest with the voice of an angel and, it must be added, a kinder heart than some, for he could have killed the Duke had he really been of a mind to do so. Cantore came on horseback with his hands tied in front of him and his feet tied together under the horse. A noose had been tied around the priest's neck and the executioner held the other end, riding slightly ahead of the prisoner. The crowd jeered at Cantore, spitting at him and tearing at his hair. On Epiphany 1507, a cage could be seen hanging from the Torre dei Leoni. Inside sat the 'fat Gascon', now a thin man in rags. A plate of bread and jug of wine had thoughtfully been provided for him as he sat dangling in the freezing wind and temperatures well below zero. The singing priest would be heard no more, for on 13 January he could be seen hanging from the top bars of the cage. It is not known whether he took his own life or whether the guards killed him. After the ritual of dragging the conspirator's naked body around the city, the duke ordered that his corpse, or the remains of it, should hang upside down from the bridge of Castel Teobaldo that spanned the River Po.

The two princely conspirators had approached their own execution, though it was not to be held in public. They mounted the scaffold as a reprieve arrived from Alfonso; they would not die on that day after all, but he had benignly sentenced them to life imprisonment.

Where there is life there is hope and never more so than with these two noble prisoners. First they were held in cells high up in the Torre dei Leoni, their food being lowered down to them on a small pallet from the high wall in each cell – this also lowered their few visitors that officialdom required. Eventually they received permission for a third room that had good views over the city. Ferrante died forty-three years after his imprisonment, and Lucrezia's nephew Alfonso II released Giulio a decade after Ferrrante's death. Upon his discharge it was noted that he was wearing the same clothes that he had worn on the day of his confinement. Giulio emerged aged eighty-one, mortified by the unfashionable rags that had been all the rage half a century earlier. He had mercifully grown a beard so long that it almost covered some of his shame.

Lucrezia had absented herself as far as possible. She had not only been fond of both the young princes, but feared that her old reputation would be given life, for she had danced with Ferrante, the groom's proxy, at her wedding to Alfonso, and Giulio had been her laughing companion during the earliest years of her marriage. The loose and far too engaging young Angela had been in Lucrezia's care and the duchess certainly wished that she had not spoiled the girl as much as she had, nor given into her caprices and left her unattended. She managed to save one embarrassing legacy from the internecine struggle: she took in the chaplain Don Rainaldo, the unwitting cause of the trouble.

As war continued to bedevil the peninsula, international forces invading from the north and south, local struggles also persisted with infrequent pauses. Julius had appointed Francesco Captain-General of the papal armies and he reappeared briefly in Ferrara during 1508. He stood before Lucrezia looking magnificent. With the confusion of treaties followed by further military action, states breaking from leagues created by like-minded dominions, each day seemed to bring a fresh change of enemy, or further outbreak of fighting.

Having proudly danced with the duchess at Ferrara, in 1508 Francesco had fallen *de haut en bas*. Lucrezia gave birth to a son on 4 April 1508, whom the couple named Ercole in honour of Alfonso's father. She received visitors while lying in the splendour of her new apartments. This baby had not required a primitive syringe of holy water to baptize it in utero; she could celebrate a healthy boy, with a snub nose and dark eyes.

CHAPTER 22

Saving Face

1515–1523

'They say great things about her life here'
GIOVANNI GONZAGA AFTER LUCREZIA BORGIA'S DEATH

Throughout her long career of diplomacy, Isabella d'Este had learned the value of that most Italian of virtues, the preservation of *la bella figura*. In the years following her husband's release from his Venetian captivity, this capacity was stretched to the utmost. Francesco by now frankly disliked his wife, and the couple were unofficially estranged; moreover, Francesco's behaviour was becoming disturbingly eccentric. A carefully measured description, dated 1515, of the Marquis of Mantua *chez lui* in the castello gives a flavour of his increasingly odd proclivities:

> Here they [the Venetian ambassadors] found the Marquis reclining on a couch by the hearth of a richly adorned room, with his pet dwarf clad in gold brocade and three superb greyhounds lying at his feet. Three pages stood by, waving large fans lest even a hair should fall upon him; a quantity of falcons and hawks in leash were in the room and the walls were hung with pictures of favourite dogs and horses.

An odour of 'rich perfumes' greeted the envoys on the threshold of the chamber. No doubt these were deployed to disguise what everyone in the Gonzaga household knew – the Marquis stank. The charming tableau painted by the Venetian visitors glosses the fact that Francesco spent much of his day in filth, surrounded by

the animals of the chase upon which he was fixated, their excrement befouling his exquisitely decorated rooms. The dwarf may
have been smartly turned out, but his master's toilette left a great
deal to be desired. While Isabella busied herself with visits from
distinguished ecclesiastics, including the writer Matteo Bandello,
and entreating Castiglione to give readings from Livy, her husband
made his own entertainments beneath the grimy folds of his rarely
changed garments.

Other family troubles derived from the Medici annexation of
Urbino. For the second time, Isabella received the dispossessed
Duke and Duchess of the Apennine city, and for the second time her
welcome was less than fulsome. After a hideous voyage, Isabella's
daughter Eleonora, her husband Francesco Maria and her dearest
old friend the Dowager Duchess Elisabetta Gonzaga made their way
to the port of Pietola. And there they remained, as Isabella was far
too afraid of papal disapproval to consider letting them anywhere
near Mantua. She did extend herself so far as to have some bedding
sent out to the distraught trio, and when the permission from Leo
X eventually appeared the two women were given a room apiece
in the dilapidated Corte Vecchia of the Gonzaga castello. Despite
promises of assistance from the marquis, they soon found themselves in dire financial straits and were obliged to melt down their
plate to raise funds. Isabella expressed her regret that she had not at
present the means to purchase two of Elisabetta's charming bronze
dishes, as it was a pity to see them go to the foundry.

Isabella's financial embarrassments were largely the consequence
of her ambitions for her eldest son Federico. In October 1515 her
beleaguered nephew Massimiliano Sforza, the elder of Beatrice
d'Este's sons, had resigned his birthright of Milan to François I of
France for the less than princely amount of 30,000 ducats, a sum
Juan Gandia Borgia had long ago seen fit to squander on a hat for his
sister Lucrezia's wedding. Massimiliano continued to send respectful letters to his aunt from his French exile, but any disquiet Isabella
may have felt about her nephew was subsumed in her desire to ingra-
tiate herself with the new ruler of the duchy of Milan. Federico was
duly despatched to do homage to the French King and was invited to
accompany the court on its return to France, where he spent lavishly,

though his funds were too meagre to indulge in the high gambling which the French aristocrats relished, and he had to content himself with impressing François with his skills at football.

Since the fact that she was unwelcome in Mantua was beginning to penetrate even Isabella's gem-encrusted hide, she now undertook a perambulation to the shrine of St Mary Magdalene at Sainte-Baume near Marseilles. Her secretary Giovanni di Cremona wrote to Federico that 'whenever Madama is seen passing through the streets, all the men and women in every rank of life ... stand still in the road, gazing in wonder at her beautiful clothes ... some people have told me that they could hardly believe that Madama was the mother of Your Excellency and felt sure she must be your sister'. Back in Mantua, Isabella's visit had reportedly caused her to lose weight, but not enough to prevent the makeshift stage erected outside the convent at Porta Pradella, where Isabella attended a play about Mary Magdalene, from collapsing under the burden of her bulk. Unfortunately the stage had been built over a lake, though Isabella reported cheerfully that no one had been killed. The lake was shallow, but Isabella's presence in it may have made alarming waves as, despite her attendants' oleaginous praises, she was now quite obese – so much so that when she was obliged to vacate her apartments in widowhood she prudently moved to the ground floor. No staircase was safe from the mighty Marchioness.

Francesco Gonzaga had now been ill for some time, and on 29 March 1519 he died. Among the letters of condolence which arrived in Mantua from all over the peninsula was one from the marquis's lover, Lucrezia Borgia. 'This bitter loss has afflicted me so deeply,' she wrote, 'that instead of being able to comfort others I am in sore need of comfort myself ... I know Your Highness will bear this grief with your well-known courage and wisdom.' Despite their estrangement, Francesco behaved correctly towards his wife at the end, confirming her annual income of 12,000 ducats and appointing her as guardian and regent for their son until he was twenty-two.

Just three months after Francesco's death, Lucrezia Borgia was delivered of a baby girl. Neither child nor mother lived long, and on 24 June the Duchess of Ferrara was dead. Shortly before her death, she was able to dictate a letter to Leo X, in which she declared: 'so great is the favour which our merciful Creator has shown me, that I approach the end of my life with pleasure, knowing that in a few hours, after receiving for the last time all the holy sacraments of the church, I shall be released ... I offer myself to you in all humility and commend my husband and my children, all of whom are your servants, to your Holiness's mercy'.

Her correspondence with Francesco Gonzaga had continued until the latter's death, though the tone of their letters had grown considerably more concerned with spiritual matters. 'It is ironic,' writes one of Lucrezia's biographers, 'that these two, one certainly committed to the sins of the flesh, the other the daughter of the carnal Alexander and sister of the amoral Cesare, should have turned towards God in their later years.' There is nothing remotely ironic about this; indeed the burgeoning Christian conscience which overtook the lovers as they recognized themselves to be near the end is entirely in keeping with the culture of their age. Just as the vices and corruption of Lucrezia's father had never compromised the personal integrity of his devout Marianism, so Lucrezia and Francesco experienced no cognitive dissonance in reconciling their actions and their faith. It is a peculiarly Renaissance conundrum that each and every deadly sin could happily join hands with the virtues, that the crimes of the body could coexist with a sincere desire for purity of the soul.

Alfonso d'Este grieved greatly for his duchess. To Federico Gonzaga he claimed, 'I cannot write without tears, so grave is it to find myself deprived of such a sweet, dear companion as she was to me, for her good ways and the tender love there was between us ... I know that you too will share my grief; and I would prefer someone to accompany my tears than to offer me consolation.'

The last years of Lucrezia's life had reflected her need for spiritual restoration and made her extremely popular in Ferrara. During the period of peace after 1519, Lucrezia had dispensed with 'the pomps and vanities of the world to which she had been accustomed from childhood and gave herself up to pious works'. But Lucrezia was never an ascetic, and had not lost her taste for beauty; so she and Alfonso worked together to restore Ferrara after the depredations of the conflict. Titian and Raphael received commissions, as did the artists of the Ferrarese school – Dossi, Garofano and Michele Costa. Lucrezia, like Isabella, owned a Cupid by Michelangelo, though she at least was aware of its provenance. In acquisitiveness, though, she was a poor rival to her sister-in-law. Lucrezia was buried in the convent of Corpus Domini with two of her children, Alessandro and Isabella, in the tomb which Alfonso d'Este ultimately shared.

Lucrezia's legacy in Ferrara is contested. Despite the pleasure she was able to take in the life of the court, in her frequent retreats to the convent of San Bernardino and the summer visits to Belriguardo, where her improvised *fêtes champêtres* became well known for the Petrarchan spirit of their elegance, it is claimed by some that 'Lucrezia never felt that she was Ferrarese'. Conversely, it is maintained, she always viewed Spain as the promised land, clinging to the belief that had she only been permitted to return to her family's homeland in Catalonia, her life might have been much happier. Certainly, Lucrezia cultivated a Spanish atmosphere within her circle. Her account books reveal almost daily gifts to Spaniards, from the jewelled cups she presented to Don Enriquo Enriques, the father of her widowed sister-in-law the Duchess of Gandia, to Miguel her goldsmith, Baldasso her groom and Sancho her carver. She received perfumes and essences from Spain – bergamot and citrus, jasmine and rosewater to flavour the delicate marzipan tarts on which she and her ladies picnicked at Belriguardo.

Yet to conclude from this that the Duchess of Ferrara was a *senorita manquée* seems wishful. Lucrezia's origins may have been Spanish, and she had spoken it with her family, but she was born and raised as a Roman princess and had never visited the country. Perhaps that fact contributed to her idealization of Spain, if indeed it existed, but her relations with the Spaniards were not unequivocally positive. It was the Spaniards after all who had betrayed her brother Cesare and contested the birthright of her son Don Alfonso Bisceglie. Rather, given Lucrezia's popularity in Ferrara and the assiduous success with which she assisted at the public functions expected of a duchess, it would be equally reasonable to speculate that she saw Ferrara as a refuge from the domineering, manipulative men who had controlled her life as a young woman, and that it was

Ferrara which provided her with the autonomy to order her life as she wished.

Isabella d'Este's reaction to Lucrezia's death was no more than formal; she reserved her real grief for her beloved secretary, Benedetto Capilupi, who also died that year, as did Lorenzo II de Medici, the recently installed Duke of Urbino. This naturally inspired her son-in-law Francesco Maria with the hope of recovering his dominions, but once again Isabella was too uncertain of the papal reaction to lend him aid. She did obtain permission for Eleonora and Elisabetta to continue their meagre existence in Mantua, but Francesco Maria was exiled to Venice and then to Verona. It was not until the death of Leo X in November 1521 (possibly precipitated by Isabella's incessant nagging about a cardinalcy for her son Ercole, which pursued him quite literally onto his deathbed) that the della Rovere couple could return. Alfonso d'Este, meanwhile, had special medals struck to commemorate his delight at the passing of his arch enemy. Isabella, though, was now engaged in a war much closer to home.

Initially, Isabella and her son worked well together. Federico was appointed *Gonfaloniere* of the papal forces, to their mutual delight, and they both supported the return of the Sforza, whose adherents had taken refuge in Mantua, to Milan. Yet when Isabella began the grandiose redecoration of the sixteen rooms of the Corte Vecchia, which were to be her new quarters, Federico hinted that he was relieved to have his mother out of the way. Isabella had shown her capacity for jealous rivalry in her reaction to Lucrezia Borgia's arrival at Ferrara, but in some ways her son's mistress Isabella Boschetti presented a more serious threat. Federico eventually had three children by this young and reputedly very beautiful woman, for whom he built the exquisite Palazzo della Giustizia in Mantua. One might imagine Isabella's rage when Titian was commissioned to execute La Boschetti's portrait; but if anything was more important to her than her vanity, it was power, and she was appalled when Federico broke off his betrothal to his highly desirable dynastic bride Maria de Monferrato and went so far as to seek formal papal dispensation to do so.

Isabella's attendants, who had learned well from their mistress, began to neglect her for the rising star of the Mantuan court, and a disgruntled Isabella found herself huddled by the hearth with a few old women while La Boschetti flaunted herself about the city streets. Isabella put on a brave face by adopting in her Corte Vecchia apartments and her country house the device of a many-branched candelabra, as used in churches during Holy Week. One by one, the candles are extinguished, until only one remains burning. Isabella was sending an explicit message with her adoption of the device and the motto *Sufficit unum in tenebris*, but it was one which Federico wilfully ignored. His mother might claim to be a loyal light in the darkness, but he was determined to shove her ever further into the shadows.

Federico made it clear that his mother had no right to interfere in his private life, nor did he wish her to continue her active role as regent once he reached his majority. Her propensity for unilateral action, which admittedly was an established habit, irritated him and when she continued to ignore his objections, the new Marquis of Mantua had his mother banned from his chancery. Isabella was particularly wounded by the treachery of her formerly trusted secretary Mario Equicola, who showed his 'perfidious ingratitude' to the woman he had served so long and who was now 'degraded and little esteemed' by conniving with Federico to hide from Isabella the diplomatic correspondence which had shaped her policies for so long. Frustrated and marginalized, Isabella began considering another visit to Rome.

Her first visit to the city, in 1514–15, had also been prompted by domestic discord. At that time, she had departed in high dudgeon due to the rising influence of her husband's favoured secretary, one Tolomeo Spagnoli, for whose counsels Francesco had neglected her own. In 1525, Isabella gave out that her motive was the promotion of the ecclesiastical interests of the Gonzaga in the Curia. After the death of Pope Leo X the project of making Ercole d'Este a cardinal had been temporarily dropped, as it was impossible that his scrupulous and devout successor Adrian of Utrecht would have countenanced such a choice; but when the conclave which eventually elected Clement VII was convened in 1523, the Gonzaga had entertained a brief hope of one of their own wearing the tiara. Cardinal Sigismondo, who indeed owed his hat to Isabella's exertions, was considered (at least by the Gonzaga faction in Rome) as a strong candidate, but Sigismondo preferred to give his loyalties to Giulio de Medici, which now gave an extra spur to Isabella's darling ambition for her son. Her departure for the Eternal City did, then, have an official purpose, but Isabella's true motivation was the 'revindication of her offended dignity'. Far from Mantua, she believed that Federico would come to his senses and recognize his dependence on his wise, experienced and loving mother.

CHAPTER 23

The Last Man Standing

MAY 1527

'A besought evil is never in excess.'
OLD FLORENTINE PROVERB

September 1523 saw the death of the last non-Italian pope until the twentieth century. Adrian VI passed away to universal rejoicing among both the Roman populace and the elect of the College of Cardinals. Unlike the majority of his predecessors, Adrian had been a truly devout man in deed as well as thought, devoting more of his time to study and prayer than Church business, frugal in his spending and irreproachable in his personal life, qualities which naturally made him extremely unpopular. The new pope, it was widely felt, ought to be a figure capable of restoring the papacy to glory, but when the conclave met to discuss the election on 1 October, their decision was complicated by the ancient rivalry of two of Rome's most powerful magnate dynasties, the Orsini and the Colonna, whose sparring had been a persistent thorn in the papal side for a century or more.

Since the fifteenth century, the Orsini and Colonna houses had been effectively holding the Eternal City to ransom. Both possessed of vast holdings in the Roman Campagna, the agricultural estates surrounding the city, they had rendered the Romans dependent on imported wheat by turning their land over to pasture for profitable meat production, a move which the papacy had continuously attempted to counter and both families perpetually to resist. If conditions were precarious, Rome could swiftly descend into starvation; but the Orsini and Colonna princes grew rich, developing cultivated courts in miniature, making powerful dynastic alliances and serving successfully as *condottieri* all over the peninsula. Two marriages, that of Lorenzo de Medici and Clarice Orsini in 1469 and Piero de Medici and Alfonsina Orsini in 1488, cemented a tradition of loyalty between the Medici and the vast clan of Orsini which set the former at odds with the Colonna. The papacy had also relied on the Orsini to keep the Colonna in check, as the Colonna, who had obtained their lands through the family Pope, Martin V, and subsequently had them revoked by Eugenius IV, were frequently in conflict with the Vatican over territories which they now held by might rather than right. Whenever the Colonna became too aggressive or demanding, the popes made use of the Orsini. By the sixteenth century, territorial disputes had been transposed into the arena of the real centre of power in Europe, the papal Curia, where the two dynasties remained at odds. Julius II had refused to appoint cardinals from either family since, in Machiavelli's words, 'those parties are never at rest when they have cardinals, for they stir up the parties both inside Rome and outside it and the barons are forced to defend them. Thus, from the ambitions of prelates, arise the discords and tumults among the barons.' In 1517, however, the Medici Pope Leo X had granted a cardinal's hat to Pompeo Colonna, one of the most capable men the family had ever produced, and who saw an opportunity in Adrian's death both for his own long-sought advancement and the chance to strike a blow against the Orsini.

The feuding Orsini and Colonna houses represented only one of the factional rivalries played out as the thirty-five cardinals took their seats in the Sistine Chapel that autumn for the papal conclave. The two houses also found themselves on opposing sides in the wider political dispute over the balance of power in Europe. In 1519, King Charles of Spain had been elected Holy Roman Emperor as Charles V, uniting the holdings of the Spanish crown with those of his grandfather Maximilian of Habsburg to create an empire which spanned over one and a half million square miles. As *condottieri*, the Colonna princes had often served the Spanish and were thus inclined to favour the Imperial cause within the Curia. In contrast, the Orsini (and the Medici) history held a preponderance of alliances with and service to France, ruled since 1515 by François I. François (and

Henry VIII, who had thrown his name in as a contender, though unsuccessfully) had been defeated as Imperial candidate by Charles; he felt that his own territories, hemmed in by Charles's disparately placed dominions leaving them permanently exposed to any potential threat from the Empire. Moreover, the two ambitious young kings loathed one another. As the conclave met, the two leading candidates emerged as Pompeo Colonna and Giulio de Medici, who latterly had departed from his family position and effectively declared himself an Imperialist. Giulio could count on ten votes, which would be enough to disqualify a lesser candidate, but not to obtain the tiara for himself. For that, he needed the co-operation of Colonna. At length, on 17 November, Colonna and Medici held a public ceremony of reconciliation, and on the 19th de' Medici was elected as Pope Clement VII.

Under Clement, at least for a few short years, Rome resumed its position as the pride and the hope of the Christian world. A consideration of the losses suffered by the crisis Clement's policies were eventually to provoke gives some sense of the unparalleled concentration of artistic and cultural wealth in the city in the period 1523–6. Libraries such as those of Gieronimo Negro, Accolti, Giraldi and Giles of Viterbo flourished, while the Sapienza University attracted scholars such as Augusto Valdo and Isabella d'Este's protégé Lodovico Boccadiferro, famed as one of the peninsula's greatest living philosophers, and Paolo Bombace, who had tutored Erasmus. Benvenuto Cellini, Raffaelo da Montelupo, the architect Baldassare Peruzzi, the painters Gianbattista Rosso and Parmigiano and Raphael's Bolognese engraver Marcantonio Rainaudi were just some of the eminent Renaissance figures active in Rome at the time. However vehemently the followers of Martin Luther's new religion denounced the luxury and corruption of the place, Rome now attracted more visitors and pilgrims than any other city, all of them awed by the magnificence of its buildings and the fabulous abundance of both secular and sacred treasures.

Yet Clement's cautious Florentine inheritance of patience – or indecisiveness – was to tear out Christendom's very heart. The emperor had initially been delighted with the election, since, as his ambassador claimed, 'The Pope is entirely your Majesty's creature.'

There was nothing Clement desired so much as peaceful neutrality in the rivalry between the Empire and France, but both sides were anxiously soliciting the favours of the city which Luther derided as the 'Great Whore'. Given Charles V's self-location in a 'half-world between the Middle Ages and the modern world, pursuing medieval ambitions by modern means', it was unsurprising that he chose to further his aims in Italy. Islam was on the march, and Charles took seriously his traditional, indeed sacred role as defender of Christianity against the infidel. Nor had he forgotten, as many contemporary Italians had, that the Spanish had only reluctantly been drawn into the conflicts on the peninsula as a counterbalance to French ambition. For Charles, Italy was crucial to his policies towards not only the Ottoman Empire, but also France and the increasing threat of Lutheran Germany. A Florentine writer according to one source claimed 'Charles's appetite is so set on this occupation of Italy that he would rather lose Austria and its neighbouring provinces than remain the loser in this enterprise'. Conversely, François I was equally determined to maintain the claims of the French royal house to its Italian holdings. Milan became the focus of the conflict between king and emperor, with Charles declaring that he and his cousin of Milan agreed at least about one thing – the possession of Il Moro's former duchy. In 1515, at the Battle of Marignano, François led a force of 40,000 men to victory over the penultimate puny remnant of the great house of Sforza, Beatrice d'Este's son Massimiliano and his Swiss allies, once more taking possession of the Lombard capital. For Charles, a French Milan meant the loss of a communication network between his territories, control over the important port of Genoa and the containment of Venice. In 1521, papal and Imperial forces routed the French and gave Milan its last Sforza duke, Francesco Maria.

Clement, who had not proved to be the Imperial puppet for which Charles had hoped, was disturbed by Charles's incursions on the peninsula, and in December 1524 joined in alliance with Florence, Venice and France against him. Charles was outraged: 'I shall go into Italy and revenge myself on those who have injured me, especially on that poltroon of a Pope,' he stormed. By February 1525, French armies were once more in Lombardy, encamped outside Pavia.

Bad French intelligence and Imperial initiative allowed François to be caught napping, resulting in the king losing his horse from beneath him and fighting on foot until he was honourably captured. Meanwhile, French forces had been simultaneously moving on Naples, along with their allies the Orsini, though their commander, the Duke of Albany, swiftly recognized that the attack was hopeless and attempted to withdraw northwards to rejoin his king. Just outside Rome, the Colonna attacked, and pursued the French and the Orsini into the streets of the Holy City, which greatly angered Clement.

While François I waited out the conditions of his ransom in a Madrileño prison, the powers of Italy tried to find a solution for ousting Charles. They were betrayed by the Marquis of Pescara, a lifelong adherent of the Spaniards whom Clement had unsuccessfully attempted to persuade to switch his allegiance, and who on 2 November led Imperial troops once more to Milan. Clement tried to assure Charles of his loyalty and in a series of letters to convince him that the only hope of peace in Italy lay in the restoration of Francesco Maria Sforza, but Charles was reluctant. He had also gained a significant ally in the figure of Charles de Bourbon, hereditary Constable of France, whose wife's estates had been seized by François I on her death, despite de Bourbon having been designated her heir. He fled to Burgundy, which was to become an Imperial dominion under the terms of François's release, and offered his services to the Empire.

On 2 February 1526, the terms of François I's release under the Treaty of Madrid were announced in Brescia, reaching Rome eighteen days later. François had bought his freedom at the price of Burgundy, the keeping of his two elder sons as hostages and the restoration of the Bourbon estates, conditions which he had no intention of honouring. He repudiated the terms of the treaty on 10 May by refusing in the presence of the Imperial legate to cede Burgundy, followed by committing himself on the 17th to the League of Cognac. In classic Machiavellian style, the aims of the League, to which France, Venice, Florence, England and the papacy subscribed, were ostensibly to defend Italy, and Charles was cordially invited to become a member if he would restore the Sforza in Milan, pay off a huge Imperial debt to Henry VIII and return François's sons. Broadly, the purpose of the League was the restoration of the Italian status quo as it had been prior to Pavia.

The position of Florence was implicated in this project. When his first attempt at the tiara had failed in 1521 with the election of Adrian, Giulio de Medici, as he then was, had returned to govern Florence. His absence in Rome had caused dissent in the Signoria, angered by the inefficiency of the Medici deputy Cardinal Passerini, but the future Pope showed that he possessed his share of the family ability to govern by stealth: 'It was the universal opinion that never since the city had been under the rule of the Medici had it been governed with greater appearance of civil liberty, or more skilful concealment of despotism.'

When Giulio achieved the papacy as Clement VII in 1523, he left a vacuum in the city republic. Cardinal Passerini was once more despatched to Florence and governed there under the direction of Clement in Rome. A new Medici Pope also influenced the life of Florence's most celebrated (though admittedly not in a crowded field) *condottiere*, Giovanni, son of Caterina Sforza and her third husband Giovanni il Popolano. Since the Medici had always been lovers of money rather than fighters, Giovanni's military prowess might well be attributed to his Sforza blood, though his mercantile inheritance was made manifest in the fact that his loyalty belonged to whoever paid the bills. Having cut his teeth fighting with brilliant success for Leo X against the della Rovere in Urbino in 1516, at the age of just eighteen, Giovanni had fought the French under the Colonna in 1520. In mourning for his relative Leo the next year, Giovanni had his soldiers wear black sashes, giving him the nickname 'Giovanni delle Bande Nere'. When Clement VII was elected, he paid his kinsman's debts on the condition that he transfer his skills to the French cause.

On 2 May 1527 a red hat, perched on a cushion, was carried from the Vatican to the Palazzo Colonna. After two years of soliciting and 40,000 ducats, Isabella d'Este had finally achieved her heart's desire. Her son Ercole Gonzaga was a cardinal. The circumstances, admittedly, were less than ideal. Some time earlier, the Dowager

Marchioness of Mantua had ignored a warning from her estranged son Federico to leave Rome, where she had been established for two years, as the armies of the Holy Roman Emperor, Charles V, were on the march. It could only be a matter of days now before they reached the Holy City, and Federico wrote to his mother that 'They already see Florence and Rome thrown down and Rome pillaged.'

The city which Isabella had made her home in 1525 was already no longer recognizable. The particular character of Rome under Clement VII, described as an 'intellectual climate [which] owed its excitement to an extraordinary convergence of talent, to a frenzy that was intensified by the meeting of individuals and ambition, to the fervour of a culture that had become self-assured and to an unusual freedom of speech and behaviour', was dying. Even as she had journeyed there in the spring, receiving the news of the Battle of Pavia en route from Loreto, Isabella was aware that the Imperialist faction in Rome was in the ascendant. With the capture of the French King François I, Clement was anxious to secure the loyalties of the Gonzaga, who ever since Fornovo had been the vassals of the emperor. As *Gonfaloniere* of the papal armies, the Marquis of Mantua had insisted in his contract that he was not to be obliged to fight his feudal Lord, and that this obligation be made public; but a secret clause had also been inserted into a separate document obliging Federico to fight whomsoever the Pope commanded. Under the pontificate of Adrian VI, Isabella d'Este had bribed a papal functionary named Pietro Ardinghelli to steal the compromising document (which was eventually bought by Baldassare Castiglione). Thus, when the time came for the contract to be renewed in 1526, it was nowhere to be found.

Isabella, her pride buffeted by her increasing marginalization in Mantua, not to mention her disgust at her son's 'immoral life', was confident that she would be able to achieve her aim of grabbing the cardinalcy for Ercole. Clement was prepared to make concessions to the Gonzaga (when, for example, he heard that the Marquis of Mantua was keen to possess Raphael's portrait of Leo X he had it removed from the Medici palace in Florence to be sent as a gift, though the painting Federico eventually received was actually a copy

by Andrea del Sarto), but in his first audience with Isabella, on 9
March, he parried her blunt request for the elusive hat. Nevertheless,
Isabella settled happily into the Palazzo Colonna, offered to her by
Cardinal Pompeo Colonna in acknowledgement of the betrothal of
her daughter Giulia to Vespasiano Colonna, and set about wearing
him down.

Initially, Isabella seemed capable of ignoring the gathering political storm clouds which were to result in what Vasari later claimed
was the greatest diaspora of artistic talent on the peninsula, and
established her own salon in Rome in imitation of her much praised
court at Mantua. Pietro Bembo was in the city and described his
pleasure at seeing his patroness: 'Only the other day, I saw the Lady
Marchioness, honourably attended by a fair and noble company,
driving about in her chariot, which is as fine as sight it is a novel one
in Rome.' The writers Sadoleto, Paolo Giovio and Chiericati became
members of Isabella's circle there, along with the Venetian ambassador Domenico Venier and the poet Molza, who came from Bologna
with a recommendation from Ercole d'Este, who knew of the
'delight' his mother took 'in the company of learned men'. Isabella
trundled about, visiting the Roman ruins and the principal churches,
cultivated the acquaintance of Michelangelo's pupil Sebastiano del
Piombo and, as ever, spent many hours beating down the antiquar-
ies of the city to add to her collection of marbles and mosaics. She
acquired ancient medallions, some valuable china vases, arrases to
Raphael cartoons and numerous tapestries and paintings, though
she was later to be accused of removing materials which were not
strictly hers to take. Julius II had placed a ban on the export of antiquities from Rome, but characteristically Isabella wrote to her agent
insisting he find a way around this. In the end, she need not have
concerned herself with the ban, as there was to be no one left to
enforce it.

The summer passed pleasantly, but in October 1525 Cardinal
Sigismondo d'Este, for whom Isabella had pawned her jewels more
than twenty years before, died. Isabella barely stopped to drag on
her mourning before rushing to the Vatican and demanding her
brother-in-law's hat for Ercole, but was vexed to be once again dismissed. Although Isabella was welcomed with the best musicians

and dinners at the Vatican, and invited to peruse its unique collection of antiquities at her pleasure, Clement had realized he could no longer make use of the Gonzaga. With the disappearance of the secret document, Federico of Mantua could truthfully affirm that he was contracted not to fight against the emperor, and the insistence of Mantovese neutrality, which Isabella had also pushed for, would mean that in the event of an invasion, Imperial troops could pass through the Gonzaga territories unmolested. Unsurprising, then, that Clement was not inclined to reward Isabella, though he may not have known the extent of her duplicity. He certainly no longer had anything to gain by giving Ercole the cardinalcy.

Much sadder news came with the death of Elisabetta Gonzaga, Duchess of Urbino, on 28 October. Ever an invalid, the shock of her brother Sigismondo's death had hastened Elisabetta's final decline, and Isabella grieved sincerely for the woman whom she had believed, in the way of the selfish and self-righteous, to have been her closest friend for nearly half a century. 'Madama,' reported the Mantuan ambassador, 'has felt the greatest distress at the death of the widowed Duchess of blessed memory, and besides the ties of blood and the singular love which has always united these two illustrious princesses, she grieves over the loss of the most rare lady whom this age has known.' The fact that Isabella had failed her friend in the hour of her greatest need and effectively stolen her possessions was forgotten in her touching display of grief.

Even this now looked to be overwhelmed by politics. In 1525 Clement had been corresponding with Charles V, in an attempt to stave off the Imperial threat, but when the League of Cognac was formed between France, England, Florence and Venice after the release of François I in early 1526, he had allied the papacy against the Empire as a counter-measure. The Colonna, who had allied themselves with Charles as part of their perpetual struggle against the Orsini, now attempted a coup, their forces entering the city on 20 September. Desperately, the Pope called the citizens of Rome to his defence, but they were ominously unwilling to protect him and he was obliged to take hasty refuge in the Castel Sant'Angelo, though his hurry did not cause him to neglect to bring a large sack of the best papal jewellery with him. Isabella, appalled at the Colonna insurrection, protested by refusing to attend the wedding of Giulia and Vespasiano in November, but she does not appear to have fully understood the gravity of the Roman position. Admittedly her son Ferrante Gonzaga was in the service of Charles V, while Mantua itself had requested papal permission to remain neutral in the matter of the League, so she may have felt sanguine about her prospects in the event of what was now agreed to be the certainty of invasion. The armies of the League had already suffered a blow in the form of the death of Caterina Sforza's youngest son Giovanni at Governato, the loss of this skirmish permitted the alliance of the Imperial troops with the forces commanded by Charles de Bourbon near Mantua itself. Even with Clement released from the Colonna threat, far graver forces were mustering, but Isabella's tenacity was not to be thwarted. She had come to Rome with a purpose, and she would achieve it, invasion or no invasion.

That Giovanni delle Bande Nere's death should have occurred in 1527 seems significant, as it ended not only the martial dynasty of the Sforza, but also the tradition of the great Italian *condottieri*, as mourned by Aretino. Their beautiful, elegant, wasteful and fool-hardy cavalry tactics were being rendered obsolete by the more prosaically efficient methods of field artillery. The poet's account of his patron's death evokes some of the horror of Renaissance doctoring. After being hit by a ball in the leg, the twenty-eight-year-old warrior was taken to the Gonzaga palace in Mantua where the surgeon Abramo prepared to perform an amputation. Ten men were requested to hold him down as his leg was sawn off without any form of anaesthetic, but Giovanni announced it would need at least twenty and took the surgeon's candle himself. He held it steady, but died a few days later. Federico Gonzaga, against whom Giovanni had fought many campaigns, received his old enemy tenderly, saying that he would 'never cease to lament the loss of so noble and excellent a prince'.

By May 1527, the Imperialists were well on the march to Rome, with the forces of the League lagging two days behind. Clement now signed a pact with the viceroy Lannoy to keep them out of Rome in return for a huge indemnity, but, having no means of raising it, he resorted as others before to simony, selling off five cardinalcies for 40,000 ducats apiece. Hence Isabella got her way, but she had a very short time to enjoy her triumph, as by 5 May the Imperials were encamped outside the very walls of the city. Her son Ferrante, along with her kinsman Marc'Antonio Colonna, commanded the pro-Imperial Italian divisions, while 10,000 German troops, the Land sknechts of fearsome reputation, were joined by 6,000 Spaniards. Incredibly, many Romans received their arrival in a remarkably relaxed manner. Clement continued to insist vociferously that Rome was inviolable, and what defences were organized were frankly pathetic. The only strategy they did manage to pull off was posting guards at the city gates to prevent cowards from fleeing. No consensus could be reached over destroying the bridges over the Tiber, and the theoretically compulsory muster of able-bodied men from each Roman district produced only a handful of destitutes, as those who were prepared to take up arms had already committed their services to the far more lucrative pursuit of security-guarding for wealthy private citizens. The smugness and incompetence of the Romans at this juncture contributed much to the horrors which befell them, but they were equally unaware of the desperate conditions of the Imperial troops.

Bourbon knew that any kind of siege would prove impossible. The Imperial artillery had been left behind on the road in the effort to stay ahead of the armies of the League, and moreover the Imperials had no supplies. The hungry, exhausted men, dressed in rags, had been spurred on by their commanders who promised them the riches of the Eternal City. If they did not attack, they risked total mutiny. Accordingly, on the night of 5 May, Bourbon sent the challenge decreed by convention to the Pope, demanding surrender and a ransom of 300,000 ducats, though both sides knew this was no more than a formality. Indeed, the Imperials were so anxious to get about sacking that Bourbon was unable to complete the traditional rousing address to the men before they began the assault on the walls.

The attack started in earnest on the morning of 6 May. In thick fog, ladders were thrown up, with the Spaniards entering at Porta Torrione and the Lutherans at Santo Spirito. Clement was praying for deliverance in the Vatican, and 'so narrow was the Pope's escape that had he tarried for three creeds more he would have been taken prisoner in his own palace'.

With a purple cardinal's cloak thrown over his own conspicuous white robes, Clement made the now familiar scuttle to the Castel Sant'Angelo, with the Bishop of Novara holding up the skirts of his cassock like a corpulent bridesmaid.

From the walls of Sant'Angelo, the great papal goldsmith Benvenuto Cellini observed with the diffidence that characterized the Roman attitude in the early stages of the sack: 'Night had fallen, the enemy was in Rome. We at the castle and above all I who have always enjoyed new things, watched this unbelievable spectacle.'

What followed seemed barely unbelievable, in the sense that Europe reeled from an assault that seemed impossible, heretical, demonic. Rome was to be left 'a cadaver of a city', in the words of the regretful Pompeo Colonna, while Sanudo claimed that 'hell itself' was a more beautiful sight to behold'. Compared with what the Imperials were about to do, the invasion of Charles VIII seemed no more than a military parade.

There was little or no street fighting to be observed, no resistance of brave citizens for the invaders laboriously to overcome, street by street, *quartiere* by *quartiere*. There was no time. The Imperialists simply killed everyone who fell in their way. The Spanish troops were noted as being *primus inter pares* when it came to viciousness; many of them were veterans of the campaign in the New World against the Aztec capital of Tenochittlán, and they sought the blood of the Romans like greedy Mexican gods. The inmates of the Ospedale di Santo Spirito went the same way as the orphans of the Pietà. Those of the Borgo prison were freed, to add their pent-up depravities to the massacre. By the time the Imperialists had penetrated as far as the Campo de' Fiori there was hardly a church, palace or major house which had not been pillaged, a pattern which soon spread over the entire city. Sapienza, Rome's celebrated university, was destroyed, while monasteries and convents were set alight. The Palazzo Montefiore, where Caterina Sforza had celebrated her first wedding feast, was among the first to be destroyed.

Those who survived the initial incursion may well have wished they hadn't. The Imperialists in particular took especial delight in attacking nuns, raping women who had barely so much as spoken to a man, or selling them as prostitutes, roped in the city squares like beasts. Torture was widespread, the cloister of San Cosimato was used to shelter animals, and the holy relics in which Rome abounded were defaced when not destroyed, or demeaned in a manner which appalled the faithful. Venerated objects such as the napkin of St Veronica were wilfully desecrated, in the case of the latter by being scornfully offered for sale in taverns. Tombs, including that of Pope Julius II, were violated, and a millennium's worth of sacred treasures looted or damaged beyond repair. In a neat irony, the Spaniards stole the silver bust of Cesare Borgia from the Ospedale di Santa Maria della Consolazione.

In the first few days of the sack, an 'unearthly silence' held over much of the city, broken only by the howlings of the now mostly drunken Imperials, who had begun to fight among themselves. A brisk trade in ransoms was quickly established, with 5,000 ducats as the going rate for a high-ranking ecclesiastic. Those who had no means of paying were killed or subjected to horrific coercement, such as one Cristofero Mercellio, who was tied to a tree and had a fingernail pulled out each day until shock and hunger killed him. When the Colonna troops arrived on 10 May, thousands of corpses were strewn around the city, with hundreds more bloating and stinking in the river. By 5 June 1527, when Clement was prevailed upon to treat with the enemy, the city was largely in ruins. Trade was extinguished, there was simply no merchandise or goods to buy or sell, and the legions of hell unleashed by Charles V were soon joined by their companions in the cavalry of the Apocalypse, famine and disease.

Although accounts of the sack may be exaggerated, there is no doubting its profound psychological effect. In an age which had so prided itself on the search for classical precedent to establish cultural authority, suddenly no precedent could be found. The shock of the attack on Rome appalled the whole of Christendom, of which it had been the centre. In modern terms, the reaction might be compared to that which reverberated around the world when Islamic fundamentalists attacked New York on 11 September 2001. It was totally unbelievable. God had abandoned His chosen city.

★

Of all the inhabitants of the city, Isabella d'Este had some reason to feel secure. The initial envoy to Clement requiring immediate Roman surrender had also brought a message for the Marchioness of Mantua, instructing her to barricade herself in the Sant'Apostoli palace and to remain there until troops could be sent to her aid. How, then, did Isabella react to the news that her champion had been killed by a shot from an arquebus in the first minutes of the assault? Even as the troops were in the city, desperate women fled to Isabella, until it was estimated that 1,200 were in her charge, joined by 1,000 citizens, including the daughter of Pope Julius II, Felice della Rovere, and the ambassadors of Mantua, Ferrara and Venice, the latter having recognized that he would not be able to reach Sant'Angelo in time. Whatever Isabella's other failings, she was no coward, and it was not until the late morning of 6 May, when the Imperials had been in the city for some hours, that she ordered her gates to be locked. The palazzo was well defended, with bastions at every doorway, and indeed was the only major palace in the city to remain unharmed. On the first day, the inhabitants pressed to the shuttered windows, squinting out to see what they could, as the guns from the fortress punctuated the screams of the dying. Towards nightfall, as the city was illuminated by the flames of hundreds of torched buildings, Alessandro Gonzaga, dressed in the Imperial colours of red, white and black, was recognized by his sister Camilla, who was in Isabella's party, running across the piazza towards the gates. Ropes were let down and he was hauled to safety, followed shortly by Isabella's son Ferrante.

Isabella, Ferrante and Alessandro quickly identified an opportunity to combine compassion with commerce. In terms of *composizione*, or ransoms, the assembled refugees were worth fortunes. The next morning business began in earnest, suggesting that 'Isabella's offer of shelter might not have been entirely altruistic and that shelter did not come without a price'. The Imperial lieutenant, Alonso da Córdoba, arrived and began to work out how much the captives (excepting Isabella herself) were worth. He demanded 100,000 ducats, but the refugees bargained him down to 52,000, of which 10,000, it was rumoured, were pocketed by the Gonzagas, which was hardly in the great Este tradition of aristocratic hospitality. Isabella stood security for the Venetian ambassador in return for 5,000 ducats, and was subsequently outraged when her 'friend' managed to escape from Mantua without coming up with the cash. Relishing his mother's discomfiture, the Marquis of Mantua wrote to the Doge of Venice congratulating him on the recovery of his envoy.

Conclusion

As Rome continued to burn, Isabella d'Este returned to Mantua. The fifty-three-year-old marchioness left by galley from Ostia on 13 May 1527, arriving a month later to a land she had not seen for two years. Her stay in the Holy City had been happy and busy. Yet all was clouded by memories of the horrid drama she had witnessed as troops, initially led by her nephew the Duke of Bourbon, rampaged through the bloody streets, committing their foul assault on the Eternal City. The Sack of Rome is certain to have shaken Isabella's beliefs in the modern world.

Mantua gave her a muted welcome. Few people of consequence remained in town. This did not represent a slight upon Isabella so much as a pusillanimous stampede of courtiers to the country to escape the early arrival of the summer plague. All the same, it meant that her quiet homecoming felt less than triumphant.

Back home, Isabella pined for the gratifying attentions she had enjoyed from the Romans, who had fêted her with so much warmth and a quite different manner from the bird-brained courtiers who still surrounded her son, Federico, Marquis of Mantua. In Rome she had cultivated close relationships among those within the Curia who counted, had been visited by artists seeking commissions (usually fruitlessly) and found herself invited to the entertainment for visiting foreign princes, grandees of all sorts and emissaries on diplomatic visits. She had felt important again.

She had also succeeded in her political aims. She had originally left Mantua for Rome with the stated intent of winning a cardinal's hat for her son Ercole, and had returned with her trophy which, combined with her other winnings, represented a splendid haul. One commentator wrote: 'For all the vexations, those were glorious days. What a lucky windfall the Sack of Rome was to collectors!' Isabella did not only bring the cardinalcy back with her, but also galleys filled with treasures she had collected. Unfortunately, though some had been lost in a storm at sea, Isabella had also made a fine profit from those who had sought her protection both inside the Palazzo Colonna, and her laissez-passer out of Rome. Deep down, however, she probably knew that, while she had won her way, it had come at a terrible price. She had watched Rome burn down, taking with it her own world.

Isabella had spent her whole life chasing the capricious goddess Fortuna: what we call Chance or Luck. She held to the Humanist belief that the vicissitudes of Chance could be managed – if not entirely, then to a greater extent than if left without her own efforts. Luck must be encouraged, and if she succeeded then the result would be Virtù. In some senses this encapsulated the meaning of the Renaissance.

Virtù had nothing in common with Christian virtue, loaded with the ideas of humility, piety, forgiveness and largely self-effacing characteristics. To those raised during the glittering age into which Isabella had been born Virtù meant success, good judgement, having perhaps outsmarted a rival, and survived the tergiversations of life's ongoing struggle against Fortuna. Virtù also translated into a fine ability to create a delicate and refined environment that came with achievement, the intelligence as well as the knowledge of how best to *enjoy* the fruits of winning.

The words might have sounded familiar to those born in the late 1300s such as Contessina de' Bardi, wife of Cosimo de' Medici, who died around the time of Isabella's birth, but by the time Isabella reached her old age, they had ceased to have their old-fashioned meaning.

Isabella spent the rest of her long life travelling. She lived partly in Ferrara as well as in Mantua, working, as ever, for the good of her state. But by the 1520s, Isabella had become a relic of the era she had also outlived. Although still driven by curiosity and ambition, she did not realize quite how much she had herself become viewed as a curiosity of her time. Still less could she know how, much later, she would come to be seen as the paradigmatic woman of the High Renaissance.

In 1530 Isabella travelled to Bologna in order to attend the coronation of Charles V as Holy Roman Emperor. As Clement performed the rites, he became the last pope ever to place the iron crown of Lombardy – once worn, it was said, by Charlemagne – upon the anointed head of his successors. Charles V's coronation included the titles both of Holy Roman Emperor and King of Italy.

In reality Charles – who visited Mantua twice – was the emperor of the vast Habsburg territories that stretched from the sea ports of the Low Countries to the southernmost tip of united Spain, and from Naples to Sicily; his easternmost states incorporated Hungary and Croatia. The northern boundaries of his empire reached far into today's western Poland, and would be enhanced further when the Conquistadors had added yet more terrain, by taking swathes of land in North, Central and South America.

Despite his onerous duties Charles V found time to elevate Isabella's marital state from a marquisate to a duchy. Before her death Isabella had the pleasure of seeing Federico married to the heiress Margherita Paleologa, Duchess of Monferrat. Nor had the marchioness neglected her natal state of Ferrara, for she lived to see her nephew Ercole d'Este, the heir to Ferrara and son of her rival Lucrezia Borgia, marry Renée of France. The daughter of Louis XII and Anne of Brittany felt underwhelmed by the connection with an Italian city state, yet in June 1528 a splendid wedding took place, joining the royal house of France with the ducal house of Ferrara.

Isabella reportedly spent the last years of her life living largely outside the city of Mantua at her house in Porto. It is said that she enjoyed visits from her grandchildren and lived out her last days in contentment. It is hard to believe that a woman as acutely conscious of all around her dandled any grandchildren on her knee with more than fleeting pleasure. It is more likely that she realized she had increasingly become a curiosity from another age, an age which she had outlived.

Isabella died on 13 February 1539. She left behind her a Christian world that had changed beyond recognition even since her birth in 1474. The patchwork of princely states that covered the Italian peninsula had been condemned, as vast empires and nations states grew up around them. Isabella, the last of the great women of the Italian Renaissance, witnessed the end of the world that she and her contemporaries had made.

Contessina de' Bardi (wife of Cosimo de' Medici and grandmother to Lorenzo Il Magnifico), born in approximately 1390, had opened her eyes during a period still considered part of the Middle Ages. Her sphere of influence remained within the home, and any power she may have wielded over her husband derived from her being a Bardi. Her daughter-in-law Lucrezia Tornabuoni lived at the beginning of the Renaissance – as was demonstrated at its most obvious level by the names of the two women: Contessina named after the martial heroine Countess Mathilda of Tuscany, and Lucrezia after the hugely respected Roman matron who killed herself after being raped. The classically influenced upbringing Lucrezia shared with her brothers would not have been considered proper in Contessina's day. Lucrezia's studies had given her a Humanist education and a love of learning for its own sake; it had also taught her ambition. Isabella represented, along with Caterina Sforza, the apogee of female power and influence in her age.

But the world in which women such as Lucrezia, Isabella and Caterina had lived was altering dramatically. The great nations of Europe were on the rise, and new cultures of courtly behaviour and piety were rising with them. Just as Spain and the Habsburg territories would soon unite, the Hundred Years' War had petered out by the mid-1400s, leaving France to establish itself as another major power. Having repelled the English, the French monarchy needed to secure their great land mass. Certain critical states such as Brittany came to France through marriage. (Anne of Brittany married two French sovereigns; her daughter Queen Claude of France and Duchess of Brittany became the first wife of François I.)

This allowed the French crown to enter a period of unprecedented supremacy and territorial security. François I had commanded that the French speak one tongue, and the Langue d'oil triumphed over the Langue d'oc. The long wars for land, people and resources that had raged throughout Christendom since the collapse of Charlemagne's empire in the ninth century had shifted their focus to the New World.

The papacy, a temporal monarchy itself, awarded titles of divinity to the ever more powerful sovereigns of France, England, Spain and the Habsburg Empire. Henry VIII became Defender of the Faith, François I the Most Christian King, and after Charles V his son Philip became the Most Catholic King. Theories of the divine right of kingship, that the men and women who ruled had been chosen by God, had begun to percolate in the minds of the rulers.

By contrast with these great nations, the Italian city states – fiercely independent, warlike and proud – began fading into obscurity and irrelevance, their former *de facto* independence gradually eroded. Their futures no longer lay cupped in the capricious hands of upwardly mobile brigands and self-made princes, nor in the finer, softer palms of ruling feudal dynasties. Rather, the peninsula became once more a battleground, torn apart by the rival ambitions of the rising nation states, until the Treaty of Cateau-Cambrésis in 1559, when the French withdrew from the peninsula almost entirely and left it under the domination of Philip II of Spain.

Italy itself would not achieve sovereign unity until the mid-nineteenth century, but even by the mid-sixteenth century one language – Tuscan – had defeated the multiplicity of tongues and dialects once spoken upon the peninsula. (In this, we can detect Lucrezia Borgia's hand since it was Pietro Bembo who promoted Petrarchasque Tuscan as the basis for written Italian, a simplified verson of which is still used today.) Slowly the individual identities of the city states were disappearing.

The frizzled ruins of Rome, having just reappeared as the Eternal City, would be restored thanks to vigorous rebuilding and restoration plans and projects. Yet just as the resurgent papacy had restored itself as the authority to speak for the Almighty, the changing world proved that it would brook no more simony, corruption, sexually

deviant behaviour or 'forgiveness for sale'. The popes of the fifteenth century had exploited the Church and misused their powers
to an extent that, when Luther's prickly denunciations decorated
church doors from Scotland to Sicily with his 95 Theses condemn-
ing the Catholic Church's abuses of power, many hearts opened to
these protests.

The 'monkish squabble', as Luther's protest was dismissed by
the first Medici pope, Leo X, adumbrated the end of the golden
age of Renaissance Humanism, a time when men and women had
both permission and the tools with which to think for themselves.
The Sack of Rome was seen as a punishment delivered by an angry
God, as the Renaissance Humanism skirted dangerously close to
heresy as they played fluently with the images of both Greek deities
and the Church's saints. No more would anyone articulate or dare
interplay, however respectfully, the Holy Virgin with Venus, or any
other of the sulphurous goddesses of the ancient world. Instead,
the classical revival gave way to a darker, vicious and bigoted war
for hearts and minds. Wars of religion occupied the minds of monarchs, overshadowing the noble quest for rediscovering long-lost
knowledge.

Yet who were the consorts and queens regnant who ruled over
the emerging nations? Many of them were descended from the
extraordinary women of the Italian Renaissance. Catherine de'
Medici became the *de jure* ruler of France upon the death of her
husband, Henri II, although she did not ride into battle wearing
a breastplate, as her namesake, Caterina Sforza, had done. In the
manner of Elizabeth of England, she wore a breastplate as a symbol
of her kingship; these two contemporaries both donned whatever
habit would inspire the men and women over whom they ruled, and
talked of the heart and stomach of a king.

Eventually breastplates, rather than protecting women on the battlefield, now became part of ceremonial wear for the ruling women
of the generations that Isabella and her like had given birth to.

Another Medici followed Catherine as queen, then regent of
France: Maria de Medici, the granddaughter of Caterina Sforza.
Maria married the first Bourbon king, Henry IV of France and
Navarre. Her son Louis XIII was not blessed with a mother with

a knack for politics in the mould of Catherine, and the royal family lived in exile for a while during her regency. And the bloodline continued: Henrietta Maria, one of Henry IV and Maria's daughters, became Queen Consort of England by marrying Charles I of England and Scotland.

But if the women of the sixteenth century reached political heights never enjoyed by the brave (and less brave) women of this book, they had fewer opportunities to assert themselves politically. The Reformation ushered in an age of greater sexual hypocrisy and squeamishness than had been enjoyed by the more libidinous age of their mothers and grandmothers of the fifteenth century.

The Golden Age of Bastards was over. Stricter laws governing the careers and positions of illegitimate children began to be enforced. Women found their military role diminishing. Caterina Sforza, who had led troops into battle, was one of the last of her kind. Rather than performing military duties, the women who descended from Caterina and her contemporaries merely enacted ceremonial imitations of them – forms of grand pageantry which were ritualized in the increasingly formal European courts, such as that of Versailles under Louis XIV, and which can still be seen today at the court of Queen Elizabeth II.

The descendants of the women in this book generally married into the royal families of the emerging nations, many of which, tragically, played a large role in obliterating the small city states from which the women came. Their bloodlines can be traced to royalty today. It is to be wondered whether Queen Elizabeth II, on her visit to Florence of May 1961, while walking up the Via Tornabuoni realized that the street had been named after Lucrezia, her direct ancestress.

The Italian Renaissance was as much an age of culture and learning as of violence and deceit. The brutally misogynistic language of some lofty humanists notwithstanding, it was also a time that allowed for female greatness. It is perhaps ironic to see learned men of the day, who arrogantly subscribed classical and pagan tenets of their gender's superiority, grovelling at the feet of those they considered by-products of a lesser clay, in the hope of obtaining protection, money and fame. At the same time, these women, whom

Ficino would dismiss as the piss-pots of humanity, planned the construction of buildings, arranged the disposition of artillery, managed estates and states, foiled attempted coups against their husbands, arranged the brilliant education of their children, plotted the interlocking relations between the greatest states in Christendom, and influenced the elevation or destruction of the men who apparently ruled their world. I hope this book goes some way to giving them their proper due.

Bibliography

ABBREVIATIONS

ACRF   Archivio Capponi alle Rovinate, Firenze
AGF   Archivio Guicciardini, Firenze
ASF   Archivio di Stato di Firenze
ASI   *Archivio storico Italiano*
ASL   *Archivio storico lombardo*
ASM   Archivio di Stato di Milano
ASMn   Archivio di Stato di Mantova
ASMo   Archivio di Stato di Modena
ASPN *Archivio Storico per le Provincie Napoletane*
DBI   *Dizionario Biografico degli Italiani*
MaP   *Mediceo Avanti il Principato*
MP   *Mediceo del Principato*
RIS   *Rerum Italicarum Scriptores*
RRIISS *Rerum Italicarum Scriptores*, new edition
SDO   *Signori, Dieci di Balìa, Otto di Pratica*

GENERAL

For Italy during the Renaissance, the classic – if, to an extent, dated – study remains Jacob Burckhardt, *The Civilisation of the Renaissance in Italy*, (London, Macmillan, 1929, and reprinted many times since). For a more recent, compelling, survey, see Lauro Martines, *Power and Imagination: City-States in Renaissance Italy* (New York, Knopf, 1979). For a thematic treatment of the period, see John M. Najemy (ed.), *Italy in the Age of the Renaissance: 1300–1550* (New York, Oxford University Press, 2004).

Our knowledge of female figures in Renaissance Italy has benefited greatly from the advent of women's studies. For some recent books on the subject, see Christiane Klapisch-Zuber, *Women, Family and Ritual in Renaissance Italy* (Chicago, University of Chicago Press, 1987); Letizia Panizza (ed.), *Women in Italian Renaissance Culture and Society* (London, Legenda, 2000). For female artistic patronage, see Sheryl E. Reiss and David G. Wilkins (eds), *Beyond Isabella: Secular Women Patrons of Arts in Renaissance Italy* (Kirkville, Truman State University Press, 2001). Still a lively read is Christopher Hare, *The Most Illustrious Ladies of the Italian Renaissance* (New York, Cosimo, 2008; reprint of the 1907 edition).

For original sources, invaluable are the collections published in *RIS*, Ludovico Antonio Muratori (ed.), 28 vols (Milan, Typographia Societatis Palatinae in Regia Curia, 1723–51); and *RRIISS*, Giosuè Carducci et al (eds), 56 vols (Bologna, Zanichelli, 1900–79). Needless to say, original sources should be approached with caution: Johannes Burckard's *Liber notarum* (in *RRIISS*, 32, 1, 1 and 32, 1, 2, 1907–11) has many juicy stories about the popes from Sixtus IV to Julius II, which continue to be gobbled up whole by many authors. However, Burckard hated Rome, Italians and his masters, and was therefore ready to devour any malicious gossip that crossed his path. His writings should always be cross-checked with those of other sources of the period.

PROLOGUE

The standard work on Caterina Sforza is still Count Pier Desiderio Pasolini's *Caterina Sforza*, 3 vols (Rome, Loescher, 1893). An English, abridged version (trans Paul Sylvester with the assistance of the author) in one volume was published in 1898 by Herbert S. Stone & Co., Chicago/New York. Pasolini further integrated his work with a documentary addendum: *Caterina Sforza: nuovi documenti* (Bologna, Tipografia A. Garagnani e figli, 1897). See also Ernst Breisach, *Caterina Sforza, A Renaissance Virago* (Chicago, University of Chicago Press, 1967); Elizabeth Lev, *The Tigress of Forlì: Renaissance Italy's Most*

Courageous and Notorious Countess, Caterina Riario Sforza de' Medici (Boston, Houghton Mifflin Harcourt, 2011).

For a flavour of the events surrounding the murder of Girolamo Riario, see Leone Cobelli, 'Le Cronache forlivesi di Leone Cobelli dalla fondazione della città sino all'anno 1498', ed. G. Carducci and E. Frati, in *Monumenti istorici pertinenti alle provincie della Romagna*, s. 3, vol. I (Bologna, 1874). There are countless different versions of Caterina's infamous gesture. Depending on the mores of the age the accounts have been subject to change, analysis and additions. The original account given of Caterina showing her 'shameful parts' is by far the likeliest. The Early Modern period had no time or space for privacy. Life and death were lived out in public by kings and commoners alike. For a discussion of the episode, see Julia H. Hairston, 'Skirting the Issue: Machiavelli's Caterina Sforza', *Renaissance Quarterly*, vol. 53, no. 3 (Autumn 2000), pp. 687–712.

ONE: POWER FROM BEHIND THE VEIL

The best one-volume book on Italy's political situation in 1471 is Riccardo Fubini, *Italia quattrocentesca. Politica e diplomazia nell'età di Lorenzo il Magnifico* (Milan, Franco Angeli, 1994). The struggle that ultimately brought Francesco Sforza to rule Milan is thoroughly described in Niccolò Capponi, *La battaglia di Anghiari. Il giorno che salvò il Rinascimento* (Milan, Il Saggiatore, 2010).

The Medici dynasty still needs a proper study, if one excludes the excellent if slim book by John R. Hale, *Florence and the Medici* (London, Phoenix, 2001). Paul Strathern's *The Medici: Godfathers of the Renaissance* (London, Jonathan Cape, 2003), is a highly readable survey. George Frederick Young's *The Medici* (London, John Murray, 1909), is still useful. From a documentary standpoint, unsurpassed are the biographical sketches of various Medici in Gaetano Pieraccini, *La stirpe dei Medici di Cafaggiolo: saggio di ricerche sulla trasmissione ereditaria dei caratteri biologici*, 3 vols (Florence, Vallecchi, 1924–5). The Medici system of power is well described in Nicolai Rubinstein, *The Government of Florence Under the Medici, 1434–1494* (Oxford, Oxford University Press, 1968).

For Lorenzo de' Medici there is a glut of biographies. One of the best, despite its age, is still William Roscoe, *The Life of Lorenzo de' Medici called the Magnificent*, 2 vols (Liverpool, J. M'Creery, 1795). See also Miles Unger, *Magnifico: The Brilliant Life and Violent Times of Lorenzo de' Medici* (New York, Simon & Schuster, 2009).

For Galeazzo Maria Sforza, the best book to date is Gregory P. Lubkin, *A Renaissance Court: Milan under Galeazzo Maria Sforza* (Berkeley, University of California Press, 1994); see pp. 98–100 for Galeazzo's visit to Florence in 1471. For the visit itself, see Cesare Paoli, Luigi Rubini, Pietro Stromboli (eds), *Della venuta in Firenze di Galeazzo Maria Sforza duca di Milano con la moglie Bona di Savoia nel marzo del MCCCCLXXI: lettere di due senesi alla Signoria di Siena (ser Baldino di Domenico da Lucignano e Lorenzo d'Antonio Venturini)* (Florence, Barbera, 1878). Machiavelli's cutting commentary on the Sforza visit is in Niccolò Machiavelli, *Le istorie fiorentine* (Florence, Le Monnier, 1857), p. 367.

For the Medici women in general, see Yvonne Maguire, *The Women of the Medici* (London, G. Routledge & Sons, Ltd, 1927). Maguire's work is solid, although sometimes her translation of original documents is faulty. For a more recent, and more feminist outlook, see Natalie R. Tomas, *The Medici Women: Gender and Power in Renaissance Florence* (Aldershot, Ashgate, 2003). Contessina, wife of Cosimo de' Medici, lacks a proper biography, but her personality emerges powerfully in her letters; see Tommaso Casini, Salomone Morpurgo (eds), *Sette lettere di Contessina Bardi (ne, Medici) ai figliuoli Piero e Giovanni* (Firenze, Carnesecchi, 1886). Translations of these letters can be found in Janet Ross, *Lives of the Early Medici as Told in Their Correspondence* (London, Chatto & Windus, 1910). For more recent finds, see Orsola Gori, 'Contessina moglie di Cosimo "il Vecchio": Lettere familiari', in A. Degrandi et alia (eds.), *Scritti in onore di Girolamo Arnaldi offerti dalla Scuola nazionale di studi medioevali* (Rome, Istituto Storico Italiano per il Medio Evo, 2001), pp. 233–59

Lucrezia Tornabuoni has fared much better. An early biographical sketch can be found in Niccolò Valori, *Vita di Lorenzo il Magnifico*, A. Dillon Bassi (ed.) (Palermo, Sellerio, 1992). For a more recent work, to a large extent informative if somewhat cavalier with its sources, see Maria Grazia Pernis and Laurie Adams, *Lucrezia Tornabuoni de' Medici and the Medici Family in the Fifteenth Century* (New York, Peter Lang, 2006). The best analysis of the relationship between Lorenzo and his mother is: Francis W. Kent, 'Sainted Mother. Magnificent Son: Lucrezia Tornabuoni and Lorenzo de' Medici', *Italian History and Culture*, 3 (1997), pp. 3–34.

TWO: THE PRINCESS BRIDE

The citation by Giovio is from Paolo Giovio, *Le vite di Leon Decimo et d'Adriano Sesto, sommi pontefici* (Florence, Torrentino, 1551), p. 22.

For the Medici-Orsini marriage of 1469, see Cesare Guasti (ed.), *Tre lettere di Lucrezia Tornabuoni a Piero de' Medici, ed altre lettere di vari concernenti al matrimonio di Lorenzo il Magnifico con Clarice Orsini* (Florence, Le Monnier, 1859). Some cutting comments on the marriage can be found in Alessandra Macinghi Strozzi, *Lettere di una gentildonna fiorentina del secolo XV ai figli esuli*, Cesare Guasti (ed.) (Florence, Sansoni, 1877), pp. 592–3. For marriage expenses at the time, see Julius Kirshner, 'Li Emergenti Bisogni Matrimoniali in Renaissance Florence', in William J. Connell (ed.), *Society and Individual in Renaissance Florence* (Berkeley, University of California Press, 2002), pp. 79–109. For spectacles in Florence, including the joust of 1469, see P. Ventrone (ed.), *Le tems revient, 'l tempo si rinuova: feste e spettacoli nella Firenze di L. il Magnifico* (Cinisello Balsamo-Milan, Silvana editoriale, 1992).

THREE: LA DAME DE PETIT SENS

The comment by Commines on Bona of Savoy is in Philippe de Commines, *Les mémoires de Philippe de Commines* (Paris, J. Renouard, 1840), p. 302.

For Sixtus IV and his family, see especially Ian F. Verstegen (ed.), *Patronage and Dynasty: The Rise of the Della Rovere in Renaissance Italy* (Kirksville, Truman State University Press, 2007).

The exchanges between Galeazzo Sforza and Lorenzo de' Medici can be found in Caterina Bonello Uricchio, 'I rapporti fra Lorenzo il Magnifico e Galeazzo Maria Sforza negli anni 1470–1473', *ASL*, XCI–XCII

(1964–5), pp. 33–49. Galeazzo Sforza's murder is thoroughly examined in Vincent Ilardi, *'The assassination of Galeazzo Maria Sforza and the Reaction of Italian Diplomacy'*, in L. Martines (ed.), *Violence and civil disorder in Italian Cities: 1200–1500* (Berkeley, University of California Press, 1972), pp. 72–103.

For Bona of Savoy, the best biography available is Daniel Meredith Bueno de Mesquita, 'Bona di Savoia, Duchessa di Milano', in *DBI*, vol. 11 (1969), pp. 428–30. For Bianca Maria Visconti, see Maria Nadia Covini, 'Tra cure domestiche, sentimenti e politica. La corrispondenza di Bianca Maria Visconti duchessa di Milano (1450–68)', *Reti Medievali*, X (2009), pp. 1–35.

For Ludovico Sforza's rise to power, see Carlo Paganini, 'Reggenza, due sconfitte e ritorno del Moro (1478–9)', *ASL*, s. 12, VII (2001), pp. 221–347.

FOUR: FAIR IS FOUL AND FOUL IS FAIR

The citation by Giovanni Battista da Montesecco is in Gino Capponi, *Storia della repubblica di Firenze*, vol. 2 (Florence, Barbera, 1875), p. 512.

For the Pazzi conspiracy, see Lauro Martines, *April Blood: Florence and the Plot Against the Medici, Oxford and New York* (Oxford University Press, 2003); Fubini, *Italia quattrocentesca*, pp. 87–206. The citation by Nardi is taken from Pernis, Adams, *Lucrezia Tornabuoni*, p. 14.

The war following the Pazzi conspiracy is understudied. For details about military operations: Piero Pieri, *Il Rinascimento e la crisi militare italiana* (Turin, Einaudi, 1970), pp. 291–304. For a more popular approach, see Marco Barsacchi, *Cacciate Lorenzo! La guerra dei Pazzi e l'assedio di Colle Val d'Elsa (1478–1479)* (Siena, Protagon, 2007). Much unpublished material can be found in ASF, *Dieci di Balìa: Responsive*, 24–6; *Missive*, 8–9; *Ricordanze*, 1. For Lorenzo de' Medici's activities, see Lorenzo de' Medici, *Lettere*, vol. III (1478–9), R. Fubini (ed.) (Florence, Giunti, 1977); and vol. IV (1479–80), N. Rubinstein (ed.) (Florence, Giunti, 1981).

For Lorenzo de' Medici's peace negotiations with Ferrante of Naples: ASF, *SDO*, 10. ASM, *Sforzesco*, 86, 229, 298–9. ASMn, *Archivio Gonzaga*, 1626. ASMo, *Estense: Carteggio ambasciatori*, 2.

Much of the above archival material has been woven into Laura De Angelis, 'Lorenzo a Napoli: progetti di pace e conflitti politici dopo la congiura dei Pazzi', *ASI*, CL (1992), pp. 385–421. 'There is no doubting that Lorenzo was in real danger' is quoted in Strathern, *The Medici*, p. 168. For the relationship between Lorenzo de' Medici and Ippolita Sforza: Judith Bryce, 'Between Friends? Two letters of Ippolita Sforza to Lorenzo de' Medici', *Renaissance Studies*, vol. 21, 3, 2007, pp. 340–65.

FIVE: MISTRESS OF THE REVELS IN ROME

For the War of Ferrara, see Michael E. Mallett, 'Le origini della guerra di Ferrara, in Lorenzo de' Medici', *Lettere*, vol. VI (1481–2), Michael E. Mallett (ed.) (Florence, Giunti, 1990), pp. 345–61; Edoardo Piva, *La guerra di Ferrara del 1482*, 2 vols (Padua, Angelo Draghi, 1893–4). See also the extensive archival sources cited in: Sergio Mantovani, 'L'assedio di Ficarolo (maggio–giugno 1482)', in *Tra terra acqua e terra. Storia materiale in Transpadana* (Ferrara, Comunicarte, 2001), pp. 13–53.

For Sixtus IV's impact on Rome, see Massimo Miglio et alius, eds, *Un pontificato ed una città: Sisto IV (1471–84): atti del Convegno, Roma, 3–7 dicembre 1984* (Vatican City, 1986).

SIX: THE VIRAGO HOLDS THE HOLY CITY HOSTAGE

For the doggerel about Sixtus IV: Unger, *Magnifico*, pp. 364–5.

For the transition between Sixtus IV to Innocent VIII, see Pasolini, *Caterina Sforza*, vol. I, pp. 144–165; Ludwig von Pastor, *History of the Popes, From the Close of the Middle Ages. Drawn from the Secret Archives of the Vatican and other Original Sources*, vol. V (London, Kegan Paul Trench Trübner & Co., 1898), pp. 228–34.

For scepticism among inquisitors about witchcraft: Giovanni Romeo, *Inquisitori, esorcisti e streghe nell'Italia della Controriforma* (Florence, Sansoni, 1993).

Lorenzo de' Medici is suspected to have had a hand in Girolamo Riario's murder, more for reasons of political expediency than to avenge his brother's death: see Marco Pellegrini, *Congiure di*

Romagna. Lorenzo de' Medici e il duplice tirannicidio a Forlì e a Faenza nel 1488 (Florence, Olschki, 1999).

SEVEN: FROM KISSING COUSINS TO KILLING COUSINS

The Neapolitan court is described in detail in George L. Hersey, *Alfonso II and the Artistic Renewal of Naples* (New Haven, Conn., Yale University Press, 1969). The torching of the Neapolitan state archives by German troops during the Second World War has to an extent stymied the production of scholarly works about the kingdom of Naples under Ferrante of Aragon, most of the papers concerning his father Alfonso being stored in Barcelona. For Joan of Aragon see Adele Scandone, *'Le tristi reyne di Napoli Giovanna III e Giovanna IV'*, *ASPN*, n.s., XIV (1929), pp. 114–55; XV (1929), pp. 151–89. For Ercole d'Este and Eleonora d'Aragona, see Luigi Olivi, *Delle nozze di Ercole I d'Este con Eleonora d'Aragona* (Modena, Società Tipografica, 1887).

There is no want of studies on Beatrice d'Este and, especially, her sister Isabella. The classic works in English are Julia Cartwright, *Beatrice d'Este, Duchess of Milan 1475–97* (Honolulu, University Press of the Pacific, 2002; reprint of the 1915 edn); idem, *Isabella d'Este: Marchioness of Mantua 1474 –1539*, 2 vols (Honolulu, University Press of the Pacific, 2002; reprint of the 1920 edn). See also Carlo d'Arco, *'Notizie di Isabella Estense, moglie a Francesco Gonzaga con documenti inediti'*, *ASI, App.* 2, 1845, pp. 205–326. For the Este girls' upbringing, see Luigi A. Gandini, *Isabella, Beatrice e Alfonso d'Este infanti: Documenti inediti del secolo 15* (Modena, Soliani, 1896). Alessandro Luzio, *I precettori d'Isabella d'Este: Appunti e documenti* (Ancona, Morelli, 1887). For Ippolita Sforza's marriage with Alfonso d'Aragona, see Carlo Canetta, *'Le sponsalie di casa Sforza con casa d'Aragona (giugno–ottobre 1455)'*, *ASL*, IX (1882), pp. 136–44. Ippolita Sforza's intellectual activities are examined in Judith Bryce, *'"Fa finire uno bello studio et dice volere studiare": Ippolita Sforza and her books'*, *Bibliotheque d'Humanisme et Renaissance*, vol. 64, 1 (2002), pp. 55–69.

For the marriage of Beatrice d'Este and Ludovico Sforza, see Gennaro Porro (ed.), *'Nozze di Beatrice d'Este e di Anna Sforza. Documenti copiati dagli originali esistenti nell'Archivio di Stato di Milano'*, *ASL*, XI (1882), pp. 483–534. Luca Beltrami, *Il cofanetto nuziale di Lodovico il Moro e Beatrice d'Este* (Milano, Allegretti, 1907); Adolfo Venturi, '*Relazioni artistiche tra le corti di Milano e Ferrara nel sec. XV'*, *ASL*, s. 2, XII (1885), pp. 227–9, 249, 253–4. Guido Lopez (ed.), *Festa di nozze per Ludovico. il Moro: nelle testimonianze di Tristano Calco, Giacomo Trotti, Isabella d'Este, Gian Galeazzo Sforza, Beatrice de' Contrari, e altri* (Milan, De Carlo, 1976). For the marriage of Isabella d'Este with Francesco Gonzaga, see: Alessandro Luzio, '*Isabella d'Este e Francesco Gonzaga promessi sposi'*, *ASL*, s. 4, XXXV, 9 (1908), pp. 40, 44–5, 51–2. For the 'competition' between Isabella and Beatrice, see Alessandro Luzio, Rodolfo Renier, '*Delle relazioni d'Isabella d'Este Gonzaga con Ludovico e Beatrice Sforza'*, *ASL*, s. 2, XVII (1890), 7, pp. 74–119, 346–99, 619–74

For Beatrice d'Este's mission to Venice, see Alessandra Massarenti, 'L'iniziazione politica di una giovane sovrana: Beatrice d'Este e Eleonora d'Aragona in visita diplomatica presso la Repubblica di Venezia (maggio 1493)', *Genesis*, Vi, 2 (2007), pp. 137–64.

For hunting, especially in the Po Valley, see Giancarlo Malacarne, *Le cacce del principe: l'ars venandi nella terra dei Gonzaga* (Modena, Il bulino, 1998). When compared to his wife, Francesco Gonzaga has always fared poorly as a patron of the arts; yet he was by no means the philistine he is commonly believed to be. On this matter see Mary H. Bourne, 'Out From the Shadow of Isabella: The Artistic Patronage of Francesco II Gonzaga, Fourth Marquis of Mantua (1484–1519)', Ph.D. dissertation (Harvard University, 1998).

EIGHT: QUEEN MOTHER OF FLORENCE AND THE PRINCESS
BRIDES

For Lorenzo de' Medici's domestic setting: Yvonne Maguire, *The Private Life of Lorenzo the Magnificent* (London, A. Ousley, 1936). Agnolo Poliziano taught all the Medici children, regardless of their sex, as witnessed by Lucrezia de' Medici-Salviati: ASF, *MP*, 380, f. 162 (Lucrezia de' Medici-Salviati, from Rome, to Cosimo I de' Medici, in Florence, 8 February 1546).

Maddalena de' Medici's complaint to her brother Piero about her husband's behaviour is in ASF, *MaP*, 100, f. 133r.

For understanding the pattern of Tuscan rural holdings, although in a slightly earlier period than this, see Sean T. Grover, 'A Tuscan Lawyer, His Farms and His Family: The Ledger of Andrea di Gherardo Casoli', MA Thesis (University of North Texas, 2009). Both Lucrezia and Lorenzo acquired numerous strategically placed holdings in Tuscany. See ACRF, XI (A) *Da Uzzano e Altopascio*, n. 8, rental contract in perpetuity (*livello*) between Lorenzo and Guglielmo Capponi, 23 August 1486; see also Niccolò Capponi, 'Dall'Ordine di S. Giacomo alla Commenda di S. Stefano: Altopascio e la penetrazione medicea nella Valdinievole, sec. XV–XVI' in Amleto Spicciani (ed.), *Guadi della Cassia. Terre di confine tra Lucca e il granducato di Toscana* (Pisa, ETS, 2004), pp. 89–103.

Although a formidable woman, Lucrazia Tornabuoni was not the only one of her kind in Florence. Indeed there appears to have been no lack of such ladies. See, for example Catherine V. De Luca, 'Guglielmina Schianteschi (1463–1536): A Tuscan Countess and Florentine Citizen', Ph.D. dissertation (University of California, Riverside, 2004). Megan Moran, 'Patriarchies in Practice: Women, Family, and Power in Late Medieval and Early Modern Italy', Ph.D. dissertation, Vanderbilt University, 2008.

Despite what one could be led to believe, neither Lucrezia Tornabuoni, nor the Medici for that, could throw their weight around unchallenged, soothing Florentine sensitivities and the need to keep a smooth relationship with Florence's oligarchy being a priority. For example, in 1476 the staunch pro-Medici Guglielmo Capponi, Master of the Altopascio, politely told Lucrezia Tornabuoni to buzz off when the Grand Dame tried to extort a chaplaincy from him for one of her protégés. ASF, *MaP*, 85, f. 99, Guglielmo Capponi to Lucrezia Tornabuoni, 4 January 1475 [1476]. For a detailed study on the attitudes of the Florentine ruling elite, see Francis W. Kent, *Household and Lineage in Renaissance Florence: The Family Life of the Capponi, Ginori, and Rucellai* (Princeton, NJ, Princeton University Press, 1977).

NINE: A WONDERFUL FAMILY MAN

Given their notoriety, it is not surprising that the Borgias have been thoroughly dissected. The best books in English on Cesare and

Lucrezia Borgia are Sarah Bradford, *Cesare Borgia: His Life and Times* (London, Phoenix, 2001); idem, *Lucrezia Borgia, Life, Love and Death in Renaissance Italy* (London, Viking, 2004). Maria Bellonci's *Lucrezia Borgia* (English edn, London, Phoenix, 2000) is a lively historical novel based on rigorous archival research. An excellent, scholarly survey of the Borgia as a family is Michael E. Mallett, *The Borgias: The Rise and Fall of a Renaissance Dynasty* (Oxford, The Bodley Head, 1969).

For Alexander VI in particular, see Ferdinando La Torre, *Del conclave di Alessandro VI papa Borgia* (Florence, Olschki, 1933); Giovanni Soranzo, *Studi intorno a papa Alessandro VI (Borgia)* (Milan, Vita e Pensiero, 1950); Giovanni Battista Picotti, 'Nuovi studi e documenti intorno a papa Alessandro VI', *Rivista di Storia della Chiesa in Italia*, 5 (1951), pp. 169–262. For his relationship with Vannozza Cattanei, see Karl I. Lawe, 'Vannozza de Cattanei och påven Alexander VI: en renässanspåvenfamilj i relation till samtidens och eftervärldens syn på celibat, prästäktenskap/konkubinat och prästbarns rättsliga och sociala ställning', doctoral dissertation (Uppsala Universitet, 1997).

For Giulia Farnese, see Carlo Fornari, *Giulia Farnese. Una donna schiava della propria bellezza* (Parma, Fondazione Monte di Parma, 1995); Giovanni Battista Picotti, 'Orsino Orsini, Adriana di Mila sua madre e Giulia Farnese. nei loro rapporti con papa Alessandro VI', *Archivi*, s. 2, XXVI (1958), pp. 133–80. For the relationship between the Borgia and Giulia's family, see Christine Shaw, 'Alexander VI, Cesare Borgia and the Orsini', *European Studies Review*, 11 (1981), pp. 1–23.

TEN: SIBLING RIVALRY

For Isabella d'Aragona, see Achille Dina, *Isabella d'Aragona duchessa di Milano e duchessa di Bari*, ASL, XLVIII (1921), pp. 269–457. Christopher Hare, *Isabella of Milan, Princess d'Aragona, and wife of Duke Gian Galeazzo Sforza: The Intimate Story of her Life in Milan Told in the Letters of her Lady-in-Waiting* (New York, Scribner, 1911).

Isabella d'Aragona is reputed to have written a poignant letter to her father Alfonso, asking him to intervene to redress her husband's situation; see Antonio Colombo, 'Il "grido di dolore" di Isabella d'Aragona duchissa di Milano', in *Studi di storia napoletana in onore di*

Michelangelo Schipa (Naples, I.T.E.A., 1926), pp. 331–46.

There is some evidence that Ludovico il Moro had an active, rather than a passive, role in his nephew's death; see Francesco Fossati, 'Lodovico Sforza avvelenatore del nipote? (Testimonianze di Simone dal Pozzo)', *ASL*, XXXI (1904), 2, pp. 162–71.

ELEVEN: PANDORA'S BOX

For the French invasion of 1494, David Abulafia (ed.), *The French Descent into Renaissance Italy, 1494–5: Antecedents and Effects* (Aldershot, Ashgate, 1995). On the Italian awareness of foreign types of warfare, see Pieri, *Il Rinascimento*, pp. 304–19.

Ludovico Il Moro's tendency to play with fire was a cause of concern for some time in Italian diplomatic circles. In 1488, Lorenzo de' Medici commented: 'Messer Ludovico should reflect carefully for this evil will not stop where it is at present but it might well arrive in a place he has not considered', AGF, V, n. 287.

For the crisis of the Florentine regime in 1494 and subsequent events, see Humphrey Butters, *Governors and Government in Early Sixteenth-Century Florence, 1502–19* (Oxford, Oxford University Press, 1985).

TWELVE: THE IMMACULATE DUCHESS LUCREZIA

For Lucrezia Borgia's first two marriages: Bernardino Feliciangeli, *Un episodio del nepotismo borgiano. Il matrimonio di Lucrezia Borgia con Giovanni Sforza, signore di Pesaro* (Torino-Roma, Roux e Viarengo, 1901). Francisco Rafael de Uhagón Laurencín, *Relación de los festines que se celebraron en el Vaticano con motivo de las bodas de Lucrecia orgia. con don Alonso de Aragón, duque de Bisceglie* (Madrid, Real Academia de la Historia, 1916).

THIRTEEN: FORTUNE'S CHILD

For the battle of Fornovo: Alessandro Luzio, Rodolfo Renier, *Francesco Gonzaga alla battaglia di Fornovo (1495)* (Mantova, Sartori, 1976); David Nicolle, *Fornovo 1495: France's Bloody Fighting Retreat* (Oxford, Osprey,

1996). The translation of Commines somewhat disingenuous comment is in Kenneth M. Setton, *The Papacy and the Levant, 1204–1571*, vol. II (Philadelphia, The American Philosophical Society, 1978), p. 494. Despite its title, Setton's work is a veritable goldmine of information and sources about Italian politics in the centuries it covers.

The diplomatic manoeuvres before Fornovo are well illustrated in Michele Jacoviello, 'La lega antifrancese del 31 marzo 1495 nella fonte veneziana del Sanuto', *ASI*, 143 (1985), pp. 39–90.

For Giovanni 'il popolano' and his branch of the Medici family: Pieraccini, *La stirpe de' Medici di Cafaggiolo*, vol. I, pp. 353–66. Allison Brown, 'Pierfrancesco de' Medici, 1430–76: A Radical Alternative to Elder Medicean Supremacy', *Journal of the Warburg and Courtauld Institutes*, XLII (1979), pp. 98–103. Breisach's comment is in Breisach, *Caterina Sforza*, p. 186.

FOURTEEN: 'YOU ARE ONLY A WOMAN. I FORGIVE YOU.'

For the French occupation of Milan, see Giorgio Chittolini, 'Dagli Sforza alla dominazione straniera', in idem, *Città, comunità e feudi negli Stati dell'Italia centro-settentrionale (secoli XIV–XVI* (Milan, UNICOPLI, 1996), pp. 167–80. Letizia Arcangeli (ed.), *Milano e Luigi XII. Ricerche sul primo dominio francese in Lombardia (1499–1512)* (Milan, Franco Angeli, 2002). For the exchanges between Alexander VI and Louis XII over the king's divorce: Michele Monaco, 'The Instructions of Alexander VI to His Ambassadors Sent to Louis XII in 1498', *Renaissance Studies*, 2 (1988), pp. 251–7.

For the dwarves and jesters at the Mantua court: Alessandro Luzio and Rodolfo Renier, 'Buffoni, nani e schiavi dei Gonzaga ai tempi d'Isabella d'Este', *Nuova Antologia*, 16, 1891, pp. 618–50.

FIFTEEN: CATERINA'S LOSS, LUCREZIA'S GAIN

Isabella d'Este's comment on Caterina Sforza is taken from Natale Graziani, Gabriella Venturelli, *Caterina Sforza* (Milan, Arnoldo Mondadori Editore, 2001), p. 263 (author's translation).

Sanudo's quote is in Marin Sanudo, *I diari di Marino Sanuto*, vol.

III, F. Stefani et al (eds) (Venice, Deputazione di Storia Patria per le Venezie, 1879), p. 38.

SIXTEEN: LUCREZIA AND ISABELLA DO BATTLE

For Lucrezia Borgia and Alfonso d'Este: Nicolò, Bendedei, *Lettera al pontefice Alessandro VI per gli sponsali di Lucrezia Borgia. con Alfonso d'Este* (Ferrara, Taddei, 1889). Pellegrino Prisciani, *Orazione per le nozze di Alfonso d'Este e Lucrezia Borgia*, ed. C. Pandolfi (Ferrara, 2004). Gianna Vancini (ed.), *Lucrezia Borgia nell'opera di cronisti, letterati e poeti suoi contemporanei alla corte di Ferrara: studi nel quinto centenario delle nozze di Lucrezia Borgia e don Alfonso d'Este* (Ferrara, Este, 2003).

For Isabella d'Este and Lucrezia Borgia: Alessandro Luzio, 'Isabella d'Este. e i Borgia', *ASL*, XLI (1914), pp. 469–553.

SEVENTEEN: LUCREZIA'S EMBARRASSMENT

For Isabella d'Este and the Montefeltro: Alessandro Luzio, Rodolfo Renier, *Mantova e Urbino. Isabella d'Este ed Elisabetta Gonzaga nelle relazioni famigliari e nelle vicende politiche* (Turin, UTET, 1893). For Guidobaldo da Montefeltro, see Bernardino Baldi, *Della vita e de' fatti di Guidubaldo I da Montefeltro duca d'Urbino*, 2 vols (Milan, Giovanni Silvestri, 1821). For Elisabetta Gonzaga and Guidobaldo da Montefeltro: Pietro Bembo, *De Guido Ubaldo Feretrio deque Elisabeta Gonzagia Urbini ducibus* (Rome, 1548). For Elisabetta Gonzaga: Maria Luisa Mariotti Masi, *Elisabetta Gonzaga duchessa di Urbino nello splendore e negli intrighi del Rinascimento* (Milan, Mursia, 1983).

The letter by Machiavelli a Francesco Soderini on Cesare Borgia is in ASF, *Dieci di Balia, Responsive*, 66, n. 369 (Francesco Soderini and Niccolò Machiavelli to the Signoria, 26 June 1502).

For Lucrezia Borgia's relationship with Bembo, see Lucrezia Borgia, *The Prettiest Love Letters in the World: Letters between Lucrezia Borgia and Pietro Bembo, 1503–19*, H. Shankland (ed.) (London, Collins Harvill, 1987).

EIGHTEEN: CESARE'S TROUBLES

For Cesare Borgia's murder of his enemies in Senigallia see Niccolò Machiavelli, *Descrizione del modo tenuto dal duca Valentino nello ammazzare Vitellozzo Vitelli, Oliverotto da Fermo, il signor Pagolo e il duca di Gravina Orsini*, in Niccolò Machiavelli, *Tutte le opere*, M. Martelli (ed.) (Florence, Sansoni, 1971), pp. 8–11. However, one should compare it with Machiavelli's original letters to the Florentine government, in: ASF, Dieci di Balia. Responsive 65, ff. 171–213.

NINETEEN: THE DUKE OF ROMAGNA AND THE BORGIA DIE OUT

Isabella d'Aragona's return to Naples is discussed in: Patrick Zutshi, 'An unpublished letter of Isabella of Aragon, Duchess of Milan', *Renaissance Studies*, vol. 20, 4, 2006, pp. 494–501.

For the events following the death of Alexander VI, see Pastor, *History of the Popes*, vol. VI (London, Kegan Paul, 1901), pp. 185–215.

TWENTY: THE MEDICI RESTORED

For Piero de' Medici's activities after his exile: Roberto Ridolfi, 'La spedizione di Piero de' Medici nel 1497 e la Repubblica senese', *Bullettino senese di storia patria*, LXX (1963), pp. 127–44.

'Instead of serving the Church' is quoted in Paul Strathern, *The Medici*, p. 244.

The Strozzi–Medici marriage is treated in detail in Melissa M. Bullard, *Filippo Strozzi and the Medici: Favor and Finance in Sixteenth-Century Florence and Rome* (Cambridge, Cambridge University Press, 1980), pp. 45–60. For Machiavelli's involvement see Lorenzo Strozzi, *Le vite degli uomini illustri di casa Strozzi* (Florence, Landi, 1892), pp. 96–7. 'She was visited', Tomas, *The Medici Women*, p. 111.

'Ogni giorno di più', Graziani, Venturelli, *Caterina Sforza*, p. 281. For Caterina Sforza's recipes see *Emilio Sani, Il ricettario di bellezza di Caterina Sforza* (Reggio Emilia, Tipografia Editrice Bizzocchi, 1954).

For the 'Pisan' council and its consequences, see Kenneth M.

Setton, *The Papacy and the Levant, 1204–1571*, vol. 3 (Philadelphia: American Philosophical Society, 1984), pp. 110–15.

The best treatment of the Battle of Ravenna is still to be found in Frederick L. Taylor, *The Art of War in Italy, 1494–1529* (Cambridge, Cambridge University Press, 1921), pp. 180–204.

For the sack of Prato and the events preceding it, see Cesare Guasti, *Il sacco di Prato e il ritorno dei Medici a Firenze nel 1512*, 2 vols (Bologna, Romagnoli, 1880), plus the three contemporary narratives of the sack published in *ASI*, I, n. 1 (1842).

For Savonarola see in particular Roberto Ridolfi, *Vita di Girolamo Savonarola*, 4th edn, 2 vols (Florence, Sansoni, 1974). Lauro Martines, *Fire in the City: Savonarola and the Struggle for Renaissance Florence* (New York, Oxford University Press, 2006). For Savonarola's legacy, see Lorenzo Polizzotto, *The Elect Nation: The Savonarolan Movement in Florence, 1494–1545* (New York, Oxford University Press, 1994).

Leo X's misgivings about sending Lorenzo II de' Medici to run Florence can be detected in the political memorandum he addressed to the young man: *Instructione al Magnifico Lorenzo*, T. Gar (ed.), *ASI*, app. 1 (1842–3), pp. 300–5.

TWENTY-ONE: LUCREZIA THE DUCHESS

For gun-casting in Ferrara see Francesco Locatelli, *La fabbrica ducale estense delle artiglierie: da Leonello ad Alfonso II d'Este* (Bologna, Cappelli, 1985). Lucrezia Borgia's managerial activities are descrive in Diane Y. Ghirardo, 'Lucrezia Borgia as Entrepreneur', *Renaissance Quarterly*, 61, 1 (2008), pp. 53–91.

For musical patronage in Mantua and Ferrata, see William F. Prizer, 'Isabella d'Este and Lucrezia Borgia as patrons of music', *Journal of the American Musicological Society*, XXXVIII (1985), pp. 1–33. For culture and politics in Ferrara: Edmund G. Gardner, *Dukes and Poets in Ferrara: A Study in the Poetry, Religion and Politics of the Fifteenth and Early Sixteenth Centuries* (London, J.M. Dent, 1904).

For the evolution of fashion: Eugenia Paulicelli, *Moda e moderno: dal Medioevo al Rinascimento* (Rome, Melterni, 2006).

A good sketch of Angela Borgia can be found in Roberto Zapperi, 'Borgia, Angela', *DBI*, 12 (1971), pp. 693–4.

For Giulio d'Este's conspiracy: Riccardo Bachelli, *La congiura di don Giulio d'Este* (Milan, Treves, 1931).

TWENTY-TWO: SAVING FACE

Isabella d'Este was a master of deception when it came to letter-writing: see Sarah Cockram, 'Epistolary Masks: Self-Presentation and Dissimulation in the Letters of Isabella d'Este', *Italian Studies*; Vol. 64, 1 (2009), pp. 20–37. There is a veritable abundance of archival sources about Isabella d'Este: in Mantua alone one may consult ASMn, *Archivio Gonzaga*, 330, 332, 400, 1890–1902, 2106–33, 2904, 2911, 2916–7, 2929, 2935, 2963, 2991–3000.

For Lucrezia Borgia's religion, see Gabriella Zarri, *La religione di Lucrezia Borgia: le lettere inedite del confessore* (Rome, Roma del Rinascimento, 2006). 'Lucrezia never felt that she was Ferrarese', is from Bellonci, *Lucrezia Borgia*, p. 310.

TWENTY-THREE: THE LAST MAN STANDING

For the events surrounding the sack of Rome, see Judith Hook, *The Sack of Rome* (New York, Palgrave Macmillan, 2004); Adrien Chastel, *Le sac de Rome, 1527* (Paris, Gallimard, 1984); Carlo Milanesi (ed.), *Il sacco di Roma del 1527. Narrazioni di contemporanei* (Florence, Barbera, 1867).

For Isabella d'Este and the Gonzaga involvement in the sack: Alessandro Luzio, 'Isabella d'Este e il sacco di Roma', *ASL*, XXXV (1908), 10, pp. 5–107, 361–425. Italo Bini, 'Il sacco di Roma e gli armeggi dei Gonzaga attorno ai capolavori predati', *Civiltà Mantovana*, n.s. 10, 4 (1985), pp. 69 93.

Pero Aretino's comments on the Italians' style of warfare are disingenuous. See Michael E. Mallett, *Mercenaries and their Masters: Warfare in Renaissance Italy* (Oxford, The Bodley Head, 1974).

The death of Giovanni dalle Bande Nere has been the subject of a film by Ermanno Olmi, *Il Mestiere delle Armi* (2001). Not always historically precise – for one, Olmi, from northern Italy, fails to capture Giovanni's Florentine sense of humour – it nevertheless illustrates well the vagaries of Italian politics in the Renaissance.

Acknowledgements

Before I thank the many people whose help, expertise and goodness made writing *The Deadly Sisterhood* possible, I should like respectfully to acknowledge the inspiration I received from the nob. Ippolita de' Medici-Tornaquinci dei Marchesi della Castellina; Don Ascanio Sforza Cesarini dei Principi di Genzano; Donna Alessandra Ruspoli dei Principi di Cerveteri; the Prince of Melissano, Don Landolfo Caracciolo; Count Dr Piero Guicciardini.

My boundless thanks go to Anthony Cheetham, a dear friend and constant supporter. Anthony spent his valuable time with exceptional generosity, if not profligacy, developing the quintessence for *The Deadly Sisterhood*. I also extend my fulsome gratitude to George Weidenfeld, whose peerless experience in publishing convinced this neophyte historian to realise Anthony's challenging vision into a book, their confidence gave me the courage to write this book,

Niccolò Capponi became my teacher, companion, sometime flatmate, and so much more, as he guided me through the complex and often apparently contradictory world of the Renaissance. Without his gifts as a pedagogue, matched by his patient and affectionate nature, I should have been lost in the epic drama that swept across Italy during the fifteenth century.

I am hugely indebted to Sarah Bradford for her encouragement inspirational and ground-breaking biographies on history's most reviled siblings, Lucrezia and Cesare Borgia.

I should also like to thank the following who have given me help and support while working on this book; HRH Princess Michael of Kent, Johannes Auersperg, Max Auersperg, Robin Birley, Saul David, Amanda Foreman, Antonia Fraser-Pinter, Paul and Marigold

Johnson, Daniel Johnson, Terry Karten, Clarissa Nadler, Count Don Francesco ('Chicco') Moncada dei Principi di Paternò, Andrew Roberts, Keith Rodriguez, Simon Sebag Montefiore, Anne Somerset, David Starkey, Max and Joy Ulfane, David Windsor-Clive, the late Mathew Carr, the late Iris Origo, and Julian, the late Earl of Oxford and Asquith.

I shall be ever beholden to my friend and confidant Ion Trewin, the original editor of *The Deadly Sisterhood*, and who kept me going when other events in my life seemed too overwhelming to permit further work on this book. My warmest appreciation goes to my editor, the intrepid Bea Hemming, who picked up Ion's editorial baton, and gave me her fullest support. I have benefitted from her imaginative approach and willingness to do whatever has been necessary; in short, far more than the duties that lie within any editor's remit: thank you. My copyeditor Linden Lawson, provides another instance of 'above and beyond': bless you. I give my heartfelt thanks to my superb agent, George Capel, whose goodness and good humour even in the face of daunting obstacles never failed. I am especially thankful to Alan Samson, and all at Orion, for allowing me all that I needed to finish my work and for their faith in this project.

Those closest to me deserve my loving recognition, for putting up with tears, nerve storms, and my sloping off to work whenever I could. In particular I give my love to David Davies, my children Lil' and Jake, my sister Anna, not forgetting Andrew, Olivia and Oscar. I also include Evelyn and Rosa – where shall we put those books? I cannot think of adequate expressions to thank you enough. To my darling mother, I owe you so much for your loving understanding despite the sorrows you had to face, and I repaid you with numberless broken dates, trips, as well as many broken promises and engagements. Thank you all with love.

Leonie Frieda.
London, 2012

Index

ABOUT THE AUTHOR

Leonie Frieda is the author of *Catherine de Medici: Renaissance Queen of France*, which was a bestseller on both sides of the Atlantic and was translated into eight languages. She lives in London.